D1173225

An Interpretation of Desire

WORLDS OF DESIRE
THE CHICAGO SERIES ON SEXUALITY, GENDER, AND CULTURE
Edited by Gilbert Herdt

Also in the series:

An Interpretation of Desire

Essays in the Study of Sexuality

John H. Gagnon

THE UNIVERSITY OF CHICAGO PRESS
CHICAGO AND LONDON

John H. Gagnon is Distinguished Professor of Sociology, emeritus, at the State University of New York at Stony Brook. He is the author, coauthor, or coeditor of numerous books on sexuality, including *Sexual Conduct, The Social Origins of Sexuality, Human Sexualities, The Social Organization of Sexuality, Conceiving Sexual Conduct,* and *In Changing Times: Gay Men and Lesbians Encounter HIV/AIDS.*

The University of Chicago Press, Chicago 60637
The University of Chicago Press, Ltd., London
© 2004 by The University of Chicago
All rights reserved. Published 2004
Printed in the United States of America
13 12 11 10 09 08 07 06 05 04   1 2 3 4 5

ISBN: 0-226-27858-1 (cloth)
ISBN: 0-226-27860-3 (paper)

Library of Congress Cataloging-in-Publication Data

Gagnon, John H.
    An interpretation of desire : essays in the study of
sexuality / John H. Gagnon
      p. cm. — (Worlds of desire)
    Includes bibliographical references and index.
    ISBN 0-226-27858-1 (hardcover : alk. paper)
    ISBN 0-226-27860-3 (pbk. : alk. paper)
    1. Sexology — Research. 2. Sex (Psychology)
    3. Identity (Psychology) 4. Social interaction.
    5. Social influence. 6. Interpersonal relations and
culture. I. Title. II. Series.
HQ60 .G54 2004
306.7'07'2—dc21

                  2003010215

For Cathy Stein Greenblat
Without Whom There Would Have Been Much Less

of Everything

Contents

Preface

No writer has ever been the first, though confusing oneself with God is a writer's temptation; and no one writes alone, though many may feel lonely when they write. The colleagueship of any text is composed of both visible and invisible coauthors. Sometimes this network of others is acknowledged as footnotes or references, or in prefaces, such as this one, in which particular people are cited as influences or helpers on a specific work. Others remain less visible, shadowy figures whose conversations with the author on the topic of the work (or more generally) were instructive or corrective but remain unacknowledged in print. Even more ghostly are authors of books read and remembered (or forgotten) that have constructed an attitude of mind toward the world. And these are but a tiny selection from the vast collective sea of unread writing in which the individual writer paddles as he or she writes. And this sea of texts is only a puddle in the ocean of talk that is more often forgotten than recorded.

This is a preface to a set of solo-authored essays written over many years, though weighted toward the present, during which the author was involved in a variety of these extended collegial relations. Some involved research and publication; some involved research that had little or no public issue; some were just composed of intellectual conversations. The essays bear the mark of those collegial relations; in the process of extending, resisting, honoring, rejecting, never are they indifferent to the influence of others. Often these essays were provoked by the invitations of others to speak or write (and I owe much to those who made the invitations), and the ideas expressed were always shaped by the situation in which they were first presented. In this sense each of the essays is local in the writer's biography, but each possesses the ambition to transcend the local, to become part of the cosmopolitan world of writing in general and to influence the ideas of others. It is part of that larger narcissistic process described by Kohut as idealizing ones ambitions and having ambitions for ones ideals.

At the same moment as I recognize the burden of collegiality, it is apparent to me that I cannot name everyone who contributed in one or another way to these essays written over a period of a quarter-century.

Thank everyone or thank no one? The dilemma is explicit. Thanking everyone would go on too long and introduce even more characters that no reader knows. Thanking no one goes against the ideology of the author. And there is no solution.

So just a few dozen names. Three from a time before these ideas were ideas: Thomas B. Stauffer, exiled from the State Department to Hyde Park and local activism; Hans Walter Mattick, with whom I spent three years at the Cook County Jail; and Frank Oliver, a criminal defense attorney in Chicago. At Indiana University in the Department of Sociology were Alfred Lindesmith, Albert Cohen, and Sheldon Stryker. At the Institute for Sex Research: Paul Gebhard and visitors Steven Marcus, Morse Peckham, and George Steiner—all of whom I owe special debts. Also there was William Simon, whom I knew for the majority of my life—all of the essays in this volume are marked by our shared work, which continued beyond that at the institute, in more modest measure, from 1973 until his death in 2000. At Stony Brook: in psychology, Gerald C. Davison and Raymond Rosen; in ecology and evolution, Lawrence Slobodkin; in sociology, Lewis and Rose Coser, Charles Perrow, Judith Tanur, Michael Kimmel, Wallace Davis, and Richard Williams; and students, some now colleagues, Jorge Arditi, Lee Clarke, William Gronfein, Gladys Rothbell, Patricia Pugliani, Patrick Moynihan, and Mathew Kowalski.

Others: the Russian—Igor Kon of the Institute of Ethnology of the Russian Academy of Sciences; some Danes—Berl Kutchinsky, Susie Haxthausen, Nini Praetorius and Karin Lutzen; the English—Kenneth Plummer and Everard Longland, Jeffrey Weeks, Laurie Taylor, Stan Cohen, Stevie Jackson and Antony Grey; the Dutch—Theo Sandfort; the French—Alain Giami; the German—Gunter Schmidt.

Before AIDS: Judith (Pepper) Schwartz, Celia Marriott, and Elizabeth Roberts. After AIDS: Shirley Lindenbaum, Martin Levine, Peter Nardi, Richard Parker, Edward Laumann, Robert Michael, Stuart Michaels, Martina Morris, Gina Kolata, Anke Ehrhardt, and Joseph Catania.

And finally, Bennett Berger, Jeffrey Escoffier, Gilbert Herdt, Carole Vance, and Gayle Rubin, and Cathy Stein Greenblat, to whom this book is dedicated.

All of these folks are principals in the conversations that form the background of this book. As Kenneth Burke put it (and he is a constant presence on the these pages):

Where does the drama get its materials? From the "unending conversation" that is going on at the point in history when we are born.

Imagine that you enter a parlor. You come late. When you arrive, others have long preceded you, and they are engaged in a heated discussion, a discussion too heated for them to pause and tell you exactly what it is about.

In fact, the discussion had already begun long before any of them got there, so that no one present is qualified to retrace for you all the steps that had gone before.

You listen for a while, until you decide that you have caught the tenor of the argument; then you put in your oar. Someone answers; you answer him [or her]; another comes to your defense; another aligns himself [or herself] against you, to either the embarrassment or gratification of your opponent, depending upon the quality of your ally's assistance.

However, the discussion is interminable. The hour grows late, you must depart. And you do depart, with the discussion still vigorously in progress. (1974, 110–11)

John H. Gagnon
Eden Beach, Nice
May 2002

Foreword

In the years after World War II, American sociology achieved an unprecedented legitimacy (if not influence), but it attained that legitimacy at a cost. It grew increasingly institutionalized—virtually every college and university had a sociology department—and came under the sway of two great organizing programs: the grand theoretical synthesis of functionalism and the empirical strictures of middle-range sociology. The authors of those programs, Talcott Parsons and Robert Merton, portrayed society as a coherent but differentiated system nearly impervious to dramatic changes or political chaos, a system that could be studied through ahistorical surveys of individuals. They failed to understand, in the words of C. Wright Mills, "the larger historical scene in terms of its meaning for the inner life and the external career of a variety of individuals" (Mills 1959, 5).

One of the consequences of that failure was the increasing irrelevance of professional sociology to public *intellectual* discourse. The great works of popular sociology of the 1950s—*The Lonely Crowd, The Power Elite, The Status Seekers, The End of Ideology*—sought to relate the inner life and social careers of ordinary people to large-scale historical changes. But these books often were the work of eccentrics, outsiders, rebels, journalists, muckrakers, ex-Communists, or ex-Socialists—that is, deviants of the profession—rather than of influential academic sociologists. Also, the hegemony of what was to become the Harvard-Columbia school of sociology discouraged the development of empirical sociological research on symbolic action and human interaction. The sociology of deviance (and in those days nearly all sex research was research on deviance) emerged as an academic subdiscipline that was a grab bag of social problems and theoretical approaches that did not easily fit into the functionalist or middle-range paradigms: empirical research on crime, prostitution, homosexuality, gambling, alcoholism, blindness, and mental illness tended to explore individual strategies and symbolic interactions (Escoffier 1998, 79–98).

Sociological research on sexuality was rarely addressed within sociology's academic paradigms. Rather, in the decades after World War II, sexuality and the social theory was most often addressed by the leading intellectuals on the Freudian Left: Wilhelm Reich, Herbert Marcuse, Erich

Fromm, Norman O. Brown, and Paul Goodman (King 1972). Although the studies of Alfred Kinsey introduced an unprecedented empirical dimension to the research, the sociological approach to the study of sexuality developed when a sociologist trained at the University of Chicago encountered Kinsey's research methodology. That sociologist was John Gagnon, who has now studied and written about sexuality for almost forty years. Gagnon has often collaborated with others, but this book brings together his most significant individual contributions that amplify and elaborate his thinking on sexuality and, in particular, the theory of sexual scripting that he and William Simon developed in the late sixties and early seventies. These essays also serve as a bridge to Gagnon's work with Edward Laumann and Robert Michael that integrates sexual scripting with theories of social networks and sexual partner choice.

That most of Gagnon's career has taken place under the sign of Alfred Kinsey is both fitting and ironic: fitting because Gagnon began his research on sexuality and, with Bill Simon, developed the theory of sexual scripting while on the staff of the Kinsey Institute, but ironic because the social theory he and Simon developed is so thoroughly in opposition to the naturalistic approach that Kinsey and his colleagues had advanced. In addition, his recent work with Laumann and Michael on sexual conduct and social networks took place over the course of collaborating with them on the most comprehensive survey of sexual behavior in American society ever undertaken.

Gagnon's entire career has taken place during what future historians of the United States will no doubt insist on calling "the sexual revolution" or perhaps even "the second sexual revolution," as opposed to the one that occurred at the turn of the twentieth century (Allyn 2000). Gagnon himself has always been skeptical of the idea of a sexual revolution—at least, when thought of in terms of rapid changes in behavior. Nevertheless, there have been immense changes in social attitudes toward sexuality, in the acceptance of sexual variety, and in the proliferation of cultural representations and public discussion of sexual issues. Sex, sexuality, and gender have been at the center of sweeping cultural shifts in the last fifty years—the changing social role of women; increased awareness of female sexuality; the emergence of social identities based on sexual preferences; the development of effective contraception; the increased prevalence of sex before marriage; and changing conceptions of marriage, divorce, and cohabitation; as well as artificial insemination, single parenthood, and new configurations of the family. Many of these dramatic cultural changes are usually included in what is described as the sexual revolution. What exactly "sexual revolution" means—when it began (if indeed it did), to whom it applied, and what changes it wrought—are highly contested subjects. The life work of John Gagnon is central to this grand cultural shift—this *longue durée* of historical time—in two significant ways. As a sociologist he has empirically mapped many of these changes, and as a theorist, he has transformed how we think about sex and sexuality as social phenomena.

Recognition of a revolution in public attitudes toward sexuality dawned slowly after World War II. The publication of Alfred Kinsey's two path-breaking volumes on human sexuality in 1948 *(Sexual Behavior in the Human Male)* and 1953 *(Sexual Behavior in the Human Female)* probably exerted greater influence on modern conceptions of sexuality than any work since Sigmund Freud's. Moral outrage and a great deal of professional hypocrisy greeted the report, but few Americans remained immune to a new awareness of the gap that Kinsey found between public attitudes toward sexual behavior and daily sexual activities. Kinsey was so struck by the extraordinary extent of individual variation in sexual behavior that he argued that any attempt to establish uniform cultural standards of sexual conduct was both impracticable and unjust. He believed that his discovery of the widespread deviation from accepted sexual standards showed that attempts to regulate sexual behavior were doomed to failure and "the only proper sexual policy was no policy at all" (Robinson 1976, 51).

Although the research in the Kinsey reports was not based on the generation that experienced the so-called sexual revolution after World War II (Kinsey had focused on those who grew up between the First and Second World Wars), the reports did come to be the symbol of sexual revolution in the popular consciousness and in the history of American culture. Indeed, the political and religious Right viewed the Kinsey reports as the cause of the sexual and sex-related changes of the 1960s. If "sexual revolution" refers to any particular behavior, it is the increase of various forms of nonmarital sexual activity. By the early sixties, shifts had begun to take place along several fronts that consolidated the sexual revolution. One of the most important was that young men and women were engaging in their first acts of sexual intercourse at increasingly younger ages. The impact of earlier sexual experimentation was reinforced by the later age of marriage. Thus, young men and women began to have more time available for acquiring sexual experience with partners before entering a long-term monogamous relationship. The growing number of marriages resulting in divorce provided another opportunity for men and (to a lesser degree) women to engage in nonmonogamous sexual activity. All three of these developments allowed the generation born between 1935 and 1945 to experience sexual activity with a larger number of sexual partners in their lifetimes than had previous generations.

If the Kinsey reports represent the opening salvo of a possible sexual revolution, the research of William Masters and Virginia Johnson represent an ambiguous resolution of some issues raised by the shifts in sexual attitudes and behavior. *Human Sexual Response* (1966) and *Human Sexual Inadequacy* (1970) were based on laboratory observations of sexual behavior and became the basis of a therapeutic practice devoted to sexual dysfunction. Nevertheless, the work of Masters and Johnson also exemplified the sexual egalitarianism of the sixties, not only in the working relationship of the researchers, but also in the image of sexual relations that they projected in their books. Their work stressed the *quality* of sexual activity. However, Masters and Johnson made the couple rather than the unattached individual the preferred unit of analysis and therapy. They focused almost exclusively on the quality of sexual experience *within* committed relationships. They never addressed the quality of sexual experience for those men and women who chose to engage in sex with casual or other nonmarital sexual partners—a group that is essential to the definition of the sexual revolution.

Finally, the early work of John Gagnon and William Simon, which began to appear in the late sixties and culminated in the publication of their book *Sexual Conduct* in 1973, offered a new way of thinking about sex and social change. In this period, Gagnon and Simon introduced a thoroughgoing conception of sexual behavior as a learned process, one that is possible not because of instinctual drives or physiological requirements, but because it is embedded in complex social scripts that are specific to particular locations in culture and history. Their approach stressed the significance of individual agency and cultural symbols in the conduct of sexual activities. "Undeniably," they wrote, "what we conventionally describe as sexual behavior is rooted in biological capacities and processes, but no more than other forms of behavior. . . . [T]he sexual area may be precisely that realm wherein the superordinate position of the sociocultural over the biological level is most complete" (Gagnon and Simon 1973, 15). No previous theorists of sexuality had interpreted sexual behavior as so completely social. Gagnon and Simon redefined sexuality, from the combined product of biological drives and social repression to an arena of creative social initiative and symbolic action. Gayle Rubin, a feminist theorist and anthropologist, observed that, in the course of their work, Gagnon and Simon "virtually reinvented sex research as social science" (Rubin 2002, 28).

* * *

John Gagnon attended the University of Chicago as an undergraduate starting in 1949 and later as a graduate student from 1956 to 1959. During the fifties, Chicago offered a rich cultural education, which included the flourishing jazz clubs in the Loop and the South Side, gatherings with folk singers, exhibitions of abstract expressionism and other modern art at the Art Institute, and, not least, drinking and talking in the bars near the campus. No doubt the excitement in Chicago and at the university stemmed not only from its great intellectual traditions and its bustling urbanism, but also from the creative mix of young men and women starting out in life and all the former servicemen (and a few servicewomen) going to college and graduate school on the GI Bill. Gagnon completed his graduate work in Chicago's legendary sociology department, although most of the generation that had defined the Chicago school in the period between the World Wars were gone by the late forties and early fifties. Gagnon was at the younger end of a generation that included Erving Goffman, Howard Becker, Albert Reiss, Joseph Gusfield, Eliot Friedson, and Morris Janowitz—a generation that, with the decline of the hegemony of the Harvard-Columbia school, went on to definitively reshape the discipline of sociology in the postwar United States (Fine 1995).

While there is some debate whether or not this postwar generation inherited and continued the great Chicago tradition that W. I. Thomas, Robert Park, Louis Wirth, Herbert Blumer, and Everett Hughes established early in the twentieth century, it seems altogether clear that the University of Chicago's sociology department transmitted a style of intellectual engagement that stressed empirical attention to the social construction of everyday life. Classical European sociology—Max Weber, Émile Durkheim, Karl Marx—had focused on the dynamic between historical processes, such as secularization, industrialization, and capitalism, and the social structures that shaped individuals and communities. University of Chicago sociologists had instead turned their attention to the writing of descriptively rich ethnographic accounts of Chicago's immigrants, blacks, hobos, prostitutes and taxi dancers, and delinquents—all those people most often overlooked or marginalized in classical sociology's grand narratives.

The Chicago tradition is to a large degree indebted to the work of philosopher and social psychologist George Herbert Mead, who explored the ways human behavior is shaped through symbolically mediated patterns of reciprocal expectations and interactions (Strauss 1977, vii–xxxi).

Mead argued that the "self," as the site of individuality and meaningful experience, is the product of social processes. During the course of social interactions, both those involving physical cooperation and intersubjective communication, human beings pursue their goals and shape their culture. At the same time, the "selves" of these social participants are also formed. In the post–World War II era, a number of intellectual perspectives emerged from this Chicago tradition, of which symbolic interactionism is only one of the most notable. These perspectives, put forward by Howard Becker, Erving Goffman, and Joseph Gusfield, for example, stressed the process of social interaction, focused on the reciprocal action of social actors, and emphasized the symbolic character of social action. Gagnon's work is fully compatible with this tradition.

In 1959 Gagnon moved to Bloomington, Indiana, where he joined the staff of the late Alfred Kinsey's Institute for Sex Research as a research sociologist. In 1965, William Simon also joined the staff of the institute as a sociologist. Together they conducted research on college students, the homosexual community, and sex education. In addition, they coedited two volumes of papers devoted to the sociological study of sexuality— *Sexual Deviance* (1967) and editions of *The Sexual Scene* (1970, 1973)— and in 1973 they published their pioneering book, *Sexual Conduct*.

Earlier theorists of sexuality, particularly Freud and Wilhelm Reich, had believed that sexual behavior was shaped by a combined development of biological and environmental factors. Both Freud and Reich had stressed the importance of biological drives while also analyzing how those biological energies were channeled by family dynamics and by social structures. The empirical research of Alfred Kinsey was similarly founded on the sexual as a primarily biological capacity, molded to only a small degree by environmental conditions. But Gagnon and Simon vigorously rejected the determining importance of biological drives or energies and instead adopted a thoroughgoing social interpretation of sexual behavior.

Sexual Conduct introduced a coherent social constructionist approach to human sexuality. In it, Gagnon and Simon sought "to bring the field of sexuality under the control of a sociological orientation. . . . to lay a sociological claim to an aspect of social life that seemed determined by biology or psychology" (Gagnon 1990, 231). In *Sexual Conduct* and in a series of theoretical refinements published in the 1980s, they elaborated the view that the doing of sex requires learning and that only because physical acts of sex are embedded in social "scripts" do they become possible. Gagnon and Simon sought to replace biological or psychoanalytic theories of sexual behavior with a social theory of sexual scripts. In this theory they argue that individuals use their interactional skills, fantasy materials, and cultural myths to develop scripts (with cues and appropriate dialogue) as a means for organizing their sexual behavior. They distinguish three distinct levels of scripting: *cultural scenarios* provide instruction on the narrative requirements of broad social roles; *interpersonal scripts* are institutionalized patterns in everyday social interaction; and *intrapsychic scripts* are details that an individual uses in his or her internal dialogue with cultural and social behavioral expectations (Simon and Gagnon 1986, 98–104). For example, interpersonal scripts help individuals organize their own self-representations and those of others to initiate and engage in sexual activity, while the intrapsychic scripts organize the images and desires that elicit and sustain an individual's sexual desire. Cultural scenarios frame the interpersonal and intrapsychic scripts in the context of cultural symbols and broad social roles (such as those based on race, gender, or class).

While Gagnon and Simon's view is certainly consistent with Mead's interactionism, the idea that sexual behavior is scripted was to some degree suggested by the work of literary theorist Kenneth Burke. Over the course of a career spanning from the 1920s to the 1950s, Burke published a series of books employing a variety of intellectual strategies, which viewed literature, art, and forms of intellectual discourse as symbolic action. He also argued that social action was not merely causal, but also communicated meaning, thus it too was a form of symbolic action. His books, especially *Permanence and Change* ([1935] 1954) and *The Grammar of Motives* (1945), had a significant impact on a number of sociologists in the decade after World War II, including Erving Goffman, Joseph Gusfield, and C. Wright Mills.

Gagnon and Simon's scripting theory is a synthesis of the Chicago interactionist tradition, the Burkean explication of social context and symbolic action, and the Freudian analysis of fantasy life and the intrapsychic aspect of sexuality. Nevertheless, its most important sociological assumption is the Meadean emphasis on "role-taking," which refers to the ability of social actors to anticipate the situationally specific behavior of their partners in action. The actor's expectations of the other's behavior allows the actor to negotiate his or her partner's interactions, but also, in a fundamental way, contributes to the actor's synthesis of his or her own reflexive sense of self. In scripting theory neither the human subject nor the social situation is the primary reality. Each is constituted in and through recurring symbolic practices. In addition, each is embedded in social structures and public cultures. The scripts that social actors activate are their interpretations of social rules, cultural myths, and forms of carnal knowledge.

***

In the mid-seventies, Gagnon and Simon's work had a significant impact on the emerging feminist and gay liberation movements, particularly on a group of young English sociologists and historians—Kenneth Plummer, Jeffrey Weeks, and Mike Brake—who were active in these movements. While many sexual radicals, feminists, and gay activists had initially turned to the work of Wilhelm Reich, Erich Fromm, and Herbert Marcuse—the Freudian Left—for insights into sexuality, the Freudian Left's dependence on a notion of biological instincts (and other forms of essentialism) was politically and intellectually unacceptable. Gagnon and Simon offered an alternative in which, as Jeffrey Weeks noted, "nothing is intrinsically sexual, or rather . . . anything can be sexualized" (Weeks 1980, 13). Some members of this group established the journal *Gay Left* (1975–1979) and developed a synthesis of interactionist sociology inspired by Gagnon and Simon and Marxist historicism. This synthesis was soon challenged by the publication of Michel Foucault's *History of Sexuality.*

Foucault's little volume is a methodological introduction to a larger project, a history of sexuality. Foucault situated his project within the lines of the "grand narrative" that he had begun to explore in *Discipline and Punish:* the rise of disciplinary power. This form of power, which used expert knowledge and moral discourses, operated effectively through a process of "subjectification" or the creation of new social identities and through social practices that shaped the subject's body. Foucault had found it interesting that sexuality was integral to a form of power that had emerged alongside new forms of the state in the seventeenth and eighteenth centuries.

Foucault launched an attack on what he called "the repressive hypothesis." His critique supported several important arguments. The main point was that sexual conduct was shaped not only by repressive mechanisms—as Freud, Wilhelm Reich, and others had argued—but also by a process of discursive construction. Foucault's attack thus sought to remove the "hydraulic" model of sexuality as a theoretical framework. Sexuality was not an essential characteristic of human nature or gender, but a thoroughly social-historical construction. The hydraulic metaphor as used by Freud, Reich, or even Kinsey implied that sex was based on biological energies. Foucault's critique shifted attention to the discursive production of sexuality.

In addition, Foucault also gave a historical account of how the discursive production of sexuality in Europe was accomplished. He considered the Catholic institution of confession instrumental in the translation of sexual desires into social discourse. The requirement of confessing one's sinful desires and deeds and evaluating their gravity by discussion generated a sexual discourse (Foucault 1978, 21). The impact of the Church's moral discourse was later overlaid by new Enlightenment discourses on population. "At the heart of this economic and political problem of population," Foucault wrote, was sex; it was necessary to analyze the birthrate, the age of marriage, "the legitimate and illegitimate births, [the] precocity and frequency of sexual relations, . . . [and the] impact of contraceptive practices" (25). Later medicine and law emerged to complement the Enlightenment doctrines of population.

The repression hypothesis is central to the Freudian account of the sexual development of the individual and the requirements of social life. "Our civilization," wrote Freud, "is, generally speaking, founded on the suppression of instincts" ([1908] 1963, 15). By relegating the repression hypothesis to a secondary status, Foucault was obliged to offer, if only tentatively, some alternative explanation of individual sexual development. He identified in the nineteenth century a dispersion of sexualities outside the heterosexual monogamy required for traditional relations of kinship. The interweaving of the discourses of law, church, and Enlightenment generated new forms, new identities, enabling the implantation of "perversions," creating new categories of marginal people. Thus, the man who committed acts of sodomy in an earlier historical period became a particular type of person in the nineteenth century, the sodomite—a precursor to the modern homosexual. Other normalized sexual identities were the Malthusian couple (practicing the unnatural act of birth control), the masturbating child, and the hysterical woman. Thus Foucault, in what is basically a very brief book, offered a sweeping historical interpretation of Western European sexuality. Moreover, he also proposed a theoretical framework that dispensed with the psychoanalytic explanation of sexual development and its social ramifications.

Foucault's understanding of sex shared much with that developed by Gagnon and Simon. Like them, Foucault argued that the self is socially constructed, and that sexuality is shaped through the bodily coordination and symbolic interaction of social subjects. Steven Seidman has argued that while sociological perspectives—particularly the work on labeling and stigmas by Howard Becker, Erving Goffman, and Edwin Schur, as well as Gagnon and Simon's theory of sexual scripts—were influential in the sixties and early seventies, by the late seventies and eighties sociologists no longer played a significant role in debates about sexuality, "in part, because sociologists did not critically investigate the categories of sexuality, heterosexuality, and homosexuality. They did not question the social functioning of the hetero/homosexual binary as the master category of a modern regime of sexuality" (Seidman 1997, 88). However, as Jeffrey Weeks noted, "the theoretical tradition represented by Gagnon and Simon and the school of thought represented by Michel Foucault have in common recognition that . . . sexuality is regulated through the process of categorisation and the imposition of a grid . . . upon the various possibilities of the body and the various forms of expression that 'sex' can take. This in turn should direct our attention to the various institutions and social practices which perform this role of organisation, regulation, categorisation: various forms of the family, but also legal regulation, medical practices, psychiatric institutions and so on, all of which can be seen as products of the capitalist organisation of society" (Weeks 1980, 14).

Although Gagnon and Simon's theory is also a theory of discursive production, it did not achieve the currency that Foucault's intellectual framework did. Despite their similarities on the social construction of sexuality, these two theoretical traditions focused attention on very different issues. Foucault and his followers concentrated their analysis on the deployment of sexuality on a broad historical terrain, while Gagnon and Simon focused on the individual's scripting of sexual behavior through a three-way dialectic of cultural symbolic systems, an individual's fantasy life, and social interactional norms. Foucault, Weeks, and the Left interactionists focused on the grand narratives of historical change, the emergence of sexual identities, and "regimes of sexual regulation," while Gagnon in particular pursued a more detailed examination of how those historical processes and those regimes of sexual regulation actually shaped people's sex lives.

With the advent of AIDS, Gagnon and Simon's scripting approach to sexual behavior gained a new urgency. Understanding the sexual scripts enabled researchers to identify the risks of HIV infection in sexual activities and develop prevention strategies. More recently, in the context of designing a national survey of sexual behavior, Gagnon, Laumann, and Michael developed an approach that integrated sexual scripting behavior with the choice of sexual partners and the operation of social networks, thus linking interpersonal interactions (scripting and partner choice) to social structures and cultural systems and extending the theoretical approach of Gagnon and Simon's initial breakthrough. The work of Gagnon and his collaborators has continued to influence sex radicals, feminist, lesbian, and gay intellectuals, and AIDS researchers—among them, Carole Vance, Gayle Rubin, Martin Levine, Anke Ehrhardt, and myself—who have sought to understand the social construction of sexual conduct and identities in its quotidian reality.

The devastating outbreak of the AIDS epidemic in the early eighties provoked a profound social and public health crisis. It was also a crisis of scientific knowledge of sexual behavior and practices. The Human Immunodeficiency Virus (HIV) was found to be the most serious and devastating of sexually transmitted diseases. As the epidemic gained momentum Gagnon increasingly turned his attention to the study of HIV/AIDS. Individually and with colleagues and friends such as Shirley Lindenbaum and Martin Levine, Gagnon undertook a series of projects that explored the impact of AIDS on various social communities within the United States. Gagnon was an important participant in three seminal conferences on sexuality and AIDS (his contributions to which are included in this volume as chapters 9 and 10 and in *Conceiving Sexuality,* which he coedited with Richard Parker) that had widespread influence on thinking about HIV/AIDS, sexuality, and culture. As a member of the National Academy of Sciences Committee on the Behavioral Sciences, Statistics, and Education's Panel on AIDS Research in the Social and Behavioral Sciences, he participated in a number of studies, organized a series of conferences, and published several important papers on the social dynamics of the epidemic.

In 1986, the National Academy of Sciences issued a report on the AIDS epidemic, concluding that "[i]nfected bisexual men and IV drug users of both sexes can transmit the virus to the broader heterosexual population where it can continue to spread, particularly among the most sexually active individuals" (Institute of Medicine 1986, 9). The report predicted a substantial number of cases of HIV infection among the heterosexual population by 1995. However, since no large-scale systematic data on sexual behavior in the American population existed, it was difficult to identify the potential routes of transmission or estimate rates of HIV infection. The uncharted epidemiology of AIDS epidemic pointed up the ignorance of sexual behavior and practices in the United States.

Soon after the National Academy of Sciences report was issued, Gagnon, Edward Laumann (a University of Chicago sociologist working in the area of social networks), and Robert Michael (an economic demographer and director of the National Opinion Research Center) won an

NIH contract to conduct a comprehensive survey of American sexual practices. Thus Gagnon returned to the terrain Kinsey had pioneered. The survey that Laumann, Gagnon, and Michael developed was the most comprehensive survey of sexual behavior ever attempted in the United States. It was soon to became, however, the center of a fierce political controversy, which included a personal attack on Gagnon on the Senate floor by North Carolina's Senator Jesse Helms. This controversy resulted in the cancellation of federal funding not only for this study, but also for another already approved federal grant to this same team of researchers. With only nongovernmental funding, the team scaled back considerably the projected size of the study. Despite these challenges, in 1994 the team published two books reporting on the survey. One, *Sex in America*, coauthored with journalist Gina Kolata, was written for popular consumption, while the second, *The Social Organization of Sexuality*, was primarily for academic experts (Ericksen 1999, 176–218).

Sexual conduct, in Gagnon's work, is neither a form of rational, "utility maximizing" behavior nor purely a form of normatively oriented action. Instead sexual interactions are creative actions drawing on cultural myths and images, personal fantasies, and rich interactional social codes (Joas 1996). As these essays illustrate, the social study of sexuality does not take us away from either the hard realities of social life—the political, economic, and social structural realities within which men and women are bound—or the biological and physical aspects of human life. All of these aspects of human life are in constant play in all of our sexual interactions. Sexual conduct is also a form of symbolic action, which is why a theory of sexual scripting is able to articulate the links between individual interactional behavior on the micro level and the larger social forces of the macro level. The work of Gagnon and his associates demonstrates how sexuality is an integral aspect of social life.

Jeffrey Escoffier

References

Allyn, D. 2000. *Make Love, Not War: The Sexual Revolution, An Unfettered History*. Boston: Little, Brown.

Burke, K. [1935] 1954. *Permanence and Change*. 2d ed. Berkeley: University of California Press.

———. 1945. *A Grammar of Motives*. Berkeley: University of California Press.

Ericksen, J. A., with S. A. Steffen. 1999. *Kiss and Tell: Surveying Sex in the Twentieth Century*. Cambridge, MA: Harvard University Press.

Escoffier, J. 1998. *American Homo: Community and Perversity.* Berkeley: University of California Press.

Fine, G. A., ed. 1995. *A Second Chicago?: The Development of Postwar American Sociology.* Chicago: University of Chicago Press.

Foucault, M. 1978. *The History of Sexuality.* Vol. 1, *An Introduction.* New York: Pantheon Books.

Freud, S. [1908] 1963. "Civilized" Sexual Morality and Modern Nervousness. In *Sexuality and the Psychology of Love,* edited by P. Reiff. New York: Simon and Schuster.

Gagnon, J. H. 1990. An Unlikely Story. In *Authors of Their Own Lives: Intellectual Autobiographies by Twenty American Sociologists,* edited by B. M. Berger. Berkeley: University of California.

———, and P. M. Nardi. 1997. Introduction to *In Changing Times: Gay Men and Lesbians Encounter HIV/AIDS,* edited by M. P. Levine, P. M. Nardi, and J. H. Gagnon. Chicago: University of Chicago Press.

———, and R. G. Parker. 1995. Introduction to *Conceiving Sexuality: Approaches to Sex Research in a Postmodern World,* edited by R. G. Parker and J. H. Gagnon. New York: Routledge.

———, and W. Simon. 1973. *Sexual Conduct: The Social Sources of Human Sexuality.* Chicago: Aldine.

Joas, H. 1993. Pragmatism in American Sociology. In *Pragmatism and Social Theory.* Chicago: University of Chicago Press.

———. 1996. *The Creativity of Action.* Chicago: University of Chicago Press.

Institute of Medicine. 1986. *Confronting AIDS: Directions for Public Health, Health Care, and Research.* Washington, DC: National Academy of Sciences Press.

King, Richard. 1972. *The Party of Eros: Radical Social Thought and the Realm of Freedom.* Chapel Hill: University of North Carolina Press.

Laumann, E. O., and J. H. Gagnon. 1995. A Sociological Perspective on Sexual Action. In *Conceiving Sexuality: Approaches to Sex Research in a Postmodern World,* edited by R. G. Parker and J. H. Gagnon. New York: Routledge.

———, J. H. Gagnon, R. T. Michael, and S. Michaels. 1994. *The Social Organization of Sexuality: Sexual Practices in the United States.* Chicago: University of Chicago Press.

Mills, C. W. 1959. *The Sociological Imagination.* London: Oxford University Press.

Robinson, P. 1976. *The Modernization of Sex: Havelock Ellis, Alfred Kinsey, William Masters, and Virginia Johnson.* New York: Harper and Row.

Rubin, G. 2002. Studying Sexual Subcultures: Excavating the Ethnography of Gay Communities in Urban North America. In *Out in Theory: The Emergence of Lesbian and Gay Anthropology,* edited by E. Lewin and W. Leap. Urbana: University of Illinois Press.

Seidman, S. 1997. *Difference Troubles: Queering Social Theory and Sexual Politics.* Cambridge: Cambridge University Press, 1997.

Simon, W., and J. H. Gagnon. 1986. Sexual Scripts: Permanence and Change. *Archives of Sexual Behavior* 15:2.

Strauss, A. 1977. Introduction (revised) to *On Social Psychology,* by G. H. Mead, edited by A. Strauss. Chicago: University of Chicago Press.

Weeks, J. 1980. Capitalism and the Organization of Sex. In *Homosexuality: Power and Politics,* edited by Gay Left Collective. London: Allison and Busby.

Prologue

An Unlikely Story (1990)

Naming the ways in which the events of an individual's life have influenced his or her works is necessarily a trickster's task. It requires a decision that, first, there is some work separate from the events of the life and, second, that the order of effect is from life to work. How much more interesting it might be if one asked how writing a certain article affected the way the author reared children or loved friends. Even as I submit to the usual autobiographical pretense that early life affects later life, that nonwork life affects the content of the work, I submit to the reader that we are conflating two temporary representations, the representation of a life and the representation of a body of works. Neither the events nor the works will be in this new representation what they were when experienced or produced.

This version will be full of denied absences and illusory presences, of voices strangled and ventriloquism practiced; it will add up to truths and fancies masquerading as each other. This creation of a plausible past must submit to at least two kinds of demands of the present, first to the contemporary selves that will recollect the past, and second to the present-day fashions of making autobiographical sense. When I think about my own past it seems to be a docudrama (perhaps a ficumentary, a doction, a faction) that I re-create, not quite on a daily basis but often enough, to

Originally published in *Authors of Their Own Lives: Intellectual Autobiographies of Twenty American Sociologists,* by Bennett Berger (Berkeley: University of California Press, 1990), 213–34. Copyright © 1990 The Regents of the University of California. Reprinted by permission.

produce a semblance of authorship for audiences of different weights and valences. There are, of course, certain epiphanies, episodes that when elaborated and condensed can be comfortably told to nearly everyone, including myself. But even these ritual professions provide only a fragile link between my recollections and the listing of works in my curriculum vitae.

Even when I reread in a current CV the small number of works attributed solely to Gagnon, I have no certain memory of having been the author of those texts. How much more suspect are the majority of citations listed as ". . . and Gagnon," "Gagnon and . . . ," or ". . . , . . . , and Gagnon." Sometimes I recall the contexts in which I wrote or talked, and the colleagues who wrote or talked with me, but the ideas and the text into which they were made are strange to me. Although I am willing to take credit and salary for that portion of "it" or "them" that others believe I have done, the portion I believe I have done is somewhat different from the institutional estimates. Whatever my transient claims to *auctoritas* might have been, it is a sense of detachment that now dominates. I sometimes wish detachment would become indifference, but one must eat.

Lately I have, with some perverse comfort, begun to think of my life as an extended example of tourism. I no longer wish to be a successful native or even a virtuous traveler. I like better the figure with camera that has just stepped down from the bus to pause for a few moments in front of everyday facades crowded with tour guides, confectionery sellers, and postcard and souvenir hawkers, whose speeches and gestures and silences will only be fragmentarily understood.

My itinerary begins with conception. I traveled, while in the womb, from a Depression-gripped mining town in Arizona to be born in a dying mill town in Massachusetts. My mother was forty-three, but I was spared visible birth defects. She was a devout Roman Catholic for her entire life and came from hardworking and temperate Irish stock. She went to work in the braid shops when she was twelve. Mary Emma Murphy was married at age thirty to a French Canadian in a town where the Canucks were beginning to fall below the ambitious Portuguese in the ethnic morality play. My father had run away from home (and the cotton mills) when he was fifteen and had returned a decade later, an atheist and a Wobbly, after hoboing and hard-rock mining in Montana, Alaska, Colorado, and Arizona—or at least so the family legend went. I think I can attest to the mining, the atheism, and the anarchism, but not to the places.

In this divided house my mother forced a decision about my fate. I was to be her child, a child of the church, a child of Irish respectability, a printer or a post office worker—no atheism, no anarchism, no working in the mines. My father honored the bargain, though as I grew older he offered me a book or two that cast doubt on the morality of the robber barons and the mining industry. Secretly he may have been relieved by not having to bear the responsibility for my fate, but he never let on.

By the time I was four we were moving again, first to a Civilian Conservation Corps camp in Vermont and then, at the bottom of the Depression, back across the country to Bisbee, Arizona, the place of my conception. Goodbye to respectable poverty; hello, raggedy-ass poor. My mother changed my birthday to get me into school ahead of my class; I thought I was born on Columbus Day for at least another five years. Comic books, *Flash Gordon, Riders of the Purple Sage,* and *Grand Ole Opry* on the radio, *Life* magazine, heat lightning in the sky, barren ochre hillsides, mining slag heaps, pulled teeth, car sickness, eyeglasses, first communion, Stations of the Cross, nightmares. My sister went away to nurse's training at Hotel Dieu in El Paso; we took a bus to visit her when she graduated, and I saw *The Wizard of Oz.* My mother and I went to church; I skipped catechism, was afraid of the nuns and God, lied at confession, and played alone. My father read books and made speeches, and they ran us out of town.

We looked like Okies, and at the Yuma crossing into California the state police treated us like Okies. They said they were looking for prohibited fruit and vegetables that might be hiding the precursors of the dreaded Mediterranean fruit fly. So my father took the mattress off the roof of the Model A and emptied out all of the boxes and pillowcases and suitcases onto the ground. The cops fingered the cotton dresses and the denim work clothes and the worn bedding, but did not find what they were looking for. Welcome to the Garden of Eden.

Long Beach during World War II was paradise. The three of us lived in a one-room, wood-sided, canvas-roofed, army-style tent for two years and shared a one-room apartment after that. My parents slept on a Murphy bed, and I slept on the couch. I do not remember a primal scene. There was an antiaircraft battery stationed in front of the apartment building, between the boardwalk and the beach, until 1943. The night sky during the blackout was disturbingly full of stars. I learned how distant they were, and I was disturbed in a different way. I started school wearing short pants and was regularly chased home by redheaded Jimmy O'Reilly, whose father had taught him how to box. My father said I had to fight my own battles, so I took to skulking home by back alleys. My mother bought me long pants, but that did not make me brave. I met a Japanese girl in the fifth grade and traded her mayonnaise-on-white-bread sandwiches for raw fish, but she was sent to a concentration camp in 1942.

In the center of town was one of Andrew Carnegie's libraries. By the middle of the war I had read my way though the children's section and was promoted upstairs to the adult books. I read without direction or discrimination; I was voracious, a cannibal of other lives. Sea stories, adventures, historical novels—I read *Beau Geste* and *Apartment in Athens* and *A Farewell to Arms* without raising my eyes from the continuous text. I thought *Moby Dick* was a book about whales and did not understand what the scarlet letter stood for. James Michener, Edna Ferber, Kathleen Winsor, Thomas B. Costain, Frank Yerby, Joseph Conrad, and Knut Hamsun had scribbled just for me. The library was a daily stop; it was safer than the alleys, and on each bookshelf there were places to hide. Books, particularly books that were not true, became (and remain) the most important source of knowledge in my life. Everything that has happened to me since then first became known to me through the scrim of text. I learned about tongue kissing when reading *Forever Amber* (a book they nearly did not let me take out) and about the thrill of looking up a girl's skirt from *Studs Lonigan*, a thrill I acquired without knowing what I was supposed to be looking at.

I caught the disease of science fiction while skipping catechism lessons for confirmation. There was a used magazine shop in a bungalow down the street from the private home in which the priest met with those of us who did not go to parochial school. I began reading *World War One Air Aces* but quickly switched to *Astounding Science Fiction* and *Amazing Stories*. I spent lovely, guilty Saturday mornings leafing through the pulp pages, disappearing into the future while worrying whether my mother would find out that I did not know the justifications for the third commandment. The musty smell of decaying paper on shelves still evokes meditative quiet in me.

As my dependence on text grew, the grip of the church weakened. It was too demanding, too frightening, too singular. I was unable to treat religious praxis with the requisite balance of indifference and attachment, to view sinning and being forgiven as part of a cycle of casual pollution and easy purity. I took it all too seriously. The version of Catholic theology preached by the Irish primitives from the pulpit of Saint Anthony's offered no comfort, only terror. After a series of minor crises, visits to the Jesuits, and the like, my spirit left, but my body continued to go to mass with my mother until I left home. "There is no God," I said to Carlfred Broderick as we walked home from Benjamin Franklin Junior High School one sunny spring afternoon. I think I made some attempt at explaining why, and I think he was shocked. I was fourteen. I went to church until I was seventeen; I worried a bit about taking the wafer in my mouth without going to confession, but that passed. When I got to the University of Chicago, I read *A Portrait of the Artist As a Young Man* and discovered a more courageous ancestor.

My father died in the spring of my apostasy. A man in a green mackintosh came to the door at about four-thirty in the afternoon and asked where my mother was. He was the designated messenger, probably having been given the nasty job because he lived nearby: They don't have a phone, Charley, so you'll have to do it. Anyway it's on your way home. I told him that my mother was at work. We stood at the open door. When would she be home? I was not sure. We shuffled about for a moment or two. Then he told me that my father had died that day at work. He said he was sorry to have to bring the message, especially sorry to have to deliver it to a kid, but he couldn't wait around because he had to get home to his family and, well, he was sorry. I called the shipyard on a pay phone, hoping there had been a mistake, but they told me no mistake had been made. My mother came back an hour later, and I told her just like that. She shrieked "Oh my God" and immediately ran away to be comforted by a neighbor woman. I have always wondered why she did not doubt, even for an instant, the truth of what I said, and why she did not pause to comfort me.

My father's death settled the covert struggle over my religious, occupational, and political fate—no atheism, no mines, no anarchy. Long after my father died, my mother said to me that she was glad that she had outlived him because he was already thinking of returning to the mines. Indeed, he had taken some of their tiny savings to buy part of a gold mine with an old comrade from the Industrial Workers of the World. She had rescued the savings, and she thought she had rescued me.

At the same time his death was the most distal cause of my attending the University of Chicago. My mother faced the choice of whether we should continue to live in California or return to Fall River, Massachusetts, where her remaining family still lived. We journeyed north via San Francisco and Spokane and then east through Chicago and New York to Fall River. These were the closing moments of the age of the train. The summer of 1946 was for me a great numinous time, a preserve of fragments only one of which is relevant to this tale. On our way back from New York to California, we had an extended stay in Chicago when the Golden State Limited was delayed ten hours. The day was full of touristic possibilities ready to be seized. First we took a luxurious shower in the white-tiled bathrooms of Union Station, sumptuous with soap, hot water, and fluffy towels, and then stepped outside to the Gray Line tour buses waiting in the August sun. Shall it be the north side of the city or the south side? The bus to the south side left first. We happily looked out the windows at train stations, black folks (who then lived in black belts), churches, and parks and then headed down the Midway Plaisance (oh, World's Fair names!) toward Lake Michigan.

Our bus slowly rolled between Harper Library on the left ("The crowns on one tower and the bishops' hats on the other symbolize the separation of church and state," said the tour guide), Burton and Judson dormitories on the right. Again on the left we passed Rockefeller Chapel, Ida Noyes Hall, and the Laboratory School—fake late Gothic stage sets. Though unlikely, it being the end of summer, perhaps William Ogburn and Ernest Burgess, and even Louis Wirth and Everett Hughes, may have been thinking sociological thoughts in their department offices at 1126 East Sixtieth Street at the very moment we rode past. But these were not names and thoughts that I would have conjured.

Perhaps it was the reverential tone of the tour guide, the hot shower, the freedom of being on the road again, going back to Eden, that made me say quite without premeditation—indeed, how could a poor fatherless child have meditated such a thing?—"I'm going to go to that university." My mother held her tongue, but thought (as she told me later when I was testing my recollection of this story), Who the hakes [heck] does he think he is? It is fortunate for our continuing affections over the next four decades that she never let on whether she had found out. I do not know, but perhaps if we had taken the north-side tour first rather than second, I might have responded with equal passion to DePaul, Loyola, or Northwestern or pledged myself to becoming a Bahá'í.

My desire to go to the University of Chicago remained only a wish that I invoked to defend myself when I was confronted by those who knew they were going to Reed, Berkeley, Stanford, USC, UCLA, or even Harvard. I secretly thought that I would go to Long Beach City College. Actually, I did not plan to go to college at all because I did not know the mechanics of going. Of course I had read novels in which people went to college, but they never said anything about how to write for catalogs or how to compose a convincing why-I-want-to-go-to-your-college-more-than-anything-else-in-the-world essay. I had never known anyone who had gone to college. That statement is not literally true; I had known many schoolteachers, but it never occurred to me that they had been licensed to teach what they taught by attending college. Our impoverishment both in money and, more important, in middle-class craft made all colleges, including the University of Chicago, seem as far away as the moon.

I was, however, rescued by a kindly man named Oakes, later registrar of the University of Chicago, who came to Long Beach Polytechnic High School on a recruiting visit. He told me how to apply to the university and may even have arranged to send me the application. Without that visit I would have gone to Long Beach City College. It perplexes me in retrospect why such a man was wandering around the United States in 1949 to recruit interested youth to the university (that is how we learned to call it, not the University of Chicago, or Chicago, just the university). Had the university put him on a train and aimed him west? Was he already in California for other reasons? It all seemed natural to me at the time. Was this not what all universities did? Much later I was told (perhaps falsely) that these recruiting efforts were part of an attempt to increase the national representation in the college. This I assume to be a code phrase for not having all of the undergraduate students—except the disappearing ex-GIs—be young Jews from Chicago and New York. I wonder sometimes who was left out when I was let in.

I went to the College of the University of Chicago as an innocent. I had not understood the plan of the university's president, Robert Maynard Hutchins (who now remembers the Hutchins plan?), nor that I was to be subjected to a week of examinations to "place" me in the course of study that would make me a liberally educated man. I recall being given a short story by Henry James and a paper on the theory of braids, both of which I was to read and on which I was to be examined in a few days. I did not understand either one. From these examinations I learned that it would take me two years to get a slightly tainted B.A. (True degrees take four years; time on task is education.) I was proud of getting the B.A. in two years until I realized that I was exactly where I should have been; the first two years of the college were meant for those who entered it after two years of high school. So much for precocity.

There was a second set of required examinations—the first complete physical I had ever been given. From these examinations I learned that I was defined epidemiologically as a wanderer. As a consequence of having lived four years in Massachusetts, one year in Vermont, five years in Arizona, and seven years in California, with asides to New York, my diseases could not have local origins. I rather liked the new label; it seemed a bit more promising than saying we moved because we were too poor to stay. I was also told my teeth were in bad shape, which was attributed to sweets, but which I blamed on the welfare dentist whom I avoided because he did not use novocaine.

These were only the first of a long series of misunderstandings between the university and me, misunderstandings often of my making, to which the university remained generously indifferent until they became a bureaucratic irritant. Kindly deans then resolved them in my favor because they thought I had promise, but of such misunderstandings and forgivenesses are disorderly careers made.

My first term in the college was exquisite. I can still recall the syllabi and I still reread many of the assigned texts. I met up with culture and personality through Freud, Durkheim, Gunnar Myrdal, Allison Davis, and John Dollard. I cannot say that they made much sense to me on first reading, nor did a career in sociology suddenly seem a sensible option when I listened to David Riesman and Philip Rieff. More appealing to my tastes were works by Thucydides, Milton, Forster, Joyce, Austen, Dostoyevski, and Huxley—works of fancy that called for response more than analysis. From there on, it was mostly downhill; I was not in any way prepared to grasp and order the opportunity offered by the college and the university to make learning into a career. I did not know how, and so each idea came to me as sweetly and individually as a flower, and on occasion I would group a bunch of ideas into a bouquet. It was good to know, but knowing for what eluded me.

It took me five years to finish the two-year program of courses for the bachelor's degree, but not because I was idle. In retrospect I seemed to have been frightfully busy, but my life was evasive and tangential rather than centered in the academy. I cannot remember any deep intellectual experience with the faculty in that entire period—except with Edward Bastian, who remained kind even as I stumbled through a fine history preceptorial that he taught. He suggested I write about the Bloomsbury group and read Anatole France. He told me something I treasured as a compliment—that I had been born old in the soul.

During those five years I attended many classes, often at the introductory graduate level, but actually I was taking courses in Harper Library, middle-class practice, the city of Chicago, and Jewishness.[1] My first job in Chicago was shelving books in the stacks of Harper Library. Shelve one, browse two. The quiet hours when I worked among the PN and PQ shelves were rather better than the doldrums of the Hs, though there were many pleasures in the DCs and GNs. The beginnings of middle-class craftiness and good manners I learned from young women, particularly two, whose families behaved with an uncommon generosity toward a young man who desperately wanted to please, did not know how to please, and hated himself for trying to be pleasing.

---

1. When I scanned this essay in preparation for this book, the scanner misread the word *Jewishness* as *Juiciness*. To take a class in Juiciness, what a treat.

But it was the membrane between the university and the city that offered the most vivid possibilities. It was a stage for the most romantic, bohemian pretenses: drinking at the High Hat or Jimmy's; listening to jazz at the Cadillac and Crown Propeller lounges on Sixty-third Street, at the Beehive on Fifty-fifth Street, or at the Sutherland Lounge on South Parkway; and listening to folk music on the Folkways record label, the local Young People's Socialist League singers, or at Big Bill and Moore's. I went to the movies without letup. There seemed to be projectors running in every rectangular room of the university as well as triple features at the Ken and the Kim on Sixty-third Street. And there was work that I did for pay on assembly lines and in machine shops, ice plants, and packing houses. The work kept reminding me of what I did not want to be, but I still did not know what I wanted to be. And it was the work that paid the rent.

If the University of Chicago had refused some Jewish applicant to accept me, a goy, it had, in an indirect sense, failed. For I was far more vulnerable to what appeared to me to be the coherent cultural claims of secular, cosmopolitan forms of Jewishness than theories of ethnoreligious origins might have predicted. In early adolescence I was already (if invisibly) detached from the religious feelings that are the core of Americanized Irish Catholicism, except perhaps the terrors of damnation. By the time I was fifteen even those fears came in infrequent surges, and finally they were replaced by an appreciation of the brute indifference of the physical world (nature signifying emptiness rather than an occasion for awe) and the thoughtful cruelties of humankind. I was also detached from my working-class world of intermittent poverty and intellectual mindlessness. As a somewhat cowardly and physically inept youth, the conventional working-class hierarchies of strength and sexual exploitation were outside my abilities even when they were relevant. At the same time I had no interest at all in Judaism, only in what I took to be a common marginality and a common interest in the book.

Being bookish took me to the university, and it was there that I first met a large number of people who were bookish beyond my dreams. They were nearly all Jews, part of that postwar release of Jews into the mainstream of life in the United States as the intensity of anti-Semitism in academic life began to fall. It was not that these young people were intellectuals; indeed most were climbers in the bureaucracies and the professions or mere careerists of the book. However, they seemed to value, perhaps only for that moment and in that context, perhaps only for purposes of gossip and belonging, the only activities at which I had talent. Had there been a place for socially mobile infidels at the universities of Cairo or Baghdad in the great ages of Islamic life, I would have become a near-Arab.

I was unaware of Jews in any deep way before that time. I did not even know the universal Christian fact that the Jews had killed Jesus. I may have missed that point since I often daydreamed during mass. Even rumors of the whirlwind had passed me by in my provincial Eden, though the death march at Bataan and Wake Island were included in the attractions at the United Artists movie house. I may have fallen in love in the summer of 1949 with a girl about whom it was said that she, a Jew, had survived in German-occupied Poland by pretending to be a Christian. I am not sure anymore whether I was in love or even whether I should believe the story, but I like remembering that she looked like Ingrid Bergman.

I am carried back by this meditation further into my adolescence, to a time when I did not understand why Nathan Tucker could not play on Saturday. He would disappear above his father's tailor shop, where on every other day of the week sailors from the Navy would come to be fitted for their dress blues and buy their combat ribbons. It was the first stage of the ritual of "getting blued, screwed, and tattooed." After my father died, Nathan's father took us fishing in the Sierra Nevada mountains, where I did not catch a fish in a whole week. It was the only extended time I ever spent with Nathan's father. I never learned his first name, but it was of course a different time, and I would not have called him by it in any case.

During the period I knew Nathan he must have been bar mitzvahed, but I was not aware of that event even as a ceremony, nor was I aware that hundreds of thousands of children our same age were being murdered in Europe. Nathan and I quarreled violently on the handball court when we were fifteen; he hit me with the ball three times, I thought deliberately. I threw the ball at him and hit him, the only Jew I ever physically attacked, but I did not know then that he was a Jew. That quarrel seemed to end our friendship. Still I do not think that we would have been friends much longer, for he was not very bookish. It is out of the university context of Jewishness that I married a Jewish woman (by parentage, not religious training) and had two Jewish children (so identified by Mosaic, Nuremburg, and Soviet laws). I worry about them, as I do about my close friends, nearly all of whom are Jewish and nonreligious. I do not think the era of pogroms and holocaust is over. That worry, the circle of people I love, and bookishness comprise my Jewishness. In this peculiar union of Venn diagrams are represented the immediacy of terror and love and the distance found in the text and the library. What then to do or feel about Zionist colonization, land expropriation, orthodox theocracy, Menachem Begin and the Stern gang, the West Bank, Shatila and Sabra? Perhaps my Jewishness has nothing to do with those matters, but only perhaps. The world fashioned by history does not allow me to choose my connections. Zionist colonization came after pogroms, Israel after holocaust—one entwined in the other, as the Palestinian Diaspora is another twist in the rope after the establishment of Israel. There is no place to stand at ease, happily convinced of the rightness of one's stand, in the midst of competing injustice and misery.

I entered the graduate program in sociology at Chicago largely as the result of failure, drift, and misadventure. My vague occupational dreams in high school had been of the hard sciences, but an inept performance in calculus and a certain penchant for text deflected me from that path. Medicine was out early, a sort of nonchoice. It was my first encounter with the ungloved reality principle at the university:

Premed adviser: Do you have all A's in the sciences?
JG: No.
PA: Is your father a doctor?
JG: No.
PA: How much money do you have?
JG: None.
PA: Forget it.

Psychology was eliminated by two short interviews on a hot August day in 1952. I suspected that the first great love affair of my life was ending and hoped that if I could make an honest man of myself, she might think more positively of our sharing the future together. So I tried to get some vocational counseling as I slithered down the occupational aspiration scale. It is difficult to communicate the fusing of heat and smell of an August day in the Chicago of the 1950s. The sky was bleached milky white, the edges of red buildings quivered in the heat, whereas the edge between shadow and light was hard, the asphalt sucked at the soles of shoes. The wind blowing from the west was thick with mutant molecules. It carried the taint from the packing houses and tanneries and the heavy metals and complex organic waste from the vents of factories. The enamel finishes baked off the cars as they spewed lead, carbon, and sulfur out of their exhausts. Future cancers were in every breath.

In back of the University of Chicago Press building were some leftover World War II barracks, one of which housed rats and rat psychologists. On the second floor I found one of the healthiest men I had ever seen. He was sitting quite composed at his desk, his brow not even damp, his shirt neatly pressed, his nose unoffended by the extraordinary stench of the place. Stretching away from us down the length of the barracks were what seemed to be hundreds of Skinner boxes in which rats were squeaking, pushing levers, eating rewards, and shitting through the grills into trays. The thousands of little clicks of the levers were being recorded by inked needles on endless loops of graph paper. There were a couple of animal tenders in white coats who seemed to be constantly engaged in filling the token dispensers with tiny pellets of food and wheeling out garbage pails full of tiny pellets of shit. The man told me that the future of psychology was now to be found in the intersect of physiology and learning, and he proposed a curriculum that sounded suspiciously like the premed program except that you did not get the golden handshake when you were done.

He asked if I minded whether he ate lunch while we talked. When I voiced no objection—indeed I encouraged him—he took out a bacon, lettuce, and tomato sandwich on white bread thickly smeared with mayonnaise. Each time he bit into it, a little mayonnaise pulsed up each of the grooves between his white, perfect front teeth. I thanked him for his time and bolted into the sunlight.

My second appointment was in a quasi-Victorian building across Fifty-eighth Street from the barracks where they kept the clinical psychologists. I climbed up four creaky flights of stairs until I reached a belfry office. The office was distinctly cooler and dimmer than the outside, and a small, dark man looked up from what he was reading to ask me what I wanted. I said I thought I might want to become a psychologist. Did I understand that many people became psychologists only to solve their personal problems? I knew enough Freud to nod appreciatively at this insight. Did I not think that it might be best to seek therapy, to set the mental record straight, so to speak, before making an occupational choice of this kind? I said that his idea had merit and thanked him and left. My suspicion that my lover might be planning to leave me for someone with better chances in life seemed sadly reasonable as I waited for the bus to take me to Continental Can for the afternoon shift.

I drifted around the university trying to avoid the fact that I had not passed the language course required for the B.A. It was also true that if I had passed the exam I would have had to give up a small scholarship that the university provided me and would have had to decide what to do when I grew up. So I sampled the graduate social sciences: a little anthropology, a disastrous sociology course from Everett Hughes, industrial relations, the history of trade unions, psychology, economic planning. Finally someone discovered that though I was still officially a student in the college, I had taken no courses in the college for a number of years, and I was making no progress toward the degree. I was forbidden to register for further courses. I was still passing as a proletarian at the aircraft engine division of Ford Motor Company, and that job paid the rent. I was now also ready to marry, but we had agreed to do so only if I finally received a degree. Proletarians may be romantic, but only if they have the promise of becoming former proletarians. I passed the course, received a degree, and married—the alternative was the fantasy of learning to play flamenco guitar in a bar in Palma, Majorca. The meaning of the past does indeed come to meet one from the future.

I then began sliding down the academic funnel toward a graduate degree in sociology. I had already sampled the early 1950s Chicago department—Hughes, Anselm Strauss, Donald Horton, Philip Hauser, and the young Otis Dudley Duncan—and then I took courses from the hybrid Columbia-Chicago department—Jim Coleman, Peter Blau, Peter Rossi, Elihu Katz, and (though they did not have the right ancestry, they did have the correct attitude) Leo Goodman, Fred Strodbeck, and Jim Davis. These were busy years since by then I was working full time at the Cook County jail for the professor-sheriff Joseph Lohman. In a fit of sentimentality I even took courses from Clifford Shaw (does anyone remember *The Jackroller?*). There is no way neatly to summarize these years. I learned a great deal of sociology since I faithfully went to classes and did assignments. But no particular idea and certainly no intellectual posture of these teachers became mine. As I reread this passage it seems arrogant, but it is not meant to be. These scholars were interested in training people in the profession (and good training it was), and whatever other mental passions they had were hidden behind their extraordinary craft. I never met any of them outside of the classroom, nor could I call any of them a friend. The fact that they spoke and I listened made them seem much older than I, though they were not. I did not know well any of my contemporaries in graduate school, though I can trot out the names of the fairly large number who have become famous in the ways sociologists become famous. I knew Philips Cutright well for a time (our first marriages took place on consecutive days), and I knew Bill Simon better than most—we helped each other at exam time and in statistics but had no sense of a shared fate.

I do not know what I learned from working at the county jail. I was only twenty-three when I started and in time was third or fourth in administrative authority. When tear gas was fired to quell a disturbance, I was sometimes fifth or sixth, as Warden Johnson, Captain Makowski, and an Italian lieutenant took priority in those circumstances. I grasp for phrases that offer a glimpse of that place that was the center of my emotional life for three and a half years—sometimes it was biffo-bongo *Hill Street Blues* with real blood, sometimes a tragicomedy in the cloacal regions; it was always the heart of darkness. And it was also a job. The only remnants of those years are absurdist fables and the love I recollect having for a man named Hans Mattick. He was the assistant warden of the prison when I arrived, and what I learned from him are those banalities of spirit about which one is ashamed to speak in these modern times. My first wife thought I loved him more than I loved her. I protested against that view at the time partially because if it were true it seemed to be a betrayal of our marriage vows and partially because she insisted on labeling it latent homosexuality (psychiatric social work has its charms). I am now persuaded she was right on the love count, though I prefer, even now when such attachments are more generously regarded, the rhetoric of friendship. As a result of helping to manage this branch of the lower intestine of urban life, I had, by indecision, evolved into someone who was believed to know something about drugs, delinquency, crime, and prisons and who had passed the Ph.D. comprehensive examinations.

My career at the Institute for Sex Research began with a visit from Wardell Pomeroy, one of the coauthors of the original Kinsey reports. He was looking for someone trained in the social sciences who was knowledgeable about working-class and criminal populations (the lower social level, ISR people called them) and comfortable with the topic. Kinsey had been dead for two years, and the current team was completing the interviewing, data analysis, and writing for the publication of a major volume on sex offenders. I was more than a little ambivalent about the prospect of sex research (about which I had read only the selection on sexual behavior and social class in *Class, Status, and Power,* edited by Reinhard Bendix and Seymour Martin Lipset, 1953), and I was about as relaxed about the topic as any other upwardly mobile former Irish Catholic man. My own sexual life was as uninspired as it could be (I later discovered the hollowness of sexual inspiration), and whatever sexual history I had accumulated was largely from individual or joint follies. I was losing my job at the jail because of an Illinois law that forbade county sheriffs to succeed themselves in office, the justification of which was that if you could not enrich yourself in a single four-year term at the public trough, you did not deserve a second opportunity. No one else was offering me a job at the time, and to return to the university would have made me a degraded student again. My wife wanted to have a child, and there was always the rent.

I knew no more about the Kinsey reports than *Time* magazine was willing to tell. Actually, the first time I heard of them was in 1949 when I went out with the male troop who hung around on the boardwalk in front of our apartment building. We visited a homosexual man who lived in a flat in Seal Beach. He gave us beer and told us about our mammalian homosexual heritage and that, according to Kinsey, one man in three had had sex with men. My compatriots had done some hustling, but I did not figure that out for nearly a decade. I had also heard Kinsey give a public lecture in Chicago just before his death, but I do not recall what he said; it must have been something about the conflict between culture, the law, and our mammalian heritage.

The first years of my career in sex research were pastoral. Blooming-ton, Indiana, where the institute is located, had peculiar powers of place, for it was at that time a world without any distractions from the professional or the domestic. In those early years I learned a great deal about sex in various species, watched films of various species doing sexual things, wandered through the collections of erotica, even learned how to interview in the correct Kinsey fashion (for a description of this arcane skill, see the section on interviewing in *Sexual Behavior in the Human Male*). It has occurred to me that if I outlive all of my colleagues of that period, I may be the last person on earth to possess that knowledge in practice. I will be a living artifact waiting to be tapped for a marginal dissertation on the history of method. As I learned more about sex, I drifted away from sociology, though Alfred Lindesmith, Albert Cohen, and Sheldon Stryker served as my disciplinary anchors as well as my friends. Daily life was full of research and lawns and babies and faculty dinners and grant applications and cocktail parties and local gossip and mortgages and swing sets and journal articles and backyard barbecues and rumors of tiny infidelities. The comforting rounds of young faculty lives worked themselves out against the shaping purposes of university rhythms. We were allowed to be thoughtless because it had all been so well thought out before.

When I arrived at the Institute for Sex Research it was dying in the quiet way most institutions die, by reenacting its old routines. Indeed, the result of my first years there was a book that was the end of a tradition, the last of the great statistical life history studies of the varieties of sex offenders. *Sex Offenders* is of some use, even though it suffers from problems of sampling and analysis and, most devastatingly, from conceptual limitations. But for me it was a project with direction, a momentum that pulled me along. Whatever my doubts about the Kinsey tradition—the fictive nature of the sexual life history, its abstraction from individual experience, the transformation of pleasure into outlet, the fantasy of the mammalian tradition—they were minor when weighted against the force of ongoing involvement. This is not a denial of my active participation in Kinsey work, only an attempt to place it at the intersection of three historical processes: the production of social science texts, the production of a career, and, now, the production of a consideration of the same texts and career.

In the spring of 1964 William Simon drove through Bloomington as he traveled from Southern Illinois University, where he was teaching, to a COFO (Congress of Federated Organizations) meeting, a civil rights movement training program at Miami University in Ohio. I was not in Bloomington then, but he stopped again when he returned west. We had seen each other a few times while he was still in Chicago, but only at the American Sociological Association meetings after he went to Southern Illinois. We had largely lost touch. For a variety of reasons he was on the job market, and for a variety of different reasons the institute was looking for a new staff member. It was a propitious pit stop, not least because a local restaurant offered us the curious delicacy "chocolate pie in season."

The institute was still winding down. Clyde Martin (one of the first of Kinsey's collaborators) had left in 1960; Wardell Pomeroy was thinking of leaving and finally left to go into private practice as a therapist in New York City in the mid-1960s. The full-time research staff would soon be down to two. Everyone was extraordinarily active, but most of the work was in the service of the collectivity and the past. The Kinsey ethos was to subordinate the individual to the goals of the collective (usually identified with Kinsey's). For example, until after William Simon and I left, no individual researcher received royalties for books or honoraria for speeches; all those moneys were contributed to the institute's own funds. The volume on sex offenders was a collective project conceived in the Kinsey era; it rested on interviews collected before 1960, and the analysis and writing of that book dominated our efforts until 1963. Research support for the institution at that time was a grant to transfer all of the original case histories (some seventeen thousand interviews) to punch cards. This coding operation required eliminating even the slightest chance of identifying subjects from the interview schedules as well as deciphering the arcane manner in which the interviews were originally coded. Even with a crew of a dozen coders the process took some three years to complete. The activities of the institute's library and archive bulked large in everyone's lives; new materials were constantly being added to the collection, and older materials needed cataloging and preservation.

At the same time there was a constant stream of notables visiting Indiana University who wished to see the collections of erotica and be taken for a tour. The tour usually began with the mysteries of the inter-view schedule ("all items are memorized by the interviewer") and the fact that the key to connecting the name file and the interviews themselves was known only by memory to senior members of the staff ("they never travel on the same plane lest the code be lost forever"). The tour guide then opened selected green cabinets containing erotic examples of Peru-vian burial pots, Japanese netsuke, and Chinese prints. The tour ended with slightly demoralized tourists looking at the spines of erotic books in the library. This was the second time I had been a tour guide; the first was at the county jail, where we took citizens' groups and various notables (Henry Fonda when he appeared in *Twelve Angry Men*, Nelson Algren after he had written *The Man with the Golden Arm*, a tough-looking gen-eral in the Shah of Iran's army) around the prison to educate them about the need for prison reform. "In this institution," we would tell them, "we have city, state, and federal prisoners, men and women, adults and juve-niles; we have a daily count of about two thousand prisoners in a building designed for thirteen hundred; all of the cells are six feet by four feet by nine feet, designed small to hold only one person, though we now have two people in more than half the cells in the institution; we turn over twenty thousand prisoners a year; 60 percent of the prisoners here have been sentenced, and sentences range from one day to five years; we have thirteen men sentenced to die—note the electric chair on your left."

In addition to the collective effort during this period, I wrote a number of unexceptional articles on sex offenders, victims of sex offenses, and sex and aging, primarily from archival data. I was committed to making the archives and library accessible to outside scholars since these represented enormous investments of time and energy that were virtually unused. The problem was to breach the barriers to the archives for outsiders, bar-riers that were created when the institute was in its initial phase of devel-opment. Can anyone today experience directly what it must have been like for Kinsey to wander through a 1940s and 1950s sexual underworld collecting erotica? To believe, and then to write, that masturbation, ho-mosexuality, and oral sex were no crime? It was a world in which the nud-ist magazine, the striptease, and the stag night were the outer limits of the erotic. It was J. Edgar Hoover's world of the sex moron and sex pervert and of the Boy Scout manual theory of masturbation. It was a world in which sex research was an academic offense. I was an adolescent in that world.

Beginning with these tours and with a certain amount of recruiting among friends, a number of outside scholars worked on problems pre-sented by the archives—though I needed to persuade my colleagues to make the archives available. Out of these efforts came Steven Marcus's *The Other Victorians* well as Morse Peckham's *Art and Pornography* (probably the best theoretical treatment of erotica to date). I helped graduate students do dissertations in a variety of areas, especially in literature and folklore. These efforts pleased me since they continued my connections to literature and the arts, if only from an underground perspective. And they allowed me to continue to acquire a varied supply of unconnected facts. I view them as having generally been a good thing, producing some of the few texts that give evidence of the peculiarities of my intellectual practice.

Bill Simon's arrival in June 1965 turned the focus of activity at the institute from inward to outward, from the archives and the past to new research and the disciplines (sociology, anthropology, etc.). I do not think that this shift would have happened without his coming to Indiana, at least not as dramatically. He was less respectful of the past than I was, better oriented toward conceptualizing problems in ways that were of interest to sociology. From his experience at the National Opinion Research Center he knew how to do survey research. We shared an interest in the work of Kenneth Burke and the softer side of the symbolic interactionist tradition (emphasis on symbolic) and a certain outsider status at Chicago, particularly as the sociology department grew more professional.

We collaborated daily from June 1965 to June 1968 and continued to work together, though with decreasing intensity, until August 1972. In the last months of 1965 we wrote three grant applications—one too many to have done them all well. I recollect some division of labor in the beginning: Bill supplied more of the disciplinary orientation, and I knew the substance of the research area. As we collaborated further, that difference grew less, and the balance and weight in contribution changed from project to project, paper to paper—indeed, from one period to another.

Each of the research projects was an attempt to bring the field of sexuality under the control of a sociological orientation. The novelty of what we did then was to lay a sociological claim to an aspect of social life that seemed determined by biology or psychology, but a claim that differed from Kingsley Davis's mechanical functionalism. The study of so-called normal psychosexual development in college students began with Erik Erikson and the crisis of the late 1960s among youth but finally turned into the ideas about the social elicitation and maintenance of sexual conduct that inform the opening chapter of *Sexual Conduct*. The research project on gay men (called homosexuals in those days) began with a distrust of etiological theories and a vision of sexual lives as determined by social factors. In the phrase homosexual banker our concern was with banker as much as with homosexual. Similarly in our tiny study of lesbians we were interested in the effects of gender on sexuality. Ideas about scripting seem to be most visible in our early writing about pornography but grew slowly to have a more central place in our thinking, replacing Erving Goffman's dramaturgy with Burke's symbolic action.

In those three years the core of my and Bill Simon's joint work was effectively completed: three edited books, a large number of papers and presentations, and the volume *Sexual Conduct*, even though it was not published until 1973. It always strikes me as strange that all of this work was completed in a period that also contained so much political and personal chaos. The antiwar movement on campus was growing in intensity (I remember hearing students shouting "Napalm!" at Secretary of State Dean Rusk as he defended President Johnson's policy in Vietnam). At Indiana the tension over issues of racism (then called discrimination and prejudice) was chronic: in 1959 the barbers in the student union building would not cut the hair of black students; in 1968 black students threatened to block the running of the Little Five Hundred bicycle race, the spring raison d'etre of the fraternities and sororities. Allen Ginsberg and Peter Orlovsky came to campus and read poetry, to the pleasure of the students and the outrage of the governor, who declared, "No more cocksuckers on campus." The Fugs, a New York rock group composed of some serious intellectuals, stood outside the office building that housed the Institute for Sex Research and sang a hymn to the memory of Alfred Kinsey while attempting to levitate the structure itself.

I was not personally ready for even this modest success. I do not think that I had planned any speeches about how I had been done in by the mindless empiricists, thus explaining away my lack of productivity, but I surely was not ready to be a cheerful member of the profession. During this period my personal life became increasingly incoherent as the disordering opportunities presented by my life course were fulfilled and found unsatisfying. In a peculiar way as my desire for professional success had increased, and indeed such success had grown more likely, my contempt for the banality of my own desires flowered as well. As the Fugs' song went, "Love is not enough, fucking is not enough, nothing is enough."

By the spring of 1967 it was clear that the effort to pull the institute out of its inward-looking posture had split the organization. By the fall of that year it was also clear that Bill Simon and I would be on the job market and that the projects we had started would have to be reallocated. We took with us the college youth study, for which the field work had been completed, and left behind the study of the homosexual community that was nearly completed in Chicago. In June 1968 Bill left for the Institute for Juvenile Research in Chicago, and I went to the State University of New York, Stony Brook, as a lecturer in sociology. Lecturer? I have forgotten to mention that during the nine years that elapsed between my leaving Chicago and my going to Stony Brook I had not finished my dissertation. Why not? As the years went by and mild successes accumulated, the student role became simply too punishing to reassume. I could not face dealing with the faculty at Chicago, even though they were unfailingly nice in my sporadic attempts at finding a dissertation topic. Just walking on campus I could feel my IQ falling. It was that most paralyzing of afflictions: I had avoided a hurdle because I was afraid to fail; I then became so contemptuous of the hurdle and the hurdle holders that it was impossible for me to jump. This twenty-year gap between entering the University of Chicago and getting the Ph.D. made me expert on why graduate students should hang around and finish their degrees at all costs, but it also made me uncritical of those who do not. I am convinced as well that a disordered career such as mine was possible only in the era in which it occurred. There is now less forgiveness in the profession than there once was. Perhaps the question might be, is a disordered career better than none at all?

I finished the dissertation after being at Stony Brook for one year. Kindly circumstances and Morris Janowitz allowed me to write a simple, but acceptable, five-variable, 180-page survey research document. Not quite Durkheim, but even at my advanced age the committee, composed of members of the third Department of Sociology at the University of Chicago I had attended, did not expect a classic. For the next four years Bill Simon and I continued to collaborate, but at a greater intellectual distance and less effectively. Both of us were caught in the daily circumstances of our lives, and our attention focused on the demands of the institutions in which we worked. We completed a number of papers from the study of college youth, wrote up our research on working-class young people, and finished a number of projects together, but the routine of collaboration was gone. Still, it had been a remarkable run. Its intellectual, professional, and emotional influence on my life I still feel directly and indirectly. We talk about collaborating again, now and then, and have even done so, in a set of four papers on scripting that are a substantial advance over the earlier work. It is not possible for me to separate what is mine from what is his. Even asking who authored what causes me pain that I want to avoid. I tend to look away, think of other things. Perhaps this experience is behind my deep distrust of the idea of *auctoritas* and authorship. Even writing about the time when we worked together seems invasive of his right to tell his version of the same events, in his own voice. Let me evade articulating my affection for him lest it require a false reciprocity from him.

Toward the end of this period I made a number of missteps. I became a dean and worked on projects in regional and environmental planning. Neither job came to much. The deaning gave me a higher salary. No publications resulted from the environmental work, but there were later benefits. In 1972–73 I was an overseas fellow at Churchill College, Cambridge, supported by a National Institute of Mental Health postdoctoral fellowship. It was a good year for me, but not for my children, who went to English schools, or for my first wife, who left her job to come to Europe.

After we returned to the United States I went back to the sociology department to teach. I worked with two psychologists at Stony Brook on psycho-physiological correlates of sexual response. I learned some psychology, but my sense was that they got more out of it than I did. I separated from my wife in 1975, and we got divorced in 1979. Also in 1975 I started to do some work in simulation and gaming, and that has now become a serious area of study for me. My kids grew up. I got older. I now live with my best friend, and I have two more Jewish children. I spent 1978 to 1980 at the School of Education at Harvard and the year 1983–84 teaching at the University of Essex. I reside in Princeton.

Why so cryptic about this recent period and so lush about the distant past? I think because the time since 1973 has been busy but indecisive. It has no re-collective plausibility: the participants are still alive; the events are only events, not yet stories; even my texts of this time have no center. When I think about this period I have a strong sense of evasion and drift, but it is too soon for it to be adequately revised and protectively judged.

Will I do anything else interesting? It would be pretty to think so.

Part One

Scripts, Conduct, and Science

Sex Research and Social Change (1975)

The field of scientific sex research, which emerged at the turn of the century with the exemplary work of Sigmund Freud and Havelock Ellis, has been complexly interactive with changing general social conditions, specific trends in sexual conduct, the content of sexual ideologies, and the developing techniques of scientific inquiry. The earliest sex researchers, although serving to bring sexuality out of the Victorian cold and into the center of human development, based their views of sexuality on control-repression and drive models. The Freudian tradition was especially influential in general intellectual matters and was probably the most important in the development of twentieth-century sexual ideologies. Beginning in the 1920s and culminating in the work of Kinsey in the 1940s and 1950s, a tradition of social bookkeeping began focusing on the sexual behavior of relatively "normal" persons. Methodologically such studies moved away from the case history and from populations who were defined as criminal or neurotic. At the same time, general social changes were occurring that were directly affecting the rates and directions of sexual conduct in the society. The work of Alfred Kinsey charted

Originally published in *The Archives of Sexual Behavior* 4 (2): 111–41. Reprinted by permission of Plenum Publishing. This essay is a revised version of the Havelock Ellis Memorial Lecture presented in London, February 2, 1973, while the author was an Overseas Fellow of Churchill College, Cambridge. The research was supported by USPHS grants from the National Institute of Child Health and Human Development (HD 4156) and a special postdoctoral fellowship from the National Institute of Mental Health (MH54372).

these changes and in turn influenced public attitudes, public policy, and research interests during the 1950s and 1960s. The work of other researchers began to fill in the picture of sexual conduct in the society using survey methods, and some workers began studies in sexual deviance that focused anew on homosexuality and prostitution. The work of William Masters and Virginia Johnson served to open the door to studies of sexual anatomy and physiology by applying well-known techniques to the laboratory study of the sexual. While the biological tradition is still strong in the discussion of the sexual, new emphases are being placed on a cognitive-social learning perspective that emphasizes the nonbiological factors in sexual development. Major changes have occurred in the sexual backdrop of the society in the 1960s, and, while changes in sexual conduct have been less than revolutionary, they have occurred in a number of areas (contraception, abortion) that have directly influenced societal practices. Sex research and the sex researcher have played an important role in providing benchmarks for sexual practices, illuminating general understanding, and providing the content for ideological debates about the right and wrong of sexuality in the society. In few areas of research have researchers had such an important role in the debate over the meaning and significance of the behavior they have studied.

One of the most sensitive and consequently elusive indicators of social change is the rate at which members of a culture become strangers to their personal pasts as well as to the historical modes of experiencing which were provided by their culture. That is, as members of an ongoing present we are detached and/or alienated from those past processes, which have created our current cultural situation. This estrangement seems to have two sources. The first is that we are the individual products of the cultural changes we seek to understand, and the cultural resources of symbols, language, and styles of apprehending which we use are themselves the results of this same process of cultural change. We lose our past because we can only experience it through present artifact and the rules of retrospection; the layers of the present conceal and distort. The second source is that our attempts to consciously set in motion planned social change are lost in the general process of social action and the outcomes of our efforts cannot be limited and controlled. This is in some measure because the consequences of complex social acts are difficult to predict, but also in part due to the indeterminate nature of such complex social activities. We offer ideas and perform acts, and despite our best attempts to constrain their meanings an active and variously motivated world takes them and puts them to manifold uses both consonantly and dissonantly with our original intentions.

In any attempt to examine the history of research on human sexuality and the interactions of that research with the sociocultural order in which it is embedded, we face these problems of estrangement from the past. As each new generation appears, the felt and experienced sexual culture, the sexual landscape of the past becomes more distant. Not only does the cultural reality of the era prior to the work of such sexual revolutionaries as Ellis, Freud, and Magnus Hirschfeld fade, but so does the reality of the two decades prior to the publication of the Kinsey researches in the late 1940s and early 1950s. The young today grow up in a post-Freudian, post-Kinseyan, and near to post–Masters and Johnson world in which the findings of sex research have been transmuted into popular culture by the alchemy of the mass media magazines, advice columns, volumes of popularized science, and the textbooks of abnormal psychology, sociology, physiology, and home economics. The climate of ideas and the cultural-historical situation that produced scientific knowledge about sex and the sense of personal mission and risks that accompanied its original acquisition and publication can be experienced only in retrospect, even by those who participated in it, for the ideas themselves are now part of our present conventional wisdom. For the majority of the young, except for those rare few who as a result of personal or academic misadventure are historically minded, these ideas in their present textbook form seem adequate. This is at one level surely appropriate, for if knowledge is to be of use to a new generation it must come partially or even totally freed from many of the historical, biographical, or cultural conditions that produced it. Yet for those who participated in that older culture and for those who actively sought its transformation, this easy acceptance can only produce a sharp sense of disjuncture and an uneasy feeling of both personal and historical inauthenticity.

Not only have the cultural conditions under which research into human sexuality began been partially lost to us, but the second source of estrangement comes into play as well. The outcome of what researchers have done or published is not received passively nor does it retain the form in which it was conceived. Research on sex or practical attempts at sexual reform enter into the world and are willy-nilly put to use by a lively culture in ways that their creators never intended. Unlike the poets, who can claim to be the parents of any interpretation that a critic finds in their poems, especially if the poets like it, scientific researchers find themselves in the difficult position of defending a "truthful" view of their own work. The near impossibility of this attempt, against the inventive efforts of both followers and adversaries, is suggested by Freud's continual struggles for doctrinal purity in psychoanalysis. But such struggles for the control of the meaning of ideas and research have far deeper implications for those who perform research on sexual conduct than for most other researchers, for the influence of their ideas flows far outside the academic sphere and in more or less accurate forms penetrates into the daily life of society. I recall from Calder-Marshall's (1959) biography of Ellis that some of the volumes of *The Psychology of Sex* found their way into the less staid Soho bookshops, their pages riffled by those seeking what Calder-Marshall calls prurient excitement. Undoubtedly, the findings of the "Kinsey Reports" have been used by young men to justify having intercourse with young women on the grounds that such practice improves the likelihood of sexual compatibility in marriage, and in an earlier day the Freudian texts were used to point out the potential psychological disorders that resulted from personal sexual inhibition. None of these men, if they had observed these unintended uses of their work, would have recoiled in shock. I think Ellis particularly would have appreciated the ways in which what he had done had been put to use in the marvelous diversity of human lives. Such practical uses he would have seen not merely as clinical manifestations or additional data, but also as celebrations of human ingenuity.

I do not wish these "practical" outcomes to be taken as the only examples of the ways that research on human sexual conduct penetrates the life of the culture and serves as an element in its change. I use them only to illustrate the various ways that the work of those who would disturb the world's slumber are received. Such uses of the work of Ellis, Freud, and Kinsey are further reflections on the meaning of sexual research and its relation to the social and cultural order in which it exists. In this sense, research on sexual conduct, which by its form and findings influences to some degree the less academic forms of sexual life in society, is itself a form of sexual conduct. As sexual conduct, academic research and publication are subject to cultural constraints; they are desired, permitted, or prohibited. The subject matter, the techniques and conditions of research, the forms of publication, and the canons of proof of sex research are cultural products with an internal dynamic as well as having connections with the larger academic, intellectual, and social world which surrounds and interactively influences them. Once the researches are completed and published, the public informed, and students trained, these new conditions have a variable influence on general sexual conduct in society by bringing to bear on that conduct new bases for judgment, and this new conduct becomes the basis for similar or different patterns of future research.

A studied concern for the role of sexuality in human life has a relatively short history, one of scarcely a century, at least insofar as that concern takes as its point of departure a scientific attempt at disclosing what people do sexually through researches performed in the spirit of intellectual and social enlightenment. This is not to say that there were not some who were concerned with the sexual, both medically and morally, earlier in the nineteenth century. There exist some fragmentary studies of the sexual life of peasants, the dangers of masturbation, and, most commonly, the social conditions of prostitution and venereal diseases. But it was largely toward the end of that century in Europe that there was a major cultural movement cast in a scientific-medical form that directly challenged previously held beliefs about the role of the sexual in human life. It was at this time that the works of Freud, Hirschfeld, Moll, and Krafft-Ebing on the Continent and Ellis in England began to appear in print. It is a difficult and perhaps fruitless task to declare the beginning of an era in more than the roughest historical terms, but it appears that in much of Western Europe and to a lesser extent in the United States in the 1890s more attention began to be paid to the formulation of alternative interpretations of the significance of the sexual in human life. It was clearly not a movement that occurred on its own, for it shared elements and overlapped with changing patterns of political and artistic thought and activity. It was part of the period in cultural history which was the source of the idea and experience of the "modern." One aspect of the modern is that it was/is a period when cultural elements that were largely insulated from the sexual in the past could be informed by and informing of its new presence. More directly than before, the sexual aspects of life could be used as material for the arts, as the basis for personal relations, and as planks in platforms for individual and political liberation.

If there was a basic common ground in the work of this generation of revolutionaries, it was that they acted to move sexuality out of the domain of the alien and the ignored—to bring sexual acts and actors into the world of the noticed. This was the major and original influence of these sexual pioneers rather than any specific formulation or program. The fundamental act was one of inclusion; that is, they took that which was largely external to the mental life of nineteenth-century culture and moved it inside. In John Le Carre's sense, sex had been brought in from the cold. But what was involved was not only the cultural *recognition* of the sexual, but through the process of cultural reformulation its cultural *invention* as well. The quality of this cultural barrier in England (and with variations, for the Continent) is expressed in the words of Sir George

Croft in George Bernard Shaw's long-banned play of the early 1890s, *Mrs. Warren's Profession* (1970).[1] Croft, in plighting his troth to Mrs. Warren's daughter, is not aware that she knows that her mother's profession is managing the brothels that Croft has financed. When confronted with the facts, Croft says: "Why the devil shouldn't I invest my money that way? I take the interest on my capital like other people: I hope you don't think I dirty my hands with the work. . . . How do you expect me to turn my back on 35 per cent when the rest are pocketing what they can like sensible men? . . . If you want to pick and choose your acquaintances on moral principles, you'd better clear out of this country, unless you want to cut yourself out of decent society." And then Croft goes on to define "decent society" in this way: "As long as you don't fly openly in the face of society, society doesn't ask any inconvenient questions . . . there are no secrets better kept than the secrets everybody guesses. In the class of people I can introduce you to, no lady or gentleman would so far forget them-selves as to discuss my business affairs." At one level I suspect that Shaw, in order to draw his archetype of Victorian hypocrisy with hard edges, makes Croft too knowing and too cynical. But to see that the same situation of respectable profit from society's dirty work still exists, we need only to examine a recent essay (Sheehy 1972) in *New York* magazine which exposes the ownership of the hotels that profit from the recent boom in prostitution: "No one in city government was willing to talk about the *owners*of prostitution hotels. It was all very embarrassing . . . a little research turned up the names of immaculate East side Wasps (White Anglo-Saxon Protestants), a prominent Great Neck heart surgeon, bona fide members of the Association for a Better New York and the Mayor's own Times Square Development Council . . . [as well as] several Park Avenue banks" (71). These two quotes are not to emphasize the continuing venality and corruption of respectable society, but to highlight the nature of attitudes toward the sexual that revolutionaries like Freud, Ellis, and Hirschfeld faced—an attitude deeply ingrained in contemporary consciousness which defined persons who were unashamedly sexual as belonging to a different class of human beings than the general run of society. Ellis's response to these conditions was to say: "I have never repressed anything. What others have driven out of consciousness. . . . as being improper or obscene, I have maintained or even held in honor" (Collis 1959, 8).

At one level these personal postures and scientific works were a chal-

1. Written in 1894, *Mrs. Warren's Profession* was first presented as a theater club performance in January 1895 but did not receive a public first night in England until March 1926.

lenge to many of the collective views of the place of sex in human life. They exposed and brought forward deeply held cultural beliefs about sexuality. The act of including the sexual into life not only as a pathological manifestation but also as it informed and shaped conventional lives was a profound challenge to that elite for whom the sexual existed outside the normal social order. Indeed, it was only through the exclusion of the sexual that many aspects of the normal social order could go forward, since its absence was required to maintain the current orthodoxy of relations between the genders, as well as being implicated in the meaning of religious, economic, and political life. The extended crisis created by the Freudian position and its vast intellectual influence resulted from the decision of its adherents to place the sexual at the center of character formation, not as a deplorable instinct that could and should be controlled, if not completely suppressed, but as a prime motive force, not only of pathology, but in its transformations bringing about the development of cultural life itself. My sense is that the fascination and continuing power of Freud and his extraordinary influence during this century have been generated by his thoroughgoing ideological treatment of sexuality in human character development—an impressive philosophical effort at totalizing and encompassing the human condition in a single system.

In contrast, more pragmatically in the English intellectual tradition, and perhaps in consequence having a more modest impact, Ellis argued differently about the role of the sexual: "The sexual impulse is not, as some have imagined, the sole root of the most massive human emotions, the most brilliant human aptitudes—of sympathy, of art, of religion" ([1899] 1936, 282).

Indeed, this difference between Freud and Ellis was permanent—an opposition grounded in differences in cultural styles and in the nature of the cultures that produced and chose among their ideas. Outside the central act of inclusion, substantial differences did emerge among the leading pioneers in the study of sex, differences that commonly grew as their scientific styles, relations to social action and reform, and strategies for promulgating their ideas changed over the ensuing decades. In the totality of Freud's thought there remained a sense of the tragic limitations of human relationships, even those that were the most intimate. Ultimately these limits were buried in the irreducible conflicts between biological nature and cultural reality. Ellis reacted against this stream in Freudian thought and shared that ameliorative tendency which characterized social and sexual reformers in England at the turn of the century and later. He focused on dispelling ignorance and superstition, and this emphasis on education and reform limited the use of his works in the interests of an ideology of either despair or optimism. [2] This difference between Ellis and Freud meant that they had quite different patterns of influence. For many purposes, Ellis's formulations were too measured; they did not provide a general and organizing base for making sense of the role of the sexual in all aspects of life. For when the sexual was brought in from the cold, it was more than an intellectual act; it had the deepest emotional resonance and for many people it necessitated integrating the new fact of the sexual into the entire fabric of their lives. The overriding significance of the sexual required a deep personal transformation and conversion if it were to be admitted at all. This experience of conversion, which characterized not only the true believers in psychoanalysis but many other intellectuals as well, as part of dealing with a revalued sexuality, is one of the measures of the alienated status of the sexual at that moment in cultural history—a status that has lasted for many persons until the present time.

While the act of including the sexual into general cultural life was deeply original, the specific formulations about the nature of sexuality offered by Ellis, Freud, and others still shared many assumptions and preconceptions about sexuality that were current at the end of the nineteenth century. No cultural innovation comes as a totally original conception; it always combines unchanged materials from the past with novel reformulations. Its linkages with the past make it at least partially acceptable in the present, providing intellectual continuity and discontinuity at the same time. In order to bring the sexual into cultural notice, it was necessary for many former beliefs about the nature of the sexual to be retained, especially the assumption that sexuality was rooted in humanity's biological heritage and a belief in the dangerous power of the sexual instinct. The passage from Ellis quoted above continues: "It [the sexual instinct] is the first place, the deepest and most volcanic of human impulses." The power of the sexual instinct, its very naturalness and the social necessity for its expression to be controlled or inhibited, continued to be a shared basic belief of most people, including the scientific sexual pioneers as well as those who populated the barricades of the sexual struggles both on the liberationist and on the repressive sides. It is in part this underlying and shared assumption about the power of the sexual that has characterized most of the continuing controversies about the impact of the sexual on human life. As a result of this unquestioned view that the sexual is a powerful and significant biologically rooted force, which some feel should be inhibited and others want more freely expressed, the char-

---

2. Evidence for this distinction may be found in Ellis's review of William McDougal's *The New Psychology*, a text deeply influenced by Freud. The review is reprinted in Ellis 1932.

acter of the public debate about sexuality in the decade between the turn of the century and the present has been largely fixed. On one side are the sexual utopians who believe that with the liberation of our natural sexual energies aberrations of the sexual instinct will disappear, that greater personal fulfillment is possible through sexuality, and that we have mutilated ourselves through the repression and inhibition of our sexual instincts. Even more radically, the liberation of the sexual has been viewed as basic to freeing human beings from the constraints of capitalism and from the distortions imposed on free human relationships by the nuclear family and as a necessary correlative to economic revolution in liberating human consciousness. Variants of these views were expressed by a wide range of second-generation sexual revolutionaries deriving from a variety of intellectual forebears, voices ranging from Wilhelm Reich to D. H. Lawrence and Marie Stopes. The opposing view of the sexual conservatives was that the sexual instinct was profoundly dangerous, held in check only by the bonds of law and custom, sexually pure environments, and the fear of hell, loss of reputation, disease, or unwanted pregnancy. Each change in sexual values or practice from the most conventional was seen as a potential for releasing the sexual beast, which would produce the collapse of the family, of religious institutions, and even of society itself.

Possibly I have parodied these two points of view, but rarely have they risen above this level of argument, and when they were publicly opposed even more sweeping simplifications were advanced. In any case, it is the basic belief that they share which is most important—an agreement about the power and significance, for either good or ill, of the sexual instinct. The continued dominance of this view meant that everything was not new in the sexual culture of the beginning of the twentieth century and that there remained a common ground on which the later controversies would be based.

Another aspect of the sexual change at the end of the nineteenth century was that this act of inclusion was largely received into an elite and literate subculture. While there did exist channels for transmission of information into the mass of the society, the first moments of sexual change were primarily important to the middle and upper classes and disturbed only a limited number of sleepers. In a societal sense, they represented a seed bed in which the proposal of alternatives could quicken the potential for change by increasing the number of possible intellectual options which could be used to interpret the present and the past or offer models for the future. As long as these modern sexual ideas were confined to the literate minority, to private discussion, or to scientific texts and did not enter the media intended for general audiences or the domain of political or social action, they were only sporadically suppressed. When modern sexual ideas, including those which involved the politics of gender, were transmitted to society at large, they were more often suppressed, retarded, and controlled. Sexual ideas in the theater or books for general circulation, as well as information and materials for general circulation about birth control or venereal disease, came under regular scrutiny and repression long after the turn of the century.

At least two dimensions can be seen in these decisions to suppress: one was the general confusion of the idea of sexual excess with that of the dangers of political disorder—a vision of the lustful mob and political unrest so nicely captured in the phrase "riotous behavior." The connection between sexual and other forms of excess was a genuine middle- and ruling-class fear, and to some extent it still is. The view that the working classes or the Irish or the Blacks are not only reservoirs of sexual license but are also potential sources of sedition is a cultural connection of symbols and meanings which governments still act on today. The second dimension was a desire on the part of sexual conservatives to protect those whom they saw as weaker and more corruptible than themselves—commonly the lower classes, women, and children—by preventing them from being exposed to sexually noxious ideas or materials. It has been largely this latter attitude which has served as the basis for the sexual censorship of various art forms and media during the twentieth century.

But as long as advanced sexual ideas were confined to narrow literate populations living in urban centers and did not intrude on the mass media or the political or social action, they were rarely repressed. This was the situation that existed between 1900 and the end of World War I. There was a steady penetration and consolidation of a modern sexual viewpoint in certain sectors of the academic world as well as in intellectual and artistic circles in the large cities of Europe. What scientific work that was proceeding was paralleled by the increasing sexual content of the arts, especially in literature and in some cases the theater. Changes in the plastic arts came far more slowly, as did changes in the mass media. The situation of those who attempted to repress these new ideas was largely that of attempting to wage a quiet, brushfire guerilla war. Their problem was that they possessed only the weapon of censorship, which was and is an exceedingly blunt instrument, and its use often attracted more controversy and public discussion than the original materials. Articulating a program of opposition meant that for the conservatives as well as for the libertarians sexuality had moved from the sacred to the secular sphere, that sex could be the subject of debate and changes of standards were therefore possible. But it was exactly such a secular debate, a debate that involved canons of evidence drawn from the esthetic or the scientific, that the conservatives wished to avoid. This left the initiative largely to the sexual libertarians and the innovators.

The sexual situation in the United States during these years was perhaps more conservative than in Europe. At the turn of the century, it remained an intellectual colony for European ideas. The ideas of Freud, Ellis, and others became modestly well known in the years between 1900 and 1920, but once again the ideas were limited to an urban and academic elite. At the same time, the conditions for changes in sexual activity or patterns of personal conduct were far more fertile in America than in most European countries. While at one level the United States may have been one of the most singularly puritanical of societies, it contained many different groups with differing sexual traditions, spread over vast geographical regions, involved in widely differing cultural experiences, which represented a great potential for change. The large-scale movement of populations to the cities, the disrupting influences of urban life on immigrant cultures, the decline in familial and neighborhood control over the processes of courtship and marriage, a marked increase in the public affirmation of the ideology of romantic love, and a democratic belief in the value of personal mate selection contributed to an erosion of prior cultural standards about the management of sexual relations, especially those before marriage. From what fragmentary evidence that exists, it appears that there was a substantial increase in the proportion of young American women who had intercourse prior to marriage in the cohort who reached marital age just after World War I and during the 1920s. These changes were influenced less by innovations in sexual ideas than by a change in the character of social relations of men and women before marriage. This was most apparent in the sections of the population involved in middle-class and urban life, which served as a cutting edge for the changes that were to occur later in other sectors of society. It was also a change that was not observed until nearly twenty years after it had occurred. For at that moment there did not exist a social science bookkeeping system that could feed back into the larger society evidence about what was occurring within it.

The 1920s in the United States was also a period during which a concern for the sexual grew more public. The popular magazines and journals recorded an image of the colleges as sinks of immorality, and the popular press was deeply concerned with the exploits of the sexual criminal. The silent cinema tested the limits of community morality with nudity, sexual themes, and historical epics, which at least possessed the potential for exotic eroticism. There appeared in both the slick and the pulp magazines drawings and photographs of nude and seminude women and, especially in the latter, tales of sexual violence playing on images of racial and bestial sexuality. During this same period, there was also a concern for sex education, which resulted in a series of what can be described as liberal publications offered from the United States Government Printing Office. The roots of these changes in the public presentation of the sexual and the shifts in personal sexual conduct remain obscure, for even though they are parallel in time it is not clear that they affected each other, and indeed, they are likely to have been the common outcome of other and larger social forces.

These changes observed in the media and in some aspects of personal conduct occurred in an extremely chaotic and complex context, for the end of the second and beginning of the third decade of the century was one of those periods during which there was a revolt of the countryside against the emerging moral and political power of the cities. It was the period when there was absolute prohibition of alcohol and the passage of laws against drug use. It was also a period when the campaign to suppress street and brothel prostitution was begun and largely succeeded. Concomitantly with this last campaign but largely influenced by other factors, there was a decline in the frequency with which men used the services of the prostitute population. By the end of the 1920s and in the early 1930s, with the coming of a national culture and film market, even the more sexually open atmosphere of the cinema and portions of the printed media reverted to a less overtly sexual expression.

It was during the 1920s that research into sexual conduct began in earnest in the United States. Partially under the influence of Freud and variants of psychoanalytic doctrine, but more directly related to the tradition of social amelioration in United States reform movement, three studies of sexual conduct of those with relatively conventional sexual lives were completed. In 1929, Katherine Davis published a questionnaire study entitled *Factors in the Sex Life of 2,200 Women*—a study begun in 1920 and initiating a tradition of the recording of the sexual lives of the college educated. George V. Hamilton conducted interviews with two hundred men and women, the results of which were also published in 1929, entitled *A Study in Marriage* (a study that was influenced by psychoanalytic theory); and Robert Dickinson and Louise Beam published in 1931 a research drawn from Dickinson's files as a gynecologist entitled *One Thousand Marriages*. All three works showed evidence of a continuing European influence, but translated by American cultural circumstances. Ellis wrote the introduction to the work of Dickinson and Beam, and from it we can judge the novelty of these works as well as their linkage to Ellis's own views on the necessity for studying the "normal": "An investigation of the sex activities and sex relationships among fairly normal people, on a sufficiently large and systematic scale to be treated statistically is quite new, and the most carefully conducted and illuminating studies . . . have been carried out in what is commonly and not unreasonably called the Anglo-Saxon culture. We owe them to American investigators who have worked among the people of the United States" (vii). Though these studies anticipated what was to become an American hegemony in sexual studies, they did not have a deep collective influence. They gained only a limited influence in the larger research community of social sciences, in the academic world, and among sexual reformist groups; but, as Ellis realized, they foreshadowed changes in the scientific style and content of research on sexuality. At that moment, the dominant subject matter of what passed as research on sexual conduct was the exotic and the curious, the neurotic, or the criminal.

The anthropology of sexual conduct dealt with what the public thought was the strange behavior of primitive peoples. The psychology of sexual conduct with the perversions of the sexual instinct and the criminology of sexual conduct nearly exhausted the remainder of the scientific tradition dealing with sexuality. Indeed, this dominant concern with sexual criminality seemed perfectly proper, since nearly all aspects of sexual conduct except for marital coitus were proscribed by legal statutes of one form or another. Although the criminal sanctions against most forms of heterosexual behavior were rarely invoked, the law and public customs cast their net widely and securely over practices that the new statistical studies suggested were moderately widespread among "fairly normal people." These three innovative studies offered a shift from a concern with the exotic to the everyday; from the behavior of those outside the pale to those at the conventional center of American society.

At the same time, these studies utilized and Ellis applauded a change in research style that carried a different sense and source of authority and plausibility. The use of constructed questionnaires (fixed modes of questioning with common questions asked of all subjects), the anticipation of scientific sampling, and the presentation of data in tabular and statistical format made these studies the direct ancestors of the Kinsey research as well as of other sexual studies of a survey nature. Much of the prior research had been in the case history or clinical form, a form that derives much of its plausibility from what appears to be a detailed presentation of reality, a presentation that takes as its model works of literature and the imagination. The differing sense of truth value and authority that arises from these different modes of procedure and presentation has been suggested in a different context by George Steiner in his recent lectures at the University of London. Steiner points out that in the work of three exemplary figures, Marx, Freud, and Levi-Strauss, citations of belles lettres are commonly used when difficult questions requiring absolute authority are to be answered. In these cases, the authority of an imaginative text is used to confirm a scientific assertion. The presentation of case histories and clinical case study techniques are combined with the cultural authority inherent in imaginative works.

At the same time, such strategies also declare the researcher's allegiance to that class of persons who produce such works. It is an adherence to the belief that imaginative art is the highest affirmation of the human spirit, more important than science, more universal than the limited world of statistics, and that acts of art or of imagination are more truthful and enduring than science. The statistical mode of presentation offered by these early researchers suggests another allegiance and other canons of proof—an adherence to the tradition of statistical method and technique in the natural sciences. What was in the balance was the weight or evidential value of two alternative modes of apprehending and coding the world, two separate constructions with different rules of procedure and styles of presentation. This opposition between the literate and the numerate recurs again and again in later intellectual controversies, not only about development of sex research, but also about the general acceptability of quantitative behavioral science in other areas. The controversies in the study of sexuality were more bitter since it was conceived to be at the center of human intimacy and affection as well as being one of the wellsprings of the imaginative act. From a literary-intellectual point of view, this could not be captured in mere numbers.

The findings of these studies, and of smaller and more fragmentary studies done in the same style at about the same time, exposed a partial picture of sexual conduct, at least in the middle class. What appeared was a picture of conventional individuals trying to work out their own sexual lives in a situation of profound personal ignorance, misinformation, and cultural isolation. While the level of talk about sex had increased, fragments of sexual information had appeared, practical sex manuals were quietly for sale, and even birth control devices began to have a small but increasing use, the sexual scene appeared to be one of difficulty and disorder. Clearly there was a self-selection among those who chose to participate in a sex research project; it was and still is often argued that those who participate are more troubled in their adjustment than the happy many who do not. The solution to such questions awaited a more accurate set of sampling procedures, but the conclusions of these studies and other more impressionistic evidence indicated to many observers that people's sexual lives were blighted by the oppressive and inhibiting character of the society in which they were living. There is no question that during the period from 1920 to 1950 (and continuing in different forms today) there was an absence of learning conditions under which a person could find out about, judge, and develop his or her own sexual interests, that the information that did exist was often false and misleading, and that what obtained in the sexual area was a condition of pluralistic ignorance. In older, more culturally homogeneous situations, persons could manage their sexual lives using false and misleading information, but only because (here was some sort of consensus) unity in error at least provided a set of stable guidelines. In an expanding and complex social world, these older, more local cultural values no longer retained their constraining power. The picture of sex in marriage that emerged from this early research was a history of fumbling and often mute struggles to find some sense of order, an attempt to place sexuality in some reasonable relationship to the rest of life and make sense of the changing relations between the genders. In a situation of change, the more content were those who believed or made do with conventional standards about the appropriate roles of men and women, the differing rights of each to sexual pleasure, and the legitimacy of received sexual standards. At the same time, the contentment eroded for many others as they faced the external circumstances of changed living conditions and the concurrent rise of alternative ideas and beliefs about the role of the sexual in human life.[3]

If the life of conventional persons was becoming increasingly troubled, the condition of those with unconventional sexual interests was far more difficult. Even such a general practice as masturbation among men remained at best a personal blot or weakness of character and at worst was believed to be physically debilitating and perhaps mentally weakening. Mouth-genital contact was a crime and a pleasure that brought with it feelings of contamination or perversion. For many persons, particularly women, sexual pleasure did not exist as an experience and in some cases not even as a potential idea. The homosexual lived in a world outside, both criminal and perverse, both sinner and biological sport. The purported science that existed about the homosexual was as oppressive in its intent as was the theology that preceded it. The sexual offender existed in a near-Lombrosian world, his behavior usually explained by the last theory that

---

3. The idea that the sexual life could be blighted in its potential development was in itself a major shift from a view that the only thing that could go wrong with sex was its sinful or criminal use.

had been discredited in nonsexual criminology. Thus, after Goddard's view that all crime was caused by feeblemindedness was disconfirmed, the sexual "moron" still existed in public and criminological theories of crime. An interest in the pornographic or the obscene—an area that still included the barely uncovered human body and birth control information—was either a private perversion or the collective interest of adolescent boys and members of all-men voluntary organizations. Sexuality as solely a man's preserve still existed in the morally wrong but permitted domains of fornication, adultery, and sex with women prostitutes. At the level of daily life, sexuality remained a world of folklore and fakelore, to be entered into at some risk and with no safety nets. One's public posture was one of virtue, while privately the sexual remained an area of tantalizing interest and power.

In the cultural sector where sexual behavior was studied and discussed, and out of which newly developed and promoted interpretations emerged to counter the omnipresent cultural vision of the sexual domain as one of contest between vice and virtue, excess and restraint, impulse and duty, the Freudian view—or at least versions of the Freudian view—became dominant among the more innovative sector of the United States' intellectual elite. It must be noted that one reason for the acceptability of the Freudian doctrine was that it shared many of the prior assumptions about the culture oppositions expressed by the sexual, but that these oppositions were transformed by it into a set of cultural symbols which expressed the same tensions in more acceptable form. Beginning as a controversial doctrine in the 1920s and finally becoming a form of received wisdom in the late 1940s and early 1950s, psychoanalysis quickly went from heterodoxy to orthodoxy. It penetrated only marginally into academic psychology and sociology, although it was a great success in anthropology, clinical psychology, and some areas of political science. But it was in its double form as a therapy for human ills and as an ideology which could be used to sort out the facts of history, politics, individual behavior, and works of art and literature that psychoanalysis profoundly influenced the character and content of intellectual life in the United States. An exact sociohistorical study of this process of cultural penetration which would clarify the reasons for the success of psychoanalytic doctrines in that cultural situation has not been made, but there are some clues. In part, psychoanalytic theory was a useful device through which to account for the newly emergent significance of sexuality as a public fact at least in intellectually advanced circles. It made sense of the role of sex in social life, and in its more vulgar forms it served as a counter statement and justification for personal sexual experimentation. At the collective and individual levels, it was what Kenneth Burke has called a vocabulary of motives: it allowed individuals to explain their own behavior and to legitimate it in the light of concerns that seemed larger than their own personal interests. For intellectuals seeking novel explanations of the changing world around them, it was a useful vehicle through which to formulate original and alternative views of intellectual issues as well as suggesting the sources of individual creativity. Psychoanalysis appeared to be rooted in an ultimately biological version of the world, and in consequence interpretations based on it could have the appeal of human universals. After the failure of Soviet communism to provide a revolutionary and moral alternative to capitalism, many Marxists retreated from the political arena to attach themselves to the less optimistic but equally comprehensive set of ideas represented in psychoanalysis. Finally, for many members of the literary intelligentsia, book publishing, mass media magazine, and advertising professions—that is, those in what has become the communications industry—the experience of personal analysis was sufficient evidence of psychoanalysis's importance to justify any attempt to promulgate its virtues.

This penetration of new ideas about sex into a series of pivotal elites and the subsequent transmission by them through the institutions of education and communication had a series of major consequences for at least some aspects of popular cultural life in the United States beginning in the late 1930s and flourishing in the 1950s and 1960s. Clearly at no point was the absolute truth value of Freud's ideas maintained. Indeed, Freud had no success at doing that even among his own disciples. The schismatic tradition of psychoanalysis had begun early with Adler and Jung and continued in the later attempts by Reich, Fromm, and Marcuse to marry psychoanalysis to Marxism. Even among the orthodox, the emergent traditions of ego analysis in the 1930s signaled a break with the original Freudian formulations and the attainment of a more optimistic and even ameliorative posture in the New World. In the same fashion, as Freudian ideas moved into the vernacular, they existed less and less as a system and more and more as cultural prescriptions for personal behavior, procedures for less inhibiting and repressive child rearing, and advice about mental illness and mental health. The advice columns of the daily press, written by lay persons and doctors, became infused with the words and formulations of psychoanalytic theory. As the significance of psychoanalysis became more pervasive in United States society, its potential for treating large-scale social ills or at least for diagnosing them was successfully argued. In this way, the psychoanalytic tradition had deep influence on the many voluntary organizations which dealt with crime, child welfare, marriage, and mental health. Indeed it was largely this tradition that was significant in the development of that branch of the United States Public Health Service that became the National Institute of Mental Health. Versions of Freud were taught in the colleges, and there was at the level of the college educated and more significantly among intellectuals an availability of words and ideas that they could use to deal with the sexual in their daily lives.

What is important to note about this enormous success of psychoanalysis in the United States during this period is that there is very little evidence that it or the other sexual studies conducted during the same period had any effect on the majority of people's personal sexual conduct. Apparently during this period from 1930 to 1960 the increase in the available language about sex at a collective level was not interactive with those processes which are formative of overt sexual activity. What this change seems to have provided was a language with which to talk about conduct at least abstractly, but a language without the power to commit persons to sexual activity. Even among those most affected by psychoanalytic doctrine I suspect that overt sexual activity remained a fearful and troubling arena of action and feeling. The verbal revolution of psychoanalysis—discourse about sex—did not confront the actual doing of sexual things and further did not penetrate to those areas of socialization and social life which were most significant in engendering sexual conduct.

In the middle of this period, when psychoanalysis and other alternative formulations of the sexual were becoming more widespread in the United States. Alfred Kinsey began his own research on human sexuality. Versions of that story are relatively well known from the Pomeroy (1972) biography of Kinsey, from John Madge's (1962) volume of essays on various groundbreaking research studies in social science, and from the introductions to the Kinsey volumes themselves. The outline is that Kinsey, already a well-known researcher in evolutionary theory based on studies of the ecology and gross morphological structure of gall wasps, was asked to give the sex instruction portion of a marriage guidance course. In his dissatisfaction with the state of knowledge about his aspect of that course, he began to study sexual behavior. First through a questionnaire given to the students taking his course and then expanding his efforts, both by using an interview format and by going beyond the confines of the campus, Kinsey began to study what individuals had done sexually during their lives. He gained the support of his university, oddly located in an extremely politically and religiously conservative region of the United States, and through a series of foundation grants was able to hire assistance. After a period of ten years he published a largely statistical volume of data entitled *Sexual Behavior in the Human Male* (1948) that quickly became known as the first of the "Kinsey Reports."

Intellectually, Kinsey's research found its sources in two separate traditions. The first was the tradition of statistical case histories in sex research begun by Davis, Dickinson, Beame, and Hamilton, but the second followed the traditions of general biological taxonomy and natural history. It was both of these influences that led to Kinsey's collection of large numbers of case histories, which were cross-classified on certain salient taxonomic variables with the final data presented statistically. This presentation of the normative statistical distribution of sexual behavior in conventional people resulted in the questioning of prevailing concepts of sexual "normality." However, Kinsey's focus on the continuity of sexual behavior across species and across cultures, and his interest in human variation, was explicitly based on a commitment to nineteenth-century versions of evolutionary theory. The complex problem which Kinsey's work raised—how to relate biological universals and the wide variation in the kinds and meanings of human sexual conduct in various cultural-historical circumstances—remained an open question.

The success of the Kinsey research was itself an indication of changes that had already occurred in the sexual situation in the United States. As has been noted, sex research is a form of sexual conduct, and the Kinsey research itself, in its range, size, and specific focus, represented a novel kind of conduct. By 1938, a major university was prepared to support a sex research endeavor even though similar efforts had met with disaster at a number of universities. It was said in the middle 1930s that if an academic wanted to destroy a career in psychology he should choose a research project on sex, hypnosis, religion, or politics. (It is interesting to note that in the 1960s and 1970s some of the central questions among the young have been the problems of sex and pleasure, altered states of consciousness, and the issues of moral and political power—all of which have served to disturb and sometimes to enlighten academic life in the United States.) In the early 1940s, it was possible for members of the National Research Council's Committee for Research on Sex to inveigle the Rockefeller Foundation to give money to support the Kinsey research by using that committee as a conduit. Scientists on this committee, such as George Corner, Karl Lashley, and Robert Yerkes, served as the scientific bona fides for Kinsey and the social and scientific value of his research. Further, it was possible for Kinsey from 1938 to 1953 to ask the cooperation of ordinary citizens in what was openly a sex research project and to receive that cooperation from very large numbers of persons—volunteers, to be sure—by offering only the reward of talking about their own sexuality in ways that they had never talked about it before.

There were other factors operating in Kinsey's favor as well. The end of the economic depression and the onset of World War II served as a cover for his research. The people of the United States were concerned with the recovery from a major depression—a depression that in itself served to drive many persons back into conventional moralities while radicalizing others—and were then plunged into a major war, the effects of which only began to recede in 1946. Another factor that prevented premature debate about the research was the absence of a mass media focus. In part, this was the result of the media being deflected from a concern with the sexual, except in the form of sexual crimes, by the enormity of the social events that were occurring at the time. Another factor was that the present-day mass media network as a pervasive source of national integration and information dissemination did not as yet exist, and this prevented what information that did leak out about Kinsey's work from being cascaded into a national event. The isolation of the campus of Indiana University was also a factor. It was insulated from the press, as well as being isolated from the psychoanalytic modes of thinking that dominated intellectual activity in the major cities. Indeed, the intellectual links that Kinsey had formed were largely within the ameliorative, social reformist tradition in sex research—that tradition that Ellis had called the Anglo-Saxon.

There was also a personal factor in the success of his enterprise. William Masters has reported that when he asked George Corner in the early 1940s about the prerequisites of being a researcher on sex, Corner replied—perhaps taking Kinsey as his model—that the researcher must be over forty, have established a major reputation in a nonsexual research area, and have the support of a major university or medical school (Brecher and Brecher 1966). What Masters did not report is that the researcher must have the image of a happy marriage, have children, and not appear to be interested in either sex or money for its own sake. Corner's advice epitomizes the tensions about the sexual and the necessary sources of personal reputation that are required to study it—the resonating symbols are science, medicine, education, accomplishment, disinterest, and personal probity. To study the unconventional one must be the very model of the conventional.

When Kinsey's first volume was published by a respectable medical house in Philadelphia (one remembers that a similar publishing house in Philadelphia first published Ellis's *Sexual Inversion* after the censorship fiasco in England), it was printed in a lot of ten thousand. In the following months, printing followed upon printing, but this signaled more than a publishing success; it was a national event. Perhaps the best example of the cultural climate that it entered is that the *New York Times* refused to take advertisements for it. In the early 1970s it is somehow difficult to recall that climate, but the two Kinsey books—Male and Female—were close to a physical shock to many members of that society. It was shock that required a response, for through an act of social bookkeeping what had been essentially collectively unknown became part of the content of daily life. It was still discourse, but it was discourse directly about sexual activity. It is only by comparison with Kinsey that the real lack of actual talk about sexual behavior in Freud becomes apparent. There was an instantaneous media response both to Kinsey the man and to what ultimately became encapsulated in the phrase "Kinsey Reports." Kinsey and his first book were the object of cartoons, editorials, a series of congressional hearings on the tax exemptions of foundations, papers by scientists on morality and by ministers on sampling and the scientific method, and finally a cover of *Time* magazine. The controversy subsided a bit between the publication of *Sexual Behavior in the Human Male* in 1948 and the publication of *Sexual Behavior in the Human Female* in 1953, but on the publication of the latter volume it broke out perhaps even more violently and continued with only some abatement in much the same tones until the death of Kinsey in 1956. These eight years were periods of direct sexual confrontation for the public at large in the United States.

No detailed study has been made of the impact of the Kinsey research and the range of its consequences, but there are some aspects that can at least be provisionally considered. Following quickly upon the publication of the first volume, there was an intense and national media response through which the "Kinsey Reports" became the best-known scientific books of the time. In the normal fashion of the media, the books were transformed into icons. Findings and ideas were taken from the context of the whole work to be given new meanings and potency in the national press. The critical items of the media were the percentages and the frequencies of the different forms of sexual activity themselves: How many men had masturbated? How many persons had had homosexual experience? How many women were virgins at marriage? What was the incidence and frequency of orgasm in marriage? What was the relationship between the rates of these sexual behaviors and such factors as religion, social class, and education? Despite methodological carping, there existed for the first time an accountancy for sexual behavior. At the same time, the public dimension of this accountancy was largely shaped by the media. For the press and the other media, which commonly operate with nearly the formal gravity and order of a Petrarchian sonnet, served to crystallize the image of Kinsey and of the volumes themselves. A review of the press clippings which appeared in the six months after the publication of the Male volume indicates that they became the basis for all publication which occurred later. Kinsey became a personification—the archetype of the sex researcher. The books were converted into reports, and other studies of sex behavior became "Kinsey Reports" as well. The sex researcher and the sex study became part of the conventional cast of characters and content of life in the United States.

Response to the Kinsey researches was extremely variable in different sectors of society. The response of the scientific community was complex. Only a small proportion of the social science community was overtly hostile, and the majority of the criticisms were of two kinds. The first were those which focused on the sampling defects of the study and the consequent limitations on generalizing the findings to a larger population. Both the lack of randomness and the largely volunteer character of the persons interviewed introduced unknown and problematic issues of interpretation. The second class of criticisms were those which stressed the limited perspective of the research, with its apparent lack of concern with either psychological or sociological factors in the shaping of sexual behavior. It was argued from this perspective that not all orgasms were equal. But perhaps the more telling reaction in the academic world was that the Kinsey volumes themselves, having opened the door of research into sexual behavior, were not followed by any increase in the numbers and types of research into sexual behavior. No further national surveys were attempted and the Kinsey information remains some two decades later as the largest body of sexual data gathered on a human population. There did ensue a number of surveys of premarital intercourse on college campuses, but it is only since 1967 that these researches have left the campus to study premarital sexual conduct in noncollege populations (Reiss 1967; Zelnick and Kantner 1972; Simon, Berger, and Gagnon 1972; Miller, Cottrell, and Simon 1973). These studies have been largely limited to heterosexual variables and to young people, so that the stock of knowledge about the married or of periods later in the life cycle remain unexplored except insofar as studies of fertility have included questions on rates of marital coitus. Just after the Kinsey period, there were a number of publications of major studies of sexual offenders which culminated in a study (Gebhard et al. 1965) from the Institute for Sex Research, which survived Kinsey. Such studies, although interesting in themselves, were cast in an older and less viable tradition of sexual criminology, which had not absorbed many of the major messages of the Kinsey researches.

It was in the realm of law and custom that the research made its major impact. If the Kinsey data were correct—and the few subsequent studies tended to confirm many of the findings—it meant that there was a serious incongruity between the law and sexual conduct. The reports indicated that many aspects of behavior which were considered criminal or deviant were in fact practiced by fairly large sectors of the populace. Even behavior which was relatively rare was practiced in a large population by large numbers of persons. Although many of these activities were not pursued by the police, since they occurred in private, it did mean that the law continued to exist as a landmine for the unwary and the unlucky. Hence mouth-genital contact, which occurred in a majority of middle-class marriages, was criminal under those statutes (existing in most states) proscribing "sodomy" and "crimes against nature." Premarital intercourse, which was a characteristic activity of a majority of men and of 50 percent of women, was a criminal offense, as was adultery, which was practiced by half of the men and a quarter of the women in Kinsey's survey. Homosexuality among men and women was a minority phenomenon, but isolated homosexual experiences were reasonably common among both genders, and the exclusively homosexual population was calculated to constitute roughly between 4 and 6 million in the total population. The view that all such behavior should be considered as criminal or a perversion of normal sexual development was subjected to a severe critical blow, and a greater continuity between what was formerly seen as "perverse" and what was formerly seen as "normal" was established. A wedge was driven into the structure of inherited formulations and assumptions about the sexual that informed the criminal law. Change, however, has been extremely slow and only in a few jurisdictions have the general sex statutes been reformed or specific legal sanctions been liberalized. In general, courage is too meager to propose legal reform even though many statutes have largely been allowed to fall further into disuse. The appeals courts, when used in recent years, have more often been willing to strike statutes that have seemed inequitable or unclear. In campaigns for legal reform or in expert testimony in courtrooms, the data from the Kinsey Reports have been pivotal evidence for the defense and for liberalizing impulses.

The significance of the Kinsey researches among the intellectual communities was at least twofold. Ameliorative reformers in law, medicine, social work, and marriage counseling (the inheritors of the traditions of

Ellis) treated Kinsey's research in some cases with adulation, but more often with measured respect. The research was seen as another important
step, in part confirming what we had known before, in part setting the
standard for research in the future. It was largely a practical reaction,
coming from that sector of the intellectual community which was involved in political sexual reform. In contrast, for other sectors of the intellectual community, the academic and literary, already liberated in their
verbal response to sex, the Kinsey studies were a mixed blessing. The contest between the imaginative-literate and the scientific numerate traditions of knowing was rejoined. Lionel Trilling (1950), in his review of the
first Kinsey study, treated it as a cultural symptom, indicating that in
these statistical tables and abstract orgasms society still insisted on treating the sexual as alien from the fundamental ebb and flow of psychological and cultural experience. Trilling's response was not unique, and it exemplifies one major posture toward Kinsey's research. In part, it was the
canons of proof that were unacceptable, the movement from imagination
to science, from literacy to numeracy was unpalatable. Another element
was the reaction of intellectuals defending their own status as cultural
brokers and their own commitments that were already in place. Their attachment to Freud had been revolutionary, researches on sex had begun
to call into question what for them was in part achieved and in part received wisdom. Further, since they felt they had already been personally
liberated, sex was for them no longer a significant topic, for no longer
could literary and intellectual reputations be made through producing
novel formulations about it.

There was merit to the reservations that literary intellectuals such as
Trilling offered, though all assumed an essentially conservative posture.
The Kinsey style had taken sex out of its social, cultural, and psychological context by focusing narrowly on sexual incidences, frequencies, and
outlets. It was largely detached from the ongoing research traditions in
psychology, anthropology, and sociology, making sex behavior almost a
special domain of its own and sustaining the existence of the nineteenth-
century field labeled sexology with its sexual expert labeled the "sexolo-
gist." In this sense, Trilling was correct in his analysis. In the cultural-
historical situation of United States in the 1940s, dealing with the sexual
seemed to require such an abstract statistical scientific approach. If
Freud's acceptability rested on a disembodied sexuality, in which the connection between mental life and a fanciful biology was unmediated by
physical sexual conduct, Kinsey's acceptability depended on a decultural-
ized sexuality, cast in an acceptable scientific mold and limited to a concern for the practices of the body that did not implicate the mind. At the

same time Kinsey and Freud shared a commitment to the biological roots of behavior (although they were vastly different biologies), and both remained committed to the role of the "natural" in defining the meaning of sexuality. Freud's naturalness was the goal of reproduction and its biological necessity; Kinsey's was the variety of evolution. In both, nature served as the unquestioned term in the argument—it made both of their works acceptable, but at the price of accepting limited biological versions of the sexual.

Kinsey provided numbers, words, and a series of conceptions, which slowly penetrated the daily speech of people in the United States. The words "premarital intercourse," "mouth-genital contact," "penis," "vagina," and "orgasm" became appropriate things to discuss or print in various social locations. At first, these discussions were relatively anxious; the words did not come easily, the discussion of sex remained and often still is suspect between men and women. But the words did not convert instantaneously into deeds—the disjuncture between sexual thoughts, sexual talk, and sexual action still exists. Yet another potential for change had been added to the general situation of sexual learning.

The two decades of the post-Kinseyan period have been marked by a myriad of sexual changes which have been relatively helter-skelter and in which no easy pattern can be discerned. Perhaps most obvious has been the vast increase in the amount and a change in character of the media representation of the sexual, ranging from the serious to the pornographic. Possibly the most radical and rapid change has occurred in the mass-audience film industry, easily, except for the radio, the most conventional of American art forms until the 1960s. During the 1960s, under the influence of the European cinema, most of the censorship barriers against the depictions of sexual activity of various kinds and in various relationships disappeared in the major urban centers. In some measure, the ease of this transition has been a result of the general decline of the cinema as the major form of family entertainment in the United States. Now television must bear the burden of maintaining a central moral tendency, although the evidence is that a wide range of topics relating to sex (venereal disease, birth control, premarital pregnancy), as well as directly sexual topics (homosexuality, blue movies, premarital sex) treated in a relatively liberated fashion, have now emerged on television. The cinema, however, with a more complex marketing structure, now offers audiences a far wider kind of cultural fare. This shift not only has brought with it a change in the amount of sexual material in presentations that are part of high culture but also has resulted in the production of a subgenre of explicitly sexual films which are offered to audiences in urban centers.

These films offer, in large screen size, what was available only as "stag" or blue movies as recently as the late 1960s.

This same process of increasing sexual content can be observed in serious literature as well as in the pornographic subgenre. Indeed, the shift in the degree of sexual explicitness largely began in books and magazines. The erotic books formerly locked in the closed collections of the library of the Institute of Sex Research, both literature and subliterature, are now available in soft cover on newsstands along with a large body of new materials. The same shift can be observed in the magazines that serve an audience composed mostly of men with pictures of unclothed young women in various postures revealing various parts of their anatomy. The movement from the magazines of the 1940s, with what now appear to be their coy models dressed in bathing suits with suggestively loosened tops, to the magazines such as *Playboy* and *Penthouse* in the 1960s, with their photographs of pubic hair, cartoons suggesting mouth-genital contact, and couples in at least simulated coital postures, specifies a major cultural shift in the erotic content of the social backdrop.

In addition, with some but not a great deal of effort, magazines containing photographs of sexual behavior may be purchased at recognizable shops in the "bright-lights" areas of most cities. Finally, there now exists an underground press of comic books and newspapers with explicitly sexual materials in text, drawings, and photographs which fill out the range of materials for various audiences. This change in cultural availability of explicitly sexual materials has not been smooth or even. The slope of change was met with various legal and quasilegal obstacles, and the major acceleration of change occurred largely after 1968. The contest over these materials and their appropriateness was (and, in those cases where there is a countermovement, is still) carried out in the terms of the differences between sexual libertarians and sexual conservatives. Indeed, the extreme arguments that have been raised in the struggle over censorship have largely not changed their assumptions or even their formal order of presentation since the 1920s. Nothing is more predictable than the courtroom or television debates over sexual censorship. This is not to say that the content of the legal decisions has not changed in some respects. Since the United States Supreme Court decisions in 1967, the legal argumentation has taken on more of the tone of a discussion of problems of public nuisance and personal privacy than it has of dangers to "the fabric of society"(Gagnon and Simon 1967b). This movement in the courts has been seen as evidence of "corruption" by those who are more conservative in their sexual postures. The conservatives still argue that each breach in the barrier of permitted sexual explicitness is a potential social disaster, and they are still opposed by those who argue either that pornography does not matter or that increase in the sexual material available in society is a desirable human freedom. The older mythologies that sex is either a healing or a destructive force still hold in the struggle over censorship. The influence of research has been felt in the decisions of the courts; Kinsey and more recently the Congressional Commission on Obscenity and Pornography are used as authorities to buttress more liberal, anticensorship arguments in legal proceedings. At the present moment, it appears that, while the pendulum of censorship may swing to a more conservative position in particular cases, a fundamental shift toward more open access to sexual materials has already occurred.

Whatever research has been done does not, however, chronicle a concomitant shift in personal sexual behavior, which had been expected to parallel the change in media explicitness by many of the contestants in the censorship struggle. In part, the general availability of materials has been too recent to test this effect, but in any case the expectations of a relation between media materials and behavior were in themselves too grandiose. Patterns of sexual activity are shaped by and based on more profound sources than the seeing of nudity or sexual activity in various media forms. Such materials fall on already existent styles and modes of feeling and action that are more powerful and constraining in their significance. At another level, the erotica that we see have already been highly conventionalized and are composed largely of the routines of behavior that many (men especially) already possess in their fantasy lives. Most pornography is in some part the concrete externalization of the men's fantasy view of sexuality, sharing and summarizing its content. Even a casual look at most pornography suggests that it possesses in crude, subgenre forms most of the cultural nonsexual conventions that already exist in relationships between the genders, readjusted to contain an increased sexual content. In this sense, pornography is in terms of its depiction of sexual relationships socially and politically profoundly conservative, at least for the majority of the men who are its audience. This does not mean that its existence in reasonably large amounts cannot have effects larger than those intended by its cultural content and form, only that these effects will be both modest and surprising.

Another aspect of sexual conduct which began to shift during the middle and late 1950s and which was in part influenced by the Kinsey researches is our consideration of the role of homosexuality in the range of human sexual action. The effects of the Kinsey researches and of later work were indirect and complex in their influence on a changed status for homosexuality, except insofar as the findings were used to buttress demands for legal change. The arguments offered were that homosexuality was a more general phenomenon than was commonly thought, that it was not linked in any direct way to criminality, that young people were in no particular danger of being seduced by the majority of homosexuals, and that the attempt to inhibit homosexuality through the application of criminal sanctions was not very efficacious and caused more ills than it could cure. These arguments were in fact quite old; they had been made by Hirschfeld and Ellis at the turn of the century and had been reiterated between the two world wars. Freud, who saw homosexuality as a perversion, felt that legal sanctions were worse than useless. It is somewhat difficult to determine why the Kinsey researches were so much more influential than the other arguments that had been made for legal change, but clearly both the climate of opinion had altered and the specific kinds of findings offered seemed more persuasive to the legislative and legal temper. The existence of the Kinsey studies had other, secondary influences on conditions in the homosexual community as well as among sociological researchers. The collective belief in the existence of a large number of homosexuals buttressed a sense of personal normality and combated the traditional psychoanalytic and medical view of homosexuality held by homosexuals, who no longer so readily accepted the notion that they were "sick."

Sociological researchers, influenced by the new respectability of the topic, entered the study of homosexuality with a concern for the nature of community life and a common culture that turned their attention away from the questions of personal adjustment and psychopathology which had dominated thinking about homosexuality in the past. While sociologists began with interests that had a primary focus on the sexual aspects of the homosexual's life and the way in which sex was important to him or her, what became rapidly apparent was the wide variety of lifestyles among homosexuals and often the decidedly second place that sexual object choice took in homosexuals' lives as they dealt with the problems of living. In the past, the entire life of the homosexually oriented had been interpreted through their choice of sexual partners. What became apparent through research was that homosexuals have to solve all the problems of living that heterosexuals do, and that in this process sexuality plays a wide variety of roles. From this perspective, locating the sexual in the context of sex seems to explain very little and to require much explanation. This posture in the study of homosexuality has led to a breakdown in the belief that the general category "homosexual" is more than a cultural construct. The focus moves from an interest in homosexuality to homosexualities, that is, the varieties of ways of dealing with a homosexual preference. Recently, this change in perspective for dealing with homosexuality has begun to affect the study of heterosexuality as well. Once the sexual is placed in a cultural and historical context, there are not only homosexualities but heterosexualities also. Previously, it almost seemed as if heterosexuality was a large wastebasket category, a residual majority which needed no explanation because it was so natural.

Paralleling and interacting with this change in research strategies toward homosexuality, there has been a change in the posture of some homosexuals toward the majority of society. As has been noted elsewhere, since its emergence in the 1950s, the organized homosexual movement has followed the path of other civil rights movements in the United States (Humphreys 1972). The movement has changed from an education emphasis in the beginning, through legislative lobbying in the middle 1960s (with a major commitment to creating social resources and social groups for homosexuals), to a pattern of direct action and personal affirmation of homosexuality in the late 1960s and early 1970s. The slogans "gay is good" and "out of the closets and into the streets" proclaim a new militancy and sense of self-respect that has impacts not only on the larger society but also on the scientific researcher. No longer can the researcher classify the homosexual as "deviant" or "perverse" with impunity. The boundaries and content of the cultural categories have been shifted; the argument now is that everybody's sexuality is either irrelevant to aspects of social judgment or, if gender preference is to be salient, homosexuality is equivalent in value to heterosexuality. What was originally a research question has become a political question, since it has become apparent to the homosexual that certain forms of research can be as oppressive as the criminal statutes. The research question is no longer one of determining the special reason for homosexuality or the special characteristics of the homosexual, but one of attempting to sort out the learning conditions which foster one or another pattern of behavior, viewing heterosexuality and homosexuality as relatively indeterminate outcomes.

While these general sexual changes were occurring, the most recent culturally significant research enterprise in the sexual area has been the work of Masters and Johnson in the physiology and anatomy of sexual response (1966) and more recently in the treatment of what have been called the sexual dysfunctions (1970). The history of their work and the societal response to it have been very similar to those that characterized the Kinsey studies, although the response to Masters and Johnson has occurred in a far lower key, with a greater degree of cultural receptivity. The salient elements are quite similar—a well-known researcher past the age of forty, with an established reputation, supported by a major medical school, using observational and experimental methods which were common to other areas of research in similar, but nonsexual, physiological and anatomical problems. The research was begun in the late 1950s, and publication began in journal form in the 1960s. Again, as with the Kinsey researches, there was a sense of shock, but of a substantially lower order than that of late 1940s and early 1950s. The lower level of shock was in part because the physiological and anatomical emphasis of the research seemed further away from the lives of individuals, in part because the Kinsey research had already prepared the way—the society already had categories for dealing with sex researchers and sex research—and in part because the research was performed under the umbrella of the medical and biological sciences.

While the findings were largely acceptable, it was the method which created the greatest controversy. To talk to people about sex even outside the clinical setting was one thing, but the observation of sexual behavior and its measurement through dials and indicators seemed a final sacrilege. Once again intellectual critics were divided, the social-ameliorative on one side, the literary-ideological on the other. It was argued by the latter that such research would lead to a loss of enchantment with the sexual—such critics came close to celebrating a romantic mystification that viewed sexuality as resting on a certain kind of ignorance that produced innocence. These reactions had a familiar ring, recalling the language of those who opposed Freud by pointing out the risks that would result from tearing the veils from an ultimate intimacy, the danger of banalizing fundamental and natural human processes by the intrusion of the grubby hands of materialist science. At the same time, in certain sectors of the scientific-intellectual community, the work of Masters and Johnson has been taken up uncritically, even as Kinsey was taken up uncritically by a small minority in the past. This enthusiastic reception largely overlooked the need for replication, different forms of biological monitoring techniques, the problems of experimental design, the issues of sampling, and the necessity for further work on psycho-physiological interactions.

In addition to the more extreme forms of reaction to Masters and Johnson, there were many restrained sets of critiques. This restraint seemed to rest on two factors. The first is the obvious importance of the work of Masters and Johnson in opening the doors to additional research, doors that might have been closed by a intense critical reception similar to that which the Kinsey studies received. Second, the role of the natural and therapeutic was emphasized by Masters and Johnson, especially in their work on sexual dysfunction, a focus that suggested that if inhibitions and self-consciousness were reduced, the natural biological reflexes would take over and assure competent sexual performance. This reliance on the reflexive and natural accorded well with the tradition of de-inhibition and antirepression of natural instincts among students of sexuality and was supported by what may be described as a biological prejudice. There was a continuity between Masters and Johnson's innovative work and the already existent views about the nature of human sexuality widely held by sexuality experts, the media, and the wider public.

Given the recentness of Masters and Johnson's work [recall that this essay was written in 1973], it is difficult to trace their influence, but there is considerable evidence that their therapeutic strategies have received a warm reception and that clinical work following either their design or modifications of their design is relatively widespread. From all the evidence so far, what is remarkable is the substantial level of success that these procedures have with such sexual problems as premature ejaculation, secondary impotence, vaginismus, and lack of orgasm. However, while what appear to be largely technical variations in clinical procedures are proliferating, there is currently little evidence of attempts to carefully understand the impact of various therapeutic procedures, to continue basic research in the psycho-physiology of sexual response, or to further research the role of developmental factors in the determination of the range and character of sexual response. It is likely that the influence of Masters and Johnson's research will be largely indirect and perhaps even slow in coming, especially in terms of basic research. The major effects will be mediated through the therapeutic professions and through influences on teaching about sex.

The problem of assessing the interaction between research about sex and the sociocultural situation has grown increasingly difficult in the United States. Outside the area of the explicitly sexual, there has been an extraordinary amount of change in the character of social life in the United States over the past decade, many aspects of which could be influential in changing patterns of sexual conduct. The sheer numbers of young people, as well as special youth movements such as the hippies and Jesus freaks, the sudden expansion of the use of cannabis and to a lesser extent other drugs, the civil rights movement and the confrontation over race, the crisis in the colleges and universities, the peace movement and the problems left from the political strife induced by the Indochina war, and the sudden renaissance of the women's liberation movement are evidence of a decade of hectic activity. Even the relative quietude of the last few years is not an indicator that these large-scale dislocations are not working themselves out in a quieter and less public fashion. Our closeness to recent events and our participation in them make accurate analysis of the relations among the events of general social change, the more personal realm of individual sexual conduct, and the world of sexual research extremely imprecise. Indeed, from much of the evidence from the past there are no neat relationships between different sectors of social, cultural, and psychological life. Changes occur in one aspect of life without affecting others, even those that we think most closely linked to them. Sex research changes without affecting sexual behavior, family life changes without affecting sexual conduct, technology changes without affecting cultural patterns. Perhaps our vision of the world is more unified and more closely knit than life is in reality.

The past decade [the 1960s] has been a period of problematic movement without much discernible issue, a period of failures and successes which have not yet resolved themselves. But if one may venture some guesses, there are certain issues which seem central to the conduct of sex, both as the subject of research and as personal behavior, in the United States. One of these issues is the necessity to scrutinize what I have called our biological prejudices in the explanation of sexual conduct. It has been part of our conventional wisdom that sexuality is a natural drive of forbidding strength that will appear in one form or another in our lives, a drive which requires either repression and control for our own protection or release so that we may realize ourselves. The ostensible naturalness of sex has been one of the central ideological items in both the liberal and the conservative responses to sexual conduct. Homosexuality is "natural" or "unnatural" depending on the point of view, orgasm is a "natural" right for woman, men are "naturally" dominant sexually, the human being is "naturally" sexual—all of these assertions are unproven and unprovable in the form in which they are put. What is required in current research is a direct interest in the processes of human learning which move a relatively unspecified organism through the various moments of social, psychological, and physiological development that occur in a specific historical-cultural period, taking no outcome as a given or necessary expression of human nature. I am suggesting researches that take persons in their cultural particularity by examining the artificial and invented character of humanity. Appeals to biology or to nature have too often foreclosed discussion or served as special pleading for ideologies. What is being suggested is a research posture that exhausts the social and psychological and cultural before making an appeal to unknown nature.

Closely linked to this research strategy and complementary to it is the changing status of women in modern societies. The appeals on both sides of these questions are often based on arguments about nature, but perhaps men more often use them in defending the status quo, frequently raising the specter of a natural human division as reflected in parables drawn either from primatology or from hunting societies in which men appeared to be selected genetically for dominance and aggression and, by a large inference, for political and social power in modern societies as well. The challenge to our conventional wisdom and to research activity comes out of the ethical and political challenge of the women's liberation movement. In this case, research is complicated by a rapidly moving social life which precludes easy solutions to complex questions. The relation between the genders is at the center of current social change in the United States, and any changes in the status of women have the deepest implications for the social order, for the individual consciousness, and for our vision of the proper content of sexual conduct. The question of what men and women are is now open and this means that the scientific issues are open as well. The significance of this particular set of questions was seen by Ellis as early as 1884, in his review of August Bebel's volume on women and socialism (Bebel [1883] 1971): "the new ideal of human life . . . is bound up with the attainment of equal freedom, equal independence and equal culture for men and women." An equally important problem is how we deal with pleasure in general and sexual pleasure in particular: who deserves it, at what cost, and at what point in the life cycle. In relation to the problem of pleasure, we seem to have the puritan mentality wrong; it is not that it is opposed to pleasure—even sexual pleasure— but that pleasure must be associated with pain or at least with effort. In this view, God is a moral accountant engaged in double-entry bookkeeping, marking up our accounts of pleasure and pain. At a deep cultural level the crisis between the old and the young in the United States does simply involve the fact that the young appear to be enjoying themselves, but more importantly that they have not paid for their enjoyment in some thankless and grubby apprenticeship in the marketplace. We are, as members of this culture, largely afraid of pleasure that seems unrestrained, unconnected with measured cost, pleasure that cannot be subject to some metrication. Adult reaction to drug-taking and sexual activity on the part of the young springs from this calculus. It is not mere jealousy or envy, although these exist in some part—it is that it disturbs our versions of moral accountancy, the cultural balance that should exist between pleasure and effort.

These three issues

1. our dependence in sexual matters on unexamined ideas about human nature and biology;

2. the shifting balance between the genders; and
3. the calculus of pleasures

will be problems at the center of cultural life and sex research over the next decade. They represent both continuity and change, old problems to be reformulated in new circumstances with a mixture of old ideas and new transformations. They are easily susceptible to ideological posturing, to encapsulation within a single system—scientific, moral, or political—offering a single solution. If there is any lesson to be drawn from the relatively continuous influence Havelock Ellis has had on sex research, it is that he avoided the sirens of ideology and system while never losing his ability to act or to take up a cause. Perhaps the best guide for research and for personal conduct (sexual and otherwise) are the words that H. L. Mencken (cited in LaFitte 1967) used to describe Ellis: "It is not his positive learning that gives him distinction, it is his profound and implacable skepticism, his penetrating eye for the transient, the disingenuous and the shoddy."

Scripts and the Coordination
of Sexual Conduct (1974)

Most sociologists are poorly equipped to deal with the problems of motivation as they are discussed among psychologists. I must confess at the outset that I share in this disciplinary deficiency. In part the difficulty arises from a certain barrier that exists between the two fields: the complex debate in psychology about the utility of the concept of motivation in explaining the genesis and maintenance of behavior—a debate that antedates the earliest of the Nebraska Symposia on Motivation—is largely unknown to sociologists. Part of the problem, both in terms of data and theory, is a consequence of the magnitude of the information involved, but perhaps more importantly, it stems from the different styles of imagining that have evolved in the actual activities of the two disciplines. Such styles of imagining which are central to a discipline's problem sense and its canons of credibility emerge from the daily practice of reading, teaching, and research, and it is through these practices that the intellectual and moral boundaries of the discipline are defined. Regardless of the formal similarities of the condensates of a field's activities as represented in journal articles, it is the shared life of doing

Originally published in *Proceedings of the 1973 Symposium on Motivation*, edited by James K. Cole and Richard Deinstbier (Lincoln: University of Nebraska Press, 1974). Reprinted by permission. This research was supported by USPHS grants from the National Institute of Child Health and Human Development (HD 4156) and a special postdoctoral fellowship from the National Institute of Mental Health (MH54372).

psychology or doing sociology that creates both the tacit understandings which allow work within a field to go forward as well as the communicative gulf between fields.

When first invited to this symposium I felt a considerable strain to examine the points of convergence and divergence that exist between the sociological and psychological approaches to motivational theory, but upon a cursory examination of both literatures it struck me that the outcome of that effort would be entirely too casual to bear much palatable fruit, and the prospect tended to be somewhat paralyzing as well. As a consequence my tactic has been to use that portion of the relevant psychological literature over which I have some command, but in general to stay within the intellectual styles with which I am comfortable, hoping that the result will be clear enough to be intelligible and perhaps useful to those outside the field of sociology.

Conventionally the starting point in a discussion of sexual conduct is at the beginning of life. This is a strategy which draws largely upon the psychoanalytic tradition and its double emphases: first, the centrality of sexual forces in ultimate character formation, and second, the primary significance of the earliest experiences of infancy and childhood in setting the limits and possibilities of future development. For those concerned with the complexities of adulthood, this perspective poses a dilemma in that it views adult life, in both its sexual and nonsexual dimensions, as schematized and overspecified by developmental constraints. In some psychoanalytic formulations adulthood seems only a reenactment of an individual's childhood history. Even the Freudian revisionists' attempts to recognize the significance of cultural and social life in human development, such as those of Erik Erikson, are both partial and limited, focusing primarily on the constancies and continuities in development rather than the changeable and discontinuous qualities observable over the total life cycle (Erikson 1963). While the processes of socialization do have a narrowing and limiting function in any cultural-historical context by increasingly specifying outcomes—that is, by eliciting and creating what is an acceptable adult in a given society—to see these processes as fixed by an inescapable human nature or by some ordained sequence of human needs is to satisfy what might be called a conceptual "rage for order" at the expense of the observable disorder. While it is not my intention to posit an alternative rage for chaos, it is important to take account of the flexibility and discontinuity in human development and to recognize the remarkable adaptive capacities of human beings as they face and create novel circumstances throughout the life cycle.

It is these adaptive capacities in dealing with novel conditions that I would like to emphasize in this chapter. Changing environmental demands, both in terms of cultural-historical change and in terms of the changing demands on a person during his or her life cycle in any culture, require the coordination and management of a wide variety of skills learned previously in a variety of contexts, as well as the creation of novel responses through the recombination of older skills. These novel activities themselves become more effortlessly managed and become parts of other goals and plans later in the life cycle. This process of discontinuous and continuous combination and recombination of cultural and psychological resources to meet adaptive exigencies consists, in part, of ways in which the culturally provided plans and goals of persons contain the motives for behavior, and of the role that these plans have in shaping and coordinating both the verbal and nonverbal activities that are involved in sexual conduct.

In another context William Simon and I have called these plans sexual scripts, which we meant to be a subclass of the general category of scripted social behavior (Simon and Gagnon 1969). The concept of scripts shares certain similarities with the concepts of plans or schemes in that it is a unit large enough to comprehend symbolic and nonverbal elements in an organized and time-bound sequence of conduct through which persons both envisage future behavior and check on the quality of ongoing conduct. Such scripts name the actors, describe their qualities, indicate the motives for the behavior of the participants, and set the sequence of appropriate activities, both verbal and nonverbal, that should take place to conclude behavior successfully and allow transitions into new activities. The relation of such scripts to concrete behavior is quite complex and indirect; they are neither direct reflections of any concrete situation nor are they surprise-free in their capacity to control any concrete situation. They are often relatively incomplete, that is, they do not specify each act and the order in which it is to occur; indeed, as I will note later, the incompleteness of specification is required, since in any concrete situation many of the subelements of the script must be carried out without the actor noticing that he or she is performing them. They have a major advantage over concrete behavior, however, in that they are manipulable in terms of their content, sequence, and symbolic valuations, often without reference to any concrete situation. We commonly call this process of symbolic reorganization a fantasy when it appears that there is no situation in which a script in its reorganized form may be tested or performed, but in fact, such apparently inapplicable scripts have significant value even in situations which do not contain all or even any of the concrete elements which exist in the symbolic map offered by the script.

Clearly, scripts vary in their flexibility and in the details that are specified (the coronations of monarchs are planned in detail, as are the plays of Molière as played by the Comédie Française), both in terms of different kinds of scripts as well as varying performances by different individuals. Scripts are manipulable, but not without limits. While the rules for manipulating symbolic versions of the world are more flexible than those for dealing with concrete situations, these rules and the scripts to which they relate arise from the cultural circumstances in the same fashion as do the concrete situations for which they serve as a map or format. The flexibility of scripts in terms of their internal order and their capacity to be assembled or disassembled in creative or adaptive responses to new circumstances is a critical element in our capacity to manage a changing internal and external environment. The history of an individual's socialization is in part the record of the creation, reorganization, and destruction of script materials, both as a response to the innovative capacities of the scripts themselves as well as a response to the exigencies of concrete situations. The capacity to use responses learned in one concrete situation in another, together with other responses learned in still other situations at other moments in the life cycle, is central to the process of human adaptation.

The view that personal motives are embedded in these scripts—that is, that our explanatory assertions are deeply associated with our behavioral plans—suggests that motives, in this context, might be called practical motivation or practical explanation. My concern is with that class of explanatory statements that persons make about themselves or to external interlocutors, including the inquiring or experimenting scientist, about why they have done something. As one moves further from infancy, the significance of these acquired theories or ad hoc reasons for behavior becomes more evident, and they become more powerful in their capacity to constrain and shape human conduct. In this sense individual actors are what might be called practical psychologists or practical sociologists; they possess and exploit culturally received sets of explanations for their own and others' behavior. The existence of these culturally provided explanations has been noted by Albert Baldwin (1969) in his discussion of the socialization of children. He raises the hypothesis that "the socialization practices of a society reflect the culture's implicit or explicit hypotheses about how children function and what influences will modify that function" (343). Baldwin describes these theories as being "naive," perhaps in contrast to fashionable scientific explanatory assertions; yet from certain points of view, especially when removed from the body of activity that generated them, it is difficult to recognize superiority between naive and sophisticated psychologies. Our tendency is to degrade the explanatory assertions that persons make about their behavior, often to the status of rationalizations, as we seek to see through or replace these explanations with assertions about people's "real" motives.

It must be noted here that there is no impenetrable barrier between the social science community and the larger society and that the explanatory statements that members of the academy create to account for human behavior can quickly become part of the motivational accounts of members of the larger community. As part of the sociologizing and psychologizing of the larger society, various alternative academic theories of behavior are now generally available to large segments of society. There is a certain reticence among members of the academy about this process, since it commonly is referred to as a process of vulgarization. The tendency to convert all introductory courses in the social sciences into undergraduate versions of graduate courses—all students must come to understand what we do in the form that we do it—is an example of a counter effort to "devulgarize" our course offerings at the expense of their intelligibility. However, in spite of our most powerful attempts to de-emphasize the application of the social sciences, nonacademics manage to take what we offer and turn it to their own devices. Indeed, there is a reverse process through which the larger community challenges our academic versions and explanations of the world, both by refusing to conform to our predictions and often by offering more promising versions of their own motives than we can conceive.

Given that my intent is to emphasize complexity, novelty, and discontinuity in psychosexual development, perhaps the best strategy is to begin in the middle of the life cycle and read backward in time, rather than forward from infancy. A description of an adult sexual performance can not only begin to suggest an alternative way of examining the problem of scripts, the coordination of concrete behavior, and the coordination that their relation implies—a coordination of physiological processes, psychological processes, cultural resources, and social events—but it can also shed some light on the manner in which prior experiences in the socialization process are relevant to current activities. I will try to describe, in some modest detail and with some marginal comment, a heterosexual act occurring for the first time between a young couple in their late teens, tracing the ways in which scripts elicit behavior and the flexibility of scripts in their relation to concrete social arrangements. I have chosen a heterosexual act because it reflects the differential socialization processes of women and men, although I could have chosen a sexual act between two men or two women as easily, and it would have illustrated common processes. However, there would have been sufficient differences in detail and potential for raising anxieties that I might have obscured the argument by linking it to the unconventional.

The following, then, is a description of a common social event, which contains the conventional cultural materials that allow us to identify it as sexual. I make this complex introductory statement because it is not always obvious, for reasons that I will consider later, that the majority of the elements in the situation which I am going to describe are cultural conventions and are the outcome of a complex of sociohistorical processes, only limited parts of which are related to the necessities of biological reproduction. Let us consider a young man and a young woman who are in a social relationship that is going to result in intercourse. It is voluntary and it involves no direct exchange of money. It is the culmination of a larger series of experiences with each other that they mutually recognize as being likely to lead to intercourse at their stage in the life cycle. Let me further specify that neither of them is very experienced in completing sexual activity in intercourse, but they are the modal conventional outcomes of middle-class and working-class socialization for sexual performance in United States society. This implies that they both possess at least a fragmentary version of the sequence of activities that they are going to perform, even though they may have had little practice.

As the couple move beyond that tipping point when the conventionally sexual becomes salient, they are very likely to be alone together, in a private place, screened from the public—perhaps his abode or hers, or a friend's if they are still living at home. They are somewhat old for the couch in the living room of one of their parents or the back seat of a car. They will begin touching each other while still clothed, and that clothing will be appropriate to the public contexts in which they have been prior to finding their way to a sheltered place. In these other contexts the couple will commonly conceal that they might be thinking of intercourse, even though they might be defined as in love or engaged, for in these other contexts sexual modesty needs to be preserved. The time could be afternoon or evening, much to the disgust of those who enforce or prescribe the times when young people should be in bed, alone. (Such constraints are only enforceable through a belief on the part of the young that sexual activity is only proper at night.) The light in the room is more likely to be dim or even dark rather than bright, offering a certain privacy in the midst of mutual intimacy.

As they begin they are likely to talk in a slightly desultory manner, probably a little anxiously, given the danger, novelty, and transgressive nature of the behavior in which they are going to participate. The shyness of their talk and its unspecific reference demonstrate the difficulty of moving easily from a public world in which the physical aspects of the sexual largely do not exist and in which sexual talk between women and men is only obliquely referential to that physical activity. The achievement of an easy transition between the worlds of the public and the private may well never be achieved—in part because we lack a legitimate speech in which we can disclose this aspect of our sexuality, even to this very small audience.

No matter how often they have made physical love short of intercourse, which is so inexactly described as petting (perhaps to indicate that something more serious is yet to happen), this moment is seen to be different. It is, to use one colloquialism, "going all the way"; it is a rite of passage, a moment of particular significance that is linked to historically specific ideas about what a critical sexual transition is. After coitus the couple will change, with reference to themselves, to each other, and to their surrounding social world. Some young women have reported an uneasy sense that after their first intercourse other people could see a change in their faces—that the private moment was somehow turned into a visible stigma.

The couple will begin by kissing, and if they have had some physical contact before, they will perhaps move quickly to tongue kissing. His hands will touch her body outside of her clothing, tentatively or more directly, depending on the history of their relationship. She may resist, at first more and then less, perhaps only because she has resisted such gestures so often before, but she indicates in her permission her own desire. They will kiss almost continuously, maintaining a sense of intimate contact and in some degree avoiding direct attention on what their hands may be doing. They will begin to undress, or rather, parts of their clothing will be loosened, unbuttoned, unzipped, conventionally hers and then his. There will be fumblings, slightly inept gestures; he may never have undressed anyone but himself before, she has rarely been undressed by others since childhood and perhaps never by a man. The initiative is still largely his; buttons turn out to be stubborn, removing her bra turns into a slightly tense ballet. Each of these moments represents a momentary stumble, a deflection of attention from the sense of passion and a break into the inattentions or differential inattentions that are part of managing the concrete activity. As their clothing is finally completely removed, usually hers first and then his (from some obscure origin there is a convention that allows her to be nude before he is), there will be a slight clammy chill as the cool air of the room touches the bare, perhaps perspiring, bodies. To master these interruptions and transitions they may kiss more fiercely. She may straddle his leg or he may intrude it between hers and they will make movements which simulate coitus, giving the act both a genital focus and predicting its conclusion.

There will continue to be distractions, both internal and external. Footsteps in the hallway, the turning of keys in locks, the sounds of passing traffic—the external world continues to make its presence felt. There is also a lingering double presence, a sense of anticipation and risk. He wonders whether he will stay erect, whether she is enjoying what he is doing; she wonders how to keep him doing things that do feel good and how to stop him from doing other things that don't, whether she will have an orgasm, whether there is any danger of getting pregnant. There will be gentle grunts and moans and whispers of affectionate fragments, words, and sentences, which they can mutually interpret to be signs of pleasure and permission.

After some time the distractions lessen and focus is held (except for nagging doubts); they test each other's readiness (more commonly he tests hers) and she opens her legs to let him enter. He may or may not have difficulty, for there is a tense moment as the erect penis begins to enter the vagina. The mechanics intrude; there may be pain for her and sometimes for him. If it is too difficult he may lose his erection; if he is too excited he may ejaculate too soon, sometimes before entry or at the moment when his penis touches her. If she feels too much pain she may close herself to him and simply endure the wanted and unwanted intrusion. And in these moments when what was subliminally coordinated fails, there is a sense of sadness, a resonance of personal failure, a hoped for and often given, but necessarily inadequate, commiseration. He is apologetic, she is disheartened. Can the failure be repaired? Should they try again? They will talk, sometimes too much, seeking to heal the damage, to make sense of the failure, and perhaps to try again, if not now, then later.

But failure only sometimes occurs. The couple is joined together; there is a set of physical sensations on parts of their bodies that have been imagined, but never experienced. It may be fumbling, to be sure: Are the limbs quite coordinated? Does it hurt? Is the rhythm of movement correct? There may return the double presence as she compares what is happening with literary or cinematic models while he tries to recall whatever sexological advice he has heard or read or picked up from his other sexual experiences about the arousability of women. They may, in a moment of inattention, become uncoupled, and this results in a spasm of activity— his hand, perhaps hers; there is an eruption of the physical into their dreaming life; the genital fluids make their undeodorized presence known. The romance in the head is confronted with a transient reminder of the reality of the regions below. They continue, he more often active but also passive, she more often passive and sometimes active, as they move, largely apart, but seeking to be together, toward orgasm. It is a dumb show in which their private passions and excitements are coordinated through quickening movements, sounds, and vague tensions, which anticipate culmination. Such inarticulate pleasures contain their own anxieties: if he has climax too soon he may loose his erection, she may remain unsatisfied. But in the best of circumstances, given our current cultural blueprint, they move relatively closely to climax, or at least they both will have orgasm. At this moment there may be vocalizations (perhaps calling upon the Deity), requests for activity, assurances of affection. The external world is largely gone—the movement of the bed, the floor perhaps creaking, the sounds of a passing and disinterested world—but even at this moment there can be that instant of double consciousness: What if the neighbors are listening? What if a roommate returns?

When they are done—and the moment and quality of doneness is often difficult to define—there is the moment of separation and awareness. The coolness of the room, the stickiness of the flesh, the world intrudes, only to be held at bay by expressions of mutual affection, talking, touching, assurances of trust, gentle reminders of the social relationship that bounds and allows the sexual moment. There is a problem of reentry into that other world, even between themselves. There is mutual nudity, his body and hers without that protecting cloak of the erotic by which they have modified the boundaries of modesty. They must clean up, remove the evidence of physical intimacy, and dress in their cold and rumpled clothing, perhaps untangling hers from his; they must share or sequentially use the toilet, washbasin, or shower. They may smoke, have a cup of coffee, talk, sit across a table and look at each other. In the end they must admit the claims of the external world, when they are together and when they are alone, when she is with her friends and he with his. There are the dilemmas of partial and total disclosure to what audiences. For him there may be the crudities of adolescent judgments and braggadocio about his conquest that will exist ambivalently with his sense of a betrayal of intimacy. For her there may be worries (more virtuous girls quietly moralizing) and justifications (she was in love, why else would she have done it?). For both of them the outcomes are ambiguous, and their scripts will be reordered and transformed to provide plans for the future and justifications for the past.

It is possible to create many such scenes which involve the sexual. This cryptic and incomplete description contains only a part of the reality of the specific act and suggests only one of a variety of circumstances under which first coitus can take place in this society at a specific historical-social moment. One can vary the ages, the personal histories, the degrees of skill, the quality of assent, the legal circumstances, and the social status of the participants and produce differences in what might be called the conventional social situation for first coitus. But even in this simple form, the extraordinary complexity of the situation and the levels of coordination necessary for finding a successful conclusion are most apparent. Within the social and psychological fields of the two young people are a wide range of subplans or script elements, in the sense that the word *plan* is used by Miller, Galanter, and Pribram (1960), that must be integrated, organized, and reassessed. These are plans that have relevance at the physiological, psychological, and social and cultural levels. When sexual conduct (of which the physical aspects are only a small part) is viewed in this manner, its explanation is not simply a matter of determining a sequence through which a kind of biological mandate is expressed. Rather, the emphasis is on psychosocial processes and cultural-historical situations which provide meaning for behavior, allow for the integration and reorganization of information and skills learned at earlier stages in the life cycle, and indeed elicit from an underspecified organism the culturally appropriate responses to novel situations.

From the point of view of socialization, little of this complexity can be predicted with any ease from the versions of developing psychosexuality, which exist in the original or revised Freudian paradigm. That version of the socialization process is excessively linear and suggests a very rapid closure to the possibilities and requirements of adaptation later in the life cycle. It is likely that the majority of cultural resources that are ultimately brought to bear on sexual conduct are learned in contexts which, at the time they are learned, are irrelevant to the ultimate outcomes or circumstances in which they are used. Human beings in response to novel or only vaguely anticipated circumstances bring to bear upon them only loosely the adaptive resources learned in other situations; the outcomes are not random, but they are also not fixed by the creaking machinery of the laws of development which are the individual equivalent of Newton's clockwork universe.

Not only sexual socialization, but many other aspects of the socialization process, which are currently described in the literature, suffer from a largely restricted historical and cultural framework. Lives of individuals not only have a sequential character (the usual pattern is infancy, childhood, adolescence, adulthood, old age), but they also exist in a wide range of sociocultural and historical contexts which serve as the local sources for learning the content of these various stages of development. Further it must be noted that even these stages of the life cycle have been notoriously flexible in their beginnings and endings, and some of them clearly are cultural inventions that have appeared at recent points in human history (Aries 1962). We are at this very moment trying to solve at the sociocultural level the emerging disjuncture between the moment when one is allowed or can gain occupational independence and when one has legitimate access to sexual activity. The problem concerns the existence of a historical assumption that occupational maturity and sexual maturity, the access to money and the access to sexual pleasure, require an orderly and sequential relationship. The fact that sexual activity, if not pleasure, is now both possible and practicable prior to apprenticeship in the occupational order, especially among college students, raises the specter of unearned pleasure prior to labor, a peculiarly irritating thought to those of a puritan bent.

The developmental process in various cultural and historical contexts contains a very wide set of expectations of appropriate learning and activities for persons of various age grades. Not only are overt activities learned (some taught, some observed, others inferred—the mechanisms are varied and differ over the life cycle), but they are associated and interactive with the acquisition of scripts that contain classes of assertions about the causes, sources, and meanings of these activities. The scripts and their embedded practical assertions about the meaning of concrete activities are learned not only in the context of the life cycle, but in particular cultural-historical circumstances. The elements in the scripts do not exist in any one-to-one relation to elements in the concrete activities, and in this sense they are not a direct map of the concrete situation. It is this loose relationship between scripts and concrete behavior that makes inferences about the meaning of concrete behavior so problematic and invalidates much of cross-cultural and historical psychologizing. However, this same flexible relation between scripts and concrete behavior is critical to the processes of development as well as to individual and social change. To be sure, scripts and their associated practical motives are directly linked to the contexts in which they were learned and to the activities that they related to at that time. The meaning of development, however, is that what appear to be similar behaviors viewed at various points in the life cycle (as well as in various cultural contexts) actually have differing scripts, and what makes change over the life cycle possible is the detachment of scripts and activities from each other to be available as resources in new combinations of scripts and activities with changed motivational assertions at later points in the life cycle.

This adaptive capacity of human beings to separate scripts from concrete situations and independently operate with scripts, script elements, and explanatory assertions outside of their contextual origins is a well-recognized and often highly rewarded skill in other areas of human endeavor. In scientific research we constantly seek new assertions about the meaning of behavior, often substituting a new explanatory model for data the gathering of which was guided by opposed or differing models. In the study of history this process of revision is constantly with us, as the events of the past, about which there may be little dispute regarding the "facts," are reinterpreted in novel and intriguing patterns. History as the record of kings and princes yields to Marxist, Freudian, or sociocultural explanation as new movements in the culture and the historical academy seek new standards for the interpretation of the past. Lest such revisionism be recognized only in the self-serving practices of Soviet encyclopeadists, the every-decade revisions of the history of the Civil War in the United States may be offered as counter evidence. Carrying such a view of significant and useful revisions to issues of individual development, including the psychosexual, follows from an existentialist tradition. The past is not a fixed quantity in current interaction but is rather a resource, for individuals are free within certain cultural specifications to edit, rewrite, anthologize, and bring to bear new explanations upon it; they make novel plans containing what were disparate elements, learned at different points in the life cycle, as they seek to adapt and design their current environment.

This process of anticipatory and retrospective "fictionalizing of the self" has been described by the novelist John Fowles in the following manner:

> You do not think of your own past as quite real; you dress it up, you gild it or blacken it, censor it, tinker with it, . . . fictionalize it in a word, and put it away on a shelf—your book, your romanced biography. (1970, 84)

> So we are all novelists, that is, we have a habit of writing fictional futures for ourselves, although today we incline more to put ourselves into a film. We screen in our mind hypotheses about how we might behave, about what might happen to us; and these novelistic or cinematic hypotheses often have very much more effect on how we actually do behave, when the real future becomes the present, than we generally allow. (295)

This process of fictionalization has to do not only with plans for the future, but with the rearrangement of the past and the present. Just as the novelist takes the past and present, both in the real world and in fiction, as part of his resources and then creates a new work—within the cultural specifications and formal requirements of what such a work should be— so the individual takes his own past and the cultural resources of the society that are available to him to create a present self in line with his plans for the future.

Perhaps a nonsexual example might suggest the power of this process. It is generally believed (or was, some years ago) that the rates of social mobility between blue- and white-collar occupations were vastly lower in England than in the United States. The extreme myth was that they were close to zero in England and unlimited in the United States. Research has suggested that this discrepancy is not the case, and as a matter of fact, rates of social mobility of this kind have been fairly similar in this century in the two countries because of similarities in their industrial and occupational structures. Where did our beliefs, then, come from? In part, at least, they arose from differences in culturally received styles of utilizing the past in current circumstances. In the United States it is still culturally appropriate to describe oneself as a self-made person; Horatio Alger lives, at least in the ways in which we distort our pasts to make our current accomplishments the function of our own efforts, desires, and accomplishments. We may tip our hats to our parents, but the tendency to see ourselves as poorer or less advantaged than we actually were and to expand the gap between then and now is a distorting mirror, if only a minor vice. In England, until the recent present, the tendency to obscure one's social origins was quite prevalent, being in part an aspect of a larger cultural reticence about one's private matters, but also expressing a sense of cultural disassociation with working-class origins. Such cultural differences are significant, for they are some of the basic factors in potentiality for change or stability, at both the individual and the social levels. The processes of cultural change in England evidenced by the decline of the Oxbridge accent and the old school tie are more than simply an honest facing up to social reality, but are part of a change in the day-to-day character of social life. In contrast, Horatio Alger, or at least his bureaucratic equivalent, still seems firmly entrenched in the United States.

A recognition of this loose and flexible relation between social scripts, the explanatory assertions that they contain, and concrete social situations is necessary to an understanding of the limitations and confusions that exist in conventional theories of psychosexual development. Hence, the observation of children in what appears to be sexual activity from the point of view of adults fails to account seriously for the differences between adults' scripts and motives and those of children. Indeed, it is only as the child becomes adult and shares both the activities and the culturally prescribed motivations of an adult that it is sensible to describe his behavior as sexual, except in the most abstract sense.

The strategy that I would like to adopt for the remainder of the chapter is to trace out a series of influences on one aspect of the sexual situation, not exhaustively, but suggestively, noting the shifting relationship between scripts, practical motives, and concrete activities as these are assembled into what is culturally acceptable heterosexual conduct in early adulthood. In this process it is possible to observe our own cultural specifications rather more clearly and perhaps to examine their origins in the interaction between individual development and psychological and cultural circumstances.

One of the problematic aspects of the fictitious young couple's sexual situation was their coordination of mutual sexual excitement and, particularly, the processes by which the timing of the movement toward orgasm could be managed satisfactorily. What is at issue is the way in which two young people attempt, through mutual stimulation and internal self-monitoring, to alter and adapt their prior experiences to enact what Masters and Johnson (1966) have called the orgasmic cycle (composed of four stages: excitement, plateau, orgasm, and resolution) in order to produce orgasm in some satisfactory sequence. There is considerable evidence from the clinical literature that the coordination of these events in coitus is not at all obvious, and even the experience of orgasm among many women is erratic or nonexistent in coitus. It seems profitable to examine the relationships between scripts and the orgasm experience as they develop over the life cycle as an uneven process of adaptation to an ambiguous cultural and personal environment.

There as some evidence that, at the physiological level, the capacity for orgasm, in the sense that there is some kind of biological competence, occurs relatively early in the life cycle. Kinsey reports observational data, from a variety of sources of mixed quality, regarding what appears to be orgasm in children of both genders under 1 and 2 years (Kinsey, Pomeroy, and Martin 1948; Kinsey et al. 1953). The external bodily signs, noted without any physiological instrumentation, include rapid breathing, vascularization, increasing body tension, and sudden release of tension, followed by resting. It is presently unclear what meaning this behavior has for the infant and whether infants who are so experienced have been set on an alternative path of development. It is also unclear whether the experience, which an external observer is describing as similar to adult orgasm, has any specifically sexual meaning (in an adult sense) or whether this experience would continually be sought, in the absence of any meaningful script. What evidence there is suggests that early childhood orgasm is relatively erratic and, from what some parents report, is largely a sedative or self-soothing practice without any script materials that would connect with similar events among adults. There is also some evidence that orgasm occurs in later childhood before puberty, but this evidence, too, is fragmentary. There are reports from some adults who have had sexual contact with children of 7 to 11 years that these contacts have resulted in the same kinds of observable excitement and what appears to be orgasm. There is also some evidence of prepubertal orgasm as recalled by adults whose experiences seem to them in memory to be similar to those which they have had after puberty. What evidence does exist suggests that there is some possibility of a biological competence for orgasm existing before puberty, but that this competence does not quickly or easily translate into social orgasm performance in the absence of specific learning conditions to give it a sought-after character. The word *competence* is used here differently than it is by effectance theorists or than it was by Robert White in his very useful and original description of psychosexual development in 1960. It is used here in the sense that Chomsky distinguishes language competence, a tendency toward a specific organization of the biological substrate that makes possible what Chomsky describes as language performance. However, in this case I would assign an overwhelming weight to the role that social and psychological factors have in converting orgasm competence into orgasm performance.

It is important to note here that the conversion of orgasm competence into orgasm performance is especially complex in women. From sociohistorical evidence it is apparent that orgasm performance among women was largely unnoticed or discounted in the eighteenth- and nineteenth-century literatures on sexuality, except, of course, in pornography, where women were not only granted an inexhaustible orgasm capacity, but an ejaculation paralleling that of men as well. It has been conventional to argue that this lack of orgasm on the part of women was a simple function of the positive repression of a natural psychosexual function; but what seems more likely, viewed from the cultural perspective of the mid-nineteenth century, is that the sociosexual definitions of women, especially those women who became the models for twentieth-century respectability, existed without any elements that could have provided the basis for learning that orgasm was part of women's adaptive physiological equipment. The sense of refinement, passivity, general submission to masculine standards of modesty, and, at least in some part, resistance to sexual exploitation by boys and men left a large blank space in the gender socialization process of women. Such a general exclusion of the sexual from social life, especially those gender and sexual scripts that we have inherited from the nineteenth century as part of our received cultural repertoire of conduct, not only existed for women but also shaped the sexuality of many men as well. The problem was not the repression of an inborn drive, but the lack of a set of eliciting circumstances, including gender and sexual scripts, primarily for women, but also for men, that would convert orgasm competence into adequate orgasm performance.

Such a cultural inheritance still serves to differentiate the gender socialization patterns of men and women out of which our sexual patterns take many of their meanings. Thus, very young children are taught the appropriate modes of initiation, control, and dominance that should exist between girls and boys, women and men. They learn social scripts about gender, how boys should behave, how girls should behave, how they should behave together, and what are the shared and differing practical motivations for conduct. Such gender scripts contain conceptions of moral value, a sense of the appropriate explanations for behavior, and some understanding of how these may be used and changed from situation to situation. What is strikingly apparent regarding the sexuality of children is how few of the elements of the adult sexual script, except in the form of constraining gender scripts, are possessed by our children. Even when young children of 7 to 9 years engage in what we call sex play, even that which imitates coitus from an adult's point of view, it must be seen through the scripts and motivational resources of the children themselves. They are not practicing adult coitus in most Western societies— the behavior is not an intrusion of the sexual impulse into childhood or the prologue to adult sexuality. The motives are embedded in the scripts and plans that are available to 7-to-9-year-olds in this culture. Perhaps even more rare than the experience of orgasm in this children's play is their engaging in the behavior with the goal of having orgasm. What is lacking during this period is any set of scripts that might include the learning of orgasm or its inclusion in any sequence of behavior. Even if general excitement occurs, involving erection in boys and perhaps even random orgasm from this generalized arousal, organized scripts do not exist which would name the reasons for continuing the behavior. It is possible, however, to create a culture in which orgasm performance would be highly rewarded and in which there were educational processes to create orgasm-seeking behavior among young children and perhaps even to cast the behavior in terms of scripts which were available to adults in the society. To do so in Western societies with their current cultural organization would not only require a radical shift in our sexual conduct, but the effects of such change would likely extend to the farthest reaches of occupational, familial, and religious life as well.

In terms of orgasm performance, the best evidence suggests that for this culture it emerges as a routine form of behavior among a majority of boys and a less frequent and more intermittent behavior among girls in conjunction with masturbation in early adolescence (from 12 to 14 years). There are some alternative patterns, varying by gender and social class, but the modal experience seems to be through masturbation. The significance of masturbation for men is not only that it produces an orgasm cycle of generalized excitement, intense arousal, and resolution, but that the behavior is accompanied by a series of more or less complex sexual narratives, the elements of which can be independently capable of eliciting and maintaining the sexual activity itself. What are called masturbatory fantasies are in fact rudimentary sexual scripts which include selected elements of gender scripts learned previously, combined with novel sexual elements that are screened in the head in coordination with genital or other self-stimulation. It is through this process that orgasm competence is beginning to be converted into orgasm performance for many men in this culture. The boy or young man has begun to develop a proto-adult masculine sexual script which contains a cast of characters (himself, young women, and, less often, other boys or men), a rough imagery of the physical activities that might be going on in the scene, measures of the moral worth of the persons involved, and an ordered sequence of the nonsexual activities and symbolic materials that are needed to produce the desired effect. It is easy to miss the nonsexual elements in these fantasies, but a more-than-casual reading of Philip Roth's *Portnoy's Complaint* suggests the necessity of combining nonsexual attributes with sexual materials in order to create an erotic ambiance. The anxiety and considerable uneasiness about the risk and dangers of masturbation arise in part from the ambivalent combination of conventional elements into unconventional conduct as well as its largely unspecified character, since both its content and practice are learned sub rosa. These two processes are perhaps more anxiety-producing than any specific prohibitions about masturbation. Indeed, most of the descriptions of the behavior embedded in prohibitory statements are so vague that they may increase anxiety without reducing interest.

The interesting problem in terms of the developmental role of emergent scripts in the coordination of physical behavior is that in the earliest stages of masturbation, this coordination is relatively poor, and boys tend to have problems of maintaining focus on the fantasy or getting the manually induced orgasm to coordinate with the appropriate moment of sexual culmination in the fantasy itself. It is only through practice of the script and the self-stimulation that a certain level of skill emerges, a level of skill that accounts for elaboration in the script elements as well as the maintenance of excitement for longer periods of time prior to orgasm. Figure 1 roughly suggests this coordination, using Masters and Johnson's graphic image for the orgasm cycle (Masters and Johnson 1966, 5).[1] There are no qualitative measures on either axis (either for time or for excitement), and the trace line itself is clearly a convenient image rather than a true depiction of either any single or combined measure of physiological events or psychological excitement. The intent is to suggest the levels of coordination involved, and that in early masturbation excitement is rapid, the plateau stage is relatively short, and the young man comes relatively quickly to climax. What is important is that a patterned relationship emerges between scripted materials and the physical activities that must be modified in nonmasturbatory sexual activities and that even the subjective experience of orgasm itself may be modified in these transitions.

The present cultural-historical conditions with reference to women's sexuality during this period are more complex, and the evidence is far more fragmentary. In addition, since there is some evidence, at least at the ideological level, that changes are desired, if not already occurring, in women's sexual and gender socialization, the current versions of early adolescence among women may well be of a transient character. At this moment the evidence is that fewer girls than boys masturbate in early adolescence and that they masturbate less frequently. There is some evidence that the script content which accompanies, permits, and elicits masturbation by girls may contain little material that is "sexual" from the boys' point of view—content such as meeting "Mr. Right," falling in love, or getting married.

However, such events contain a romantic and anticipatory excitement for young women that may parallel the excitement produced by thinking about coitus among young men. Further, a recent study by Ruth Clifford of the Department of Psychology at the State University of New York at Stony Brook suggests that some young women masturbate to orgasm without knowing either the labels for masturbation or for orgasm. They have the experience but do not know its sexual content. It might be pos-

---

1. The trace line used by Masters and Johnson is a very useful pictorial device and is largely in accord with the subjective sense of the orgasmic cycle, but does not describe any specific physiological process. See Masters and Johnson 1966, p. 5, fig. 1-1.

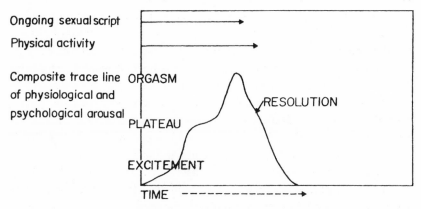

FIGURE 1. An example of levels of coordination and possible durations of segments of the orgasmic cycle in boys' adolescent masturbation (conventionally performed in private, manually, with a concurrent sociosexual narrative).

sible to speculate that this activity is similar to and perhaps follows upon prepubertal self-stimulation that is tension reducing or soothing without a sexual component in associated cognitive material. All of the evidence at this time points to the conclusion that self-stimulation with and without orgasm and the possession of a script with explicit sexual content are more sporadic among women during this period, and this behavior, when it occurs, is less well linked with the kinds of overt physical sexual activities that women will need to coordinate, under current cultural conditions, later in their life cycle.

It must be pointed out that masturbation is not a necessary element in the emergence of orgasm performance or ultimate coital success in either gender. There are some cultures in which masturbation is relatively rare in incidence and/or frequency. The Kinsey data, as well as that of other researchers, indicate that in the United States about 10 percent of men never masturbate and many working-class men do so only rarely (Kinsey, Pomeroy, and Martin 1948). This suggests the multiple pathways and the different scripts and experiences that can be sequentially assembled to produce acceptable adult sexual performances. Adolescent masturbation is given its meaning and connectivity by the cultural context in which it occurs. In this culture, with the very few practice situations in which orgasm performance can be learned and with the differential experience of the two genders in masturbation, it attains a peculiar salience. In cultural situations in which coital activity is generally legitimate for both genders, either in early adolescence or even in later marriage, orgasm performance is likely to be easily attained.

It is largely in patterns of sociosexual interaction in middle adolescence that women begin to formulate and build into their romantic scripts about woman-man interaction elements that contain a specifically sexual component. Most young men by this point have at least a theoretical knowledge of the sequence of behaviors that are presumed necessary to get through a coital act. In this sociosexual interaction boys and young men begin to initiate at least some of these behaviors, and in such interaction young women begin to learn a reactive version of the young man's primitive sexual version of women. Girls and women learn a pattern of responses not only to men, but to themselves (he is turned on by touching my breasts; I must be turned on by being touched on the breasts).[2] In this fashion, generalized excitement is specified to body parts, and the local cultural sequence of physical intimacy and heightening excitement begins to be formed. But there are constraining elements in this process. The masturbatory script as well as the content of adolescent boy-boy interaction contains a cast of personae in which the girls and women are commonly marked by their bad character, evidence of which can be found in their sexual accessibility. There are parallel beliefs among young women who are perfectly aware of this moral division between the sexually accessible and sexually inaccessible. A conception of the good girl/bad girl distinction comes long before any specifically sexual content is built into it. Rules about nudity and cross-gender touching and vague images of men's and women's virtues have already been set in place, even for the girl who has no idea of what the act of coitus might entail in any direct or concrete sense.

In middle and late adolescence, falling in love serves as a novel mechanism through which this constraint on sexual experimentation may be overcome. A new script element is added which serves to allow many forms of cross-gender intimacy, including the sexual. At the beginning of adolescent petting, a beginning marked by social and sexual ineptitude, anxiety, and fears about general masculinity and femininity as well as peer-group standing, there is a relatively wide separation between the genders. Often young men and older boys have a relatively advanced sexual script, reinforced by peer-group values, relatively coordinated with the experience of masturbatory orgasm, and integrated with general cultural prescriptions, which is now linked to the sexual, about men's initiation and dominance. Young women and older girls have a relatively more

2. This is, of course, only one of a variety of learning circumstances in which a special character can be given to the breasts in the sexual-response cycle. A sense of the significance of breasts as an indicator of maturity or personal worth is also provided by the mass media, as well as by girl peers (Kinsey, Pomeroy, and Martin 1948).

restricted sexual script. Their conduct is often constrained by the gate-keeper role, they are less likely to have autonomously sought orgasm in masturbation, and they are usually bound to a commitment to wifedom and motherhood as a fundamental goal. However, the availability of the adolescent script for falling in love offers a potent and facilitating basis for sexual experimentation.

If we recall adolescent petting in any detail, we remember that it is a rhythm of increasing general intimacy between pairs which peaks at various kinds of sexual activities linked to age grades, the possibility of falling in love, and marriage. It is an activity of extraordinary subjective excitement, with each performance often extended over long periods of time and commonly completed without orgasm. This pattern is suggested in figure 2, with the dotted trace line suggesting the possibility of declines in excitement and the rare possibility of orgasm. The plateau is long sustained, and in the absence of orgasm, the resolution is long drawn out, often with young men and young women feeling some pain or discomfort in the groin or genitals. Once again, there are no quantities involved; what is important is a recognition of the differences in cycles of excitement and the conditions under which sexual learning goes forward, as well as the difference between durations of various parts of the orgasmic cycle when compared with prior orgasmic practice on the part of men.

This physical cycle is repeated over and over again, and only as couples get older and closer to marriage is it likely to result in the scene of first coitus that I described above. In these situations of petting, young people learn an enormous facility in kissing and a reasonable repertoire of non-coital skills. Both young women and young men learn to tolerate relatively high levels of psychological excitement and physiological tumescence without orgasm. That such petting does not terminate in orgasm is quite worrisome to some adults (Kinsey was one of them), but both young men and young women find it a remarkably pleasant activity in itself, even though it may not terminate in orgasm or coitus. Such restraint is sometimes difficult for young men in that they had experience of orgasm as an appropriate culmination in masturbation, but there is no easy translation of the solitary, autonomous, fantasy-impregnated experience of orgasm to the dyadic, dependent, exploratory situation of petting. By contrast, young women, whose bodies are now increasingly invested with erotic meaning derived from the young men with whom they pet, learn that arousal is possible and pleasurable through the sequence of activities that young men attempt and in which they ultimately cooperate. They learn in the context of love a sense of the physicality of sexuality and its role in sexual gratification.

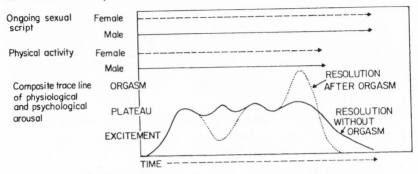

FIGURE 2. An example of levels of coordination and possible durations of segments of the orgasmic cycle in middle-adolescent petting (similar trace line for both genders) (conventionally performed in private or semipublic locations, with separate gender-specific scripts and motives and a division of labor in patterns of mutual physical stimulation).

What must be obvious is the infrequency of the dyadic practice of the complete orgasmic cycle. The young man is involved in sexual excitement that does not end in orgasm while engaged in concurrent masturbatory behavior which does result in orgasm. At the same time the scripts for these masturbatory performances are being modified by the concrete content of the experiences of petting as well as by materials from other sources, such as the media. The young woman retains a generally inexperienced role as far as the completion of the orgasmic cycle is concerned, but possesses an increasing awareness of its potentiality. It is in the late teens or early twenties that first premarital coitus usually occurs, a description of which I essayed earlier. It is no wonder that its performance seems so error ridden. The event has rarely been practiced, its subelements are badly integrated, the couple is anxious, and they are unsure of each other's and their own responses. At the moment they attempt coitus they have very little concrete experience to go on. What they do possess are scripts that are quite imprecise and badly articulated.

As in the relation between masturbation and petting, the mastery of the sexual excitement cycle and the attendant scripting in petting does not translate directly into the mastery of the same processes in coitus, and the practice of the sexual excitement cycle without orgasm in petting only in part anticipates the general complexities of the coital situation. Petting does provide, however, a direct practice round for some aspects of the coital situation: there is some practice in mutual disrobing, learning the social skills to secure privacy, developing the ability to focus on the body of the opposite gender, and the like.

While I am in some disagreement with the generality of Erving Goffman's (1971) description of the problematic nature of first trials for many kinds of behavior, especially those for which there has been substantial support or rehearsal, his words do apply to sexual experimentation: "It should be . . . evident that almost every activity that any individual easily performs now was at some time for him something that required anxious mobilization of effort. To walk, to cross a road, to utter a complete sentence, to wear long pants, to tie one's own shoes, to add a column of figures—all these routines that allow the individual unthinking competent performance were attained through an acquisition process whose early stages were negotiated in cold sweat. A series of formal tests is likely to have been involved and solo trials, that is, distantly supervised practice under real, and hence fateful conditions" (248). Goffman overstates the case (how many people feel anxiety at a cold-sweat level and in how many activities is, of course, variable), but he points to a valuable lesson: ultimately competent performances conceal the processes of learning not only from observers, but from the person who went through the process. In part, the possession of a sufficiently powerful goal embedded in a script gives a person the capacity to overwhelm the cold sweat, to submerge error, and to forgive incompetence. Indeed, the tenacity of young people in continuing to engage in premarital sexual activity, given its problems of logistics and coordination and the low level of social support, suggests the power of learned social goals and the capacity of scripts, with their associated motives, to overcome the friction of brute reality.

In figure 3 there is an example of the two orgasmic cycles of the young couple I described, suggesting the differences between the two genders in the duration of the various elements of their response to the sexual situation. One may compare these with the figures for masturbation and petting to get some inkling of the commonalties and differences involved. The trace lines again do not stand for quantitative measures, although there is some evidence that a young man will become excited more rapidly than a young woman, and there is some evidence of a rising and falling subjective sense of arousal in both partners. Where one puts the moments of disrobing, intromission, and other contingencies on this trace line is dependent on the concrete situation. The durations of the various phases of the orgasmic cycle will vary across individuals and in the lifetime of a single individual. If one looks forward in time for this young couple, it is possible to predict that the quality of the coordination of the phases of the orgasmic cycle will become better, that is, it will meet the culturally specified definitions of good performance. Part of this

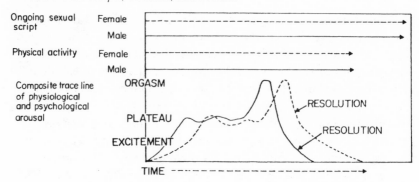

FIGURE 3. An example of levels of coordination and possible durations of segments of the orgasmic cycle in late-adolescent and early-adult coitus (separate trace lines for each gender) (conventionally performed in private, with differing anticipatory and concurrent gender-specific scripts and a division of labor in patterns of mutual physical stimulation).

improvement will result from practice together, in greater assurance about the sequence and order of pleasing each other. It will be possible to achieve a certain lack of attention to many aspects of the behavior: the risk of losing an erection will be less problematic; if she wishes something to be done she can indicate it by signs or words; the subelements of the final behavior will be integrated as routine sequences. Such sequences of concrete behavior will become largely conventionalized, having a normal order and character between any couple.

Since there is a reasonable level of cultural agreement and specification in the learned order of sexual conduct, it will be possible for the members of any pair to move to new partners and behave with a fair level of accomplishment. This transition is rarely without minor crises or problematic elements regarding both physical coordination and changes in the social situation, which require changes or additions to the script elements that are brought to bear on the situation. Thus, intercourse under conditions that do not involve love or which arises out of a summer affair requires the addition of a new set of script elements including novel practical motives for the performance of behavior. Intercourse with persons between marriages or, more complexly, with extramarital partners also requires additional script materials to allow for a successful performance in the concrete situation.

Few persons manage these transitions without some concern or disruption in concrete performance, but even so, the possession of the script and the capacity to manipulate script elements allows one to move from one concrete situation to another with (hopefully) a minimum of distress and error. This relationship between mental scripts and their role in or-

ganizing behavior—especially the loose relationship between script specifications and each subelement in the concrete situation, such as the duration of the plateau phase in the sexual excitement cycle—has been use-
fully explored by Michael Polanyi (1964):

> A mental effort has a heuristic effect: it tends to incorporate any
> available elements of the situation which are helpful for its pur-
> pose. . . .
>
> These actions are experienced only subsidiarily, in terms of an
> achievement to which they contribute . . . This is how you invent a
> method of swimming without knowing that it consists of regulat-
> ing your breath in a particular manner, or discover the principle of
> cycling without realizing that it consists in the adjustment of your
> momentary direction and velocity, so as to counteract your mo-
> mentary accidental unbalance. Hence the practical discovery of a
> wide range of not consciously known skills and connoisseurship
> which comprise important technical processes that can rarely be
> specified. (62)

The emergence of new scripts to coordinate behavior in new circumstances, a process that Polanyi describes in its polished form as connoisseurship, has a series of interesting adaptive consequences. In the process
of transforming and performing previously learned skills (in my example, the coordination of the sexual excitement cycle in differing circumstances), the skills themselves must have the possibility of being removed from the contexts in which they were originally learned and put
to use in novel concrete circumstances often far removed from the contexts of original learning. Hence, the coordination of fantasy, sexual excitement, and orgasm that occurs among adolescent boys is not directly
applicable to the coital situation, in which there is another person and
sometimes a concern for the sexual pleasure of the partner. The relatively
rapid movement from excitement to orgasm on the part of the boy or
young man in masturbation is not initially coordinated with the behavior
of many young women who are just learning in coitus to identify and develop skills which were not learned earlier in the life cycle. From the point
of view of the relation between sexual scripts and concrete sexual behavior, the beginning of coitus involves a young man possessing a developed
script and set of coordinated concrete behaviors who interacts with a
young woman with a differing and less well developed script and a relative absence of subsidiary concrete skills. The problem for young women
is not so much one of direct repression as it is a lack of circumstances in
conventional socialization which would provide content and connection

between mental scripts and concrete action. For men of all ages, the issue may be the overdetermined relation between scripts and concrete activities.

This forgetting of the past which is involved in the dynamic process of the behavioral coordination of scripts and behavior at various moments in the life cycle has contributed to our dependence on linear and/or biological models of sexual development. In the process of editing, rewriting, and reorganizing our scripts to meet new concrete exigencies, we not only lose the older scripts that were linked to prior circumstances, but we also lose the relationship between these older scripts and the skills that were being learned or coordinated through the existence of such scripts. The capacity to coordinate and elicit the sexual excitement cycle in adolescence was dependent on the existence of the scripts that existed in that period of life. The skills that emerged, both directly and subsidiarily, which were of direct interest at that time are now either deleted or become subsidiary, often unnoticed, elements, especially if the coital performance is to succeed in the present situation.

This adaptive capacity—indeed, this adaptive necessity—for scripts and concrete skills to be detached from the original contexts in which they were learned and then to contribute flexibility to the new situation conceals from us the conditions of learning that existed before. This leads to two kinds of problems. First, since our own pasts are hidden from us and we now organize the world through our new scripts, in which are embedded our assertions about motivation, we begin to impose on persons at other moments in the developmental cycle our versions of the world. Second, since we lose the older connections and contexts, in which the scripts and skills coexisted, we tend to simplify the processes by which our current stage of development came to be. In the absence of a clear-cut contact with our earlier experiences, a simple reproductive or drive-based sexual teleology is substituted for the complexity of learning situations, making adult sexual experience the outcome of biological imperatives, independent of historical and cultural contexts. As the historical and cultural situation changes, the inputs from that portion of the world also become lost, and we impose upon the past our current explanations, thinking that they have some universal applicability. At the same time we constrain the future by imposing the present upon it, reducing the potential variability of behavior as individuals encounter novel circumstances and engage in symbolic manipulations in order to adapt to them.

An example of this changing learned relationship between sexual scripts and concrete sexual performances may be found in the recent therapeutic work with various forms of sexual dysfunctions carried out first by Masters and Johnson (1970). In their work (and more recently in the work of other clinicians), the problems of secondary impotence, premature ejaculation, and lack of orgasm are being treated quite successfully through a combination of behavior modification techniques in a general context of individual security and permission for sexual conduct. An outstanding feature of these therapeutic endeavors is that they offer situations in which both scripts about sexual conduct and specific skills and errors in sexual performance may be changed. In some of the clinical cases, the success or failure of certain subsidiary concrete elements in the sexual performance is given a great deal of attention: the woman worries about whether she is going to have an orgasm, the man worries about whether he is going to stay erect. In other cases there are problems regarding the kinds of sexual scripts that the patient may possess. The scripts may contain elements that the patient thinks are discordant with the behavior to be performed (I would note that most of the patients, at least from the Masters and Johnson case histories, suffer problems that would be familiar to Freud in their symbolic content), or there may be a failure in the coordination of the sexual excitement cycle between the couple. It should be noted that all of these problems were present in the experience of first coitus that I described earlier in the paper and that they are ordinarily solved or mastered in nontherapeutic circumstances. The quality of these solutions is clearly variable, but there are at least some persons who move through this inchoate and disordered socialization process to achieve what they, at least, view as satisfaction. In part, this level of satisfaction may well be the counsel of despair—the couple covertly agreeing that what they have attained is the best they can hope for in the circumstances. It is evident that most Western cultures have very low standards for sexual connoisseurship. Indeed, connoisseurship in sexuality is commonly defined as either nymphomania or Don Juanism.

While the specific treatments for the dysfunctions vary in this clinical approach, there is a common core of general permissiveness (sexual conduct is not dirty or wrong). Therapists teach specific sexual skills, simultaneously allowing attention on elements that will become subsidiary while not directly attending to the performance element that is dysfunctional. Couples are instructed not to attempt to complete the entire sexual excitement cycle, but to attend to elements of general eroticism or specific skill learning. At the same time there is a revision of specific script elements if they interfere with performance; for example, those inhibited about their own bodies are taught massage and those who are unable to deal with the concreteness of the body are given a learning situation in which bodily exploration is allowed. There is a studied inattention to a completion of the entire sequence of sexual excitement, often even a prohibition, in order to bring into focus the failure of coordination.

What is important about this emphasis on skill learning and symbolic change is that it highlights the significance of learned materials in the coordination of sexual scripts and the performance of concrete sexual acts. Masters and Johnson have largely interpreted their results as being the consequence of releasing natural processes by decreasing the anxiety and self-censoring brought about by conditions of sexual repression and inhibition. I prefer to argue that what they are doing is not releasing a natural process, but rather engaging in sexual reeducation, an additive rather than a revelatory process. The preference is based on the prior argument that successful performance of the sexual excitement process is an elicited and learned social-psychological process shaped by cultural and historical conditions. This emphasis on learning now needs to be carried beyond the domain of those who are willing to be treated for what they experience as sexual difficulties; the approach is also necessary for an examination of the processes by which competent sexual performances occur, independent of therapeutic interventions, in ordinary situations (that is, in the artificial circumstances of a specific culture and at a moment in history, which is only transiently something that we can call "natural").

Regarding motives, it is important to note another problem. Sexual conduct shares with other aspects of human conduct the dilemma of the divergences in the scripts and the practical motives between parties involved in the most successful concrete performances. Women and men may come together sexually for goals and for practical motives that involve love or lust, exploitation or commiseration, self-aggrandizement or self-loathing, and even with the widest differences in scripts, they may manage to engage in what both experience as extremely successful activity. The practical motives are a variable part of the script, but once the subsidiary skills are learned, it is possible for persons to perform a concrete conventional sexual repertoire with all of the thoughtless grace of dancing a minuet. But this success should not blind us to the importance of sexual scripts, for they exist as a bridge, as sustaining heuristic devices to promote novel conduct and to solve problems of uncoordination. Their flexibility allows us to move from situation to situation and to recognize why one situation is the same as another or why another situation is different. The script is crucial, since it is through using or changing it that gaps in concrete life are managed and levels of connoisseurship are attained. This is implied in graffiti I found on a toilet-room wall (attributed there to John Barth): "Technique in art is like that in lovemaking, heartfelt ineptitude has its appeal, as does heartless skill, but what is wanted is passionate virtuosity." All of these are possible in the relationship between our sexual scripts and our concrete sexual acts. The fictional couple I described were characterized by the first, we have deep cultural reservations about the second, and the last may represent the limits of our present personal and cultural vision.

Reconsiderations:
The Kinsey Reports (1978)

Sexual Behavior in the Human Male, by A. C. Kinsey, W. B. Pomeroy, and C. E. Martin

Sexual Behavior in the Human Female, by A. C. Kinsey, W. B. Pomeroy, C. E. Martin, and P. H. Gebhard

I learned of the first of these two books, whose existence has conditioned so much of my professional life, when I was a teenager unsuccessfully hanging out on the fringes of the local working-class, street-corner society. One night in 1949 a group of us went to the apartment of a young man, previously known to my more sophisticated comrades, who plied us with beer and evidence from the "Kinsey Report" showing that although homosexuality might be a crime and a sin, it was statistically common, phylogenetically normal, and might indeed be pleasurable and profitable.

This was my first experience in the use of sexual science for practical goals, though I discovered in college that a certain vulgarization of Freud could persuade a young woman that she was inhibited or that sex was natural, and further, that the case histories in Richard von Krafft-Ebing and Havelock Ellis had an erotic value in a world that spent more time in sexual fantasy than in sexual activity. It was not until considerably later in my life that I could treat works of sexual science with the "cool attention . . . and scientific equanimity" recommended by Alan Gregg in his introduction to *Sexual Behavior in the Human Male.*

This split in my own response to sexual science—the immediate and the practical as opposed to the distant and theoretical—exemplifies what might be described as the double life of these volumes. The first is their existence as notorious objects and as media artifacts that called forth a

Originally published as "Reconsiderations" in *Human Nature* 1 (10): 92–95.

major reaction from society. The notorious objects are known as the Kinsey Reports, and Alfred Kinsey, their principal author, became our prototype of the sex researcher: The other, more private, existence that these books have, in their complete forms as *Sexual Behavior in the Human Male* and *Sexual Behavior in the Human Female,* remains almost overlooked—with the exception of Paul Robinson's serious consideration of them in *The Modernization of Sex.*

This double existence invites two different responses—the first is to the Kinsey Reports, which exist as a psychic unity in our collective memories; the second is to the complete books as intellectual and moral records of a society.

The first volume intruded on the national consciousness suddenly, startling all those who had lived their lives against the sexual landscape of the 1940s and earlier. The two volumes sold about 500,000 copies and remain probably the most talked about scientific books since Darwin's. The reports became a presence in the society, a presence both consolidated and disseminated by the mass media. Scientific sexuality could be publicized, but erotic sexuality could hardly be mentioned. The scientific framework allowed public discussion of premarital sexuality, oral-genital sex, homosexuality, penises, vaginas, and orgasms. Putting a percentage in front of the topic made it speakable.

Kinsey and his colleagues had obtained quantitative reports from their ventures into the sexual lives of those whom Ellis had labeled "fairly normal people." The reports appeared to be a mirror in which society could look at its sexual reflection. In a world of sexual ignorance and secrecy, even a distorted reflection was desperately desired. By providing members of the society with a collective version of their sexual lives, the reports served as a precursor of what is now a major role of the human sciences. As local cultural traditions have largely dissolved, people in modern industrial societies use the theories and evidence of the social and behavioral sciences to explain their conduct. The absence of a publicly shared sexual culture in the United States meant that the Kinsey findings flowed into a vacuum created by ignorance.

The impact of Kinsey and his reports was conveyed and shaped by the existence of a mass-media system that had matured during the years of World War II. The national media took the works of an obscure Midwestern biologist and his colleagues and made them into front-page news, the subjects of long articles in magazines, jokes on the radio, and cartoons. In so doing they carried a sexual message into every home in the society. Whatever sexual standards or patterns of conduct existed in various regions and enclaves, the Kinsey data became a national portrait. A review of newspaper and magazine responses to the two Kinsey Reports shows that the media's view of Kinsey and the reports crystallized with considerable speed. By time the long-awaited volume on female sexuality appeared in 1953, the automatic responses in the media had become an acceptable substitute for the actual book and its authors.

The media selected the portions of the books that were most intelligible: the percentages of who was doing what. And these numbers quickly became grist for routine quarrels between the sexual middle and sexual right: quarrels over method (Was it a sample? Who were these six thousand people? Would you tell the truth to the interviewer?), quarrels over morality (Would the books signal a moral decline in the society? Should the foundation that funded the work lose its tax-exempt status?), and quarrels over personality (What was Alfred Kinsey really like?). At the same time fragments were pulled from the books in order to legitimize a particular sexual behavior, to convince legislatures to change laws, to justify the publication of sexually oriented magazines, and to argue for more (or fewer) sexual activities of various kinds.

The presence of the reports and the sexual conversation and debate that they created were a prelude to a major increase in the publicly sexual character of society that occurred in the late 1960s and early 1970s. The reports had no direct effect on sexual conduct, but they did provide a basis for public and private talk that helped lead to some changes (particularly among young people) and the wider discussion of sexual matters in the mass media. Indeed, if the media's description of sexuality prior to the reports underrepresented the sexual conduct of members of the society, since the publishing of the reports, the media may be overrepresenting the importance of sexuality to people in the United States.

The Kinsey Reports were created in this process of public use, and the books as coherent intellectual and scientific response were obscured. The very titles of the books proclaimed a point of view; the phrase "in the" in their titles suggested the magnitude of the task they were written to perform. Modestly described, they were books about some aspects of the sexual conduct of a perhaps atypical collection of mostly white, middle-class, youngish women and men who were interviewed in the United States during the end of a great depression, during a world war, and during the recovery from that war. But the books were meant to be more—they were meant to embody a theory of sexuality and to bear witness to the necessity for social change. Both the volume on men and the volume on women are deeply felt, moral books—this is their overriding quality—but the tone of that morality dramatically shifts from the first to the second. The volume on men is both innocent and contentious, convinced in its prose and in its science. The four introductory chapters give sufficient warning. In these Kinsey extols the taxonomic method as the "best" kind of knowledge, which can be gained only by sampling large populations. He denigrates studies of the single case and participant observation (social science tourism, he calls it)—nothing will do but "large and well selected samples of the sort the modern taxonomist employs." In his enthusiasm for adequate samples Kinsey even writes the criticism that others will apply to his own works. He warns of researchers who have not studied a representative group of people: "Conclusions based on such studies are applicable only to the particular sample which was available to the particular investigator, and it is practically certain that no one will ever again meet, at any other time, in any other place, another group of persons similarly constituted." Kinsey never mentions prior studies of sexual behavior that lack statistics; the key to science is the "statistical sense" without which one is "no scientist."

Kinsey firmly believed that he had the right method, both in terms of sampling and in terms of interviewing; and using the right method, he believed that he had asked nature the right questions. As a consequence nature had given him the right answers. The answers showed that the social arrangements devised by moralists run contrary to the reality of sexual nature. Kinsey concluded that cultural values that oppose biological facts are social errors. The contest between the demands of a culture and those of imperious sexual nature was as vivid in Kinsey as it was in Freud—but Kinsey took nature's side.

Kinsey made his crucial argument in the following manner: "The homosexual has been a significant part of human sexual activity since the dawn of history, primarily because it is an expression of capacities that are basic in the human animal." For "homosexual," Kinsey could have substituted any form of sexual activity—oral-genital sex, aggression during sex, masturbation—for he regarded it all as part of biological potential and mammalian heritage.

It should be pointed out that what Kinsey meant by nature was clouded by prejudices. For instance, he viewed less-educated people as closer to nature, less sophisticated, and less artificial than the well educated in their approach to sex. Thus he regarded premarital petting without intercourse (which was prevalent among the well educated) with some suspicion—it appeared to deflect the true aim of sexuality. In harmony with this view, Kinsey argued (from preliminary data that turned out to be wrong) that working-class women are more likely to have orgasm than are middle-class women because the former are less inhibited in their approach to sex. This "naturalness" was further reflected in Kinsey's belief that working-class and criminal populations are likely to tell you "the straight of it" because their motives for being interviewed are direct and uncomplicated.

The reductionism in Kinsey's arguments is obvious, but it is not a reductionism that seeks to explain all behavior by appeal to some more satisfactory level from physiology or physics. It is in fact reductionism for ideological purposes; Kinsey wished to justify disapproved patterns of sexual conduct by an appeal to biological origins, to the power and wisdom of nature. This appeal is based, however, on evidence that contains no direct measures of biology—unless self-reported rates of sexual activity can be construed as direct indicators of biological activity, potential, or purpose. The powerful factors in the volume are sociological: the impact of social class, marital status, religion, and aging on sexual activity in a specific culture.

Kinsey's urgent sense of scientific and moral correctness, which was so patent in the volume on men, was severely moderated in the volume on women. It is not clear what happened in the five years between the publications of the two volumes to produce this shift. It may have been in part the critical response of the scientific community to the first book, but it may also have been evidence contradicting that volume, which emerged from the researching and writing of the volume on women. The evidence of this erosion of surety can be found in the opening chapters—the collection of cases (that no one would ever meet again) is more modestly described, and its limitations are spelled out; the interviewing procedures are described again, but without the earlier volume's passionate belief in their accuracy. The early chapters concern themselves more with practical matters (sexual problems of the young, of the married, of sex offenders) and less with the ability of taxonomy to show society the error of its ways. But Kinsey was still unprepared to give up his conviction that truth comes from a commitment to science: "There is an honesty in science which leads to a certain acceptance of the reality. [This phrase is repeated at the head of three consecutive paragraphs.] There are some who, finding the ocean an impediment to the pursuit of their designs, try to ignore its existence. If they are unable to ignore it because of its size, they try to legislate it out of existence, or try to dry it up with a sponge. They insist that the latter operation would be possible if enough sponges were available, and if enough persons would wield them." The moral flame was dimmed, but it was not extinguished. Kinsey was deeply pained that "in an age which calls itself scientific and Christian" (note the order of faith) we are unable to mediate social and individual interests.

If the certainty is muted, it is perhaps because there had been erosion of Kinsey's faith in biology as the determinant of sexual conduct. The explanatory factors in the volume on women remain dismayingly social, and only when Kinsey refers to the mammalian heritage does he seek other sources for the existence or working of sexual arrangements. In the volume on women the factors of religion, decade of birth, and age at marriage (premarital intercourse was closely associated with when women married) were all critical in explaining women's sexual conduct.

Perhaps the major source of the shift in Kinsey's tone was the fact that Kinsey (unlike Freud) had to face in an extended fashion the problem of the sexuality of women. The volume on men is time and again prosexual, and prosexual in a way that emphasizes the frequency, intensity, and search for variety that is exemplified in male sexual conduct. Kinsey contrasts males and females in the first book in the following way: "The female is on the average slower in developing sexually, and less responsive than the male. She is in consequence, more easily affected by, this training in the niceties of restraint." As a measure of Kinsey's honesty, he yields before the new evidence in the volume on women:

> Clinical advice has sometimes exceeded our scientifically established knowledge. It has been difficult to interpret the problems which are involved when we have not understood how nearly alike females and males may be in their sexual responses, and the extent to which they may differ.
>
> We have perpetuated the age-old traditions concerning the slower responsive of the female, the greater extent of the erogenous areas on the body of the female, the earlier sexual development of the female, the idea that there are basic differences in the nature of orgasm among females and males, the greater emotional content of the female's sexual response, and still other ideas which are not based on scientifically accumulated data—and all of which now appear to be incorrect (Chapters 14–18). It now appears that the very techniques which have been suggested in marriage manuals, both ancient and modern, have given rise to some of the differences that we have thought were inherent in females and males.

If the sources of the sexual differences between men and women—who have been treated almost as separable sexual species by sexual scientists—cannot be explained by the evidence of biology, then they must arise from effects of damned custom. As we know, customs vary according to time and place. Customs, which are merely what people believe to be right and wrong in some locality and at some moment in history, *are* the arbiters of sexual conduct. If this is so, then the desire to liberate sexuality, to prevent its repression by older custom, is merely an attempt to institute some new custom. What began as a moral crusade based on biology ends in a near recognition of the fundamentally social and arbitrary character of sexual conduct. The attempt to create a new sexual morality by appealing to the wisdom of biology had foundered.

It is possible to feel a certain sense of sadness when reading this quite remarkable volume on women. For the most part it is actually full of exceptional good sense. The last chapters anticipate nearly all of Masters and Johnson's studies on the female orgasm (some findings were based on films taken by Kinsey's group, but this was not admitted), and there are long and interesting discussions of the right to research and the right to disseminate knowledge to everyone. At the same time, although the second volume was a far better and more sensible book than its predecessor, it was treated with the utmost critical ferocity.

It was as if everyone had spent the five years between the two books writing their reviews and then had printed them without having read the second volume. This problem derived from the other existence of the books; they existed as Kinsey Reports rather than as intellectual and moral records of a major transition in the social and sexual life of a modern society. As Kinsey Reports they required a collective response. The interplay of moral purpose and scientific intent, the changing character of Kinsey's effort, was lost in the necessity of striking a posture.

It is very difficult to make the experience of a sexual life lived prior to the 1950s clear to the young, who did not share that time. History rapidly slips away from us, and only through the most strenuous application of our sense of past times can Kinsey's passion for righting the sexual condition be understood. A description of that vanished time (which is perhaps more applicable to the present than we might like) can be found in the preface by Alan Gregg: "As long as sex is dealt with in the current confusion of ignorance and sophistication, denial and indulgence, suppression and stimulation, punishment and exploitation, secrecy and display, it will be associated with a duplicity and indecency that lead neither to intellectual honesty nor to human dignity."

Science and the Politics
of Pathology (1987)

De Cecco (1987) has identified an important continuity with traditional scientific homophobia in his discussion of recent biological and socio-logical research on gender preference in erotic relations. Historically the strongest supporters for the belief in either the genetic, hormonal, or early childhood origins of gender preference in adult erotic relations could be found among those who were seeking evidence for the patho-logical origins for what they believed was a pathological outcome. The following point apparently needs constant reiteration: Most of the inter-est that has been expressed about the origins of same-gender erotic pref-erence has derived not from its scientific interest but from social and political struggles over the moral value of "homosexuality."

I have used "gender" rather than "sex" because it is my position that we desire a person's gender (that is, the socially constructed complex of masculinity or femininity), not their biological sex. The complex phrase "same-gender preference in erotic relations" is an attempt to deconstruct (or make manifest by contrast) the assumptions in usages such as sexual orientation and sexual preference as well as in homosexuality and het-erosexuality. The argument is:

1. We desire persons' gender, not their sex;
2. This desire is socially constructed, not biologically driven;

Originally published in *Journal of Sex Research* 23 (1): 120–23. Reprinted by permission of the Society for Scientific Study.

3. We, in the complex social sense, "prefer" the other—we are not oriented to the other;

4. This preference is unstable and changeable across the life course;

5. This instability is both internal (what we desire in the other person changes) and external (we can come to desire other-gender persons as well as same-gender persons).

6. All sexual preferences are not gender preferences—we can have race preferences, technique preferences, beauty preferences, context preferences, etc.;

7. *Erotic relations* is meant to specify what relationship is being discussed in contrast to gender preferences in friendships, work relations, love relationships.

If our interests were purely in the scientific questions—What aspects of adult conduct are fixed early in life and under what circumstances?— we could find a wide variety of phenomena that could be studied far more easily than gender preference in erotic relations and which could be approached with more secure methodologies.

There is in Western cultures a deep-seated prejudice that the conduct of socially problematic individuals (criminals, mad persons, the inept, the perverted, the retarded) can be best understood as the result of some defect in the individual's origins. The grip that "normal" people have on their "normal" selves seems to depend on the distance they can create between their selves and their origins on the one hand, and the selves and origins of these aliens on the other. Since scientists (and science) are an integral part of our culture, it should not surprise us that one of their major goals would be to discover why problematic persons are different from the unproblematic. It should further not surprise us that when these crucial differences have been "discovered" (or invented) that scientists would then seek to eliminate the problematic conditions or persons (Gould 1981).

So it is with "homosexuality." It is commonly believed, even by persons who are not individually homophobic, that "homosexuality" as a form of adult conduct in all cultures and historical periods must be caused by some fundamental and singular defect that is possible to isolate by contemporary scientific research. Further it is believed that this defect must reside in the biological make-up or the earliest experiences of the individual. Finally, it is thought that "heterosexuality" is the product of normal biology or normal early learning, a normality that will become known when the defect among the "homosexuals" is discovered. It is only the cultural strength of this view that can explain the continued efforts of serious scientists to locate this defect. The decision to identify the origins of men's "homosexuality" with a "feminized" brain is only one further step in the process of searching for a special physical stigmata for the "homosexual." I would argue that such dedicated searches for the defective origins of problematic individuals seems to be fundamental to modern science and modern culture. As far as one can predict, such a search for the biological origins of problematic conduct is so strongly programmed into our culture that no amount of negative evidence can prevent a continuation of research for the alchemical origins of same-gender erotic desire.

If there were no connection between such scientific efforts and specific cultural prejudices (homophobia in the narrow sense), one could afford to be untroubled by what would otherwise be a harmless, culturally induced obsession. However, the ways in which scientific hypotheses become the basis for or informing of a vulgar belief in the defective origins of the "homosexual" poses a more complex question. Thus the study by Gladue, Green, and Hellman (1984) referred to in De Cecco's (1987) critique was greeted in the *New York Times* as "Homosexual Study Cites Hormone Link" (Brody 1984). No matter how the authors protest that they are not responsible for press reactions to their work, they are surely knowledgeable about the tendency of the press to use them and their findings in these ways. Thus in the earliest days of the AIDS epidemic the headlines was "New Homosexual Disorder Worries Health Officials" (Altman 1982), and the second headline response to the publication of *Sexual Preference* in the *New York Times* was "Kinsey Institute Study Finds Fundamental Predisposition to Homosexuality" (Brody 1981). In the cases of Gladue, Green, and Hellman 1984 and Bell, Weinberg, and Hammersmith 1981, there were more than subtle invitations to these headlines. In the former case, the only point of the study was to examine whether gay men seemed more like women than men in their response to a specific hormone preparation. In the latter, the authors specifically chose biological arguments without any empirical evidence.

When these issues are pointed out to scientists who conduct this research, their responses are well within the rhetoric of normal science: First, it is argued such research provides information about heterosexuals as well as homosexuals (i.e., to know something about the latter tells us something about the former); second, it is argued scientists cannot be responsible for press coverage of their work; and third, it is pointed out that some members of the gay community would prefer a theory of homosexuality that is biologically based. Of the three arguments, it is probably only the scientific issue that is not true—it is only a presumption that heterosexuality and homosexuality are polar opposites and therefore should be studied as if their causations were somehow opposite of each other. Using heterosexuals as a "control group" or comparison group in such studies makes an unexamined "scientific" truth out of what is a contemporary cultural prejudice. That is, the invention and acceptance of the idea that heterosexuality and homosexuality (like masculinity and femininity) are either polar opposites on a continuum or dichotomized essences has structured research programs into a search for confirming examples of difference. Indeed, the acceptance of a need to disconfirm such instances of "differences" continues the viability of the assumption on which the original program of research is grounded. Moreover, each time a prior "difference" is disconfirmed (e.g., gay men are not pseudo women), new ones are found (e.g., the influence of prenatal hormones).

The wish of some gay men and lesbians to locate the origins for their desires in unchanging and unchangeable biology or early experience deserves a respectful response even though I think it to be wrong. Such a preference in explanation rests on two grounds: the first is personal, the second, political. On personal side, any gay or lesbian life, happy or unhappy, open or closeted, is a life that has been created and sustained, sometimes at great cost, in a world dominated by heterosexuals and homophobes. A social constructionist argument that same-gender erotic preferences are simply cultural artifacts vulnerable to changes in culture, history, and the life course often does not meet with the felt experience of the actors. It is thus believed that something more important must be going on than make-believe, since life has often been too hard to be just play-acting. My argument is that all of life, the best and the worst, is pretense with consequences.

On the political side, the protections offered by purported biological or other irreversible causes of adult desires or statuses are surely ephemeral, as any reading of the historical record of the eugenics movement in its savage or benign forms will suggest. Further, a plea for exemption on the basis of an early and irreversible cause will only support a defect theory of same-gender erotic desire, a theory that will ineluctably lead to more violent forms of scientific intervention (Schmidt 1984; Sigusch et al. 1982). Attempts to placate the oppressors will only invite further persecution. The source of freedom in everyday life for gay men and lesbians is continued vigilance and practical political action.

Support for this freedom among scientists should be recognition in their research of the complexity of gender and desire rather than an attempt to find "the cause" of some singular essence labeled "the homosexual" or "the heterosexual."

Gender Preference in Erotic Relations: The Kinsey Scale and Sexual Scripts (1990)

The contemporary study of "homosexuality" "bisexuality" and "heterosexuality," or more generally "sexual orientation" or "sexual preference," *is* in a muddled state.[1] It is tempting to call the current scientific situation of these topics "revolutionary," or more mildly, "interparadigmatic," but that suggests a more coherent program of research than has previously existed and presumes an equally coherent, though differently ordered, program may follow (Kuhn 1970, 1977). In addition, the interdisciplinary character of sexual studies makes the vocabulary of paradigms seem less plausible than it appears to be when applied to marked changes within a delimited subfield of a larger discipline that has conventionally acceptable boundaries. The issue is both more diffuse and more complex and is perhaps better indicated by the quotation marks that have been placed around what are commonly taken to be scientifically unambiguous terms.

The quotation marks are meant to suggest the coexistence of confidence and doubt. The routine use of terms such as *homosexuality* and *homosexual* in a variety of scientific and lay contexts expresses a widely held, perhaps near universal, belief that we know what these words in-

Originally published in *Homosexuality and Heterosexuality: Concepts of Sexual Orientation*, edited by D. H. McWhirter, S. A. Saunders, and J. M. Reinisch (New York: Oxford University Press, 1990). Copyright © 1990 by The Kinsey Institute. Reprinted by permission. My thanks to Professor Cathy Stein Greenblat for her comments on this chapter.

1. The name *homosexuality* was given to same-gender erotic relations in the mid-nineteenth century as part of the general medicalization of sexual nonconformity. *Heterosexuality* as a label appeared somewhat later (Katz 1963).

struct us to think and to study. At the same time there is a tendency within a number of fields concerned with sexuality to believe that these received classifications are in need of unpacking, so that we might approach the conduct that they identify not as universals or singular essences, but as complex assemblies of human conduct that may be fundamentally unalike in different cultural spaces and historical times. This argument recognizes the importance, in some cases the priority, of the terminological, for it is the names that we are called that justify the sticks and stones that hurt us.

What is proposed in this chapter is to set forth an alternative conception of the relation between sexual studies, sexual conduct, and the cultural-historical context and to examine two examples of the ways in which this conception can lead to a different consideration of both sexual theory and sexual conduct. This will involve three tasks. The first is to discuss the relations between sexual science and its objects of inquiry as well as the culture of which both are constituents. This discussion will emphasize the multiplicity and interdependency of these relations rather than their singularity and independence. The second task is to apply the results of this discussion to Kinsey's treatment of homosexuality and heterosexuality, particularly as embodied in the heterosexuality/homosexuality scale. Kinsey's treatment of these matters is at the midpoint of the history of sexual studies and represents the first major break from the medical and psychoanalytic conceptions that dominated prior thought. The third task is to consider recent developments in sexual theory, particularly those associated with sexual scripting, and to discuss how these developments can be used to richen our understanding of the transformations in the conduct of gay men and lesbians since the middle of the 1960s.

Sexual Studies and Cultural Context

SEXUAL STUDIES AND SEXUAL REFORM

Until very recently sexual liberals commonly believed that the emergence of a scientific sexology at the end of the nineteenth century was an unalloyed triumph of "truth" over Victorian repressiveness (Weeks 1981). Placing sex on the agenda of science meant that a new attitude of mind, as expressed in the scientific method, would provide an objective version of human sexual needs or capacities. This scientifically authorized version of the sexual would in turn serve as the basis for appropriate social reform. Freud did not entirely subscribe to this positivist vision of sexual redemption through science, although he was committed to those reforms that his theories and limited optimism could envisage. However, it was a matter of faith among the late-nineteenth-century sexologists such as Magnus Hirschfeld, Albert Moll, and Havelock Ellis that scientific knowledge would combat the antisexual values of those speaking for the cultural majority (Robinson 1976).

In the period between the turn of century and the present, this reformist spirit has continued to animate most sex researchers, including many psychoanalysts, in the United States, which has been the major center for research in sexuality. Whatever disputes might have existed among sex researchers about the particular explanations of different sexual practices, what all (here including Freud) would have agreed upon was the privileged character of the scientific enterprise. To them, science and its methods represented an independent and self-correcting system of knowledge production; though dominant groups in a culture could decide not to implement what scientists knew, they did so only out of error.

Despite the expressed views of many researchers that they only dealt with "what is" and not "what ought to be," from its beginnings this attempt to take a detached and "value-free" stance toward sexuality has always resulted in a constant struggle between the researchers and various religious and political groups. These latter groups correctly perceived that the existence of a secular attitude toward sexuality when embodied in independent scientific institutions would fundamentally erode the social dominance of the traditional cultural scenario in which gender and sexuality were exemplary moral functions. And indeed the practice of sex research has modestly contributed (though always in combination with other social forces) to changes in the discussion of the moral and legal status of various sexual practices. Even the proliferation of new dichotomies with which we label conformity to or violations of rules governing sexual life attest to the role of sexual studies in changing the debate over the sexual landscape. What were once solely questions of vice/virtue or the unnatural/natural (e.g., the practice of oral sex or masturbation) have been transformed into issues of more variable moral intensity. Indeed, oral sex is now treated by many of the sexually unadventurous (excluding the Supreme Court) in the United States as a matter of competent sexual technique rather than as sodomy (Gagnon and Simon 1987). Practices that were once examples of the perverse, the infantile, the abnormal, the deviant are now treated, among many social groups, as mostly matters of convention or taste.

That there now exists in most Western societies a spectrum of opinion on sexual matters ranging from vice to taste is in part the result of the success of liberal sexual ideologies and the legitimation of a variety of sexual practices (the prevalence of which often preexisted the legitimation).

However, these continue to coexist with traditional sexual ideologies that have a less benign vision of even the limited set of sexual practices that they allow. While the weight of opinion has shifted in a more liberal direction, a shift supported by scientific "sexology," most of the social orders in which such sex research programs have emerged remain deeply divided about many aspects of sexuality. In most large Western societies the erotic is simultaneously promoted and denied, homophobia remains the norm, the genders are segregated in many domains of social life, anti-woman practices and values are widespread, and there is usually no widely approved system for acquiring and practicing a sexual life at any stage in the life course. These conditions continue to shape not only the sexual lives that sex researchers study, but the ways in which sex researchers think about those lives. As a consequence, research reports on pornography, scientific books on sadomasochism, studies of the internal secretions of homosexuals and heterosexuals, and reports on the erotic experiences of women cannot be treated as merely the results of disinterested inquiry, but they represent moral and political acts in larger dramas of liberation and repression.

THE SCIENTIFIC CONSTRUCTION OF SEXUAL LIFE

The recognition that sexual studies are ineluctably part of a larger arena of moral and political struggle and that debates about scientific knowledge (even those among scientists) are concerned with more than scientific knowledge is, however, only the first step in understanding the larger conceptual and intellectual difficulty within sexual studies. It is now better understood that the right to explain social phenomena is not neutral and that who explains a phenomenon and how it is explained are central to the control, or more strongly, the construction, of that phenomenon (Foucault 1978, 1979; Peckham 1969, 1979). The analytic distinction between control in the weak sense of participating in the social management of a phenomenon and control in the strong sense that involves the social construction of a phenomenon is one of emphasis. Clearly, one merges into the other; medical doctors, when diagnosing and treating "homosexuals," participate both in the management of the behavior of the patient and in the maintenance of the cultural category "the homosexual."

In both of these senses of control—management and construction—scientists and their explanations are part and parcel of the phenomenon that they study. The research they conduct contributes to and is responsive to change in that phenomenon. While only some members of the community of scientists who deal with sexuality are directly involved with social control (e.g., psychiatrists who formulate diagnostic manuals, therapists who treat individuals and couples, those who castrate sex offenders), the majority indirectly influence the social order by providing the attitudinal and factual content of various forms of media (textbooks, television shows, science reports in the newspapers) and by affecting (again, indirectly) institutional practices and procedures in the public and private sectors (Scheff 1968; Szasz 1961). Even the promotion of a decline in traditional forms of social control over sexual practices based on scientific studies (e.g., repealing laws against obscenity) serves to change, at least in some modest ways, how sexual life is controlled (in the widest sense) in a society.

This understanding that sexual studies are an active ingredient in social control is not difficult to understand and is fairly widely understood. Indeed, in the weak form of social management it is not in opposition to a positivist view that the results of the scientific enterprise are privileged in terms of their truth value. Even a constructionist perspective might allow that explanations and facts based on a scientific method might be, in some sense, more "true" than those based on folklore, common sense, or religious praxis. However, what has been a less popular perspective (at least until the last decade) is that explanations of sexual conduct in the human sciences have a number of other, deeper connections with the surrounding cultural order. Probably the most important of these is the one that they share with all forms of human conduct, including those they claim to explain, which is that they bear the permanent mark of the time and place in which they are created. This historical grounding of explanatory statements, including scientific paradigms, places a fundamental limitation on understandings between different cultures and between the present and past in any culture (history being a variant of cross-cultural research) (Darnton 1984). Members of the present are limited in their ability to understand the past in both its collective and individual dimensions because of fundamental cultural constraints on what can be known. These constraints mean that in any culture the not-knowable is a domain created by that which members now know and the conventional explanatory network that holds that knowledge together (Fleck [1935] 1979). The not-knowable is composed of the past worlds we have lost, the future worlds we will never inhabit, and contemporary worlds that are so alien that they cannot be thought except by those who are natives. Members of all cultures, including the culture of science, share with Veblen's engineers the "trained incapacity" that is the mark of the native (Veblen [1914] 1964).

This view that the theories, techniques, and observations of the separate scientific disciplines (indeed, even the existence of "separate disciplines") are historically and culturally situated and change in interaction with that historical and cultural situation has been most frequently discussed in the social studies component of sex research. It is most commonly held in sociology, anthropology, clinical psychology, and certain areas in historical studies, where the traditional boundaries between fields are weakening and where even the weak positivist assumptions about "science" are becoming more suspect (Geertz 1973, 1983). In these fields it is recognized that the human beings who are the objects of inquiry of these disciplines change both in interaction with and independently of changes in the disciplines themselves. Indeed, it is proper to observe that many of the conceptual difficulties that are treated as internal to the study of sexuality have actually resulted from changes in what have been treated as the field's "objects of inquiry." Thus, changes in the social, political, and economic status of women and their ideological correlate, feminism, have been the primary grounds for constituting a field called the study of gender. Similarly, the political and ideological efforts of gay men's and lesbian liberation have transformed the study of gender preference in erotic relations.

THE CULTURAL SPECIFICITY OF GENDER PREFERENCE

In the study of gender preferences in erotic relations (otherwise known as heterosexuality or homosexuality, gay sex, lesbianism, straight sex, or sexual orientation), the characteristics of the sexual actor and his or her conduct is increasingly recognized as a specifically cultural and historical artifact. Whatever the similarity in the arrangement of the sexes and their genitals, it is apparent that sex between men and women, men and men, and women and women is not the same in differing cultures or at differing moments in history. More specifically, neither the sexuality between married men and women nor the sexuality of older men with young men nor the sexuality praised by Sappho in classical Greece can be made comparable, without significant acts of translation, with married heterosexuality, man-boy love, or the sexual lives of lesbians in the modern United States (Gagnon and Simon 1973). The conduct could not have been learned in the same contexts, it is not practiced for the same purposes, it is not maintained by the same social forces, and it does not cease to be practiced at the same moments in the life course for the same reasons. The social construction of sexuality (and even if sexuality exists as a separable domain in a culture) and its connections to nonsexual conduct are specific to the cultural and historical circumstances of a particular social order.

What this means for the study of gender preference in erotic relations is that the facile application of modern "scientific" explanations of how persons in another time or place acquire, maintain, transform, and extinguish their "homosexuality" or "heterosexuality" and the relations of that sexuality to the larger social order usually involves unrecognized acts of translation and reconstruction. In most cases this makes the other historical moment or culture into a puppet through whose mouth the scientific ventriloquist speaks. Thus, the application of contemporary psychoanalytic, sociobiological, sociological, or biological theories of the origins of gender preference to sexual practices among the classical Greeks (Dover 1978), the monks of the Middle Ages (Boswell 1980), early-nineteenth-century romantics (Crompton 1985), or the natives of Melanesia (Herdt 1981, 1984) is an act of theoretical hubris. Even the decision to apply modern names to the conduct should require, though it usually does not, a certain delicacy since these usages bring with them the assumptions of the time and place in which they were invented. Is it appropriate to call persons with same-gender erotic preferences in other times and places "gay" or "homosexual" or "lesbian"? In what sense do they possess a "sexual orientation" or a "gender preference"?

It is possible to argue that such terminological niceties are unreasonable or excessively strict and might result in our only using the natives' words for such conduct. And indeed there is some debate among contemporary natives about which of their words should be used for same-gender and other-gender erotic preferences: homosexuals, heterosexuals, gays, sodomites, fags, dykes, breeders, clones, woman-identified women, straights. It could be claimed that everyone knows what we mean when we label someone homosexual and at least it has the virtue of being widely used. More subtly it could be suggested that *homosexual* is the contemporary word and thus culturally applicable to the natives and the practices that it has served to name. Thus, *homosexual* and *homosexuality* could be construed to be merely provisional and weakly held labels for what everyone recognizes is a more complex reality. What is required, however, is more than a certain caution in naming, though such a caution would be an advance. What is required is a constant recognition that acts of usage and explanation are acts of social control in the strong sense, that "homosexual" and "homosexuality" are names that have been imposed on some persons and their conduct by other persons—and that this imposition has carried the right of the latter to tell the former the origins, meaning, and virtue of their conduct.

This issue of names and explanations is thus linked to the conflict between the rights of members (in this case gay men and lesbians) and the rights of nonmembers (in this case psychoanalysts, sociologists, biologists, and other currently "authorized" scientific explainers) to explain the conduct of the membership. Within Western societies certain occupational groups have gained possession of explaining rights for same-gender erotic preferences, and the individuals and the conduct so marked are possessed as part of that group's turf. Such explanation rights bring, in addition to the pleasures of complex and dominating thinking, such material benefits as career advancement, research grants and fellowships, professional deference, and opportunities for performing in the mass media. While these rights are always in contention and there are constant within- and between-group struggles over what individuals or professions have such rights (e.g., biologists versus sociologists, feminists versus psychoanalysts, fundamentalists versus secular humanists, psychologist M versus psychologist E), there are often fairly long periods (though they have grown shorter in recent times) during which one voice or another drowns out the rest. In modern societies with the availability of message multipliers (the print media, radio, and television), such explainers can be widely heard and sometimes believed. The point is that authorized explainers, whoever they might be, are in the process of inventing social and psychological facts as often as they are discovering them, and such authorized facts are often "disproved" or at least "disbelieved" when a revisionist group of authorized speakers seizes the means of communication.

PRIVILEGED AND EVERYDAY BELIEFS

In modern societies authorized explanations often become the basis for everyday belief, replacing in mass media dominated societies what would have been systems of folk belief. In the area of sexuality this is most evident among the college educated, whose exposure to the clichés of authorized social science in various university courses provides them with scientifically acceptable "explanations" of conduct. Such explanations are often refinements of beliefs acquired from vernacular sources earlier in life (though these are often contaminated with media-based elements), but in some cases beliefs that are entirely novel are added to a student's repertoire of explanation. One consequence of this intimacy between explanation producers and explanation consumers is that future researchers are likely to hear answers to questions that are entirely congruent with prior explanations given in introductory textbooks. That a large body of scientific knowledge represents no better guide to action on the part of individuals (here think of volumes on the impact of child-rearing practices on personality development) than grandparents' tales or folklore has no bearing on the extent to which such knowledge is believed. Indeed, in many cases the formulation in the human science literature is folklore renamed and justified by "research data" (e.g., masturbation is not only a vice, it is a sign of mental disorder).

The historicity and culture-boundedness of scientific ideas, the intimate relation and mutual influence of scientific ideas and everyday ideas, and the power over the subjects and subject matter held by institutions and ideas of science all belie claims to the cumulation of privileged knowledge, the detachment of the scientist, and the disinterestedness of both the research enterprise and its practitioners. However, few in the human sciences wish to accept such "limitations" on their theoretical ambitions. Perhaps driven by what Ellul (1964) has observed as the drive for domination in Western science and technology, many human scientists strive for general and universal explanations of social and historical conduct. They have what psychoanalyst Heinz Kohut (1977) described as "ambitions for their ideals," and having idealized their ambitions, they wish to impose their ideals on others. Having created a simulation of the world, they then wish to impose that simulation on the world itself (Baudrillard 1983).

This desire for the universal and eternal on the part of the essentially transient is perhaps reason for the continued attractiveness of the great collective dramas of nineteenth-century romantic social thought, the tragic and hopeful visions subsumed under the names Marx, Darwin, and Freud. A more tempered vision can be found in the following social constructionist statement: "I no longer believe that there is some ahistorical entity called homosexuality. Sexuality is socially constructed, within the limits imposed by physiology, and it changes over time, with the surrounding culture. There was no thing such as a Castro clone, a lesbian feminist or a Kinsey 6 a century ago, and 100 years from now, these types will be as extinct as Urnings" (Califia 1983, 27).

The correlative point is that the explanations of contemporary sexual studies that have helped to create these types will become fossils in the verbal record as well. The types, their conduct, and the explanations will become historical artifacts. In the same way that contemporary explanations of contemporary types fail to explain the extinct Urnings of the nineteenth century, theories of whatever "homosexuality" will be called a century from now will not explain the Castro clone, the lesbian feminist, or the Kinsey 6.

The Kinsey Scale

THE CULTURAL CONTEXT OF THE KINSEY RESEARCH

The attempt to richly recollect past experiences in periods of even moderate collective and individual change—to locate the selves, the others, and the social contexts and to script them into plausible narratives—strains the limits of most people's skills at *verstehen*. It is thus very difficult for those who lived through the period from World War I to the end of World War II, and perhaps impossible for those who did not, to accurately experience the pleasures and pains of sexual life in the United States during those decades. The changes in sexual life that have occurred since the 1950s have perhaps permanently estranged us from a world in which the underwear advertisements in the Sears, Roebuck catalogs were the source of rural and small-town boys' erotic fantasies, when nudist magazines were sold in brown wrappers in certain bookstores in larger cities, and when a bare breast in a photograph was the grounds for an obscenity trial. It was a time when J. Edgar Hoover was an expert on sex crime and pornography, and the sex moron and the sex fiend graced the pages of urban tabloids. Pluralistic sexual ignorance was the norm, carrying with it the usual corollaries of sexual guilt and misadventure. The literary, visual, and interpersonal landscapes of the times were filled with good girls and boys (June Allyson and Andy Hardy) and bad girls and boys (the young Jane Russell and Studs Lonigan), who enacted quite traditional tales of sexual excess and constraint and experienced community exile and redemption. Even the voices of present-day religious fundamentalists carry only a faint echo of a period when the views they now espouse were those of a confident majority occupying the American Protestant center.

These decades were also a period in which new social forms for desire were being created, especially for the young. The independent girl with her bare legs and short hair, young people dancing first to jazz and then to swing, double-dating in cars while listening to the sounds of Glenn Miller and Guy Lombardo, and the exquisite pleasures and anxieties of truly forbidden and dangerous unbuttonings and touchings were all inventions of this period. These spots in time and space for romance and sex were detached from immediate community and familial surveillance and the usual religious constraints. For the majority these delights were perhaps more often offered at the movies than in real life, but holding hands and (for that passionate minority) necking while watching the screen in the great dream palaces was thrilling in any case. A sexuality created out of glimpses, denials, fears, going only part of the way, and waiting for true love certainly had its appeal.

These sexual lives that now seem so far away, even to those who lived them, were conducted in a nation that was in the process of radical social and cultural transformation. The United States entered the 1920s a nation composed of cultural regions, of natives and immigrants divided by ethnicity and religion, and of urban dwellers segregated from those who lived in small cities and towns and on farms. The four decades of the 1910s through the late 1940s saw the country transformed, by economic and political upheaval, internal migration, and the mobilization of the society for purposes of two world wars, into a national economy and polity that, increasingly stratified by class and education, offered the potential for a national culture. The sexual recollections of this period, whether journals, autobiographies, or other fictions, usually entirely or in their early passages record the sound of these regional, even local, accents. It was only toward the end of the period, when the tide of immigrants had been stemmed and their children provisionally Americanized and when radio and the cinema had begun to create a national character for the new middle classes, that a national culture actually began to emerge.

THE IMPACT OF THE KINSEY STUDIES

The lives of those interviewed by Alfred Kinsey and his colleagues exactly span the concluding years of this first period and the first years of what was to be the next cultural epoch in the history of the United States. Kinsey conducted his first interviews in 1938 and continued to interview throughout the end of the depression and during World War II. It is remarkable that no one has commented on the fact that during what was thought to be a total mobilization for war, it was possible to conduct a major sex research project (involving travel, research grants, and face-to-face interviewing) that was irrelevant to the war effort. There has been no discussion of the impacts on Kinsey's findings of the large numbers of men who were in the military service (for example, such impacts as delaying marriage, separating spouses, increasing sexual permissiveness because of the wartime climate). Indeed, about 34 percent of the men and 48 percent of the women were interviewed during the war years. Equally remarkable are the facts that such research could have been conducted at a site universally considered to be politically and religiously conservative[2]

2. Indiana University is located in Bloomington, Indiana, forty miles south of U.S. Route 40. The entire state was historically characterized by old-time religion and Republicanism, and its southern portion was long characterized by Bible Belt conservatism. Until 1935 the university

and that the research did not receive serious public notice until the publication of *Sexual Behavior in the Human Male* in 1948 (Kinsey, Pomeroy, and Martin).[3]

Kinsey and his work—the volume *Sexual Behavior in the Human Female* (Kinsey et al.) was published in 1953; Kinsey died in 1956—represent an important marker in the historical transformation of United States society from a regional to a national culture. Sexuality in the largest sense was out of the closet; words previously unspoken outside of professional groups and those privy to the culture of psychoanalysis and never written in the popular press became part of the national discourse. *Penis, vagina, oral-genital contact, orgasm, homosexual,* and *extramarital coitus* dropped from people's lips and appeared on the printed page.[4] Conduct heretofore unmentioned, or mentioned only in the most negative terms, was reported to be exceedingly common: nearly all men masturbated and so did a majority of women, oral sex was practiced by lots of married folks, about a third of men had had a homosexual experience, perhaps 5 percent exclusively desired such experience, half of women were not virgins when they married, and a quarter of those married had sex with men other than their husbands (the number of men in the last category was much higher). Kinsey was violently assailed by religionists, conservative congressmen, and some methodologists; he and his work were caricatured in the press; and the sex researcher and sex research were freely lampooned. This backlash may well have shortened Kinsey's life; what it did not do was to discredit the work itself (Pomeroy 1972). The Kinsey studies, whatever their weaknesses, came to

administration fired all faculty who divorced, and until 1960 the barber shop located in the Indiana Memorial Student Union did not cut the hair of what were then Negro students.

3. The success of the research enterprise may have been aided by the turmoil of the times during which it was conducted. The decade of research\ activity contained the end of the depression (1938–1940), the preparation for and conclusion of World War II (1940–1946), and the period of massive family formation and occupational resettlement between 1946 and 1948. It was a period in which persons were far too seriously engaged in making critical life choices to be concerned with such minor issues as sex research. This intense involvement of people in their own lives also prevented many of them from being swept away by the moral panics of anticommunism, antidrugs, and antisexuality that marked the late 1940s to middle 1950s. The physical isolation of the Bloomington campus also meant an insulation from the still heavily regionalized press and radio news systems. It was not until the mid-1960s that the privacy of cultural life disappeared in the face of a fully developed and voracious national television and print system that began to treat behavioral science topics of various sorts as newsworthy.

4. This process was of course not completed in that period. The word *penis* did not appear in the *New York Times* until the mid-1960s, and discussions of anal sex in print and on television had to await the advent of AIDS. Thus the televised statements of the Surgeon General and the National Academy of Science in October 1986 have contained reasonably explicit references to same- and other-gender anal practices.

be treated as a national report on the state of sexuality in the United States.

It is in the larger framework of social change that Kinsey's general treatment of sexuality needs to be understood. Kinsey reported upon the conduct primarily of what was then an emergent national middle class that was being detached from region and ethnicity. It should be pointed out that nearly all studies of sexuality from Freud to Masters and Johnson have been conducted on this changing social formation, and the social formations that it has supplanted are worlds we have lost. Kinsey's subjects were predominantly young, native born, and college attending or college educated (Gagnon and Simon 1987). And the audience for his work were members of that same growing class, many of whom were already alienated from or resistant to traditional sexual values. What Kinsey supplied, under the banner of science, was a legitimation of the sexual lives that many middle-class persons were already living. His findings suggested that the dominant cultural scenarios for sexual conduct of the period from 1920 to 1940 only weakly applied to the actual sexual lives of the new middle class. If Kinsey offered a mirror to the society, it was restricted to this expanding social formation, and it reflected far more of the society's future than its past.

KINSEY AND THE RELATION OF HETEROSEXUALITY AND HOMOSEXUALITY

Kinsey's treatment of the relation between heterosexuality and homosexuality was more than a simple mirror in which conventional persons could recognize themselves. Unlike his views of premarital sex, heterosexual erotic techniques, and even extramarital experience, Kinsey's view of homosexuality dealt primarily with the experience of an outcast minority. Even though many men reported having a few homosexual experiences in their early and late adolescence, homosexuality remained for the vast majority of Americans a matter of sin and abnormality. It was exactly the dichotomies between sin and virtue and normality and abnormality that Kinsey attacked on the level of both sexual theory and individual experience. Theoretically, he argued specifically against prior conceptions of the homosexual and homosexuality, and by creating the 0 to 6 scale (or, as it was called at the Institute for Sex Research at that time, the H-H scale), he proposed that people's heterosexuality and homosexuality could be best understood as the proportion of other-gender and same-gender sexual acts (here including fantasies) in which they had engaged.[5] The relation between heterosexuality and homosexuality was to

5. It is rarely noted that the 0 to 6 scale contained an additional category, X, which meant no sexual activity at all. Kinsey reported that at age 15 one boy in five had no overt sexual activ-

be treated as continuous rather than discrete, and individuals could move from one place to another on the continuum by adding new acts of the two different types.

What Kinsey opposed was the theoretical belief, well-established among psychiatrists and psychoanalysts, that persons with substantial amounts of same-gender erotic experience represented a unitary category of persons with similar psychological or biological biographies whose lives were entirely governed or at least strongly influenced by the gender of the persons they sexually desired. Assimilated into this "scientific" conception was a prior folk belief shared by both everyday "heterosexuals" and "homosexuals" (and enacted by some of the latter) that "homosexuality" was grounded in a gender defect (either constitutional or learned). This defect meant that homosexual men were somehow insufficiently masculine (and therefore effeminate) and that homosexual women were insufficiently feminine (and therefore masculine). More complex readings of these relations between psychosexual normality, gender, and sexual desire were formulated (e.g., the obligatory, the situational, the masochistic, the situational homosexual), but at the center of the theory was the assumption of a common class of persons whose pathological conduct depended on common pathological origins (Socarides 1978).

Kinsey's theoretical counter to this view that each homosexual was possessed of a defect in biology or very early education was to take a strong biological line, but one that emphasized the evolutionary history of the species rather than the defective status of the individual. This is essentially the theoretical position he took about *all* sexual conduct, approved and disapproved. He argued that homosexuality, masturbation, and oral sex (to take the triad he most often discussed when dealing with these issues) were common activities in the "mammalian heritage" as well as among human groups where cultural repression of the sexual was not the norm. Hence such activities represented the diversity of nature rather than perversities and deviations from a biological or cultural standard for the sexually correct individual (Kinsey, Pomeroy, and Martin 1948). This is an argument of extraordinary originality, one that allowed

---

ity and no psychosexual reactions (about one in twenty for the entire period from age 16 to age 20). There is no separate definition of the X category in the 1948 volume (Kinsey, Pomeroy, and Martin, 641); however, it is defined in the 1953 volume (Kinsey et al., 472) because of the large number of women in this category throughout the life course (Ibid., 499). Xs account for 15–20 percent of the never-married respondents, 1–3 percent among the married, and 6–8 percent among the previously married. The gender preferences of these large numbers of sexually inactive persons should be treated with some caution.

Kinsey to bring what was thought to be unnatural under the umbrella of a larger and more copious nature. It shares with the Freudians a view that there is a severe tension between the offerings of nature and the strictures of culture; however, Kinsey's vision of what nature offers is closer to Rousseau's than it is to Hobbes's.

The moral and political legitimacy of homosexuality could thus be created by treating it as part of a natural world that should not be limited by the artifices of culture. Kinsey's opposition between nature and culture thus rests on a distinction between the bounty and variety of the natural world (read here the diversity of species in an unmanaged nature) as opposed to a civilized world of agriculture in which nature is pruned and limited. In much the same way as agriculture gives the fields over to mono-crops, sexually repressive cultures cultivate procreative heterosexuality as their sole flower, treating all else as weeds. Kinsey remained true to his prior evolutionary and ecological concerns; it is in the biology of abundance and adaptation that he found the template for the normal, not in the individual organismic views that characterize the defect-finding traditions in psychiatry, psychology, and biology.

THE H-H SCALE: ACTS AGAINST ESSENCES

The H-H, or 0 to 6, continuum rests at least in part on Kinsey's understanding of nature. As he wrote: "Males do not represent two discrete populations, heterosexual and homosexual. The world is not to be divided into sheep and goats. Not all things are black nor all things white. It is a fundamental of taxonomy that nature rarely deals with discrete categories. Only the human mind invents categories and tries to force facts into separated pigeonholes. The living world is a continuum in each and every one of its aspects. The sooner we learn this concerning human sexual behavior the sooner we shall reach a sound understanding of the realities of sex" (Kinsey, Pomeroy, and Martin 1948, 639). That continua are as much human inventions as dichotomies and that there is, for certain purposes, a utility to distinguishing between sheep and goats are reasonable intellectual responses to Kinsey's positivist view that the continua in the mind mirror the sexual facts in the world. However, the important issue is Kinsey's decision to make heterosexuality and homosexuality a question of acts rather than a question of common origins, common personalities, or common behavioral performances (in the case of men: effeminacy, artistic temperament, a broader pelvis, occupational preference, scores on the Terman-Miles MF scale) (Kinsey, Pomeroy, and Martin 1948, 637). It is the mixture of heterosexual and homosexual performances that impressed Kinsey; the record of "experience and psychic reactions" (639) that fluctuates across the life course, even within a single sexual occasion.

It is this record of experiences and psychic reactions that were collected during the sex history that became the basis for placing an interviewee on the 0 to 6 scale. Interviewers returned from the field and counted up, necessarily in somewhat crude ways, the frequency of sociosexual experiences, with and without orgasm, with the same or different partners (independent of marital status and other factors) that occurred with people of the same or opposite gender. In addition, the frequency of sexual dreams with and without orgasm that could be classified as having same-gender and other-gender content and the proportion of masturbation accompanied by same-gender or other-gender fantasy were estimated. These calculations were somewhat less precise than those from sociosexual experience for a variety of reasons, most significantly the result of weaker attention given to fantasy in the interviews. Such counts were made for each year of life and cumulated for the life span as well as for shorter periods in the life course.

Perhaps the best analogy for this method would be to think of each year of a person's life as a jar into which a white ball is dropped for each heterosexual experience and a blue ball for each homosexual experience. The total number of balls is then divided into the number of white balls and a place on the continuum is assigned for that year. What this does not account for is the total volume of sexual experience, so that someone who had 10 other-gender sexual experiences with the same person and 10 same-gender sexual experiences with 10 persons in a single year would be a 3, as would someone who masturbated 150 times with only homosexual fantasy but who had marital coitus 100 times and coitus with women prostitutes 50 times in a single year. This actually suggests a greater accuracy of counting events than could be attained from the sex histories and a rather more mechanical practice in the assignments than was practiced. A good deal of judgment was involved in the assignments, and researchers often estimated the "importance" of different kinds of sexual activity when assessing their contribution to the final number assigned.

The scale is an empirical attempt to undermine all of the usual sharp distinctions that were made between individuals who had sexual contacts with the same gender and those who had sexual contact with the other gender. By focusing on flexibility and change in conduct across the life course, it counters arguments that same-gender erotic preferences start early in life, are fixed across the life course, and are influential in all spheres of life. By focusing on acts rather than persons Kinsey tried to protect those who are persecuted as "homosexual" because of a few homosexual acts as well as to counter the argument that there is an essential homosexual personality. Thus a single act or a small number of same-gender erotic acts does not a homosexual make. (Kinsey did not make the corollary argument that a single or small number of heterosexual acts did not a heterosexual make.) More trenchantly, there is no such thing as a homosexual person, only persons with various mixtures of acts. Kinsey remained quite consistent in arguing that the intermediate numbers on the scale are not to be treated as a social type called "bisexuals," but are rather persons with a mixture of homosexual and heterosexual acts.

THE SUBVERSION OF THE KINSEY SCALE

Kinsey actually did not propose a specific theory of the acquisition, maintenance, or transformation of either heterosexuality or homosexuality in his 1948 volume. The closest he came was to argue, "If all persons with any trace of homosexual history or those who were predominantly homosexual, were eliminated from the population today, there is no reason for believing that the incidence of the homosexual in next generation would be materially reduced. The homosexual has been a significant part of human sexual activity ever since the dawn of history, primarily because it is an expression *of capacities that are basic in the human animal.*" (Kinsey, Pomeroy, and Martin 1948, 666, emphasis added). As in nearly all discussions of heterosexuality and homosexuality the central focus was on the latter, with the former treated as a residual category. In the volume on the women, largely in response to critics of this argument, he wrote: "The data indicate that the factors leading to homosexual behavior are (1) the basic physiological capacity of every mammal to respond to any sufficient stimulus; (2) the accident that leads an individual into his or her first sexual experience with a person of the same sex; (3) the conditioning effects of such an experience; and (4) the indirect but powerful conditioning which the opinions of other persons and the social codes may have on an individual's decision to accept or reject this type of sexual contact" (Kinsey et al. 1953, 447). The grudging readmission of what was at least a stripped down version of the roles of psychology and culture in sexual life was an important shift, one that was characteristic of a change in Kinsey's views as he wrote about women's as opposed to men's sexuality (Gagnon 1978). Culture remains, however, only responsive to the mammalian heritage and the accidents of experience and conditioning.

What is problematic for Kinsey's view that persons are mixtures of acts is that most individuals with same-gender erotic experiences actually behaved in terms of the social types that Kinsey fought so hard to dissolve. Persons with same-gender erotic experiences viewed themselves and were viewed as enacting or resisting the social roles provided in the contemporaneous existent homosexual culture. Being a sissy, queer, dyke, fem, butch, trade, or faggot was experienced as a real state. No one has ever experienced himself or herself as a jar filled with 50 percent heterosexual and 50 percent homosexual acts. Contra Kinsey, persons with what they thought to be equal desires for or experiences with women and men have labeled themselves "bisexuals." It is one of the ironies of research history that some of these persons have now substituted Kinsey "numbers" for such labels as exclusive homosexuality or bisexuality. Thus "bisexuals" might refer to themselves (in front of a knowledgeable audience) as a 3 or as a Kinsey 3. Most commonly these labels will be used by persons with predominantly same-gender partners as a summary measure, "I'm a Kinsey 6." A recognition of the extent of this knowledgeability is evident in recent studies that use various forms of the Kinsey scale as the basis for self-ratings of respondents (Bell and Weinberg 1978). What was once an "objective" count of experience has become part of the culture of gay life and part of self-labeling by members of that community.

It would raise our confidence in the scientific enterprise if it could be argued that Kinsey's ideas, as embodied either in his theories or in his scale, had some deep impact on the main strands of work that followed his publications. However, neither his notions of the importance of the "mammalian heritage" nor his treatment of heterosexuality/homosexuality as a mixture of acts independent of the existence of role packages has been deeply influential. What have been consequential are Kinsey's arguments against the negative essentialism of psychoanalytic and psychiatric formulations and the belief, based on his interviews, that same-gender erotic conduct was fairly common as an exclusive desire and very common as incidental conduct.

During the 1950s and 1960s, the way was opened for a series of studies that emphasized the importance of social oppression and local cultural circumstances as critical to the life-ways of persons with same-gender erotic preferences. In addition to scientific interest, there was an increase in political activism with what was to become the community of gay men and lesbians (Humphreys 1972). This activism was interactive with the activities of liberal social scientists, and in many cases the activists took over an important role both in performing research and in transforming the subjects of research. In its early phases this work focused on four themes: (1) that same-gender erotic preferences were not acquired through special or pathological pathways and that there was no evidence of special or frequent pathology among persons with such preferences that could not be explained by social oppression; (2) that the importance of origins was, in any case, both overemphasized and probably insoluble given the weakness of recollection and the enculturation of gay men and lesbians by dominant psychoanalytic theories; (3) that the observed similarity among persons with same-gender erotic desires did not result from common individual origins but was a function of group membership (learning how to be gay in a specific culture) and enhanced when performing for others in contexts specific in the culture (clones are more masculine in clone bars and health clubs); (4) that the nonsexual aspects of such persons' life-ways were often more important in shaping their sexual lives than vice versa (Gagnon and Simon 1973, chaps. 5 and 6).

This research activity during the 1950s and 1960s and the increase in social activism associated with "homosexual activists" were rooted, at least in part, in the existence of Kinsey as a persona and the publication of his numerical data ("how many homosexuals are there") rather than being responsive to either his theory of mammalian origins or his H-H scale. It was Kinsey and his research as a societal rather than as a scientific event that provided an opportunity to develop quite different programs of research and social activism from those he foresaw. This confluence of research and activism became the basis for the creation of the new cultures and communities of gay men and lesbians that emerged in the 1970s.

Changing Scripts for Same-Gender Desire

SOCIAL SCRIPTS FOR SEXUAL CONDUCT

The social scripting perspective on sexual conduct was first articulated in the late 1960s. Its specific conceptions were framed by the larger intellectual traditions of sociological symbolic interactionism, the dramatistic analysis of literature and culture, and a view of human action and the human life course as understandable only in specific historical and cultural contexts (Burke 1936, 1966, 1984; Mead 1934; van den Berg [1961] 1975).[6] The examples of the scripting of conduct were primarily drawn from the sexual realm and were thus heir to all of the advantages and limitations of responding to the particular scientific and intellectual conditions of that field at that time. Scripts were most often treated as heuristic devices to be used by observers to better interpret sexual conduct

6. As the careful reader has noted, there is no necessary relation between the idea of scripting and these larger traditions except perhaps for dramatism. These traditions shape the way that scripts are thought of, what they contain, and how variable they are rather than the choice of the script metaphor itself.

at three levels: cultural scenarios (such as pornography and the cinema), interpersonal interactions (as in specific sexual acts), and intrapsychic processes (e.g., sexual fantasies, plans, remembrances). When interpreting concrete role enactments, for instance, persons were thought of as engaging in sequences of interaction that are scripted in terms of who persons are, what is to be done, when and where it is to be done, and perhaps most importantly, why it is to be done. This first wave of work dealt in most detail with the heterosexuality of young people and young adults, with the sexual conduct of gay men, lesbians, imprisoned persons, and women prostitutes, and with pornography (Gagnon 1973; Gagnon and Simon 1973; Simon 1973).[7] More recent formulations of these conceptions have more explicitly recognized that using a scripting perspective to interpret conduct is not solely the activity or property of privileged observers. Many everyday actors, particularly those aware of popular approaches to understanding conduct, self-consciously "script" or near script their own interactions as they negotiate their lives (Berne 1966; Gagnon, Rosen, and Leiblum 1982).[8] Thus in making plans, people often script the interactions that are to take place and practice conversations for the purpose of self-control and to manage the conduct of the other persons involved. The ubiquity of this internal rehearsal, even among those shielded from pop-soc and pop-psych interpretations of conduct, suggests the closeness of the practices of the scientific observer and the everyday actor in scripting conduct (Steiner 1984). What one would hope distinguishes the majority of scientists from the majority of laypersons is that the former are more systematic and self-conscious in treating the script as a molar unit that can be used to package roles, contexts, expectations, and motives into plausible narratives.

7. A quite different concept of scripting has been used in artificial intelligence research, and distinguishing that usage from social scripts may serve to further clarify the latter (Schank 1982; Schank and Abelson 1977). In research on computerized story interpreters, which involves programming computers to read narrative and make choices based on their interpretations, the word *scripts* refers solely to fixed sequences of action. For example, in a restaurant script, when the meal is finished the computer is expected to "understand" that the next move is to ask for the check. Scripts in this context are the lowest-level units in a hierarchy of modular units. Scripts are the basic elements that are assembled into plans, which in turn become the elements in schemas, and so forth. The higher the modules are in the hierarchy, the more general and flexible they are thought to be. In social scripting, a script is the sole molar unit that is descriptive of all actions; as scripts can be used to interpret mental processes (e.g., plans for the future, remembrances of the past), the guidance of public interactions, and the semiotic structure of environments. They are nonhierarchical in the sense that they are not a "level" in a larger information-processor/decision-maker or personality system. They are also variable in terms of flexibility, ranging from the ritualistic to the improvisational, depending on cultural and historical context.

8. The tradition of transactional psychotherapy explicitly used the metaphors of script and game as heuristics for patients to analyze their "self-defeating" conduct (Berne 1966).

SCRIPTING SAME-GENDER DESIRE

The social scripting perspective converges with Kinsey's work on homosexuality by accepting his empirical findings that in this culture and at this moment in its history there is a great variety in the types of persons who have homosexual experience, that such experience is not the expression of a specific pattern of early learning, and that it is quite common for persons to change their gender preferences in erotic relations across the life course. At the same time, this perspective rather diverges from Kinsey in rejecting his conception of homosexuality as an inheritance from humanity's mammalian ancestors, a legacy that is expressed either in cooperation or in conflict with the surrounding culture. From the perspective of scripting theory, same-gender erotic preferences are elicited and shaped by the systems of meaning offered for conduct in a culture. What is usually construed as "culture against man" or "culture against nature" is thus actually conflict among differently encultured individuals or groups. Another major divergence is from Kinsey's belief in the continuous character of the relation between heterosexuality and homosexuality as represented in the heterosexuality/homosexuality scale. This connection fails to account for the felt experience of most persons in Western cultures that having sex with a person of the same gender is qualitatively different from having sex with persons of the other gender. Persons usually experience themselves and others through relatively discontinuous social types (and stereotypes), even when confronted with a "continuous" variable such as age.

The scripting perspective treats the causal history of homosexuality and heterosexuality (Why are you homosexual or heterosexual?) and the motivations offered for proximate performances (Why did you have sex with that particular man or woman?) as culturally plausible accounts, whether they are offered by scientists or everyday actors (Peckham 1969, 1979; Rorty 1979). In general, such motivational accounts are offered only for same-gender conduct (being heterosexual is not a "marked" form of conduct, though some types of heterosexual conduct, e.g., extramarital sex, may well be), and as such they are usually restricted to causes or motives that are drawn from the conventionalized domains of sexuality or gender. It is also not uncommon that historical accounts are conflated with motives for current conduct. Thus, the proximate motive for a man having sex with another man is treated as being verbally equivalent to being "caused by" (where cause means "motivated by" as well as "explained by") having had a seductive mother and a detached hostile father at critical moments in childhood. Such ways of explaining conduct should be understood as cultural conventions rather than scientific truths. The instability of such causal or motivational statements (e.g., whether fire starting is seen to express a sexual or an economic motive may depend on whether the analysis is conducted by a psychoanalyst or the arson squad) should suggest that they serve more than purely scientific interests.

Struggles over explanation are central to cultural change. They are engaged to reconstruct the past, to justify the present, and to propagandize for alternative futures. The idealized and gendered explanations for women's sexuality offered by some lesbian feminist intellectuals have been countered by the lesbian sex radicals who have proposed an ungendered and erotic set of motives for same-gender erotic conduct among women.[9] "It is odd that sexual orientation is defined solely in terms of the sex of one's partners. I don't think I can assume anything about another person because I have been told they are bisexual, heterosexual or homosexual. . . . For many people, if a partner or a sexual situation has other desirable qualities it is possible to overlook the partner's sex. Some examples are: a preference for group sex, for a particular socioeconomic background, for paid sex, for S/M, for a specific age group, for a physical type or race, for anal or oral sex" (Califia 1983, 2). It is increasingly plausible to provide histories and motives for same-gender and other-gender erotic preferences that are entirely independent of either sexual desire or gender. Thus, the promotion of social mobility, the opportunity to earn money, the desire for personal security, assuaging terror in the midst of battle, the chance to participate in religious communions, and the desire to bear children are all nonsexual motives for sexual conduct. Such motives can be read as explaining or motivating either the acquisition or the maintenance of same- or other- gender preferences.

This perspective, with its emphasis on the socially constructed and culturally and historically variable character of sexual conduct, indeed all conduct, seems more appropriate to the understanding of the lives of sodomites, pederasts, and homosexuals, as well as gay men and lesbians, than do perspectives that emphasize essentialist continuities in the biography and conduct of the "homosexual." In part this appropriateness is a consequence of the rapidity of ideological and, to some extent, behavioral change within the communities of gay men and lesbians since the early 1970s (Levine 1987a; Plummer 1981; Warren 1974; Wolf 1979). The decision of gay men and lesbian/feminist activists and intellectuals to re-

9. The complexities of this debate among feminists, whatever their gender preferences, about the role of sexuality in women's lives and what sexuality is correct in hewing to various political lines are exceptionally passionate and often intellectually dense. It would be too easy to dismiss all of these debates as merely sectarian (which they often are) since they are full of very important ideas about the problems and processes of cultural reconstruction.

name themselves and to play an active role in reconstituting their selves and their culture has been critical in recasting the conduct of nonelites in the gay men's and lesbian communities. The actions have also resulted in the decline of scientific privilege in naming and explaining same-gender erotic conduct and in a change in the mass-media representation of the "homosexual." Debates over the importance of early fixing of "sexual orientation," the stability of gender preference in erotic relations over the life course, and the gender bases for differences between the lifestyles of gay men and lesbians are no longer quarrels among scientists but part of intense political-ideological debates within the gay men's and lesbian communities. It is part of the ideological ferment of the contemporary situation that it is even possible to find strong support within the gay men's and lesbian communities for a "neo-essentialist" gayness or lesbianism.

SCRIPTS BEFORE AND AFTER STONEWALL

In the post-Stonewall era, the changes in what was to become the gay men's and lesbian communities (as opposed to the homosexual community) changed not only "who" gay men and lesbians thought they were (in the sense of gay identity and gay pride) but also changed the scripts for sexual and nonsexual encounters among gay people as well as relations with straights.[10] The pre-Stonewall "homosexual community" was for many persons, who for one reason or another were unpersuaded by or uncomfortable with heterosexuality, their first point of access to a collectivity that they might join. In most locales this quasi-underground community was an anonymous collection of public meeting places (usually bars and taverns serving alcohol and therefore restricted to those "of an age to drink") predominantly utilized by a somewhat fragmented collection of individuals primarily for sexual contacts and transient sociability. Many homosexual men and some women found their friends and lovers in the community as well. When coupled affectionate and sexual relationships were going well, individuals often withdrew from the community. If such coupled relations broke up or became sexually unsatisfying, individuals often returned to the public life of the homosexual community. This cycle of withdrawal and reentry gave untutored observers the idea that a constant search for new sexual partners was characteristic of all homosexual men. However, this penumbra of more stable affectional relationships could be found around a more constant population of regulars and workers for whom the institutions of the homosexual

---

10. The Stonewall riot, in which gay men defended themselves against the police, is the mythic historical marker that divides the homosexual epoch from the gay epoch. It's like dating the moment when the Roman Empire "fell."

community were primary sources of identity and provided social and economic well-being.

Except in the very largest of cities, the homosexual community was dominated by men with few all-women institutions. It was also a community with few of the resources of other communities, and one that emphasized, particularly among men, the virtues of youth, sexuality, and attractiveness. Many of its members were "in the closet" to most of the significant others in their lives; they were properly fearful of the police, their own families, and their coworkers. Such fears often extended to the people with whom they were having sex, since blackmail and violence were both endemic and not reportable to the police. At the same time, the homosexual community was one of the sole ports of entry to friendship and affectional relations and sometimes to jobs and social mobility. It also provided a place in which persons could be what they thought were their real selves. For those who were lucky—the affluent, the talented, and the beautiful—there also existed zones of tolerance, often in the arts and other culture-producing institutions, in which a more open homosexual lifestyle could be enacted. The scripts for same-gender erotic relations among men were learned and reinforced, indeed given content, in this secretive and persecuted community. The identity and experience of the lesbian was far less dependent on this community, in part because it was far less visible to most women and because it was dominated by men's cultures. As a result, lesbianism remained far more tied to traditional women's gender values, was often come upon by accident, and was often enacted within isolated pairs and small friendship circles (Gagnon and Simon 1967a).

The contemporary gay men's and lesbian communities in the major metropolitan centers are far more than just a "sexual marketplace," though prior to the AIDS crisis, the gay men's community was that as well.[11] There are now specialized institutions for both gay men and lesbians: newspapers, magazines, political groups, restaurants, counseling organizations, bookstores, travel agencies, physicians, housing cooperatives, and neighborhoods as well as intellectual/political elites. Surrounding this open community is a radically changed climate of public discussion in the nongay media of the existence of gay men and lesbians. Well

11. The impact of the AIDS crisis on the gay men's community will not be well understood for another decade. It is clear, however, that there was a rapid adoption of "safe sex" practices among most gay men. This change in sexual practices was strongly supported by the media institutions of the gay community, and the community itself has become the primary source of support for those afflicted with the syndrome. The ability of gay men to change their sexual practices supports a view of same-gender erotic preferences as relatively loosely structured both as intrapsychic and interpersonal phenomena.

in advance of the AIDS crisis, homosexuality and homosexuals, gay men and lesbians had become part of public discourse. The publicity afforded same-gender erotic desire, both in the majority media and in the existence of a gay and lesbian cultural apparatus, has not only changed the very character of the process of "coming out" (acquiring a gay or lesbian self-definition), but it has also offered the possibility of "being out" to a wide variety of audiences. Being gay or lesbian is now a more reasonable possibility, often a positive alternative to what heterosexuality offers, and there is now the opportunity for both anticipatory socialization in and practical experimentation with gay and lesbian role enactments that require relatively modest levels of erotic commitment.

Since this environment offers new attractions to wider audiences, there have been changes in which, when, and why individuals are attracted to it (White 1980). This is particularly true among the young, who now know about gay and lesbian possibilities at an earlier age and who are better informed about the content of these lifestyles. The existence of a richer and more complex gay and lesbian culture also sustains the interest of those who would have been put off by what they saw as the oversexualized or culturally impoverished character of the homosexual community. Older women and men, including those formerly married and with children, more easily find a gay or lesbian commitment plausible. These enlistees from a wider base of persons with more various biographies and life experiences may well reduce the power of the community to shape and homogenize gay and lesbian identities. Moreover, their presence will further falsify in cultural practice the belief that gay men and lesbians have similar biographies and common personalities.

THE FLEXIBILITY OF GENDER PREFERENCE

A more varied set of new members and a more diffuse pattern of conceiving of oneself as having the capacity for same-gender desire and erotic relations have also influenced the stability and fixity of same-gender erotic relations. In the very recent past many persons reported that they had had the experience of first knowing "who they really were" or being "at one with themselves" when they first publicly identified themselves as homosexual. This dramatic revelation could be produced by what now appears to be the very simple act of going to a gay bar and being in the company of others "like me." These experiences of rapid identity crystallization were often treated by those who experienced them (and by observers) as evidence that an individual had found his or her "true identity." This felt sense of "belonging" needs to be understood not as evidence of a prior hidden identity now properly expressed, but as a result of the oppressive sexual climate of the period that produced intense personal sexual isolation among nearly all adolescents and young people regardless of the usual gender of their erotic preferences (White 1983). Anxieties about sexual matters were (and are) endemic among young people; these included anxieties about most aspects of sexual performance as well as preference itself. Even a marginally competent sexual experience was more often a relief from anxiety and doubt than it was an expression of intense and innate desire. It is only a cultural and scholarly prejudice that the acquisition and early enactments of other-gender eroticism are not treated as a form of "coming out."

This is not to argue that the acquisition and enactments of same-gender desire were not more sharply felt than their other-gender correlates. That the culture was (and is) generally antisexual should not blind us to the fact that it was violently antihomosexual. For the majority, a same-gender preference in erotic relations was usually constructed in a context of extraordinary ignorance, doubt, avoidance, and fear.[12] As the content of the desire became better understood, its fatefulness in terms of traditional relationships became apparent, as did its consequences, for an individual's life chances in general. As a result of what were often long periods of isolated intrapsychic scripting of the self (Who am I?), it was common for many individuals to treat their desire as permanent even if no one else knew of it. The pain of the process of taking the ego-alien into the self (to mix two discourses) was sufficient evidence of the condition. The disclosure of the private label to other audiences, both the rejecting conventional and the accepting nonconforming, was important in confirming but not initiating the preference. Thus, prosecuting and stigmatizing an individual may help to limit his or her return to the larger community, but negative labels are not the sole agent in this adhesion (contra the work of some labeling theorists following the work of Howard Becker [1973]). Once the public disclosure is made, however, the individual, the new membership group, and the conventional community cooperate in constructing a mutually plausible biography for the marked condition.

Other aspects of the sexual conduct of "homosexuals" in the pre-Stonewall period could be understood in terms of this climate of persecution. Thus, the vigorous pursuit of sexual partners by "homosexual" men during this early period of commitment (given the argot name "honey-

---

12. This is a generalization that is probably true for many of those with same-gender erotic desires, particularly during their early adolescent and young adult years. There are persons, however, who report wonderfully cheerful and satisfying same-gender erotic lives even during adolescence and many more who report lives of great personal and sexual fulfillment during their adulthood. Considering the level of sexual oppression, it is remarkable how many happy "homosexuals" there turned out to be.

moon") must also be understood as a response to specific historical conditions of becoming a homosexual in the homosexual community. The
scholarly emphasis on the sexual aspects of the coming-out period conceals the difficulties of the action of the major elements of being an accomplished "member" of the homosexual community—sexual skills, argot, jokes, differentiation among partners, falling in love, coupling,
falling out of love—none of which are acquired "naturally."

Under contemporary circumstances a conception of same-gender desire as an irreversible orientation is less plausible to many gay and lesbian
individuals as well as to scholarly opinion. It is now possible to recognize
that changes in gender preference in erotic relations, both in fantasy and
conduct, may occur throughout the life course. This instability seems
particularly prevalent in adolescence, when gender-appropriate sexual
scripts are in the process of acquisition. While it is possible "after the fact"
to know how a large number of persons have become distributed in terms
of gender preference, it is quite clear that during the ages of 12 to 17 the
gender aspects of the "who" in the sexual scripts that are being formed
are not fixed (Kinsey, Pomeroy, and Martin 1948). A deeper complication
is that it is not obvious whether it is the gender aspects of the "who" that
have provoked the nascent desire or even if the desire is linked to a "who"
at all. The desire may be focused on someone who is successful, someone
whom others or we desire for his or her purity, or someone we can dominate or by whom we can be dominated. The "who" in these circumstances may be genderless, or gender may be important only insofar as
success, purity, and domination are linked to gender itself.[13]

CHANGES IN GENDER PREFERENCE DURING ADULTHOOD

In addition to gender-preference instability among the young, there is
evidence that in recent years a substantial number of previously married
men and women have been publicly entering the gay and lesbian communities. (It is estimated that one gay man in five has had children; this
estimate increases to two in five among lesbians (Bell and Weinberg
1978). This represents an important addition to the pathways into same-
gender erotic relations, particularly for men. It is likely that some of these
men under earlier historical conditions would have been "tearoom trade,"
that is, men who would have sought secretive and transient sexual contacts in public toilets and parks (Humphreys 1970). With changing atti-

13. Paralleling the relative diffuseness of the gendering of erotic desire during this period, it
is also likely that romantic love is less gender specific in this period for both boys and girls. Passionate friendships with persons of the same or the other gender are actually quite common for
both boys and girls; the ways in which such patterns of love and admiration facilitate same-
gender preferences in erotic relations are not well understood.

tudes toward divorce and same-gender erotic relations, such men have been able to make a less concealed choice of their objects of desire. Many of these men also appear to have been disproportionately selected from the more affluent and from those who were able to sustain relations with their children after divorce and becoming openly gay.

Similar changes in gender preference have historically more often come later in the life course for women, largely as a result of women's ignorance about lesbianism and the salience of love, marriage, and children in women's lives. The disappointments of other-gender relations (e.g., violence perpetrated by men, emotional indifference, and erotic incompetence) as well as the attractions of women's emotional and interpersonal company have always been the grounds for women to change their gender commitments. There is, however, an increase in the number of women moving into lesbian roles among those women who would have formerly remained celibate or who would have remained in an undemanding other-gender marriage. The increasing cultural complexity of the lesbian community now provides reasons to adopt a lesbian commitment other than the emotional support offered by sororal communities or even same-gender erotic desire.

These new patterns of enlistment, in terms of who enlists and when in the life course they enlist, undermine the general essentialist positions, whether they are held by traditional scientific theorists or by gay men or lesbian neo-essentialists. There is little evidence that these persons share a common biography, that they are recognizing their true identities, or that they have common psychological profiles as measured through standard psychological inventories. In actual fact, there was little evidence that such commonalities characterized those in the homosexual communities of an earlier era. Such homogeneities that did exist were the consequence of community membership and not historical or contemporaneous psychological commonalities. It was often the similarities produced by cultural conformity to available "homosexual" roles that scholars treated as the result of similar personal histories.

There is also evidence that more persons with previously exclusive or near exclusive same-gender erotic preferences are experimenting with other-gender erotic conduct. In some cases these are transient erotic encounters, but equally often these sexual relationships are conducted for reasons based on gender differentiation, social conformity, desire for marriage, physical beauty, mental health, romantic love, even reproduction. Many lesbians who wish to have children are now engaging in coitus solely for this purpose. There is also evidence that numbers of persons with predominantly same-gender sexual histories are experimenting with other-gender erotic relations for ideological reasons. Hence: "I have no way of knowing how many lesbians and gay men are less than exclusively homosexual. But I know that I am not the only one. Our actual behavior (as opposed to the ideology that says homosexuality means being sexual only with members of the same sex) leads me to ask questions about the nature of sexual orientation, how people (especially gay people) define it, how they choose to let those definitions control and limit their lives" (Califia 1983, 2).

It is difficult to estimate how often such shifts from exclusive same-gender erotic commitments (the Kinsey 6) take place, but the amount of interpersonal and ideological policing of this kind of conduct suggests that many gay men and lesbians feel an acute sense of personal and political vulnerability when confronted with such conduct. The strong negative reaction to "bisexuality" and "political Lesbians" and the construction of identity tests for culturally "correct" gayness or lesbianism represents a recognition by some members of the gay men's and lesbian community that the community is itself relatively permeable and that the preferences that have organized it are potentially very unstable. Conducting research on this movement from same- to other-gender erotic preferences is very difficult in that the persons involved may be treated as socially dead by the gay and lesbian communities. Such persons are also declared to have been false group members, never to have been truly homosexual, since the mark of the true native is his or her total commitment.

It is among those who have been traditionally called "bisexuals" that these mixed patterns of gendered eroticism have been best documented. The evidence is that these shifts in desire and practice are mediated by both nonerotic and erotic factors. Thus, the changing weight given to nonsexual exigencies such as love, children, or occupational aspirations may shape which gender preference is salient. In more specifically sexual contexts, individuals may exhibit different erotic "preferences" when enacting sexual scripts that specify different "whos." A young man who is a straight hustler to men and who uses the money he is paid to take out his woman friend, the woman who is a lesbian for feminist reasons and who has a man lover, and the wolf or jocker in prison who views being fellated as "heterosexual" since the man who does it is "like a woman" are all enacting gender-appropriate, but gender-segregated erotic scripts (Gagnon 1977). These patterns may mean that bisexuality as a gender-indifferent erotic preference may be relatively rare or is being constructed as a general cultural possibility at the present moment (Duberman 1974).

Conclusion

In the period from 1950 to the present there has been a remarkable shift in thinking about same-gender erotic relations and in the conduct of those relations. The complexity of the relation between changes in thinking and changes in conduct needs to be constantly kept in mind since the relation has been constantly dialectical. The pre-1950s essentialist theories influenced the thinking of "homosexuals" about who they were and indirectly sustained the repressive machinery and attitudes of the larger society toward the "homosexual." Such essentialist theories underrepresented the actual variety of homosexual lifestyles that existed even within the narrow cultural repertoire of the homosexual community and homogenized the biographical origins of those who were identified as homosexual. Kinsey and his colleagues offered a new empirical view of the homosexual that emphasized their biological normality and their personal diversity. Following Kinsey, a number of primarily sociological researchers focused empirically on the conditions of the homosexual community, the processes of "coming out," and the psychological normality of members of the gay community and theoretically set out to deconstruct psychoanalytic and other essentialist theories.

By the late 1960s these views were widely held among homosexual intellectuals and became part of the ideological apparatus of resistance to heterosexism. With the transformations of the homosexual community into the gay men's and lesbian communities, these social constructionist views of gender preference in erotic relations were widespread. In addition, a large number of gay scholars, including persons with and without professional licenses, began to participate actively in the construction of the history, psychology, and sociology of gay men's and lesbians' lives. During the late 1970s and early 1980s the intellectual weight in scholarly research began to shift from the "objective and disinterested" heterosexuals to publicly identified gay and lesbian scholars.[14] The intimacy between theory construction and culture construction is now far more complete, as self-conscious intellectuals attempt not only to discover, but to construct culturally that which was once thought to be only an expression of nature.

The instability of gender preference in erotic relations, both in its recognition and in fact, must be seen as part of a general decline in the

14. Journals such as *Journal of Homosexuality, Speculum, Signs,* and *Chrysalis* all include works by persons who identify themselves as gay or lesbian. The works of gay and lesbian historians, sociologists, psychologists, and literary figures represent most of the useful work now being conducted on the relation between culture, community, and the self.

constancy and rigidity of appropriate role packages in the society. As the traditional gender, race, age, religious, and ethnic prejudices have weakened, so too have prejudices against variations in sexual conduct weakened. Changes within the sexual domain have thus been driven not only by theories about sex and sexual factors, but also by changes in the larger culture, particularly in the area of gender theory and practice. The recognition of the extraordinary complexity of the relation between gender and sexuality is in part the result of the collapse of both folk and traditional scientific views that were part of their social construction and social management. The result of moving the primary sources of explanation of gender and sexual conduct into the domain of science, which is the least stable source of explanation in the culture, may be that theory will now change far more rapidly than practice.

This chapter, which started out as a discussion of same-gender and other-gender erotic relations, has focused, as do all such works, on the minority preference. Given this bias, one might ask if there is anything interesting to be said about the origins, acquisition, maintenance, transformation, and disappearance of heterosexuality in persons' lives. This turns out to be quite difficult when the discussion begins in a contrastive or polarized mode. In the traditional folk and scientific views of the mid-nineteenth century to the mid-twentieth century, heterosexuality was treated as the normal pole of a gendered opposition; it existed as a moral and biological monolith requiring no explanation. Kinsey kept the two poles, but turned the dichotomy into a continuum and made its entire length normal. From a scripting perspective it seems best, at this historical moment, to treat the interpretation of other-gender erotic relations and same-gender erotic relations as independent puzzles. It may well be that our understanding of why men and women desire each other is obscured by thinking that it is analogous to why men and men or women and women desire each other. It may be our belief that they are related in some deep way that has made the preference so critical in moral, political, and scientific debates. To return to the deconstructive mode: "I live with my woman lover of five years. I have lots of casual sex with women. Once in while I have casual sex with gay men. I have a three year relationship with a homosexual male who doesn't use the term gay. And I call myself a lesbian. . . . I call myself a fag hag because sex with men outside the context of the gay community doesn't interest me at all. In a funny way, when two gay people of opposite sexes make it, it's still gay sex" (Califia 1983, 25).

The Explicit and Implicit Use
of the Scripting Perspective
in Sex Research (1991)

Scripting as Theory and Research

The relationship between the complex set of ideas that make up the theory of social scripting (as well as the ideas that underpin them) and empirical research is a difficult one since it raises the entire problem of the proper relation between theory and research. In general in the social sciences the accepted cultural scenario for this relationship is that theory should produce the occasions for research and research should offer the grounds on which theories can be rejected or modified (Merton 1957a, 1957b). Theories themselves are often thought to be composed of a hierarchy of increasingly inclusive statements, crowned by law-like sentences that ultimately account for the many layers of explanatory sentences below. The demands of such a scenario are rarely met in a concrete world of research activity; more often than not the closest plausible relation that exists between research and explanatory statements resides at the level of the empirical generalization, and the majority of theories are often nonhierarchical and fragmentary in their applications. Methodologically sound studies that find that events occur with a given frequency in a given population can sometimes produce relatively unproblematic observations (e.g., the finding from a well-crafted probability sample that the average income of European Americans exceeds that of African Americans can

Originally published as "The Implicit and Explicit Use of Sexual Scripts in Sex Research in *The Annual Review of Sociology*, vol. 1, edited by J. Bancroft, C. Davis, and D. Weinstein (N.p.: Society for the Scientific Study of Sex, 1991), 1–41. Reprinted by permission.

be readily believed). Higher-order statements that attempt to "explain" this observation run into immediate difficulty if they are closely examined. Such alternative explanations of income discrepancies (such as the "inheritance of slavery," "IQ differences," the "matriarchal family," the changing labor market for entry-level jobs, the existence of an "underclass," and institutionalized racism) each represent explanatory complexes (i.e., sets of interlocking and mutually implicating statements that are accepted by some persons and not by others) which face ideological and philosophical, as well as empirical, difficulties.

It is quite clear that in a postpositivist world the same sets of acceptable findings can be given quite different explanations and that the choice between these explanations cannot be ultimately submitted to an empirical or philosophical test (Rorty 1979, 1989). As the philosopher Imre Lakatos has persuasively argued, it is always possible to offer a defense for a strongly held theory in the face of any set of evidence and that any "program" of scientific work is ultimately nonrefutable (Lakatos and Musgrave 1970). It appears that the choice of a set of explanations for a phenomenon rests not on "the facts," no matter how adduced, but on the consensus among workers in a field who share common understandings about what are quality techniques and observations and what explanations plausibly account for these observations (Kuhn 1970). This pragmatic description of how science is done is supported by a philosophical tradition which argues that there can be in principle no relation between theory and experiment and that theories are not descriptions of the world, but instructions to scientists about what to observe in the world.

None of these observations make it impossible to engage in the activities that we describe as science, which as a human activity simply involves a community of workers with a common thought style who as far as possible engage in work that is publicly observable, who work in a community that is open to all trained comers, and whose members avoid sacred prerogatives (Fleck [1935] 1979). As long as scientists do not insist that they are religiously seeking the "truth" in some absolute sense, such a pragmatic vision of the knowledge-producing enterprise is quite satisfactory and requires no additional ideological underpinning.

On the other hand such a pragmatic definition does create both difficulties and opportunities for those who would theorize and attempt to suggest a relation between their statements and the results of empirical research. Under postpositivist conditions the role of theory is both more modest and more grand. It is more modest in that it admits that it is local and transitory, based on what seems plausible and persuasive rather than on what is "true" (Feyerabend 1976; Geertz 1973, 1983). It is more grand in that it seeks to "make sense of the world" and is willing to go about reinterpreting the meanings of studies and findings and integrating them into an alternative body of thought. Theories are ideal systems of belief that are tentatively believed by a community of actors who explore their points of contact with the world. It is a map that desires to become the world, but it remains a map that is not to be believed, or held on to fiercely, or forced on anyone else. It is a way of constructing or inventing a world rather than discovering it.

And this is the way the article that follows should be read. It is an argument for a way of thinking about sexuality that makes sense to the author and some others. The empirical work cited comes from a variety of fields and points of view, but has been assembled here to provide a sense of facticity to the argument. In many examples of the implicit use of scripting the authors may have never thought their work was related to scripting theory at all (e.g., Masters and Johnson [1966] and their description of the orgasm cycle) (Gagnon 1974), whereas others who explicitly use the word *scripts* or cite a body of theoretical work would not have exactly the same understanding of the theory that is presented here (Abelson 1981; Berne 1966).

The Ideological Underpinnings of Scripting Theory

The development of a scripting perspective on sexuality in the late 1960s and early 1970s was embedded in a larger intellectual exercise that was an attempt to reframe a number of important ideas about the sexual (a partial history of that attempt may be found in the citations of and references to the joint and solo papers by the author and William Simon from 1967 to the present). This larger intellectual effort involved a somewhat integrated attempt both to reject a number of traditional views about the sexual and to propose a series of alternative conceptions that anticipated the emerging social constructionist and postmodernist traditions in the social and behavioral sciences (Foucault 1978, 1979; Tiefer 1987; Weeks 1981). It is important to spell out these ideas since they serve as the basis, at least in part, for the ideas about the scripting of sexual conduct that will be used in this article. In actual historical fact, the development of scripting theory and the ideas that now serve as its basis occurred interactively. It is only at this point that one can identify which of these framing ideas appear necessary for the content of scripting theory as it now stands.

The larger intellectual enterprise involved the following basic reconceptualizations:

1. Sexuality is not an "exemplary function" or universal phenomenon which is the same in all historical times and cultural spaces. This means that one cannot treat the social and cultural arrangements around the sexual as simply responses to a biological or developmental sexual imperative that will express itself in all eras and places. This also involves a rejection of the widely held view that the human condition is defined by an inevitable struggle between individual needs and cultural proscriptions, a struggle that is most commonly accepted as characterizing the sexual arena. Countering these views it is argued that sexual life is like all social life: an activity elicited by social and cultural circumstance and an activity that differs from one historical era to another or from one culture to another (Gagnon and Simon 1973). The felt importance of sexuality by collectivities and individuals in Western cultures is consequence of the specific sociogenic significance it had been given in this historical cultural milieu (Simon 1989).

2. Despite the similarity in the limited repertoire of bodily activities usually associated with the sexual, there are no similarities in the meaning of the conduct by individuals or collectivities in different cultures or eras (Gagnon and Simon 1973). More concretely, the receiving of an erect penis by a vagina did not mean the same thing to properly acculturated individuals in the Trobriand Islands before Western contact, in the suburbs of Edinburgh in the nineteenth century or in southern California at the end of the twentieth century (Simon 1974). Further, such conduct has different individual and social meanings depending on the social attributes of the persons involved and their social relationships (examples of the first are age, ethnicity, class, etc.; examples of the second are levels of social intimacy, family relationships between persons, etc.). Sexual conduct of all kinds, no matter how studied, has to be understood as local phenomena with specific meanings and purposes in particular cultural-historical contexts (Gagnon 1990a). Cross-cultural comparisons must always be addressed with great caution and are primarily cited to suggest variability in conduct rather than similarities (Ortner and Whitehead 1981; Marshall and Suggs 1971).

3. The sciences that studied sexuality are themselves historical cultural products (Gagnon 1975, 1983; Irving 1990). Thus the set of explanations and techniques and observations that make up the paradigms of the scientific enterprise are themselves cultural phenomena, not a privileged set of tools through which the world can be objectively examined. Thus when a Western social scientist (even

one recently trained) goes to visit a people, he or she is not in possession of a set of absolutely correct lenses through which to observe the natives (Freilich 1970). Similar caveats need to be made about sociologists, political scientists, psychologists, and other behavioral scientists who engage in research in their own society, research which is conditioned by the taken-for-granted ways of science and the social order as a whole. Indeed even the metaphor of lenses (and optics) is probably incorrect since it implies that with proper correction the distortions introduced by the culture of origin of the scientist could be unbiased.

The point is that a scientist has a set of interests and ways of constructing the world that is a combination of being a participant both in a specific scientific community as well as in a larger culture which is science-based, and these interests cannot be adjusted to the interests of those studied. The result is the necessary struggle between one set of interests and the other. Thus the idea that there is some set of describable observables in the world, such as homosexuality or heterosexuality, is the joint result of the changes in social life (including sexuality) in Western societies since the early 1800s and the rise of a scientific apparatus for thinking about the sexual which is itself the consequence of the same historical processes (Katz 1983). Heterosexuality, homosexuality, and the science of "sexology" are the common products of the changes in Western life over the last two hundred years (for an extensive discussion of this point, see Gagnon 1990a). Sex research thus invents social facts as well as helping to promulgate them. This "inventiveness" is extended to scripting theory as well as other scientific perspectives (Wagner 1981). Changes in the choice of scientific perspective involve changes in what the observables are, how they are measured, and how they are explained.

4. That the actual experience of the sexual as well as what is done sexually by individuals is a result of the particular learning circumstances of a specific culture. The domain of what is learned includes every aspect of the sexual including the reading of physiological events relevant to sexual arousal, sexual pleasure, and sexual climax (Gagnon 1974, 1977). Persons learn how to be sexual in specific cultures and in specific social groups within any culture. To the degree that cultures are small, homogeneous, and expend effort on stabilizing and producing conformity in sexual conduct across the life course, individuals will conduct themselves sexually in accordance with accepted social roles. Cultures that are large, heterogeneous,

and do not expend effort on stabilizing and producing conformity in sexual conduct will have many variant patterns of sexual conduct which will involve both satellite cultures and idiosyncratic patterns of individual behavior. The United States is an example of a society which (a) is composed of many ethnic subcultures and immigrant groups with viable sexual cultures (including sexual minorities), (b) does not invest in direct training in appropriate sexual conduct, and (c) provides many conflicting messages about sexuality to both young and old. As a consequence it is a society with high levels of sexual variability at the individual and cultural levels and intense, but sporadic, conflict about proper sexual conduct.

5. In most societies sexual conduct and gender conduct are linked to some degree (DeLamater 1987). That is, what men and women do sexually is often different, and there are specific prescriptions and experiences attached to sexual conduct by gender (Snitow, Stansell, and Thompson 1984; Vance 1984). These gender differences are often treated as biological in origin, and in consequence differences in sexual conduct by the two genders are viewed as having similar biological roots or as being determined by the gender differences produced by prior biological differences. What has been confused in this debate is the difference between reproductive conduct, gender conduct, and sexual conduct. Clearly reproductive conduct is organized in part by biological differences between men and women, but pregnancy and childbirth are often a small component of reproductive conduct, have only a limited influence on gender conduct and sexual conduct, and do not determine either except in those cultures which enforce their congruence. Appropriate patterns of reproductive, gender, and sexual conduct are all products of specific cultures and all can be viewed as examples of socially scripted conduct. Western societies now have a system of gender and sexual learning in which gender differentiated scripts are learned prior to sexual scripts but take their origins in part from these previously learned gender scripts (Gagnon 1979; Thorne and Luria 1986). There are two important points: the first is that both gender and sexuality are learned forms of social practice, and the second is that looking to "natural differences" between women and men for lessons about sexual conduct is an error (Rubin 1975, 1984).

These five major conceptions were therefore the underpinnings for the concept of sexual scripting: (1) sexual conduct is entirely historically and culturally determined; (2) the meaning of sexual conduct does not reside in a reading of the bodily activity of individuals; (3) sexual science is historically and culturally determined in equal measure; (4) sexuality is acquired, maintained, and unlearned in all of its aspects and is organized by social structure and culture, and (5) gender and sexuality are both learned forms of conduct and are linked differently in different cultures. It is important to note that in this view all conduct is scripted and that scripting theory is not merely to be applied to sexual conduct, but to all social conduct.

A Conception of Scripting

The original extended formulation of scripting was stated in the following somewhat negative form: "Without the proper elements of a script that defines the situation, names the actors, and plots the behavior, nothing sexual is likely to happen. One can easily conceive of numerous sexual situations in which all or almost all of the ingredients of a sexual event are present but that remain non-sexual in that not even sexual arousal occurs" (Gagnon and Simon 1973, 17). The point of this passage was to suggest that (a) sexual conduct involved an organized cognitive schema (which we called a script) needed by actors to recognize that this was potentially a sexual situation, (b) such a recognition involved a complex interaction between person and context rather than a simple response to universal sexual signs, and (c) sexual conduct is elicited by context rather than driven by internal states (it is negotiated rather than automatic or driven). More positively it was argued: "Scripts are involved in learning the meaning of internal states, organizing the sequences of specifically sexual acts, decoding novel situations, setting the limits on sexual responses and linking meanings from non-sexual aspects of life to specifically sexual experience" (Gagnon and Simon 1973, 17).

The script is what connects feelings of desire and pleasure or disgust and disintegration with the bodily activities associated with physical touching and physical signs of arousal. As a consequence erection does not automatically connote pleasure, nor does orgasm. The sequence of what ought to be done in a sexual act depends on the preexistence of a script that defines what is to be done with this or that person, in this or that circumstance, at this or that time, and what feelings and motives are appropriate to the event (horror or delight, anger or nurturance). At the same time the script provides guidance as to what is or is not a sexual situation and contains those elements that link erotic life to social life in general (e.g., knowledge about age scripts, what is an adult or a child, is a guide to what are appropriate sexual partners). But scripts are not merely the cognitive possessions of single actors, they must exist as part of the social structure: "the script is the organization of mutually shared conventions that allows two or more actors to participate in a complex act involving mutual dependence" (Gagnon and Simon 1973, 18).

In this early formulation scripting was viewed as operating primarily on two levels: the intrapsychic and the interpersonal; that is, on the level of mental life (construed broadly as plans for the future, guides to current action, and schemes for remembering) and on the level of social interaction (as used in the accomplishment of sexual activities). In further early work both of these dimensions were explored in greater detail. In the paper "Scripts and the Coordination of Sexual Conduct" (Gagnon 1974) the relationship between a naturalistic description of sexual conduct using conventional narrative forms and the Masters and Johnson description of the sexual arousal and orgasm cycle was analyzed. A number of points were at issue here. The first was the degree to which the stages of the orgasm cycle as described in words by Masters and Johnson depended upon the culturally acceptable script for sexual conduct so that arousal, plateau, orgasm, and resolution did not describe discrete biological states so much as discrete mental states (indeed no specific biological markers indicate state changes). The second was the degree to which scripts coordinated the actual doing of sexual acts during a sexual partnership (here the concern was with the relation between the interpersonal and the intrapsychic). The third was the degree to which scientific representations of the sexual underestimated the role of nonsexual elements in the doing of what appeared to be quite simple sexual activities.

The treatment of scripts in Gagnon (1974) was at the interface between mental life and social action and tended to treat scripts as if they were largely well-organized cognitive plans or heuristic devices to guide and correct action. In contrast Simon (1974) explored the notion that the conventional dramatic narrative form is appropriate only when applied to external sequences of action. When dealing with erotic elements in the intrapsychic, we are dealing with a more complex set of layered symbolic meanings which has much more to do with nonnarrative traditions in literary representation and imagery. What is arousing may not be the plan to have sex, but fragmentary symbolic materials taken from mass media or more local experience. Here the proper modes of analysis of mental life should be from a more surrealistic tradition, from poetry or from other sources of more condensed forms of meaning. Thus Stoller's conception of the "microdot" which, when accessed, produces arousal and sexual activity is a somewhat similar conception (Stoller 1976). In the theater of the mind the actor is responding to a smell, a prior experience, the body of another person, or a fetish object which provides the motivation for competent marital intercourse. This view suggests two stages of mental processes in dealing with sexual desires. There exist the erotic mental "fragments" and "emotions" that are the sources of feelings of the erotic. These are subsequently encoded into more organized cognitive scripts which form the guides for concrete interactions with other persons. This need for internal scripting occurs during all sexual conduct that involves the coordination of mental life with social behavior. This includes masturbation, which involves the coordination of fantasy with the self-manipulation of one's own body (Gagnon 1977).

In addition to the levels of scripting at the intrapsychic and interpersonal levels, more recent work has focused on the need to identify scripts at the cultural level as part of the scripting perspective. These were first considered in 1973 (Gagnon and Simon, chap. 9) in the analysis of sexually explicit representations but not fully treated until somewhat later. The analysis of sexually explicit representations (or pornography, as we called it then) suggested three important points:

1. Such representations, while usually of a highly limited literary and visual genre, included a large variety of social clues that indicated to readers and viewers that it was appropriate to be aroused by or to imagine doing sexual things with these "people" (thus it is viewed as appropriate in American cinema or television to murder women who are in the sex industry or who have casual sex).

2. Sexually explicit representations and fantasy had a close relation, but many individuals had fantasies that did not appear in these representations, and many persons who fantasized did not accept the sexual representations that were offered to them (there is an important contrast here between women and men) (Snitow, Stansell, and Thompson 1984; Vance 1984).

3. Sexually explicit representations within Western cultures was a highly iterative and boring commodity which was consumed irregularly by most customers (Kutchinsky 1973).

From this perspective even a single photograph showing oral sex or a close-up of the genitals in coitus is part of a scripted event rather than an essentially meaningful erotic sign. In some cases, the social context of viewing (e.g., a group of boys passing around a sexually explicit photograph) provides the erotic meaning and tension for the photograph. In others the well-trained observer even in private will supply the script to surround the single image to have it make narrative sense and will look for clues in the picture to suggest why this penis is in this mouth. The youthfulness of the woman/man, penis size, hair color, makeup, the "look on the faces" will all be interpreted to give meaning to what is a highly abstract arrangement of colors or light and shadow.

Sexually explicit representations were the first closely analyzed example of a "cultural scenario"; that is, instructions on the cultural level about how persons should and should not behave sexually. The problem was not simply a matter of abstract norms, rules, values, or beliefs, but how those normative and attitudinal elements were integrated into the sexual narratives to which the name *scripts* was given. Persons learn about life by being given directions about how to act that are embedded in stories with good outcomes and bad outcomes (such stories identify what is to be done [or not done], where it is to be done, when it is to be done, with whom it is to be done, and why it should be done). So it is with sexuality; persons are told if they do this or that, with these people, at these times and places, it will have a consequence. Officially the masturbator will grow feeble, socially withdraw, stunt his or her growth, and so we have the tales of Struwelpeter in German folklore or the example of Uriah Heep in Charles Dickens (Atwood 1981). Similar negative cultural scenarios about masturbation exist in the scientific literature and in instructions for youth. Cautionary tales about sexuality and gender are particularly common. Thus, the woman who does not marry or is unselective about her sexual partners is murdered by a pickup in a bar *(Looking for Mr. Goodbar)* or eaten by a shark *(Jaws)* as punishment for violating the appropriate gender/sexuality scenarios of marriage and fidelity.

Cultural instructions about sexuality, however, do not exist merely in the form of literary texts; reference is made to them simply because they are easiest to analyze. Such cultural instructions are embedded in the organization of social institutions and in the practice of everyday life in those institutions (see Roberts, 1980). The family, the schools, the churches, the military, business organizations, universities, medicine, and, perhaps most explicitly of all, the law and the criminal justice systems are all instructional systems about sexuality, both in terms of what is officially said and how they are organized. Thus the law, in modern Western societies, contains within it the codifications of what the state believes is proper and appropriate sexual conduct (Gebhard et al. 1965). The policing system, in a rather intermittent and selective manner enforces these proscriptions by arresting, incarcerating, and stigmatizing various persons. The mass media re-happens these events that are generated by the actions of the law enforcement system by re-presenting them on television and in the press.

Similarly other institutions in their everyday practice offer formal and informal instruction in sexual scenarios: schools offer sex education and segregate boys and girls in various gender tracks; churches offer versions of what is sexually good and bad; business organizations repress or tolerate sexual harassment; medicine, a man-dominated institution, deals with the sexual problems of men and women with a technologized sexism; and universities foster disciplines which provide conventionalized research and pedagogy on sexuality. In complex societies such cultural scenarios for sexuality are not monolithic or hegemonic, even within institutions. Instead there is a constant struggle between groups and individuals to foster their own scenarios. Some groups and individuals are more powerful than others, but no individual or group or institution is in entire control of the sexual scenarios for most Western societies.

Sexual scripts can thus be described as having three levels: the intrapsychic, the interpersonal, and the cultural scenario (Simon and Gagnon 1986, 1987). There are two ways of considering these levels: the first involves a static description; the other an examination of the dynamic and interactive relations between levels in differing cultures and across the life course. In the more static conception, in which sexual scripting exists on three relatively discrete levels, cultural scenarios can be thought of as the instructional guides that exist at the level of collective life. Thus all institutions and institutionalized arrangements can be read as semiotic systems though which the requirement and practice of specific roles are given. The instructions for roles are embedded in narratives (the scripts for the specific role), and they provide the understandings that make role entry, performance, and exit plausible. In this case the individual can be treated as a more or less active member of an audience for social instruction and depending on a number of variables (e.g., age, class, ethnicity) may be more or less receptive to such instruction.

Interpersonal scripts operate at the level of social interaction and the acceptance and use of such scripts are the basis for continued patterns of structured social behavior. In this case the individual is an actor meeting the expectations of other persons and guiding his or her conduct in terms of the conduct of the other. It is this usage of the concept of scripts which is most cognitivist and marks the interface between interaction and mental life.

Intrapsychic scripts represent the content of mental life, in part the resultant of the content of cultural scenarios and the demands of interaction and in part independent of them. The problems of connecting meaning (culture) and action (social interaction) are played out in the domain of the intrapsychic. Hence intrapsychic scripts have a number of origins. They are often made up of versions of cultural scenarios, which have been improvised on and sometimes permanently revised to meet the exigencies of concrete interaction. In many cases both the ideal version of cultural scenario (how one ought to behave) and the pragmatic variants are concurrently held in the mind of the individual. Such scripts can range from the most orderly cognitive narratives to fragments of desires, memories, and plans. As one moves closer to interaction, intrapsychic scripts usually become more orderly, looking more like plans or schema, though the mental elements motivating the interaction may not be very prominent. The individual in the case is a playwright, scripting his or her conduct to meet the problematic nature of interaction.

In the practice of social and cultural and mental life, the levels of scripting are dynamically interactive. At the interface of culture and mental life the individual is audience, critic, and reviser as the materials of cultural scenarios are imported into intrapsychic scripts. At the interface between interaction and mental life, the individual is actor, critic, and playwright. In the private world of mental life, the individual also acts as fantasist, memorialist, and utopian (or dystopian), working with the materials of interaction and culture to create innovative alternatives to the given cultural scenarios and contemporary patterns of interaction. Some individuals attempt to make manifest these new combinations of meaning and action by creating new forms of culture through interaction. It is important to note that there is no direct interface between culture and interaction; these effects are entirely mediated by mental life (or the intrapsychic).

This interaction between levels of scripting has historical, cultural, and individual dimensions. There are cultures and historical eras in which there is no conflict between received cultural meanings and opportunities for interaction; cultural scenarios serve as proper templates for interaction and the individual simply monitors the quality of a performance.

However, even in the seemingly most traditional social settings, cultural scenarios are rarely predictive of actual behavior. Cultural scenarios, in order to serve their very function, must be too abstractly generic to be consistently applicable in all circumstances. . . . The very possibility of a failure of congruence between the abstract scenario and the concrete interactional situation must be solved at the level of interpersonal scripting.

. . . [T]he necessity for creating interpersonal scripts transforms the social actor from being exclusively an actor trained in his or her role(s) and . . . adds the task of being a partial scriptwriter or adapter as he/she becomes involved in shaping the materials of

relevant cultural scenarios into scripts for context specific behavior.
(Simon and Gagnon 1986, 98–99)

The point of these quotes is that we are socialized first as audiences to or
learners of cultural scenarios, but as we are required to enact these scripts,
we must modify them to meet the demands of the concrete situations in
which we find ourselves, including the requirements of the other persons
in that situation and our other relationships to them. We move in these
circumstances from being pure actors reading our lines to an improvisational actor with elements of being a playwright. Such modifications may
be minimal with high levels of congruence between what the cultural ex-
pects and what the concrete circumstance demands, but various degrees
of improvisation may be required. In radically novel circumstances we are
required to make it up as we go along, but we make it up with previously
available scripted materials, not de novo. "Where complexities, conflicts
and/or ambiguities become endemic at the level of cultural scenarios,
much greater demands are placed on the individual. The need to script
one's behavior; as well as the implicit assumption of the scripted behavior
of others, is what engenders a meaningful 'internal rehearsal in the first
place,' an internal rehearsal that can become significant only where alternative outcomes are possible. . . . It is this that creates fantasy in a very
rich sense of that word: The symbolic reorganization of reality in ways
that make it complicit in realizing the actor's many layered and sometimes multivoiced wishes" (Simon and Gagnon 1986, 99).

Intrapsychic scripting is that mental activity which is required when
simply being an adequate social actor or even modifying the given materials of the cultural scenarios has become more difficult. It is clear that the
relation between cultural scenarios, interpersonal scripts, and intrapsychic scripts is complex and differs not only across cultures and eras, but
within subgroups in cultures and across individuals within cultures and
subcultures as well. Some individuals faithfully reproduce in their everyday conduct the instructions of the cultural scenarios without uneasiness
and often with enthusiasm. Others find the demands of the culture alien
and disturbing and are unable to enact the roles required or to create ways
of insulating themselves from the demands of the culture or roles. In
these latter cases the response may be crime, madness, art, or science.

Scripting in Research

Scripting plays a variety of both explicit and implicit roles in sex research.
In some cases researchers self-consciously adopt a scripting perspective in

the design of studies and in the analysis of the data that are gathered (e.g., Gagnon and Simon 1987; Matalene 1989; McCormick 1987), but even in these cases the data gathered are relevant to only parts of the general theoretical issues addressed by the theory. The aspects of scripting may be limited to one or another level of scripting (cultural scenarios, interpersonal scripts, or intrapsychic scripts) or to relations between two specific levels. More often the perspective may be used to reanalyze data that were gathered for other purposes and with other theoretical perspectives in mind (Gagnon 1974). In the case of theorizing, a number of researchers have adopted elements of the scripting perspective that they have found useful (e.g., Person 1987).

In a majority of cases, however, the presence of scripting is implicit. Researchers either design studies that (a) depend on the prior scripted character of the conduct of the individual, (b) depend on the presentation of scripted stimulus materials to research subjects that understand the scripts, or (c) assume that individuals can disaggregate and reaggregate script instances to answer specific questions about their conduct. Even sex therapy is itself dependent on the preexistence of a valued normative script (vaginal intercourse between men and women should produce orgasm for both parties) toward which the behavior of the dysfunctional couple is directed. In each of the sections below, examples of each of these implicit uses of the scripting perspective are present.

It is important to point out that there are many dimensions of sexual conduct that are not treated in this chapter. The selection of topics was based either on the volume of work, the illustrative value of the case, or the general recalcitrance of the topic to the scripting perspective (the more recalcitrant, the more likely to be chosen). Other topics were excluded for a number of reasons. The topic of extramarital sexuality was excluded even though there is a body of work that examines this behavior from a scripting point of view (Atwater 1982; Bell, Turner, and Rosen 1975; Reiss 1983; Richardson 1985; Singh, Walton, and Williams 1976; Spanier and Margolis 1983; Thompson 1983). Much of this behavior can be understood (with some variations) as part of the sexual scripts for sexual relations between women and men. Prostitution of women and men is obviously a set of scripted sexual performances, which are released by the exchange of money. Same-gender sex among women is not discussed here partially for reasons of space, but also because a closer look is needed at the changing character of sexual relations within the lesbian community and the relation of that community to the sexuality of all women in the same culture (Wolf 1979). Masturbation is also not dealt with here, though there is very good reason to view it as a solitary, but entirely social form of behavior (Atwood 1981; Atwood and Gagnon 1987; Gagnon 1977, 1985, 1987).

The Restructuring of the Scripts for "Other-Gender" Sex in Youth Populations

There is a substantial body of evidence that cultural scenarios and the interpersonal scripts for youthful sexual conduct (that is, the period from the early teens to the early twenties) have undergone considerable change in the United States over the last thirty years. Data from a variety of studies directed at examining issues of the contraceptive use and fertility of adolescent and youthful women suggest that since the early 1970s the age at first coitus, the proportion who have had intercourse by any age, and the numbers of sexual partners that these young women report have steadily increased (Chilman 1978; Gagnon and Greenblat 1978; Hofferth and Hayes 1987; Hofferth, Kahn, and Baldwin 1987). It appears that the pattern of premarital sexual behavior identified in middle-class populations by Kinsey and in studies of premarital sexual attitudes by Reiss that had been consolidated in the baby boom years after World War II had begun to change rapidly in the years of the late 1960s and early 1970s (Kinsey et al. 1953; Reiss 1960, 1967).

There existed three competitive cultural scenarios for premarital heterosexuality in the period (1900–1950) that were recorded by the Kinsey studies (Modell et. al. 1978). The first were the official moral and legal scenarios that required a single standard of premarital chastity for both women and men in which young persons were to select their future marital partners with some consultation with their parents, and while they were expected to "fall in love" with this future partner, they were not expected to engage in more than simple hugging and kissing before marriage. Both the statutes which criminalized fornication and statutory rape (intercourse with underage young women) and the dominant religious dogmas embodied these standards for conduct. A second scenario more in line with the everyday beliefs of the population assumed the existence of a double standard of sexual practice, with men having the opportunity to engage in sexual activity with women while women were expected to be chaste. This required dividing the world of women into two groups, the sexually virtuous and marriageable, and the sexually sinful and unmarriageable. The third and emergent scenario among the middle class, a scenario recorded by Kinsey, was that as part of the process of serious mate selection, a young woman and young man might have intercourse as part of sealing a sexual affectional bargain just prior to marriage. Premarital sexual intercourse was truly pre-marital in that it was preparation for getting married.

The findings of Kinsey and his colleagues that one-half of the middle-class women that they interviewed had had intercourse before marriage, but that the majority of these did so with their future spouses in the six months prior to marriage, confirmed a changing cultural scenario for the relation of sexuality to marriage in the United States (Kinsey, Pomeroy, and Martin 1948; Kinsey et al. 1953). What the Kinsey statistics represented was an aggregation of a vast number of scripted sexual encounters between couples that were characterized by such summary measures as age at first intercourse (a scripted sexual event), the numbers of times intercourse took place (a number of scripted sexual events), the sexual practices that occurred in various sexual encounters (a summary of a scripted set of behaviors that proceeded from kissing to coitus) and the number of partners a person had (the changing of the "who" in a sequence of sexual scripts).

This survey approach to sexual practice (not only in adolescence) would offer a summary of many sexual encounters that were in reality sequentially distributed over the time period from the early teens to later young adulthood (Gagnon and Greenblat 1978). Thus any single-individual would have a history of coupled relationships which would usually start at some point in the mid- to late teens. The earlier pair relationships would less often involve coitus than later ones and each relationship would be composed of encounters (dates) that would involve increases in the extensivity of sexual techniques. Relationships might involve only a single encounter with varying levels of sexual intimacy— when coitus takes place these are described as "casual sex" or "one-night stands." These events are more often reported by men. A "coupled relationship" would take place over a course of time which would be characterized by "meetings" or "dates" of varying levels of formality and during these meetings or dates young people would engage in sexual activities that were somewhat regulated by issues of age and emotional intimacy. Each "coupled relationship" would have a beginning, middle, and end, and within each relationship there would be an increase in sexual intimacy to some limit. As such relationships approached the usual age at marriage for a particular social group, sexual intercourse became increasingly likely. The important fact is that each encounter and each relationship was socially scripted, and these scripted events were ordered by a larger set of societal expectations (scenarios) about adolescent and youthful sexuality.

In the early 1970s an increasing number of surveys chronicled the changes in these scripted encounters by showing that there was an increase in the number of coupled relationships in which there was intercourse (characterized as the number of sexual partners) and that intercourse was taking place at an earlier point in time in the sequence of relationships (Cannon and Long 1971; Clayton and Bokemeier 1980; Miller and Simon 1974; Kantner and Zelnick 1972). By the 1980s there existed a sufficient detachment of these early coital relationships from marriage that it was reasonable to argue that sex between young women and men in their late teens was occurring independently of expectations of marriage (Furstenberg 1982; Turner, Miller, and Moses 1989). This meant that the sexual techniques and affectional intimacy that existed in these relationships were for the purposes of the relationship and not for the purpose of some future state for which the sex was some guarantee or preparation.

At the same time that the surveys were indicating that there had been a restructuring of the timing and ordering of sexual conduct early in the life course, both in terms of cultural expectations (scenarios) and in terms of interpersonal conduct (interpersonal scripts), two additional themes became more prominent in the understanding of youthful sexuality. The first was the continuing relevance of differential gender scripts which underpinned sexual interaction between women and men, and the second, the scripting of sexual violence and its consequences for the sexual lives of women (see the discussion of sexual violence below). It was clear from the Kinsey research and from research on the double standard during the 1950s that men and women had different scripts for their shared sexual encounters (Kinsey, Pomeroy, and Martin 1948; Kinsey et al. 1953). Kinsey's original interpretations of the behavioral differences that he observed were based on a belief that the sexual drive of women was more easily inhibited than that of men (perhaps because of some difference in the brain), however, he seemed to drop these views when confronted with the complexity of women's sexuality as represented in the volume on women (Gagnon 1978). Here, as with homosexual relations, he had to face the fact that orgasm and outlet were not the sole measures of sexual experience, since both women and men with same-gender sexual preferences had many sexual encounters without orgasm. These differences have now been reinterpreted as the consequence of both the differential social elicitation and sanctioning of women's and men's sexuality in terms of both socialization and the immediate cultural and social environments for sexual expression.

Scripts for sexual encounters from the opening phase to the couple separating are now acknowledged to be entirely gendered, with men conventionally expected to conduct themselves assertively, to make the first move and to lead in the subsequent steps, and to be knowledgeable in the ways of sexual practice (though women can offer openings to such encounters with considerable success). Women are expected to be more passive, more compliant at the beginnings of sexual interactions, and pleased and responsive as such interactions progress (see Fine 1988 for a critique of these views). In the study of concrete interactions, even at the present time, interpersonal scripts seem to accord with cultural scenarios in these matters (Clark and Hatfield 1989). These gendered tactics for managing sexual encounters at the interpersonal level involve "come-ons" and "put-offs" that are well known to young people and a number of different verbal and physical pathways that lead to different levels of sexual activity and/or emotional intimacy (LaPlante, McCormick, and Brannigan 1980; McCormick 1979; McCormick and Jesser 1983; Straver 1980). The fact that these encounters are scripted from the moment of meeting to the smallest details of physical sexual interaction and feelings of sexual pleasure should be easily generalized to tactics and interactions that lead to sexual conduct among any set of potential sexual partners at any moment in the life course.

The Scripting of Sexual Techniques

The sequence of physical behaviors that constitute a usual sexual encounter between women and men in the United States and Western Europe seems so natural and reasonable to many that they seem to require little thought, particularly scientific thought (similar cultural prejudices exist around the idea of "erogenous zones"; see Gagnon 1977). This lack of reflection results in two defective conceptualizations (or perhaps two failures of the imagination). The first defective conceptualization is that this culturally local sequence of sexual behaviors is treated as both universal and necessary. The sequence is universal in the sense that it is believed that all persons who engage in sexual acts should conform to such a sequence of actions (hence the acts and the sequence are normative) and that this sequence of actions is part of the cultural practice of most, if not all, cultures. The sequence is necessary in that it is often believed that sexual arousal follows the practice of these activities, and that in the absence of these activities sexual arousal and orgasm will not occur. The second defective conceptualization is that the arousing part of a sexual encounter rests entirely upon the obviously sexual elements of the encounter. There is a good deal of evidence that the scripted physical sequence is embedded in a larger scripted sequence of social behaviors which is as likely to be productive of sexual arousal: The anticipation of the encounter, the dressing up, the dinner and dancing, the cinema going, the drinking, and public displays of affection are themselves provocative of arousal and set the stage for and permit the physical sexual activities that then follow.

Even if attention is limited to what are conventionally believed to be the "sexual components" of the larger social encounter, one immediately encounters difficulties with a universalist approach to the character of sexual techniques. A simple examination of this behavioral sequence immediately bears this out. In the usual course of things a sexually well-acculturated and practiced couple in the opening stages of a relationship are likely to start the sexual component of a social encounter when they are clothed, and they will undress in the course of the sexual interaction (see Gagnon 1977 for more details). Sexual couples that are better established (the married and others with longer histories of sexual interaction) may undress prior to sex and begin the sexual activities when nude. Most couples, regardless of the duration of the relationships, will usually go through a moderately predictable opening sequence of actions, starting with hugging and kissing and then proceeding to mutual touching of the clothed body, first above the waist and then below. This is followed by a middle phase of fondling and kissing each other's semiclothed or nude bodies, commonly including the manual fondling of the genitals. At this point, however, there are a number of potential branches, the choice of which is variable across couples and occasions, some couples on some occasions may proceed to coitus, one or both individuals may engage in oral-genital contacts (before or after coitus), and the couple may also engage in various forms of anal sex.

The time given to each of these activities, their sequencing, and the levels of sexual arousal felt will differ depending on the sexual history of the individual and the sexual history of the couple (Peplau, Rubin, and Hill 1977). Thus an inexperienced adolescent will be deeply aroused by simple hugging and kissing, as may a more experienced person with a new sexual partner. However, as persons grow more experienced or relations last longer, expectations about what is normally part of sexual interaction will change and intense levels of arousal will be keyed to the more intimate forms of conduct. In many cases behavior will become more routine and the sequences of interaction will be fairly predictable, as will the levels of arousal. In some cases persons will restrict what they will do sexually with various partners depending on levels of intimacy, while others will have a preset sequence which they perform with all partners.

Just this simple description of this process should suggest how complex the process of acquiring and maintaining a competent set of sexual techniques must be. Young persons who are trying out the activities for the first time and in new relationships must be concerned with how long to engage in any of the activities, whether the partner is enjoying them, whether they should go on to what are thought to be more intimate practices, and how much they should be aroused by these activities (this involves a management of the intrapsychic and the interpersonal) (Gagnon 1972; Simon, Berger, and Gagnon 1972). These choices often represent an extremely anxiety-producing set of experiments. Similar feelings and trepidations are felt among adults of all ages with new sexual partners. The management of sexual technique within the encounter also has connections with nonsexual aspects of the relationship and the future social relations between the members of the couple. The more closely we examine the actual sexual interactions persons have and their practice of sexual techniques, the more complex the process becomes. When describing the sequence of activities, a simple normative script appears. But when the script is put into action with a real sexual partner, a wide variety of competence-testing improvisations are required. It is apparent that many persons avoid these competence-testing aspects of sexual performance either by restricting what they do or by restricting the numbers of persons with whom they will do them.

The evidence is that similar problems are faced by same-gender couples as well. Young persons who are beginning to have physical contact with persons of the same gender find that what is to be done with whom and to what effect is often difficult to decipher. Such difficulties appear to be somewhat greater for young women than they are for young men, whose experiences either with older men or with self-masturbation offer opportunities to learn what to do either in practice or by analogy. For young women the movement to genital stimulation appears to take somewhat longer and, from the limited data on sexual techniques among lesbians, oral sex appears only in some relationships and at a somewhat later point than do similar techniques among men. Similar issues attend the practices of oral and anal sex among men who have sex with men. There are individuals and situations in which only one technique is preferred or allowed. For example there are men who do not like the insertee role in anal sex and who are not aroused by it, and there are sexual interactions in which only a specific technique is proper (e.g., between the masculine-appearing hustler and his paying partner, in which the latter only fellates the former) (Reiss, Anderson, and Spoonagle 1980).

There is only a modest amount of evidence for the changing character of the sexual scripts that structure the use of sexual techniques. Perhaps the two best-documented examples have been in the changing role of oral sex in "other-gender" relationships and the balance between oral and anal sex in relationships among gay men. There has been a recent increase in the scientific interest in the incidence and frequency of anal sex in heterosexual relationships, but because this increase has been driven primarily by the AIDS epidemic, there has been little interest in the scripting of this conduct (who does it, when do they do, why do they do it, etc.).

Changing Scripts for Oral Sex among "Other-Gendered" Couples

The place of oral sex in "other-gender" sexual interactions has always been complex. In terms of traditional sexual scenarios it has always been an "unnatural activity" which seemed to deflect from coitus as the proper culmination of sexual interaction, and it was treated by the law and religion as either criminal or sinful. Kinsey inverted the biological argument in this position by making the counter argument that oral sex was widely manifested in the mammalian realm and therefore it was part of the bounty and variety of nature that was repressed by civilized life. In the more advanced social thinking of the secular marriage manual, oral sex seemed to be an activity which had a number of virtues: it was a prelude to coitus that expressed a heightened level of interpersonal intimacy ("I wouldn't do this for just anybody"); it was an activity which mechanically increased lubrication and hence the ease of coitus; and finally, it was an activity which seemed to produce (for a variety of reasons, both mechanical and psychological) more intense levels of psychological arousal. In the most liberated arguments, often made by feminists, oral sex to the point of orgasm, particularly for women, was an end in itself and somewhat better for purposes of sexual satisfaction than coitus. All of these arguments are evidence for changing cultural scenarios for oral sex (Gagnon and Simon 1987).

The limited survey data on oral sex suggest that indeed it is more common than in the past and that it occupies a common if not frequent place in the sexual encounters of both the single and the married in the United States. There is some additional data that suggest that oral sex is often the technique of choice among men who use the services of prostitutes and, for different reasons, among prostitutes themselves. While there has been an increase in the proportion of the populations who engage in oral sex, there is evidence that it retains a problematic character both for sexually experienced adults and for young persons who are just putting together the elements of a competent sexual script (Shostak 1981).

In a review of the data gathered by the Kinsey group on a convenience sample of largely white, college-educated, and youthful persons interviewed mainly during the 1940s, it was found that among the unmarried, oral sex was largely restricted to the coitally experienced, and while more men were coitally experienced, the coitally experienced women reported more oral sex than did the men (Gagnon and Simon 1987). In addition the more often women had had coitus, the more likely they were to report oral sex. What this suggests is that in the period this data was gathered (the late 1940s) oral sex became part of the sequence of techniques after coitus occurred, and that as coitus became more frequent, the likelihood of oral sex increased. There was in the Kinsey era a substantial discrepancy between the reports of the men and women about oral sex: that is, the men studied reported more nonmarital fellatio and less cunnilingus than the women. The excess in nonmarital fellatio suggests that men were either overreporting this practice or having sex with what were termed "loose women" or prostitutes, thus producing an excess of experience with oral sex in contrast to what the more conventional women reported in the volume on women. But in the most recent cohort interviewed by Kinsey, the proportions of women and men who reported oral sex in marriage reached close to 70 percent, and while not frequent, oral sex appears to have been part of the conventional sexual script for the educated married by the late 1940s (Gebhard and Johnson 1979; Kinsey et al. 1953).

In more recent data from studies of youthful populations in the United States there seems to have been substantial increase in the proportion of young men and women who had oral sex before marriage. In a national study of college students conducted before 1970 these figures were 30 percent for men and 25 percent for women (Gagnon and Simon 1987). In a study in one city of college and noncollege students, this rate increased to 60 percent and 57 percent, respectively (DeLamater and MacCorquodale 1979). These years saw a dramatic increase in the proportion of young women who had intercourse (in all studies), and it was among these young women that the rise in the experience of oral sex occurred. What is as important is that there is an equality in the proportion of women and men reporting nonmarital oral sex, which suggests a change in the premarital practices of men and a new reciprocity at least in the techniques used in sexual encounters. Other, more recent studies of youthful populations suggest that for younger adolescents, oral sex may be occurring among those who are not coitally experienced, with the pattern being for the boy to introduce the behavior in order to induce the girl into either oral sex or coitus, and for the girl to engage in oral sex to avoid coitus (Coles and Stokes 1985; Newcomer and Udry 1985). The difficulty of organizing a sexual script is suggested by reports that the young women report performing oral sex in order to "satisfy" the boy rather than for their own pleasure. This suggests the difficulty of integrating the interpersonal with the intrapsychic in the early stages of sexual learning. While a strong pro–oral sex literature appeared in the 1970s as part of the general rhetoric of technique encouraged by such volumes as *The Joy of Sex,*this does not seem to have penetrated into the adolescent or youth segments of the U.S. population.

It appears that oral sex has a number of uses and meanings in the scripts for sexual encounters. At different times and in different relationships the same physical movements may be performed to avoid coitus, to express intimacy, as a sign of erotic competence, or as an act of power or degradation (Simon and Kraft 1990). The statistical evidence is that oral sex is more common both in terms of the number of relationships in which it occurs and in terms of the number of encounters within each relationship (Blumstein and Schwartz 1983). This should not suggest to us that this is a return to the natural, but rather that oral sex is a sexual technique which is characteristic of better washed and more experimental social groups in which the erotic serves as an affirmation of interpersonal relationships.

The Changing Role of Anal Sex in Gay Relationships

The influence of environmental and ideological forces on the scripting of sexual techniques is dramatically demonstrated in the changes in the role of anal sex in gay men's relationships over the last twenty years. Prior to the advent of gay liberation and gay pride, the majority of "same-gender" sexuality for both men and women occurred under extremely repressive legal and social conditions (Hooker 1966). Most "homosexuals," as they were called in that medicalized language of the period, were in some version of the "closet." That is, they often concealed their erotic interests from the majority of the important persons in their lives (e.g., family, coworkers, friends) because of the danger that they would be ostracized and condemned. For many, who for one reason or another were not persuaded by or uncomfortable with heterosexuality, the pre-Stonewall "homosexual community" was their first point of access to a collectivity that they might join (Dank 1971). In most locales this quasi-underground community was an anonymous collection of public meeting places (usually bars and taverns serving alcohol and therefore restricted to those "of an age to drink") predominantly utilized by a somewhat fragmented collection of individuals primarily for sexual contacts and transient sociability. However most "homosexual" men and some women found their friends and lovers in the community as well. When coupled affectionate and sexual relationships were going well, individuals often withdrew from the community. If such coupled relationships broke up or became sexually unsatisfying, individuals often returned to the public life of the "homosexual" community. This cycle of withdrawal and reentry gave untutored observers the idea that a constant search for new sexual partners was characteristic of all "homosexual" men. However, this penumbra of more stable affectional relationships could be found around a more constant population of regulars and workers for whom the institutions of the "homosexual" community were primary sources of identity as well as providing social and economic well-being (Warren 1974). Outside of this community, in extreme cases, some men and women were in the deep closet, some were married and lived their entire lives with only limited personal or erotic contact with persons of the same gender, while still others became asexual (Humphreys 1970).

For those who participated in the "homosexual" community, there were always acute dangers. Many persons were blackmailed, robbed, assaulted, or murdered by sexual partners or by heterosexual thugs without recourse to the police; others were arrested in bars or sexual meeting places; still others lost their jobs or were drummed out of the military (Bell and Weinberg 1978; Gagnon and Simon 1973). Religion condemned the sodomite, the law and the police prosecuted "the queers," psychiatry treated the "pervert," most parents recoiled in horror that their son was a "sissy," and many normal men were ready to beat up the "faggot." The fears and anxieties that were generated among "homosexual" men and women by such conditions of oppression were themselves interpreted as evidence for the mental and social instability of the persecuted.

This environment for sexual expression created a situation in which anonymous sexual activity often went on in public and quasipublic sites, and even when in private the encounter was often between two persons who knew little of each other and might never have sex together again. Oral sex was far easier, particularly in more public circumstances, and while many men had anal sex, it was only sometimes the preferred practice. In addition there was a tendency to view the person who was a preferential insertee in anal sex as effeminate and unmanly. This latter difficulty is both interpersonal and intrapsychic: many men would not choose a partner who was too "effeminate," and many men who like anal sex found it difficult to integrate their desire for anal sex and their sense of self as masculine. In contrast to other societies where anal sex was common because of a clear-cut symbolic gender split between inserters and insertees—the former were "men," the latter were "women"—the situation in the United States was far more ambiguous, with masculinity and femininity more loosely (and sometimes playfully) related to gender preference in erotic relations.

Other aspects of the sexual conduct of "homosexuals" could be understood in terms of this climate of persecution. Thus the vigorous pursuit of sexual partners by "homosexual" men during this early period of commitment (given the argot name *honeymoon*) must also be understood as a response to specific historical conditions of becoming a "homosexual" in the "homosexual" community (Dank 1971). The scholarly emphasis on the sexual aspects of the coming-out period conceals the difficulties of acquiring the major elements of being an accomplished "member" of the "homosexual" community—sexual skills, argot, jokes, differentiation among partners, falling in love, coupling, falling out of love—none of which are acquired "naturally."

With the advent of gay liberation, the substitution of the label *gay* for *homosexual,* and the creation of new and more open communities of gay men and lesbians in a number of major cities, the environmental context for the sexual lives of at least some gay men changed (D'Emilio 1983; Humphreys 1972). As the environment for sexuality changed, it was possible, even in anonymous contexts (e.g., the bathhouse), for men to spend enough time together and with sufficient privacy for anal sex to occur (though privacy was not always necessary) (Bell and Weinberg 1978). In addition, the ideological climate was changing. With the emergence of clone culture, a new cultural scenario for gay life emerged which emphasized masculine display and masculinity, and in consequence effeminacy, effeminate displays, and the fear of effeminacy dramatically declined (White 1980). The new ideology was that gay men were first of all men, and the sexual acts that they preferred did not reduce their manliness. As a consequence the inhibition on anal sex was only personal and preferential rather than having a basis in ideology and material conditions. In the 1970s there was a dramatic rise in the amount of anal intercourse in the gay men's community and in consequence a rise in a number of sexually transmitted diseases that resulted from anal sex.

It is plausible to argue that these changes in sexual practice, that is, an increased reciprocity in anal sex and an increase in the rates of anal sex, were the behavioral seedbed for the AIDS epidemic (Wiley and Herschkorn 1990). However, with the advent of AIDS and the recognition of the role of unprotected anal sex in HIV transmission, what has been observed is a dramatic decline (at least in those cities where competent research has been conducted) in both the general rate of anal sex and, in particular, the rate of unprotected anal sex (Connell and Kippax 1990; Hessol 1987; Joseph 1987). These declines are evidenced not only by self-report data, but from declines in other sexually transmitted infections transmitted through anal intercourse.

The increase and then decrease in the rate of anal sex among gay men suggests both the flexibility of the scripting of sexual techniques and how immediately responsive many sexual scripts are to social and historical circumstance. At the same time the increase in anal sex was complex in character and involved changes in cultural scenarios (breaking the linkage of anal sex to effeminacy and the rise of a masculinized gay men's culture), changes in social context (from extremely transitory encounters to the bathhouse), and the intrapsychic management of new identities (from "homosexual" to gay man, from sissy to clone). The decline of anal sex is both a result of AIDS as well as another set of ongoing changes in the gay community, which involves an increase in the number of coupled relationships, a decline in sex on the first date, and a movement away from a "hot" sex lifestyle to a more relationship-oriented gay lifestyle (Levine 1988; McWhirter and Mattison 1984). These changes in lifestyle were in fact observable in the early 1980s, before the AIDS epidemic became a public matter. As the baby boom component of the gay men's community aged, it was possible for them, under the new conditions of gay life, to adopt more open, public, and affirming coupled relationships. This was removing them from the more active sexual community. At the same time the existence of a gay community meant that "coming out" was not merely a sexual matter for young people, and they felt less need to engage in sexuality in order to confirm their identity. The new complexity and public nature of the gay community meant that it had become more than a collection of sexual actors; it was now a community to which young people could feel belonging. It may be that the general effect of the AIDS epidemic was to accelerate a general social change that was already underway, while its more limited effect was to reduce the rate of anal sex. This process has already been identified by Martin Levine as the "the heterosexualization of gay desire" (1988).

The changes observed in sexual technique have to be seen as part of a general decline in the rigidity of scripts for sexual conduct over the past forty years. A "homosexual" was at one time a person whose behavior was entirely defined by his or her sexual orientation, and the scripts for same-gender sexual conduct seemed to flow directly from this orientation. More contemporary views are summed up by Pat Califia: "It is odd that sexual orientation is defined solely in terms of the sex of one's partners. I don't think I can assume anything about another person because I have been told they are bisexual, heterosexual or "homosexual."... For many people, if a partner or a sexual situation has other desirable qualities it is possible to overlook the partner's sex. Some examples are: a preference for group sex, for a particular socio-economic background, for paid sex, for S/M, for a specific age group, for a physical type or race, for anal or oral sex (1983, 2)"

The complexity of gender preference in erotic relations, both in ideology and praxis, must be seen as part of a general decline in the constancy and rigidity of appropriate role packages in the society. As the traditional gender, race, age, religious and ethnic prejudices have weakened, so too have prejudices against variations in sexual conduct weakened. Changes within the sexual domain have thus been driven not only by theories about sex and sexual factors, but also by changes in the larger culture, particularly in the area of gender theory and practice.

The Scripting of Sexual Aggression and Violence

Most of both folk and scientific considerations of violence and aggression between individuals are substantively similar to folk and traditional scientific explanations of sexual conduct (for a review of these views see Stearns and Stearns 1986 and Tavris 1982). Both are thought to be drives which can have impulsive or uncontrolled expression in the presence of provocative environmental stimuli, and in both cases the absence of the expression of the drives is a function of either an adequate level of self-control or the absence of provocation. While in some narrow range of circumstances sex and aggression are appropriately expressed (in that they are directed toward some social good), they have the potential for impulsive or uncontrolled disruptions of the flow of normal pacific and unaroused interaction. At the individual level, and especially among men, the emotions of anger and rage which are thought to be prior to acts of violence (as lust is prior to sexual acts) are viewed as in need of constant control since they can be easily provoked. Like the "male" sexual "drive," which is at risk of being released by improper sexual display, aggression is treated as a constant potential waiting to be released by threats to the honor or security or possessions of a manly person (Simon 1982).

These shared elements in the conventional cultural scenarios for thinking about sex and violence result in similar conceptual problems. The belief that sex and aggression are drives that are held in place by self-control (the internalized version of social constraint or rules) and that both can be activated by certain kinds of environmental provocation has two important consequences. The first is that persons who violate rules about the expression of aggression or sex (or both together) can be the targets of various kinds of social blaming strategies. The second is that the victims of violence or sexual assault can be blamed for provoking them. This activates a struggle for virtue (a blaming contest) between perpetrators and victims (even the very names begin the contest, as perpetrators seek not be blamed and victims seek to establish the legitimacy of their victimage) that may be carried out in a number of areas, especially the courts.

In recent years a more complex approach to aggression (including sexual) and its associated emotions has followed in the path of the social constructionist and scripting approach to sexuality. It has become apparent to many social scientists that aggression and violence (like sexuality) are socially patterned forms of conduct and that they occur on occasions appropriate to them (Averill 1982, 1984; Tavris 1982). Fighting on the streets, soccer hooliganism, territorial struggles among gangs, and fights between husbands and wives or parents and children are socially scripted encounters. They do not occur all of the time, but are temporally organized, have precursors and sequelae, and have an internally organized character. Even the explanatory statements that persons make after such occasions of violence or aggression are entirely socially conventional. In addition the emotions which are attributed to these events (which appear to cause them) are themselves situationally evoked. This view is in keeping with a large amount of recent work on the social psychology of the emotions, which treats them as heightened levels of arousal that are evoked and named in situations appropriate to them (e.g., the feeling of grief at funerals and joy at weddings) (Hochschild 1983).

Aggression and violence are social acts and are scripted in the way that all social action is scripted. Individuals' reported experiences of being overwhelmed by aggressive feelings (here one can also read *sexual*) or were provoked beyond their own limits of control are both learned scripts of how to be aggressive and how to engage in post hoc justification and explanation. The fact that the conduct is scripted and explainable in social terms does not mean that we cannot act as if someone is to blame and behave toward them in ways that will reduce the likelihood that they will do it again. Even in a socially determined world it is perfectly reasonable that some persons will attempt to eliminate behavior that they do not like either through attempts to change cultural scenarios and/or interpersonal and intrapsychic scripts.

Scripts for Sexual Violence against Women

The issue of sexual violence against women has been on the agenda of sex researchers since the late 1960s with the rise of the current wave of feminist activism in the United States. This concern for all aspects of sexual violence against women produced a number of research agendas: (1) a renewed interest in the study of sexual offenders which involved both diagnosis and treatment; (2) a concern for determining the actual prevalence of rape and sexual assault in the population and differentiating between differing types of rape situations (e.g., rape by strangers, dates, or spouses); (3) determining, among the general population of men and women, the extent of attitudes and values (and to some extent behavior) that appeared to promote rape; and (4) the laboratory study of relationship between sexually explicit representations (both nonviolent and violent) and subsequent displays of aggression.

This research program was developed during a period in which there was a five and one-half–fold increase in the rate of reported rapes in the United States (from 16,860 in 1966 to 91,111 in 1987) (Baron and Straus 1989, 3). There is considerable debate about the proportion of this increase that should be attributed to an actual increase in the number of rapes rather than to the increased willingness and ability of women to be able to report these crimes to the police. Efforts by feminists to make law enforcement agencies and court systems more friendly to the rape victim have undoubtedly increased reporting, as have media representations that positively depict women's attempts to deal with rape, including its reporting to the police. At the same time the numbers of women living independent lives with and without children and working outside the home has increased the numbers of women in the society who are at risk for sexual assault. This author's current resolution of this problem would be to argue there has been a modest increase in the rape rate, but that the bulk of the increase is probably the result of increased reporting.

At the same time, the evidence is that rape remains the serious crime that is least often reported to the police. Indeed, there are data from sample surveys of the general population that suggest that only half or less of all rapes are reported to the police. A close examination of these surveys suggest there may be some difficulties in these numbers as well.

There is evidence that when comparisons are made between law enforcement agency statistics and survey data, there are reports to the former that are not included in the latter, suggesting that the latter are not picking up all of the nonreported events. This is, at least in part, a function of using "proxy" reporting in such surveys in which a sample person in the household reports on rates of victimage of other members of the household. This assumes that the sample person knows about the victim experiences of other members of the household. Further, the surveys, for reasons reported below, do not appear to pick up what are called "acquaintance rapes" any more efficiently than do law enforcement surveys. Debates over the size of the problem notwithstanding, there is consistent evidence from all data sources that sexual violence and coercion are relatively common among all women and that some women are relatively continuously vulnerable to such violence and coercion. Indeed, data from the third wave of interviews with the women respondents in the National Survey of Children (conducted in 1987, when the respondents were largely ages 18 to 22) indicate that 7 percent of the sample responded affirmatively to the question "Was there ever a time when you were forced to have sex against your will, or were raped?" (Moore, Nord, and Peterson 1989).

The confrontation with these facts has raised a number of serious issues about the scripting of the sexual relationships between boys and girls and women and men in the United States. The problem is whether these high rates of sexual violence and coercion are the results of the influence of cultural scenarios on interpersonal scripts or of defective patterns of interpersonal relationships. The cultural scenario arguments have focused on three factors: (1) men and to some extent women accept a series of cultural beliefs about men's and women's sexuality and women's responses to sexual overtures that promote the acting out of violent sexual scripts (Burt 1980; Fine 1984; Jackson 1978); (2) the representations of women in the media in general, but more particularly in sexually explicit representations, lead, either through modeling effects or through creating a general climate of disrespect for women, to acts of sexual violence (Lederer 1980; Malamuth and Donnerstein 1984); and (3) the United States is a generally violent society where much of this violence is legitimated in various ways, and the violence against women is simply a "spillover" effect (although macrosociological studies of this factor have not borne out its effect on rape rates at the state level; Baron and Straus 1989). Correlative with the second argument is that gender inequality (or the scripts for gender relations), independent of sexual influences, fosters contempt for women that may be expressed in the sexual realm. Research on interpersonal scripts has examined the differences between the relationships of women to the rapist (was he a stranger, an acquaintance, or a spouse) and has looked at the way in which the management of the particular interaction is productive of violence.

The studies of the influence of cultural scenarios and sexually explicit depictions on sexual violence have most often been experimental studies which have manipulated a number of elements in scripted sexual materials in attempts to examine whether these script differences produce differences in either sexual arousal or aggression. This work built upon prior research which measured subjective and physiological sexual arousal of men and women in response to nonviolent erotic materials of different kinds (romantic versus erotic scripts) and with different modes of presentation (audio tapes, slides, film). The majority of experimental studies focusing on cultural beliefs and representations of women in sexually explicit materials have examined the ways in which certain kinds of scripted stimuli produce differences in either behavior or attitudes. Studies of cultural beliefs (often measured using Rape Myth Acceptance and Acceptance of Interpersonal Violence Scales [Burt 1980] or some variants thereof) have focused on the impact of various elements in sexual scripts on those scripts' ability to produce arousal or to neutralize inhibitions. In one experiment, in which subjective measures of arousal were used, subjects were presented with mutually consenting scripts versus scripts that contained coercive elements, including scripts in which the coerced woman experienced involuntary orgasm and/or pain (Malamuth and Check 1980; Malamuth, Heim, and Feshbach 1980). Findings from this and other similar studies were that belief in the rape myth tended to produce higher levels of arousal to rape representations and that if elements of the rape myth (that women who are forced to have sex will become aroused despite themselves) were included in presented scripts, such arousal would occur even among ostensibly normal men and women.

An overlapping similar research tradition has developed around the presentation of scripted erotic materials and attempts to examine whether the inclusion of aggressive elements influences behavioral and attitudinal outcomes (Malamuth and Donnerstein 1982, 1984). This research was motivated by concern that sex (treated as a "powerful unconditioned stimulus and reinforcer" by these researchers) was being fused with aggression in the mass media and in "pornography" with potential for changes in attitudes and behaviors. The substantive results of this body of work have been problematic, though they have cast some light on the ways in which scripted representations can be manipulated to create different levels of arousal in normal populations, both young men and young women. In addition the research itself depends on sexual behavior being scripted in different ways for its effect rather than being a "powerful unconditioned stimulus and reinforcer." What is remarkable in this research is how much arousal is dependent on the character of script that is presented. In general there is no evidence that sexually explicit materials without aggressive elements produced a higher rate of aggressive conduct, no matter how measured in experiments, and the findings for the impact of sexually explicit material with aggressive components were mixed, with some treatments showing an effect and others not (Linz 1989). Perhaps what is most problematic is the lack of fit between the laboratory script for the use of sexually explicit materials and the script which governs its use in nonlaboratory situations. There has been a lively debate about this issue (see Mould 1988 and replies from Donnerstein and Linz [1988] and Malamuth [1988], as well as an earlier article by Berkowitz and Donnerstein [1982]). There is substantial evidence that when sexually explicit materials are viewed alone and in private the result is usually masturbation. When such materials are viewed in nonexperimental or public settings (movie theaters or arcades) or by men in groups (stag parties or other similar contexts), the actual outcomes are more ambiguous and there is little empirical evidence one way or the other. One might hypothesize that individual men after viewing such materials would not be easily provoked to sexual assault. However, the evidence for men in groups, particularly those who have been drinking, is not as clear.

The scripting of sexual conduct which involves aggression appears in a somewhat different guise when studies of sexual coercion are examined according to the nature of the relationships in which they occur. There is irrefutable evidence that rape, as defined legally, occurs at some frequency in nearly all relationships between women and men—between strangers, acquaintances, spouses, coworkers, and relatives—and that sexual coercion and harassment occur far more commonly in these same relationships. The representation of these types of relationships in surveys does not represent their frequency in the world. Underreporting of rape and sexual coercion, both in surveys and to the police, is common except for those relationships in which the offender is a stranger. Even in self-report surveys, nonstranger rape and coerced sexual activity with nonstrangers is underreported in part because of an unwillingness to describe coercion within relationships as sexual violence or criminal behavior.

Each of these relationships in which sexual coercion and rape occur involves different types of scripts based on differences in the role relationships that are involved. Sexual assaults and coercion that occur between men and women who are in an ongoing nonmarital affectional and sexual relationship appear to occur when prior expectations of sex on the part of the man are denied. Circumstances when a couple have not had sex before and the man believes that the woman initially agreed to have sex and then changed her mind are particularly fertile for sexual coercion (Byers 1988; Check and Malamuth 1983; Murnen, Perot, and Byrne 1989). In marriages rape seems to appear most often in two types of relationships: first, and most common, those in which the woman has been physically battered and the sexual violence is part of the larger picture of spouse abuse; and second, where there have been prior difficulties over how often to have sex or what techniques are appropriate in the marital sexual encounters (Finkelhor and Yllo 1981). In each of these cases there are particular variants on the cultural scenario for the "legitimate" use of force, but they all share the common feature of the man with legitimate rights to sex (because of the relationship) that are frustrated by the woman's denial of these rights. The rights of the man to use coercive measures to have sex tend to be treated as more legitimate as the relationship takes on greater levels of permanence and legality.

The circumstances described above can be treated as examples of sexual coercion that occur with women who have a "protected" status; that is, a woman in sexual or potentially sexual relationship with a man who has personal and social obligations to her which should require that he treat her as a "good" woman and should protect her from his and other men's predatory sexual interests. Other examples of "quasiprotected" women who are the targets of sexual coercion are coworkers, employees, students, and other women in conventional, nonsexual relations with men who often have some power over them. In these cases the girl or woman is construed to be in the power or control of the man, and this vulnerability may channel whatever sexual interest the man has in the woman. The cultural scenarios and the interpersonal scripts for sexual relations between boss and secretary or professor and student are well known, and the fairly large volume of what are treated as consensual sexual relations between women and men in these roles operate as models of legitimacy for other men.

The rape and sexual coercion of "unprotected" women involve somewhat different script elements than those with "protected" women. In these cases women become a target for sexual violence and coercion because they have attributes (e.g., demeanor, dress, race) or are in places which define them as sexually accessible. Thus women who occupy jobs in the sex industry, who have histories of sexual activity that are well known to men, who meet sexual partners in bars or clubs and when drinking, who are divorced, or who live independent lives are all more vulnerable to rape and coercion than women who are met or known in "protected" roles or statuses. Such women are particularly vulnerable to harassment, sexual coercion, and rape when they come into contact with men in groups (this risk spans encounters with men at every social level and includes middle-class college students, working-class gangs, construction workers, and military personnel on leave). Women who are alone are harassed by groups of workmen; a woman who gets drunk and has sex with one man in a group is likely to be approached and sometimes raped by others; and in some cases gangs of men or boys will rape women who are strangers to them.

Rape by strangers of women previously unknown to them fits the stereotype of violent sexual relations between men and women, and such men are often treated as if they were entirely unlike other men in important individual psychological attributes. As has been noted, such rapes are the easiest for the victim to report, and the conduct of such men, especially if they have a history of prior rapes, can be most easily construed as the consequence of individual psychopathology that results in the failure of sexual self-control (Groth 1979). Considerable research effort has been devoted to finding psychological differences between rapists and other violent, but nonrapist offenders or normal controls, and some attention has been paid to determining the particular psychological attributes of the serial or multiple rapist (as with the serial or multiple burglar or car thief). In general such studies do differentiate between rapists and various controls, however, little of this work has practical policy outcomes in terms of incarceration or treatment programs. In addition this approach does not account for the very high levels of coercion and sexual violence experienced by women from men who do not meet either the legal or psychological criteria of a rapist. Reasoning from these studies, one would have a pool of "true" rapists and then a large number of men who for one nonpathological reason or another coerced women either psychologically or physically to have sex with them. These cases would then be treated as accidents or normal sexual interactions that have somehow gone wrong.

A theory of sexual violence and coercion at the level of cultural scenarios for gender has been suggested by a number of feminists (Brownmiller 1975; MacKinnon 1987). They argue that the current structure of gender relations in the United States (the condition of patriarchy), in which women occupy inferior roles in all dimensions of social life, infuses the cultural scenarios, interpersonal scripts, and intrapsychic scripts for sexual conduct. That is, all sexual conduct, on the part of all individuals in the society, women and men alike, is shaped by the power that men have over women. This, argues MacKinnon (1987), includes the experiences of sexual arousal and pleasure. Rape is simply the end-point expression of that power, and rapists represent the end of men's continuum of conduct toward women. This argument points out that coercion is endemic in sexual relations between women and men (indeed many women report simply "going along" with many sexual relationships which men believe to be eagerly sought). Such coercion ranges from the very lowest level of the folk belief (a cultural scenario) that "when she says no, she means maybe," which encourages men to continue to try to get sex from an unwilling woman, to coercion by husbands of their wives ("it is my right"), to sex between unequals in power (students and teachers), to violent sexual assaults by strangers. While the individual script that is called upon in each relationship may vary, offering distinctions between types of encounters, what underpins all of the acts of violence and coercion is the patriarchal cultural scenario. Indeed it is argued further that as women grow more independent of men, socially as well as sexually, the rates of violence should increase because more women will be of "unprotected status" and because men will be increasingly threatened by the loss of their power over women.

All perspectives on sexual violence and coercion use, explicitly or implicitly, the concept of sexual scripting. Experimentalists offer subjects "scripts" which vary in character for purposes of provoking arousal, and they assume the existence of cultural scenarios which promote or inhibit sexual violence. Survey researchers assume that respondents can report on scripted encounters which contain elements of violence, and they design scales that tap, through a series of items, the existence of cultural scenarios. Diagnosticians use the responses to scripted sexual stimuli to differentiate between criterion and control group, and feminists assume the existence of hegemonic cultural scripts that govern interpersonal and intrapsychic scripts.

Scripts and the Practice of Sex Therapy

It is clear that sexual problems come in many kinds, ranging from those that are dealt with primarily by the criminal law (sometimes with the help of medicine), others that are dealt with by psychiatry as forms of mental illness, and still others that are dealt with by a mixed bag of psychological and medical healers. These sets of problems can be described as sex crimes, psychogenic sexual disorders, and sexual dysfunctions, respectively. It would be nosologically comforting if the content of these sets would remain constant, however, over the last one hundred years there has been a constant struggle to determine what forms of sexual conduct should be viewed as problematic and, if it is problematic, how it should be labeled and what professional collectivity should be responsible for it. A couple of examples of this struggle should suffice.

Rape has remained a crime for a very long time, but marital rape has only recently been made a statutory offense, and acquaintance rape is only now being successfully prosecuted (Finkelhor and Yllo 1981). For about one hundred years rape has been considered to be both a crime and a psychogenic disorder, and the police and the criminal justice system and the medical profession have struggled over who has the right to explain the conduct of the rapist and who has the right to treat him. In the 1930s new medicalized responses and institutions were developed for the dangerous sex offenders (the sexual psychopath and the mentally abnormal sex offender), but rapists were rarely confined in such programs (Gebhard et. al. 1965). Feminists have entered into this debate by insisting that rape is not a "sex" crime, but a crime of violence, since this reduces the stigmatization of the victim, and they have resisted the creation of a psychiatric diagnosis for the rapist in order to keep the behavior a crime (the diagnosis of "rapism" was proposed for the recent revision of the American Psychiatric Association's *Diagnostic and Statistical Manual*).

"Same-gender" sex was a crime defined by the act (sodomy) and the object of desire in canon and criminal law but was only intermittently aggressively pursued over the past one hundred years. Medicine turned sodomy into homosexuality and concerned itself with the personality as well as the act. By the 1920s a full-fledged theory of homosexuality had been constructed. The talking therapy was introduced for the middle class, while the less fortunate went to prison or were publicly degraded (Katz 1983). During the 1950s preliminary efforts were made to decriminalize and demedicalize "homosexuality," while behavior therapists were trying to cure homosexuality through aversive conditioning. With gay liberation in the 1970s came a new social category, and gay men and lesbians have emerged as part of a new quasiethnic community that resists therapy and criminality but may seek treatment for sexual dysfunctions (Nichols 1988).

Impotence has long been a concern among men but was never thought to be a crime. Its psychogenic sources were recognized early by Montaigne (Matalene 1989), but by the early decades of the twentieth century it was a terrain over which the urologist and psychiatrist (as well as the primate endocrinologist with monkey gland transplants) struggled. In the 1960s it was renamed an erectile dysfunction and various behavioral treatments, diagnostic labels, and techniques have now been developed (the squeeze technique, systematic desensitization, reductions of performance anxiety and penile implants, inhibited sexual desire, sleep diagnosis) so that there is enough work for everyone (Tiefer 1986).

In these brief descriptions three processes can be identified: (1) the changing level of stigma and social control aimed at specific forms of sexual conduct; (2) the social agents who are responsible for explanation and treatment; and (3) the changing character of the therapeutic practice. These changes are part of the change in the cultural scenarios which instruct us how to respond to these "problems" or "nonproblems" and the interpersonal scripts in which the conduct is expressed or dealt with as problematic. At the same time intrapsychic scripts are changed as individuals think about what they are doing sexually in different ways for various audiences. Thus the rapist or man with erectile difficulties who is treated as if he is suffering from a "psychological problem" will behave and think differently if the problem is treated as one of bad character rather than inadequate hormones. The gay man who worries about suicide will interpret these worries as linked to his current life situation (or the oppression of heterosexuals), not his desire to have sex with men. The "homosexual" in contrast can be persuaded that the lack of self-worth that he feels is a function of his perversion (Socarides 1978). In these cases the diseases that people have are a function of the treatments they receive.

Given these changes in the larger set of social relations in which sexuality is embedded, during the 1960s the emergence of a new treatment tradition might have been predicted. The general rise of "here and now" therapies which focused on the current issues in people's lives rather than the etiology of the disorder emerged not only from behaviorist tradition in psychology in the United States, but from psychologists who were revolting against the psychoanalytic tradition (Davison 1968; Lobitz and Lopiccolo 1972). The extension of these techniques to sexual problems came during the years after 1960 and were consolidated in the public and scientific mind by the work of Masters and Johnson (Masters and Johnson 1966, 1970). The therapeutic procedures appeared to rest soundly on the descriptive laboratory research on the sexual response cycle, and there was a cycle of publicity that was quite similar to the response to the work of Kinsey.

What Masters and Johnson proposed was an attempt to rescript an older domain of sexual problems that they recategorized (the first step in rescripting) as sexual dysfunctions, though they never used the word *scripting*. What they observed (and what other therapists since have observed) is that many couples with dysfunctions (erectile disorders, premature ejaculation, painful coitus, lack of orgasm) were engaged in inept or misguided or emotionally aversive sexual activities that had become embedded in their relationship. Unable to talk about the problem between themselves or having engaged in talking therapies that dealt with the problem as the sole property of one member of the couple or the other, the problem had become chronic. That is, the lack of orgasm or impotence had become scripted into the relationship, both at the level of the individual and at the level of the couple. Masters and Johnson believed that what they were doing was stripping away the inhibitory or defective developmental history of the relationship and revealing the natural sexual processes which could then be enacted without difficulty by the couple. What they were actually doing was to educating or reeducating the couple by legitimating old and new sexual practices, eroticizing (or reeroticizing) the relationship, and teaching a standard set of skills and techniques to maintain sexual focus (Gagnon, Rosen, and Leiblum 1982).

This package of techniques, which, in increasingly modified ways, has become the basis for direct sex therapy, is based on quite standard behavioral and cognitive techniques. Such techniques assume that patterns of sexual behavior have been previously scripted and that under appropriate learning conditions that they can be rescripted to better meet the expectations of the individual or the couple. Using primarily a social learning model, the behavior of the individual or the couple is assessed (i.e., what is wrong with the script?) either in interviews or using paper and pencil procedures, a plan for behavior change is instituted, and couples are given the opportunity to do "homework" in order to learn the new scripts or to insert various behavioral elements into the script (Lieblum and Pervin 1980). The use of different gender cotherapists is a recognition of the gender basis of sexual scripts. In general such procedures appear to work more effectively with a dysfunctional individual than do more traditional "talking therapies," since they provide occasions for low anxiety practice of sexual activities.

The breakthrough to these procedures has depended on fundamental changes in the cultural scenarios that governed sexual activity in the society. Therapists had to feel that they had the right to prescribe "practice sessions," "homework," and in some cases use the services of a sexual surrogate for the currently unpartnered. Masturbation, which had been one of the most condemned of sexual practices, has been increasingly imported into sex therapy regimes for the purposes of diagnosis and treatment (Lobitz and Lopiccolo 1972). Erotic representations have been used as stimulus materials as well as for purposes of increasing levels of sexual fantasy and responsiveness (Barlow 1973). Increasingly gay men and lesbians have been treated for their sexual dysfunctions rather than for being gay or lesbian. The ability to move to direct sex therapy itself depended on changes at the level of the culture in terms of what was and was not appropriate both for therapists and for their patients.

It is clear that the script difficulties that individuals bring to treatment exist at the intrapsychic and the interpersonal levels, and most, though not all, interventions involve changes in both (McCormick 1987; Rosen and Lieblum 1988). Scripts may be assessed in terms of their complexity, rigidity, conventionality, and satisfaction or to the degree that they match some ideal for sexual behavior that the couple or the individual possesses. Troubles may be located in the cognitions that persons have (fantasies that produce guilt or anxiety), in the relation between the cognitions and the performance (fantasies that seek to become reality without the shared desire of the partner), or in the performance itself. Rigid, simple, conventional conduct on the part of one partner may result in lack of satisfaction on the part of the other. Only a few therapists have self-consciously used sexual scripting as the basis of their procedures, however, they use such techniques implicitly as they attend to interactional difficulties of the couple or to fantasies that seem inappropriate either to the therapist or the patient.

As the set of treatment techniques for the traditional dysfunctions have been more or less consolidated, the issue of inhibited or low sexual desire has taken center stage as the sexual illness of greatest significance. In general such cases come to the therapist because one or the other partner in a relationship reports that he or she wants more sex than his or her partner does, or in some cases when patients report that they seem to want sex less than they feel they ought to. Such cases could only begin to emerge once there existed some cultural standard, no matter how diffuse, that people ought to have sex and enjoy it. In this climate of opinion it is possible for members of a couple or for individuals to feel that they are not performing at an adequate level. A number of approaches to this difficulty have been taken, but the majority have been at the level of the individual or the couple (Lieblum and Rosen 1988). Less commonly analyzed are the absence of social support for high levels of sexual desire and the cultural scenarios that exist for producing periods of high levels of desire in individuals and couples. High levels of desire among adults are associated with being youthful, having a new sexual partner, violations of conventional erotic norms, and detachment from conventional social obligations. Treatments of individuals and couples for low levels of desire often fail to recognize the mismatch between cultural scenarios and structural opportunities for high levels of desire and the actual context of sexual performance in the society.

Most individuals and couples, even under the rather peculiar learning conditions for sexuality which exist in the United States, become fairly adequate sexual performers in a number of sexual relationships. Most of this learning goes on in relationships in which couples work out for themselves what is adequate for them. Most of these relationships fall short of the absolute goals set by such volumes as the *Joy of Sex*, however, only some persons find the difficulties which they experience in their sexual relationships as requiring sex therapy. Most settle for what they have, reduce the amount of sex which they find unsatisfying, or seek other relationships. Those who come to therapy are obviously selected in a variety of ways that do not relate directly to the level of difficulties which they have in their relationships. As a consequence the distribution of difficulties found in therapy cannot be generalized to rates or distributions of difficulties found in the general population. The importance of this observation is that the level of sexual satisfaction in the society depends as much on the level of discontent that individuals and couples have with their lives as it does on the quality of the actual sexual performances in which they engage.

Conclusion

Examining sexual conduct from the perspective of scripting allows one to organize and link together what people think, what they do, and how they are affected by the sociocultural context in which they live. Seeing the conduct as "scripted" on the interpersonal and intrapsychic levels gives the behavior the quality of a narrative in which conduct is composed of events ordered in time, events that occur with sufficient regularity that individuals recognize them when they occur, often wish to participate in them, and remember them when they are over. At the cultural level instructions for conduct do not stand alone as "rules" or "norms" but are rather embedded in narratives of good and bad behavior, things to be done, things to be avoided. Changes in the cultural scenarios are changes in the instructional systems for conduct. Such changes provide opportunities for individuals to reorganize what they think about the sexual and offer them different goals when they engage in sexual activity. As individuals come together sexually they are required to change what they do in practice and what they think about themselves as a consequence.

Two important conceptions flow from this perspective. The first is that all social behavior is scripted, including encounters between researchers and subjects in sex research and therapists and patients in sex therapy and authors writing about sexuality. These encounters are composed of intrapsychic and interpersonal scripts and are in part ordered by cultural scenarios about how researcher and subject, therapist and patient, writer and reader will govern their conduct. Similarly when researchers provide erotic material to arouse a subject, they are depending on prior scripts as well as creating a new script; when therapists prescribe the squeeze technique or a surgical implant, they are inserting new elements into the sexual script of a couple or an individual; and when writers write about sex, they are attempting to change the cultural instructions about sexuality. The elements of the particular performance may be pulled from the context of the script, but it is the script that gives the elements their meaning. The second conception is that sexuality is more than individual behavior, and what happens in the sexual arena in any society is a consequence of culture and the structure of sexual and nonsexual opportunities which exist prior to any individual. Sexual scripts exist, as do all scripts, at the levels of the individual, the interactional, and the cultural. The performance of sexual acts draws upon scripts at all three levels, and potential changes in sexual conduct can emerge from changes at any level of scripting.

Appendix: Alternative Uses of the Concept of Scripts

A number of variations of the scripting concept have been developed in cognitive psychology as well as in the therapeutic tradition of transactional analysis. One of these is use of the idea of scripts in research on computerized story interpreters, which involves programming computers to read narratives and to make choices based on their interpretations (Schank 1982; Schank and Abelson 1977). In such research *scripts* refers solely to fixed sequences of action. For example, in a restaurant script, when the meal is finished the computer is expected to "understand" that the next move is to ask for the check. Scripts in this context are the lowest-level units in a hierarchy of modular units. Scripts are the basic elements that are assembled into plans, which in turn become the elements in schemas, und so weiter. The higher the modules are in the hierarchy, the more general and flexible they are thought to be.

In other work by Abelson (1981), scripts are treated from the point of view of human actors but with a continuing focus on the idea of a script as necessary for situational understanding. "The understander is hypothesized to possess conceptual representations of stereotyped event sequences, and these scripts are activated when the understander can expect events in the sequence to occur in the text" (715). In the case of the restaurant script, "[t]hat script contains a standard sequence of events characterizing typical activities in a restaurant from the point of view of the customer." There are strong scripts (those that are highly interconnected and sequential) as well as weak scripts (which are merely a bundle of inferences).

Abelson points out, "There are scripts in understanding and scripts in behavior. To behave in a script, that is, to take a role such as a customer in a restaurant, one must not only understand that such a possibility exists, but commit oneself to the performance of it. (I invoke the concept of commitment deliberately here. Starting a script performance usually entails the commitment to finish it. One does not readily leave a restaurant once seated or walk out of a dentist's office before the dentist is through.)" (719).

From Abelson's perspective, script performances can involve many of the following: (a) equifinal or substitutable actions (one can kiss or hug, have oral sex or coitus) which produce similar results; (b) variable choices at a given moment in a script, but once the choice is made the next steps are more predictable; (c) specified script pathways in which steps can be skipped or limited; (d) selection of scenes which will set the level of script strength (the orgy may be a weak scene and unpredictable); (e) various tracks or subscripts such as the variation between sex for pay and sex with a spouse (each is subset of the man/woman coital script); (f) the potential for interferences and obstacles—the doorbell or phone may ring or there may be no condoms; (g) large distractions, such as fires or earthquakes; and finally (h) free behaviors, in most scripts, which allow for imputing to the action new meanings or for the inclusion of novel behaviors (the power lunch or a woman penetrating a man).

In other work that uses the concept of scripting, the script represents routine sequences of actions which are repetitively performed. Individuals are presented with routine and nonroutine script sequences, and their memories for each are assessed. In nearly all cases persons remember nonroutine scripts more readily and in many cases persons read into scripts routine elements which are not present in the stimulus materials (Smith and Graesser 1981 and many others). The relevance of these findings for retrospective recall in survey research is apparent. A variant of this research focuses on the relation between knowledge bases and action, assessing whether knowledge of scripts prior to action increases effectiveness (Gioia and Poole 1984). In some cases the routinization of the action is so complete that a state of mindlessness in performance is proposed (Langer 1978; Langer, Blank, and Chanowitz 1978).

In the work of Tompkins, the scene is the basic unit of analysis, a connected set of scenes is a plot, and a script is a basic set of rules for predicting, interpreting, responding to, and controlling a set of scenes (Tompkins 1978). The script is thus an organizer of subunits of behavior. Tompkins has raised the idea of nuclear scripts which are acquired in childhood and which may have lifelong consequences (Mosher and Tompkins 1988). In this case scripting has a more developmental and perhaps clinical dimension than its use in cognitive psychology.

The tradition of transactional psychotherapy explicitly used the metaphors of script and game as heuristics for patients to analyze their "self-defeating" conduct (Berne 1966). This has become a highly elaborated theoretical perspective primarily used within the community of transactional analysis (see *Transactional Analysis Journal*).

In social scripting, a script is the sole molar unit which is descriptive of all actions; as such scripts can be used to interpret mental processes (e.g., plans for the future, remembrances of the past), the guidance of public interactions, and the semiotic structure of environments. They are nonhierarchical in the sense that they are not a "level" in a larger information processor/decision maker or personality system. They are also variable in terms of flexibility, ranging from the ritualistic to the improvisational, depending on cultural and historical context.

Part Two

The Quest for Desire

Disease and Desire (1989)

Making satisfactory predictions about the short- and long-term impact of HIV disease on sexual life in the United States would require substantive knowledge about both the "change agent" and the domain of social practice that the change agent affects. Neither of these factors is well understood now, either empirically or theoretically. This is not to say that we do not know a great deal about the virus. Intense effort and vast expenditures are going into the attempt to understand the virus and the immune system, to develop chemoprophylaxis for those who are ill, and to discover vaccines to prevent the further spread of the disease.[1] However, our data on the numbers of persons who are infected with the virus, the frequency of the forms of conduct that spread the disease, the differential efficiency of transmission by any of these activities, and the variability of the latency period still do not allow us to make a definitive statement about the natural course of the disease and its epidemiology in the population of the United States (Turner, Miller, and Moses 1989, chap. 2; Institute of Medicine 1988).

The figures on the number of persons who are HIV positive and the sensitivity of these figures to the manipulation of the variables that are used to estimate them is an important example of this indeterminacy. The

Originally published in *Daedelus* 118 (3): 47–77. Reprinted by permission of the American Academy of Arts and Sciences.

1. See the October 1988 special issue of *Scientific American* for an accessible update on the biomedical advances made in understanding the HIV virus.

Coolfont report estimate that from 1 million to 1.5 million persons had been infected with HIV was based on speculative arithmetic (U.S. Public Health Service 1988). That the Domestic Policy Council reported a similar figure some three years later, after a certain amount of admittedly limited research, suggests that the advances we have made in grasping the dimensions of the epidemic are still modest (U.S. Public Health Service 1987).[2] Estimating the number of persons infected from the numbers of persons who have AIDS rests on several factors: estimates of the latency period, the accuracy of the AIDS reporting system, estimates of the number of deaths associated with having HIV disease before it was defined as AIDS, as well as estimates of the number of men who have sex with men and the number of needle-sharing intravenous drug users in each AIDS locale. Conflict in New York City over revised estimates of the number of men who have sex with men suggests the complexity of this task (Loomis 1989a, 1989b).

If we are to make some sense of the impact of HIV on sexual practice in the middle term (say, ten years), we must make some assumptions about the shape of the epidemic up to this point and prophesy what it will eventually look like. With the evidence we have now, it is possible to characterize the transmission characteristics of HIV in the United States in the following way: HIV disease appears to be difficult to transmit except through blood-blood or semen-blood contact. Even in these circumstances the chance of transmission is low (far lower, for instance, than for the transmission of the hepatitis virus). In the vast majority of the diagnosed cases of AIDS and HIV transmission in the United States and Europe, frequent anal intercourse and needle sharing associated with intravenous drug use can be identified as the primary means of transmission. Blood-blood transmission via contaminated blood products accounts for the infection of transfusees and hemophiliacs. There are some cases of transmission among health care workers through needle sticks. In a far smaller number of cases there is heterosexual transmission through vaginal intercourse of an infected person with a regular sexual partner. The degree to which other cofactors are influential in the transmission via vaginal intercourse in the United States have not yet received definitive study (degree of infectiousness of the sexual partner as measured by stage of disease, prior or current infection with sexually transmitted diseases that may make transmission more efficient, lack of circumcision of

2. Data on how many persons in the society report knowing someone with AIDS can be found in the reports of the National Center for Health Statistics in the AIDS supplement to the National Health Interview Survey. In the most recent reports, about 10 percent of the population report knowing someone with AIDS.

the man partner, and other as yet unknown attributes of the uninfected partner).

If HIV disease remains what we observe it to be now—a disease that is relatively hard to transmit, that requires certain sexual practices for sexual transmission, and that afflicts primarily men who have sex with men and minority group members via sexual contacts with intravenous drug users who share needles—then it will have one sort of impact on sexual practice in our society. If on the other hand there is another, still secret HIV epidemic concealed from us by very long latency times or through spread into previously uninfected groups that are not being well monitored and who will appear with the disease seven to eight years from now, then it will have another sort of impact. We do not currently have evidence of an imminent wildfire epidemic among heterosexuals, regardless of what segment of the society they represent. If such an epidemic is in the offing, it will occur some years into the 1990s, and a new scenario will have to be written for the change agent and its impact on sexual life in the United States.

Research and Representation

It is difficult to characterize the nature of the change agent for reasons other than incomplete scientific evidence. The way in which the collective representations of the epidemic (as distinct from the epidemic itself) have evolved is another reason. Most of our society comes in contact with the epidemic indirectly, through its representation in the mass media, which both report and reshape the scientific evidence. Only some of us know people in our extended social networks who have HIV disease.[3] Even fewer of us have close friends or lovers who are HIV positive or have AIDS. A still smaller number of us receive salaries or other gratuities to work directly on the AIDS epidemic, though this number may perhaps approach the number of new cases of AIDS in any year. Even persons with AIDS are widely split into different social groups.

In the present dominant representation of the sexual dimensions of the epidemic, the emphasis is on the dangers of multiple sexual contacts and of sexual contact with those in high-risk groups and those who are HIV positive or who have overt AIDS. In this view the use of certain sexual techniques and of condoms and other safe-sex practices, including abstinence, are promoted. (Certain high-risk groups are usually identified

3. See for example the very large-scale demonstration outreach projects directed at sexual partners of high-risk populations supported by the National Institute of Drug Abuse under the title, "AIDS Research Demonstration Projects."

as gay and bisexual men and intravenous drug users, though we are as-sured that there are no high-risk groups, only high-risk practices.) Also considered to be at risk are those who are in the sexually active periods of their lives or who are regularly sexually active with multiple partners: adolescents, young adults prior to marriage, persons who are uncoupled later in life, women and men in the sex industry, persons having sex out-side marriage, and until recently clients of women in the sex industry. The image ranges from one of low-level danger of infection with "an in-variably fatal disease" for most persons to acute danger for those with a "fast track" sexual life. In addition, risks such as the use of alcohol and drugs, which decrease prudential behavior, are cautioned against, and the possible cofactors of other sexually transmitted diseases are noted but not emphasized. It is this representation of the sexual dimensions of the epi-demic that will have an impact on the sexual practices of most persons in the society in the short term.

It would be fairly easy to measure the impact of both the epidemic as it is and the epidemic as it is represented if we had baseline data with which to measure change in sexual practice. If we knew what the sexual practices of various groups in the society were and had explanations for why persons conduct themselves in certain ways, we could employ the usual methods of social science to monitor how behavior changes as both the epidemic and its representations change. Both the baseline data needed and adequate theories of sexual conduct, however, are in short supply (Gagnon 1988). To point out that the data gathered by the Kinsey group are between forty and fifty years old is now commonplace, yet they were used in the absence of other observations to estimate various sexual parameters relevant to the natural course of the disease as well as its epi-demiology (Kinsey, Pomeroy, and Martin 1948; Kinsey et al. 1953). Al-ready when these data were collected, persons of some methodological sophistication were recognizing the limitations of using these observa-tions for such purposes (Cochran, Mosteller, and Tukey 1953). At the same time the Kinsey studies did open up the area of sex research and of-fer a number of directions for work over the next decades.

The sex research agenda that dominated the period from Kinsey to the onset of the AIDS epidemic was primarily driven either by the social problems associated with sexuality or by the mass-media interest in various sexual practices. The scientific investigation of this period con-cerned the virginity and fertility of young people (primarily of young women), the changing lives of gay men and lesbians, the impact of erot-ica and pornography (particularly after the early 1960s), the identifica-tion and treatment of sexual dysfunctions (after 1964), and sexual violence and sexual abuse (after 1975) (Turner, Miller, and Moses 1989, especially chap. 3). The mass media were interested in reporting findings about these matters as well as in generating advice about sexuality, particularly for women, about such topics as the female orgasm, sexual dysfunction, sexual technique, and maintaining relationships with men. Men were also being advised, but the advice was being packaged in somewhat different ways (contrast *Playboy* with *McCall's* treatment of these subjects). While research was also done on sex offenders, female prostitution, sexually transmitted diseases, extramarital sex, and masturbation, it was more intermittent and fragmented.

This was the small body of sex research that existed in 1980. Once they saw that the AIDS epidemic had a major sexual dimension, people nearly immediately recognized that this database was inadequate. As the new AIDS-driven research agenda has evolved, it has been discovered that there are a distressing number of empty or near-empty files that need to be filled, that there are others that have to be relabeled, and that many new files have to be made up and filled. Depending on the duration and extent of the epidemic, the new agenda for sex research set by the epidemic will contribute to society's representation of sexuality.

As the epidemic has evolved, the targets of research interest have shifted from the spread of the disease through various social groups to the expectations of where the disease may spread next. The focus and intensity of research vary as the estimate of the potential for spread outside the currently infected groups grows and as effective political groups make successful claims on the AIDS dollars. Thus, the level of research interest rises and falls as groups are identified as more or less at risk and appear to endanger "the general population," "the heterosexual community," and "those currently at lower risk."

AIDS and Gay Men

Since the disease was first identified in members of gay communities in large cities, the first sets of questions about sexual conduct focused on this group. Was it what these men were doing sexually that spread the disease? And if the disease were spread by sexual contact, what elements of their sex lives were critical to transmission? Given how little was known and how esoteric the gay community appeared to most investigators, nearly everything was suspect, including the brands of lubricants used in sexual relations, the drugs that enhanced sexual arousal, and the specific sexual techniques that were common practice (Shilts 1987). As the epidemiological search among gay men identified certain sexual practices as

potential routes of transmission, and since number of sexual partners appeared to correlate with likelihood of infection, concern about changing
these forms of conduct grew.

As an attempt was being made to fit what was being learned from epidemiological studies of the disease in a few major urban centers into a set
of larger understandings about men who had sex with men, it became
clear that even the most basic information was lacking. While the Kinsey
estimates of the numbers of men who had sex with men were widely disseminated (more than a third of men, 10 percent having sex with men exclusively for three years and 4 percent having sex only with men up to the
time of the interview), and the belief that one man in ten was exclusively
or nearly exclusively homosexual was widely held in the gay community,
these were not scientifically robust estimates (Fay et al. 1989). In the absence of a satisfactory sample survey in which individuals could safely
disclose a sexual preference that was against the law, no accurate figure
was available.

In addition, the social, psychological, and cultural world of those labeled homosexual underwent profound transformation from the early
1950s to the 1980s (Humphreys 1972; D'Emilio 1983; Plummer 1980). In
part, this transformation depended on other groups questioning authority: black liberationists, the civil rights movement, the various phases of
youth revolt from 1964 to the mid-1970s, the women's movement, and
environmentalists were all part of the ferment in which gay liberation
flourished. It is not clear the degree to which social science research during this period contributed to these developments, though the language
challenging the tenets of psychoanalysis, which had provided the medical
justification for homosexual perversity, came from a general sociological
challenge to such theories of individual deviance (Hooker 1966; Gagnon
and Simon 1967; Simon and Gagnon 1967). Homosexuality was socially
constructed, reported the social scientists, lived out in ways that were determined by culture and history rather than by biological factors or early
warping of the personality. Whatever psychological difficulties gay men
and lesbians might have, they were the consequences of oppression (later
"homophobia"), according to the scientists, rather than the pathologies
thought to be associated with same-gender desire.

By the early 1970s, a number of community studies based on convenience samples and ethnographies had been conducted that chronicled the
development of gay and lesbian lifestyles in the great cities of the United
States (Warren 1974; Wolf 1979). What was primarily a sexual marketplace in the 1950s had been transformed into full-fledged cultural communities, somewhat separate for men and women, with their own poli-

tics, commercial institutions, cultural life, and housing patterns—communities that had developed quite new relations, at least in some cities, between themselves and the larger communities in which they were embedded. During the 1970s, the research momentum faltered and the intellectual and scientific understandings of these communities were largely transferred to what were previously the "objects" of heterosexual inquiry. In this new research climate, gay scientists and intellectuals began a research agenda in sociology, psychology, history, and even psychoanalysis.

Central to the development of this new community and identity was an openness of sexual expression and a new cult of manliness. It appears that numbers of sexual partners increased (though convenience-sample data from the late 1960s and early 1970s, as well as the original Kinsey interviews with men who had sex with men nearly exclusively, suggest that having many sexual partners was not uncommon in earlier generations). The incidence, frequency, and reciprocity of anal sex increased. The institutions of this sexually liberated group offered a kind of sexual life for many men who had previously lived lives of emotional and sexual repression. The cities in which these new institutions operated most openly became national and regional meccas for gay men. Gay men migrated to or vacationed in such cities as New York, Los Angeles, San Francisco, Houston, and Miami (White 1980).

The difficulty certain political leaders and segments of the gay community had in recognizing the dangers of the AIDS epidemic rested at least in part on the important role that sexual liberation had played in personal and political liberation. Those promoting a "safer" sexual life that seemed consonant with the gravity of the AIDS epidemic often did not recognize that the price being paid for changes in sexual behavior was more than sexual pleasure, important as that was (Shilts 1987). Safer sex was, at least for some groups and individuals and in the early stages of the epidemic, a repudiation of a cultural norm embedded in a nascent community. Less visible but coexisting with these norms was another lifestyle—a conception of gay life as one of permanent couples. Modeled on the notion of the faithful emotionally constant couple recommended to heterosexuals, a stable same-gender couple represented an alternative to the more intensely sexual lifestyle of multiple casual partners (McWhirter and Mattison 1984).

This alternative lifestyle has now become recommended as part of gay life in the United States. Dating rather than "cruising," affectionate relationships as well as or in place of "hot" sexual contacts, and socializing in friendship circles rather than in bars are aspects of the preferred if not always dominant gay male lifestyle. An increase in this pattern (which has always existed among men who have sex with men) was already observable in the early 1980s and has been accelerated in the epicenters of the epidemic by the severe toll the disease has taken. In addition this is also a pattern that is characteristic of men at a later stage in life, and like the rest of the baby-boom generation, the gay male community is an aging one. What we do not know is how deeply these changes in sexual conduct have penetrated the lives of young persons beginning to participate in gay life at present or how characteristic the practice of safer sex is outside the urban centers of the epidemic. Whether micro-epidemics have begun in other communities is also unknown, though it is knowable through research.

All this is particularly important to know in the cultural and geographical communities that are outside the main centers in which research has been conducted. We do not know what the situation is for men in minority and working-class communities who have sex only with men, and the extent of the spread of HIV disease in such cities as Houston, New Orleans, Detroit, Denver, and Tucson remains a mystery except as indexed by reported cases of AIDS. At this time research has been conducted on white male, moderately well educated gay communities. Everyone and everywhere else is terra obscura.

What is apparent is that gay life has sustained itself and that new social forms have been created to sustain the connectivity of the community life. Working on the epidemic has become the focus of many persons in the gay community. Volunteering and political action are widespread, as is caring for the sick and dying through friendship networks. The public manifestations of sex are more muted. There are many persons now in couples who probably would not have been a decade ago, or at least not so constantly in couples. About half the gay men in the epicenters of the epidemic between thirty and forty-five are HIV positive (U.S. Public Health Service 1987). We do not know how many men who are younger or older than this group are HIV positive. It is clear, however, that substantial numbers of young persons are entering the gay community with no experience of AIDS except seeing it among their older friends. It is also clear that the HIV virus is now well-seeded in these communities and that safer sexual practices will have to continue for many decades.

The future of gay men's sexuality is deeply entangled with the more complex issues of gay men's identity and gay men's culture. Illness and death from AIDS is very much present in the consciousness of even the youngest gay men. The cultural movement toward the lifestyle of couples (what Martin Levine has called the heterosexualization of gay desire) appears to be widespread (Levine 1987a). The majority of the gay press and other gay cultural institutions support safe sex and disease-proof lifestyles at the individual and community levels. The gay population, at least in the epicenters of the epidemic, seems to have adapted to the realization that HIV is endemic in its community.

What has been learned from the experience of gay men and AIDS is quite complex. From research based on AIDS, very little has been learned about same-gender sexual desire and the social and psychological complexity of the lives of gay men. Narrow, disease-focused epidemiological studies have not contributed to a basic understanding of men who have sex with men. However, new knowledge has come from the ways in which the new gay male identity was formed in the context of sexual freedom and the rapidity with which that identity was transformed by the AIDS epidemic. The flexibility and openness to change that have characterized individuals in the gay male community may give us the most instructive information about the nature of sexuality as an element responsive to culture and context rather than something fixed and immutable. That all these sexual changes occurred in the context of community support indicates the importance of social connectivity in maintaining and changing sexual conduct.

The Bisexual Bridge

Among the first concerns expressed after the extent of the epidemic had been identified among gay men was the potential for spread of the disease from that population to the population of heterosexuals through bisexuality, having sex with both men and women. The concern about transmission induced the usual epidemiological questions: How many bisexuals were there? With whom did they have sex? How many bisexuals were currently infected? Did they use the sexual techniques that had been identified as risky?

Such questions quickly melded into a concern about behavior change: How could bisexual groups be identified? Were there different channels of education that needed to be accessed for different groups of bisexuals? How secret were their practices, and how difficult would it be to locate such persons? Some investigators worried that even with universal testing of blood donations, this collection of individuals might pose a special danger to the blood supply.

Earlier work offered only limited directions: the files were largely empty and arranged in somewhat unhelpful ways. On the other hand there were indications that the term *bisexual* might be too homogenizing. Clinical and criminological studies had early identified a variety of persons who had sex with both men and women, but whose conduct seemed unlike what was described in the language of psychoanalysis as typical of true, obligatory, or exclusive homosexuals. In contrast, Kinsey treated bisexuals as unproblematic. He saw them simply as persons who had sex with both men and women and considered their conduct well within the biological potential for sexual action (Kinsey, Pomeroy, and Martin 1948). From this perspective, bisexual conduct did not seem to express some underlying pathology or personality type, though there were social contexts or periods in the life course when a mixture of same- or opposite-gender sexual partners appeared more likely.

Later ethnographic work and interviews with convenience samples of various kinds (that is, unsystematic collections of volunteers) identified a very wide variety of persons as having had sex with both men and women as a result of their social and cultural contexts. A number of investigators identified a group of young men who for money or gifts had sex with older men (Reiss 1961). Some of these young men were delinquents; others were in military service and away from home; others were down on their luck. All had sexual relationships with young women. The investigators found other young men, including those who had sex with young women as well as those whose sexual desires were more exclusively directed toward men, operating in the world of male prostitution, selling themselves on a regular basis to other men and living in a demimonde marginal to the more conventional world around them. This was a complex world involving a system of prostitution not unlike that of women prostitutes—prostitution on the street, in bars, on the phone; call boys and male companions who were supported like mistresses. Unlike these groups were the men in prison who had sex with other incarcerated men. Here the mixture of motives was certainly as complex as similar patterns in the community. For many men, sex in prison with men was simply a surrogate for sex with women in the free world and often met the same psychological need for dominance and control (Gagnon and Simon 1973, chap. 8).

In addition to these groups of men there was still another that was far more difficult to study: men with entirely secretive sexual lives with other men. This included those who were married and had families but had anonymous sex with other men in public places (baths, parks, and public toilets) (Humphreys 1972). These men did not participate in the homosexual community except as sexual transients, often when out of town and in anonymous public settings. Such men surfaced on the police blotter and in little scandals that broke up families or resulted in therapeutic interventions. In more recent times at least some of these men have worked out new adjustments, some joining the gay community while attempting to continue relations with their former wives and children. Few studies of this population exist, and while it is suspected to exist in minority communities as well as among the white majority, it is only on white men that research has been conducted.

During the late 1960s concern about bisexuals as a potential new social type appeared in the literature (Duberman 1974; Schwartz and Blumstein 1977). Some persons who had had sex with both men and women reported that they had done so because they enjoyed sex with people of both genders and because the satisfactions they received from one gender were not equivalent to those they received from the other. In the sexually experimental climate of the times, bisexuality became a way for some to try out several identities. These persons argued that their interest in sex with people of both genders was not a way station from heterosexuality to homosexuality or from homosexuality to heterosexuality. As large numbers of gay men and lesbians were interviewed in the early and mid-1970s, it became evident that substantial proportions of the groups had been married and that many (particularly lesbians) were raising children. Bisexuality was becoming one of the increasing possibilities of sexual adjustment. The research literature of the period began to depict these new patterns as the development of new sociosexual identities in a changing world.

With the onset of the AIDS epidemic, bisexual men who were having sex with men very quickly became identified as a potential bridge for infection from the community of gay men. Given this early concern, it is not clear why research on bisexual transmission has been so spotty. A study of women with partners known to have had sex with men, based on a variety of case-collection methods (newspaper advertisements, notices in sexually transmitted disease clinics, friends of friends), was initiated in California and still continues as a research and education effort (Padian et. al. 1987). It was this study that early identified seroconversions among women who had had anal sex with partners who had had sex with other men. In the cohort studies of gay men, undertaken to determine the rates of seroconversion, specialized studies have not been conducted on men having sex with both men and women. One study of black men in San Francisco reporting sexual experience with both men and women is in its early stages (Peterson 1989). None of these studies has been undertaken to understand sexual phenomena, but rather to measure the risk of seroconversion and the effectiveness of prevention efforts. Such purely AIDS-driven work does not provide any estimate of the numbers in any population group who are having sex with both women and men and forces researchers to follow outbreaks of the epidemic rather than to anticipate its course.

As the AIDS epidemic has evolved, two additional patterns of bisexuality have become especially salient. While these have been noted in minority communities in the United States, the patterns are not unique to these communities. One pattern is based on a larger cultural pattern in which gender divisions are profound and in which men who prefer to have sex with men are socially defined as "women" in men's bodies. This pattern is common in Latin America and many regions of the Mediterranean basin. In this culture (now including some U.S. groups of Hispanic origin), a man who has sex with women is a man, a man who inserts his penis in a man partner remains a man, but the man who is receptive is socially defined as a woman. The inserter (the "activo") is a man; the insertee (the "passivo") is a woman (Carrier 1976). The complex of general cultural values is the frame for this kind of bisexuality, and other social groups in the United States share it. Since such men do not think of themselves as homosexuals, they are not accessible to programs of behavior change aimed at gay men.

If the first pattern is based on an accentuated difference between women and men, the second pattern is based on minimizing the distinctions between the objects of desire and increasing the importance of the impulse. This is a pattern the research subjects have described as "messing around." While this pattern has been recently identified among some black men, it also appears in other groups of men as well (particularly when they are in all-male contexts). There is an indifference to the gender of the sexual partner under various conditions, which include drinking, drug use, and feeling sexually aroused after an evening of unsuccessful sexual pursuit of women when sexual pursuit is restricted by fatigue, lack of time, or income. Women are preferred, but men are acceptable under certain conditions. "Getting your rocks off" or "getting your ashes hauled" is traditional men's argot for sexual contacts which do not involve affective involvement and which are motivated by a desire indifferent to its object. In these circumstances the form that questions might take in eliciting information about such experiences from men is fairly ambiguous.

Bisexuality represents as serious a scientific problem to the sex research driven by the AIDS epidemic as it did to sex research from psychoanalysis onward. It resists being easily categorized so that one cannot develop a singular protocol either for the study of disease transmission or for the control of the disease. As a consequence, the various types of diverse conduct that are covered by the label will be of interest only so long as they appear to have some relevance to the control of disease spread. If there does not appear to be any major risk of transmission to those who are currently uninfected in a specific bisexual subgroup (e.g., hustlers, prisoners, closeted men, activos), research concern with that subgroup will disappear. If on the other hand such behavior turns out to be important in the spread to the currently uninfected, efforts at funding and control will increase, but probably in fairly clumsy ways exactly because of the social and cultural diversity of these subgroups.

Nearly all these forms of bisexuality have a future. Only a few appear to be particularly important in disease transmission (though this impression may rest more on scientific ignorance than evidence), and these result from the use of sexual techniques that have been responsible for transmission primarily among gay men. Thus, the youth who provide sex for pay or gifts (now often runaways or throwaway children), the married men who have closeted sexual lives with other men, activos in the Hispanic community, and men who just "mess around" may be potential bridges for infection to sexual partners. If transmission is more efficient in frequent passive anal intercourse, then it is those with this practice who are particularly at risk.

The Prostitution of Women

The possibility that women who have sex with men for pay might transmit the HIV virus was recognized once the sexual character of transmission was identified. (The likelihood that these women might be infected by customers seemed less significant to researchers.) The number of sexual partners a woman prostitute has varies according to her occupational niche and the social class she serves. In general, she makes only limited discrimination among partners. The frequency of the use of barrier contraceptives was unknown, though it was suspected not to be very common and that customers could eliminate the use of a condom by paying more. With the advent of AIDS, and given the numbers of unknowns about transmission, the woman prostitute (and by extension, the sexually very active woman) quickly became a group about which considerable concern was expressed.

Complicating this public health interest was the fact that prostitution in the United States is nearly everywhere against the law and in most places primarily managed by the criminal justice system. The conditions surrounding the prostitution of women are all socially marginalizing forces: the occupation is illegal and dangerous; it is associated with drug use; the workers are exploited (there are no OSHA rules); and most come from the ranks of the unskilled, the poor, and racial minorities (Gagnon 1968; James 1977). No wonder the data needed for conclusive research were not available.

What was available came from the police and the health agencies, from reports on sexually transmitted disease and intermittent journalistic studies (some of quite high quality), and from relatively rare ethnographic reports of social scientists and the autobiographies of prostitutes. The study of the prostitution of women languished in the social sciences following World War II. After the Kinsey reports provided evidence on the decline in the rates at which middle-class men went to prostitutes between the two World Wars, the systematic study of women's prostitution as part of either the sexual economy or the money economy became limited to a very small number of noncumulative studies. A revival of interest in prostitution came with the growth of feminist scholarship and the intense debate among feminists and between feminists and sex workers (as prostitutes came to label themselves) about the legitimacy of women's labor in the sex industry (Delacoste and Alexander 1987). This is an issue that has yielded a new perspective on sex work, linking it in one direction to work of women in the industries connected with sex appeal, e.g., modeling, exotic dancing, acting, and in another direction to the similarity between sex for pay and sex for love and marriage in a patriarchal society. Unfortunately, this debate has yielded far more scholarly historical research and intellectual polemic than it has research about contemporary sex work.

Immediately after the onset of the epidemic there was a hue and cry about the dangers of transmission of HIV from women who provided sex for pay, and in a number of jurisdictions there were implementations of the police power to test for HIV seropositivity among sex workers or to otherwise constrain sex for pay—constraints imposed entirely on women. The initiatives were taken without any evidence at all to support them, and in some cases the AIDS epidemic appeared to be used as an opportunity to impose moral values under the guise of disease control.

At this time the Centers for Disease Control undertook a collaborative study of HIV seroprevalence among women who had sex for pay in a number of sites around the country. The research itself was somewhat rough and ready in its methodology (recruitment to the convenience samples differed from site to site, the quality of interviewing varied, and the interview instrument was disease driven). However, the data gathered on HIV seroprevalence was remarkably consistent. Most of the women in the study who were HIV positive were also intravenous drug users, and of the women who were not intravenous drug users, few were HIV positive. There is no evidence that there has been a sudden increase of HIV disease in the clients of prostitutes in this country, in contrast to what we know of prostitution in Africa (Darrow et. al. 1987; Turner, Miller, and Moses 1989). While the Centers for Disease Control study focused primarily on women who worked in public locations (except for bordello workers in Las Vegas) and therefore does not represent women who work with a more affluent clientele in off-street locations, it is likely that the findings of the study can be generalized to these groups as well.

A number of factors might account for these findings, some of which are relevant to the disease process and some to prostitution. First, a good deal of the sexual contact between customers and prostitutes may be oral sex, which appears to be a far less efficient way to transmit the virus than vaginal or anal sex. Second, there is some evidence that many sex workers have their clients use condoms and that this practice may be increasing, at least in sites where there is an education program and women have control over their work conditions (Cohen et. al., 1988; Day, et. al. 1988). Third, it may be that heterosexual transmission depends on multiple exposure to those who are very ill with HIV disease or on the presence or the aftereffects of other sexually transmitted diseases.

On the other hand it is not impossible that the infection might be beginning in other groups of women who have sex for pay but do not use intravenous drugs, particularly in individuals with histories of HIV cofactors, such as sexually transmitted diseases. An upsurge in other such diseases among these women might contribute as a cofactor to HIV transmission, as it has in Africa (Piot et. al. 1987). Given the apparent limitation of HIV infection among prostitutes in the United States to those who are also intravenous drug users, the transmission of HIV out of these groups seems to result more from drug-related than from sex-related behavior.

The occupation of prostitution and its role in the sexual economy do not appear to be affected by the AIDS epidemic. If evidence shows that sexual transmission is fairly uncommon in this group, research interest in AIDS will decline in Western societies. Business will not be quite as usual—condom use may increase, sexually transmitted disease rates may fall—but sex work will remain the temporary occupation of unskilled working-class and minority women. Whatever changes are observed in erotic or occupational characteristics of prostitution will depend more on the efforts of sex workers and feminists to transform its legal and symbolic status than on the epidemic. The epidemic will affect only the lives of prostitutes who use intravenous drugs. Since the evidence that the disease spreads from these women to their clients is small, residual interest is likely to focus on the regular sexual partners of drug-using women, partners who are drawn from the same social milieu.

The Endangered Young

The best-documented area of sexual life since the Kinsey reports has been the changing sexual lives of adolescents and young adults, particularly those of young women. One of the critical findings of the Kinsey research, and one of the most publicized, was that half the married women interviewed by the Kinsey team had had intercourse before marriage. Many commentators seized on this fact as evidence of the general moral collapse of the society. In the early 1950s there was an intense debate about the dangerous effects of petting on the young. What was most interesting about the Kinsey data was the degree to which this intercourse was truly premarital, that is, that the majority of the young women linked sex to getting married. Half of these young women engaged in intercourse only with the men they ultimately married, and only a small proportion reported having intercourse before marriage with more than five partners (Kinsey et. al. 1953).

What these findings signaled was that a new role for sex had developed as an integral part of the mate-selection process. Sexual activity between two young persons who were in love was evidence to each that the relationship was truly intimate. The willingness of a young woman to have sex with a man was a measure of emotional commitment, and the man in turn was expected to recognize the seriousness of this transition in the relationship. This pattern developed in the new middle-class after the turn of the century and became a national norm after the Second World War. It was expected, though not entirely approved, that young people would pair off, fall in love, and have certain levels of sexual intimacy appropriate to their age group and closeness to marriage. There was always some variability in this process and some risk for those who were too sexually "advanced" at early ages. However, this was the expected pattern during most of the baby boom from 1946 to 1964, when early marriage was characteristic.

A large number of sociological studies recorded the existence of this pattern among the young and focused particularly on the correlates of what was then called premarital permissiveness (Reiss 1960, 1967). For nearly two decades American sociologists investigated the conditions under which young people believed it was appropriate to have intercourse. They found that boys were in general more permissive than girls but that there was an increasing convergence between the genders toward a common standard of permissiveness with affection, that young people felt that love justified intercourse, particularly as they approached an appropriate age for marriage. The few studies that actually asked about the prevalence of premarital intercourse still found a substantial difference between the experience of young men and that of young women. Far more of the men reported engaging in premarital intercourse than did young women. From 1950 to 1970 the proportion of young women who had intercourse early in life increased slowly but significantly, and the close link between first intercourse and marriage eroded further. Having intercourse before marriage and after falling in love replaced the traditional expected sequence of pairing off, falling in love, marrying, and then having intercourse.

The social changes of the late 1960s along with the coming of age of the first wave of the baby boom, an increase in age of first marriage, and the sexual revolution as represented by the mass media accelerated the adoption of this new pattern. From 1965 to 1975 appears to have been the critical period. Studies conducted prior to 1969 suggest that there was a steady increase over the 1960s in the proportion of young women who had intercourse during their late teenage years. Studies undertaken in the first years of the 1970s and continuing into the 1980s reported a sharp increase in numbers of young women having intercourse before age twenty (indicating that the average age of first intercourse had sharply declined) and that the numbers of coital partners for these young women had increased (Cannon and Long 1971; Chilman 1978; Clayton and Bokemeier 1980). The data were often not as detailed as might be desired, but they were consistent. By the early 1980s some 75 to 80 percent of young woman had had intercourse before marriage, with some two to three sexual partners (Hofferth, Kahn, and Baldwin 1987). At the same time the evidence was that intercourse in early and mid-teen relationships were actually quite infrequent and that frequent and regular coitus appeared in the late teens and early adulthood. This increase in youthful sexual activity was widespread, though class and racial differences remained. Young women of middle-class origins started intercourse later than did those from less advantaged classes, and young white women started intercourse later and had fewer partners than young black women.

What makes this picture incomplete is the lack of data on young men. Sex research on young people during the 1970s was nearly entirely driven by the serious problem of adolescent pregnancy. In spite of the existence of effective contraception, the access of the young to contraception was neither universal nor easy, and the numbers of children born to unwed teenagers in all social groups grew rapidly during the decade (Hofferth and Hayes 1987; Jones et. al. 1980). A number of researchers found evidence of a steady convergence in the patterns of early heterosexual behavior among many young women and men, the young men accepting at least in part the necessity of an emotional relationship surrounding the sexual activity.

The data on the misadventures associated with this early sexual activity (unplanned pregnancies and births, sexually transmitted diseases, psychological trauma, sexual violence) indicated that young people in the 1980s were starting their sexual experience as ignorant of what it entailed as had their parents' generation. Starting earlier simply meant that more trouble could be expected. At the same time the increase in the age at first marriage meant that these early sexual experiences could not be automatically treated as truly premarital sex but now had to be addressed as part of growing up (Furstenberg 1982). Few contemporary young people (except the most naive) expect that a sexual relationship beginning in the mid-teens is very likely to result in marriage.

Complicating this picture has been the steady increase in cohabitation as a pattern of pairing off prior to marriage. For some young persons premarital sex may have transmuted into precohabitation sex. Increasing numbers of studies suggest that cohabitation is quite common among young persons and that while some of these cohabitations result in marriage, many of them dissolve. Living together (perhaps more than one time) has become part of marital partner selection (Bumpass and Sweet 1988; Willis and Michael 1988).

This was the developing picture of young adult sexuality when the AIDS epidemic was identified. Immediately there were fears that the epidemic would spread quickly among the young because of the evidence that while sex was common, caution was rare. Proposals were made to educate young people about the dangers of sex, especially those activities that were high in risk (e.g., anal sex), and to recommend the use of condoms to those who could not "just say no." This educational effort was immediately entangled in the preexisting debate about the appropriateness of sex education for the young, about who should teach the subject and what its content and goals should be. Despite studies to the contrary, many have believed that sex education increases rather than inhibits sexual activity among the young. It has been argued, correctly, that abstinence among the unmarried and sexual fidelity in marriage would be a perfect mechanism for reducing disease transmission. That the social changes required to produce these results would be extremely difficult to inculcate in the general population has not been understood, however. Because so many propose abstinence as a solution to contemporary sexual problems, it would be useful to identify the social changes necessary to inducing all members of the society to adopt the traditional sexual lifestyle.

Many national agencies are now engaged in school-based AIDS education, but if the past is any guide, the results in the classroom will be highly variable.[4] Educational programs must pass muster at many levels (the state, the school district, the school, parent groups), and each level will modify the program in various ways. Whether even the threat of HIV disease will change a situation in which nonjudgmental and complete information about sexuality can be given to young people in age-appropriate ways is unknown. Given the paucity of curriculum and trained teachers, future education seems like more of the same. Education for youth who are out of school can be explicit, but they are hard to reach. AIDS education for those of college age is likely to be sporadic simply because it is neither required as part of the college curriculum nor provided as a matter of course in the environment.

Efforts to provide accurate information about AIDS and HIV disease are in competition with both the mass media and the everyday sociosexual life of the young. The mass media now include many more references to sex than even two decades ago. Homosexuality as well as vaginal, oral, and anal sex and the role of safer sex in reducing disease transmission are regular topics. Television and theatrical films are remarkably explicit about sex, and TV soap operas are now based nearly entirely on nefarious sexual adventures. What would have been evidence for the fall of our American Rome in the 1950s is now accepted as part of our culture. The content of sex education as it relates to desire has become the responsibility of the mass media. The onset of the AIDS epidemic has simply intensified the preexisting public discussion of the sexual.

It seems very unlikely that the shape of adolescent and young adult sexuality will be fundamentally changed by the AIDS epidemic as it is being currently played out. Only the most optimistic think that the impact of AIDS on the sexual behavior of the young will be very great, except in some degree to encourage the use of condoms. The inertia against changing social practices will blunt the effectiveness of directed education

---

4. The School Health Education to Prevent the Spread of AIDS (SHEPSA) program is part of the Office of School Health and Special Projects of the Center for Health Promotion and Education of the Centers for Disease Control. It has created collaborative programs with national educational organizations as well as with state and local education agencies and has funded the development and dissemination of AIDS-relevant educational materials since early 1987. How these efforts will fare at the classroom level awaits assessment.

efforts as well as the impact of representations of AIDS in the mass media. Young people are far more influenced by each other and by the sexual practices current in their environment than they are by what adults tell them. Influencing their conduct will require a major effort to confront young people about their current sexual behavior and recognizing that telling them to just say no is unlikely to have much effect.

The research programs under way among young people are largely aimed at assessing the current state of their conduct (whether they are having sex and how often) and evaluating the impact of educational programs. None of these studies will illuminate very clearly the processes of psychosexual development and the ways in which sexuality comes to play an important role in the lives of young people in U.S. society.

Drugs and Sex

"AIDS, Sex and Drugs: Don't Pass It On" is an advertisement posted in both English and Spanish on the New York subways. Illustrating this message is a picture of a man and woman joined face to face into one body inside a syringe. Out of the needle comes a stream of blood that ends in a blob, inside of which there is a fetus. While not explicitly showing the most common sequence of transmission, which begins with the sharing of needles during intravenous drug use, continues in sexual transmission to a partner, and eventually results in transmission to the infant, the advertisement presents the problem dramatically. Immediately after the realization that the HIV virus (not known to be the cause of AIDS at that time) was appearing in intravenous drug users, primarily members of racial and ethnic minorities, epidemiological studies quickly identified needle sharing as the source of transmission. Secondary sexual transmission appeared to be very likely, and serious concern was expressed about transmission to sexual partners who were not drug users, and then from those partners into populations at lower risk. It remains difficult in many cases to disentangle whether transmission is a result of sharing needles or sexual activity since many of the sexual partners of intravenous drug users also use drugs and may share needles. There is, however, firm evidence of independent, though variably efficient, vaginal transmission of the virus.

The intravenous drug user is perhaps the most marginal figure in the AIDS epidemic. Most intravenous drug users are black or Hispanic. Many of them live in poverty on the edges of urban life. They fill the prisons and jails and are usually described as weak-willed, pleasure-seeking hedonists, unable to control themselves, willing to do anything for a fix, unreliable when offered treatment. In the fifteen years before the opening phase of the epidemic, New York had estimated that it had 200,000 intravenous drug users, but drug-treatment programs had ossified and no new treatment slots were being created. Waiting lists were long and programs unevaluated. The drug-use problem was securely in the hands of the criminal justice system. Public concern about drugs rose and fell with media campaigns, and those mugged or burglarized complained, but with little consequence. Drug use was one of the accepted miseries of urban life.

When the epidemic began, interest in the intravenous drug user suddenly surged and focused on the danger of needle sharing and on the availability of treatment (Turner, Miller, and Moses 1989, chap. 4). As the AIDS-drug agenda has evolved, concern has grown about the sexual conduct of drug users. Studies have been initiated, but little data have been published. At this moment, interest in behaviors that promote transmission and in educating persons to use safer sex procedures shapes nearly all data-gathering efforts.

In the past, continuous heroin or other opiate use was believed to inhibit sexual activity, particularly for men. This belief was based on only a small amount of unsystematic data. There was some evidence that women who were intravenous drug users worked as prostitutes to support their addiction (and perhaps the habits of their steady partners as well as their children). With the advent of crack has come anecdotal reports of young women exchanging sex for drugs. In extreme cases, young women stay in crack houses and have sex with a large number of men in order to keep up a supply of drugs. Until systematic research on these practices is conducted, it is reasonable to be cautious in drawing conclusions about the extent of their use and the aphrodisiac potential of crack and cocaine.

The recognition that intravenous drug users have steady affectional and sexual partners as well as families may well be one of the most important discoveries resulting from attempts to intervene in sex-related transmissions. Like most persons who live on the social margin, intravenous drug users usually have conventional social relationships in which they spend a good part of their lives. These relationships are attenuated by the exigencies of drug use (and now by HIV disease among those who are infected), but they often rebound during periods of nonuse.

Class, ethnic, race, and religious influences will no doubt alter the sexual practices of intravenous drug users as well as those of the rest of society. Drug users may turn out not to be such strangers to the rest of the society if we examine the ways in which their behavior overlaps that of the majority, who do not use intravenous drugs. In the absence of large-scale policy changes, however, many drug users will be infected with HIV. Most will die. To wish for AIDS to solve the problem of intravenous drug use is to ignore the steady recruitment of new users (and perhaps new needle sharers) over the course of the epidemic.

"The Heterosexual Community"

Many of the efforts at disease control have been directed at preventing HIV transmission into the heterosexual segment of the population, often mislabeled "the heterosexual community." This misnomer conceals the fact that heterosexuals are not organized into a community based on their sexuality. Heterosexuality is taken for granted. Most men who desire women and most women who desire men do not think of themselves as heterosexuals. The troubles they have with sex are sexual troubles, not heterosexual troubles, though it might be helpful if they began to think of such troubles as having their basis in their heterosexuality.

Persons can be heterosexual in many ways. Just as studies of gay men and lesbians have come to be studies of homosexualities, the study of heterosexuality needs to be reinterpreted as the study of a wide variety of sexual lifestyles. There is a tendency to see heterosexuality as having a life of its own, expressed in adolescence, in marriage, during divorce, and in old age. It may be fruitful to see heterosexuality as a dependent variable serving different social and psychological needs when it is expressed, for example, among young people, those in coupled relationships, those having sexual activity concurrent with a primary relationship, or those providing sex for pay. These relationships have different scripts. While the sexual object is constant, little else of importance may be.

Heterosexuality varies across social strata and social networks. Sexual practice between men and women is influenced by class, race, ethnicity, and religion, as well as by marriage, children, divorce, health, and occupation. The Kinsey studies probably demonstrated only one finding about which there could be no doubt: that the variation of sexual expression in the United States was nearly entirely controlled by social factors (gender, class, religion, education, and marital status). Thinking about heterosexuality in these ways creates a far more formidable task for research than does a more traditional perspective, which sees heterosexuality as an undifferentiated essence waiting to be expressed.

The Kinsey group had asked a wide variety of questions about sexuality and set a standard for coverage of sexual items that has not been matched since. While coverage was extensive, however, it was often not intensive. Kinsey reported that a large proportion of those divorced had intercourse in the post- or intermarital periods, but beyond incidence, frequency, and sometimes the number of partners, there was little reported on the relation of that sexual activity to the process of divorcing and reconstituting new relationships. The Kinsey reports made similar limited findings about extramarital and marital sex but did not relate them to other factors.

In the period between the Kinsey studies and the early 1980s a wide variety of studies was undertaken to examine the role and importance of sex during marriage, in marital dissolution, and in recoupling and having second families. These studies show that sequential patterns of cohabitation, marriage, divorce, and remarriage are now normative in our society. Sexual activity moves from the relatively constant, when persons are in relationships, to the relatively inconstant, when those relationships break up. Between couple relationships there is an increase in sexual partnering as persons eagerly seek new relationships. A number of important social forces underpin this pattern, forces very unlikely to be countered by the current pressure of the AIDS epidemic.

As excellent as some of the research studies are that outline this trend, it would be hard to argue that there existed a systematic and reliable body of sample-based quantitative data on any of these processes at the time the epidemic was recognized. The epidemic has now posed its own questions about the structure of sexual relations among the heterosexual majority. These questions are quite different from those posed by researchers in the prior three decades. Earlier researchers on extramarital sex were concerned about how such conduct affected the stability of marriage, the logistics of affairs, and the psychological impact of infidelity. They also attempted to estimate the prevalence of extramarital sex, numbers of partners, and frequency of sex in relationships, but such studies were rare and based on adventitious collections of respondents (Atwater 1982; Reiss 1983 ; Thompson 1983; Bell, Turner, and Rosen 1975). It was exactly these questions of prevalence, number, and frequency on which the epidemiologists focused, for this was the information that would be predictive of whether the virus would spread in these populations. How many partners people had and how often they had sex together over some period of time was the kind of data needed for predicting the course of the AIDS epidemic in the general population.

In addition the epidemiological modelers needed data on the structure of sexual networks in the society (Turner, Miller, and Moses 1989, chaps.

1 and 2). Who has sex with whom is a question of social structure, since persons do not mate randomly. Depending on how precise the data needed for the differing models may be, it becomes important to know numbers of sexual partners, frequency of sexual activity, and sexual techniques in each type of contact, as well as the social attributes of sexual partners. How much interracial sexual contact is there, and how constrained by social class and religion is sexual partnering? Is sexual contact in or out of stable and monogamous relationships, and does it involve more or less risky sexual techniques? Are the patterns different for male-male sexual relationships in contrast to female-male contacts? Are there differences between relationships for pay and relationships with one-time or casual partners?

Such questions direct research interest away from the image of the sexual individual to the sexual transaction between two or more individuals (Laumann, Gagnon, and Michael 1987, 170). Even more than the Kinsey approach, such research emphasizes the social dimensions of sexual conduct and the ways in which microsocial networks organize and offer opportunities for sexual activity. The interest in AIDS has stimulated an alternative image of the ways in which sexual life is organized. Prior network approaches to the study of needle exchange, social support, friendship, and scientific influence have now extended to major studies of sexual conduct. The needs of the epidemic have thus produced an alternative approach to the study of sexuality.

Studies of the general population are now being undertaken, as are specialized studies of minorities. Such studies will not begin to yield data until the early part of 1990 or later. There is evidence from some surveys that household sample surveys are yielding lower prevalences of sexual conduct than have other surveys based on convenience samples (Fay et. al. 1989; Michael et. al., 1988). If these preliminary data are correct, it may well be that the U.S. society displays less sexual behavior than previously thought and that the collective representations of sexuality in the mass media are far more erotic than the lives of those who see these representations.

At this moment we have not learned a great deal about the sexual life of the general population from AIDS-generated research. We are at the front edge of such studies, and while many will be more narrowly focused, others will attempt to map the larger terrain of sexual life in the United States at the end of the twentieth century. In the absence of such data it most reasonable to adopt the strategy of the weatherman and say that tomorrow's sexuality in the general population will look much like today's.

Conclusion

As with all continuing problems it is difficult to offer final conclusions about the relation between sexuality and the AIDS epidemic. If the epidemic maintains its present course in the United States, it is most likely to become primarily a disease of the poor and minorities. The virus will be transmitted more commonly in populations that are already burdened by many health and social problems, and there may be some relatively infrequent infections of other segments of the population through sexual activity and shared needles.

The impact on the sexual life of the society will largely be restricted to reshaping the lives of gay men so that they will tend to live as couples in a less erotic way of life. Anal sex has already become less common and less a marker of the boundary of gay identity. The research programs that have been conducted in the gay community have largely been devoted to disease issues and are less often relevant to gay identity and gay community life. The record of the impact of AIDS on gay life is far more likely to be found in small-scale studies in the intellectual gay press, and in novels and autobiographies.

It is unclear how the epidemic will affect the sexual conduct of either bisexuals or women in the sex industry. AIDS-driven studies of these population groups in the sex industry have usually not directly addressed issues of desire and occupation. In some studies of minority men who have sex with both men and women, the concern has been to find cultural determinants of sexual conduct. In a few studies of women prostitutes there has been an effort to understand their lives as part of an occupational milieu managed largely by men. In some of these studies research and education have been based on understanding that these women often have children, lovers, leisure time, parents, and nonprostitute work histories. Not much further research on prostitutes is to be expected, though additional research is likely to be conducted on bisexuals because of a potential danger to the blood supply.

HIV is primarily a threat to the young via intravenous drug use and sexual relations with users who are infected. It is not clear whether middle-class or otherwise conventional young people are in grave danger of infection. Education to reduce risky behavior is unlikely to eliminate much sexual activity, though the use of condoms may make a comeback in youthful populations. If so, it will have the beneficial consequences of reducing pregnancy and the transmission of other sexually transmitted diseases. It is extremely unlikely that there will be major reductions of numbers of sexual relationships among the young even by the most determined AIDS education programs. Young people may get more accurate information about sex as a result of AIDS these days, and their sexual lives may be better chronicled and perhaps better understood than before, but making behavior change effective is only a hope.

The greatest promise for AIDS education lies in working with targeted groups in clinical settings where health services to those most at risk are delivered—drug treatment centers, family planning centers, health maintenance organizations, sexually transmitted disease clinics, emergency rooms. Even there, only limited goals can attempted—people may use condoms but are unlikely to stop having a number of sexual partners. The cycle of coupling, uncoupling, and recoupling is now accepted as the dominant sexual pattern in the United States. Changing it will take more social science understanding and political will than is likely to be mobilized. As long as the representations and the reality of the epidemic remain as they are, the trajectory of sexual change will remain much the same.

Doing good research may or may not lead to a more reasoned vision of sexuality in the lives of individuals and our culture, but we may be sure that without the knowledge this research would give us, that vision will be impossible.

Theorizing Risky Sex (2000)

Introduction

When the two words *sex* and *risk* are used together, as in the phrase "risky sex," they conjure up in most people's minds hazy visions of heedless individuals engaging in sexual practices that will put themselves and others at risk for the transmission of HIV and other STIs (sexually transmitted infections), inappropriate pregnancies among unmarried young people, and the extramarital sexual contacts of politicians. That this view is common in the populace should not be surprising since it has been widely promoted by a number of interested constituencies in cooperation with a pliant mass media, and it conforms with a widely held vernacular theory that sexual problems are caused by out-of-control individuals. One consequence of this promotion of "risky sex" as a cause of disease transmission and adolescent pregnancy has been the granting of a limited license for scientific inquiries into the nature of "risky sex," its causes and consequences, and the development of public policy to reduce its prevalence and thus the prevalence of the health and social problems that are believed to be consequent upon it. Such scientific inquiries are expected to include theories of risky sex to guide the collection and analysis of

Originally published in *The Role of Theory in Sex Research,* by John Bancroft (Bloomington: Indiana University Press, 2000), 149–76. Reprinted by permission. Support for this research was provided by the College of Arts and Sciences of the State University of New York at Stony Brook and a grant from the Ford Foundation. During the time this work was being completed the author was a consultant at the Center for Health and Policy Research.

data, and such theories are expected to be part of the basis for the selection of social policies.

The license that is given to theories, inquiries, and policies based on social science research is limited because other interested constituencies believe that the causes of "risky sex" are already well known and that certain policies, if diligently applied, will eliminate all sex that involves negative health and, more important, moral consequences. Such interested constituencies believe that sexuality does not need to be, indeed should not be, the object of scientific study. The existence of separate and equally important constituencies with quite different methods of theorizing sexual problems and with quite different policy proposals should alert us to the important political and ideological aspects of dealing not only with "risky sex," but with all issues relating to sexuality in the United States.

Contention between various groups interested in sexual matters needs to be understood as the cultural framework inside of which all troubles which seem to be associated with sex are theorized and defined as problems requiring solutions. One set of constituencies, primarily secular in their methods of solving sexual problems, look to the theory-constructing and fact-gathering procedures of various social science disciplines to provide the basis for social policies relevant to sexuality. The other set of groups, primarily religious in their orientation, use various dogmatic texts as the basis for theorizing about and dealing with sexual matters, and they pressure the state to conform to these "sacred texts" when public policies about sexual conduct are imposed.

That these groups are in contention about the appropriate ways to theorize and solve sexual problems and about the policies to be applied does not mean that they are not in agreement about various matters related to sexuality. Secular and sacred theorists often share the beliefs that certain sexual troubles are sexual problems and that the solution to those problems resides primarily in changes in individual conduct. Indeed, they share an underlying cultural theory about the nature of sexuality, though they use a somewhat different terminology to describe the origins and expression of sexual conduct.

Sacred and secular conflict about sexuality is rooted in the historical and cultural development of the United States and is present in all contemporary public debates about all aspects of sexual life. That is, it is not possible to have a public policy debate about "risky sex"; pornography; child abuse; sex before, outside of, between, and after marriage; sexual techniques; and so forth without this conflict being engaged. This same conflict is also present in discussions of the proper role of women in society and issues of reproduction and family life.[1]

It is possible for a purely secular scientific discussion of the sexual to go forward in the United States only by ignoring or setting aside discussion of the attitudes of dominant religious traditions toward the sexual. Even as such points of view are desacralized by being treated as secular data for purposes of scientific inquiry (i.e., the measure of serious religious belief may be tapped by survey questions that ask about "frequency of church attendance," "devoutness of religious feeling," or whether a respondent has been "born again"), such points of view must be engaged as social realities when public policies are proposed. Indeed, it is the secularization of religious belief as just another belief system by the relativistic social sciences that fundamentally conflicts with notions of a sacred and transcendent realm of sexual meanings and values.

Even though there is a cleavage between the sacred and scientific theorizing of the sexual, the secular traditions themselves cannot be treated as a uniform and coherent body of theories, methods, and findings. It should be recognized that within the secular scientific study of sexuality there are profound conflicts between the disciplinary entities that claim the right to study and, in some cases, manage sexuality. These conflicts are both methodological and theoretical and as a consequence different disciplines treat different sexual troubles as problems and propose different solutions for them. Perhaps the penultimate cleavage in the sciences (the ultimate cleavage is between dogma-based and data-based explanations of the sexual) is between theories of sexual life based on nature or nurture, between the biology of the organism or the social and cultural environment. This contemporary debate has been shaped by the century-long conflict between theorists within biology and medicine who have emphasized the priority of reproduction and the importance of innate sexual drives or impulses in the organization of sexual activity and by theorists who have emphasized the role of nonreproductive purposes in sexuality and the priority of culture and society in determining the organization of sexual conduct. This debate has theoretical aspects, but it is primarily about the historical role of biology and medicine (now

---

1. There is a growing movement in academic circles (primarily in the humanities) to "theorize" sexuality independent of social science fact gathering (which these humanists treat as ideologically suspect). This movement is also antidogmatic as well as antiempirical, which places them in a third intellectual position with reference to sexual theorizing. The existence of postmodernists complicates only the lives of secularists, because of their place in the academy.

biomedicine) in supporting the repression of sexual diversity and in constituting most aspects of sexuality as illnesses.[2]

The practice of theorizing about sex exists in an arena of conflict within separate secular disciplines, between secular scientific disciplines, and between the secular scientific tradition and other contenders for the right to manage our sexual lives. Theorizing about sex is not an abstract process, separated in time and space from the messier aspects of social life, but is an ideological practice grounded in the conflicts of particular historical moments and cultural situations. One can act "as if" such theorizing is solely a scientific activity only at the price of increasing the problematic status of sexuality.

Is There a Problem in This Trouble?

What stance should we take toward a trouble when it is presented to us as a problem? The distinction made here is between something that is troubling (we wake up with a pain in our lower back) and our treating this trouble as the symptom of an identifiable problem (e.g., sciatica or arthritis), which requires that we do something about it (call a physician). The situation of a young girl having a baby out of wedlock is directly troubling to her, her family, the young man involved and his family, and perhaps to the baby and others implicated in the event. A young man dies of a new virus after having passive anal sex with a number of men partners. This is directly troubling to the young man, his sexual partners, his friends, his family, and a variety of others in his social network. Doing something about these troubles means identifying (in the taxonomic sense of classifying) the trouble as a specific type of problem and calling upon specific experts with expert knowledge (persons with theories) embedded in particular social institutions to provide a solution.

Clearly the first issue to be considered is whether this particular trouble should rise to the level of a problem. This choice is pretheoretical, at least in the formal sense that theory is used within a disciplinary context. However, a pretheoretical choice is a necessary step in the process of fully understanding the context in which disciplinary theorizing resides. What I am expressing here is a recognition that this theoretical choice is

2. A deeper and more profound cleavage can be found between the social sciences and sociobiology, a cleavage that is not precisely the same as nurture and nature and lies between an emphasis on proximate causes (whether they be biological or social) and an emphasis on what are called ultimate causes (which are based on evolutionary principles or the primacy of the gene). A full analysis of the religious character of neo-Darwinian thought in its provision of a guiding principle for human life has not yet been attempted.

part of a sequence of often unanalyzed decisions that lead to the assignment of "the trouble as problem" to a specific disciplinary matrix. These pretheoretical choices are essential to understanding the larger social situation in which "theory" is elaborated and applied.

This first choice requires a certain amount of delicacy, perhaps even caution, since deciding that a trouble is a problem of a specific kind will unleash a whole series of theoretical, data-gathering, and policy consequences. This decision is often extrascientific because it involves asking two sorts of political or ideological questions: the first about individual and collective actors, the second about the cultural climate in which the translation from trouble to problem is made. The first sort of question is often ruled to be out of court or illegitimate or ad hominum within scientific discourse since these questions raise other questions about the motivations or interests (as individuals, members of social groups, or organizations) of those who have identified this trouble as a problem that merits a solution. The question of how the promoters of the problem (i.e., problem-identifying entrepreneurs) will profit (and not only in filthy lucre) must always be considered when public attention is called to "a problem that needs solution" (Nathanson 1991; Becker 1973).

The second sort of question is similar, but these questions focus on the cultural context in which the questions are formulated. A question such as "Do individuals vary in their propensities to engage in risky sexual conduct?" is already ideological. Why do we start with individuals and propensities? What is it about "individuals," "internal propensities," "risk," and "sex" that seem to go so naturally together? Is there a prejudice in the culture (note here my view that all cultural arrangements are prejudgments) that links together "individuals," "internal states," "sex," and "risk"? That is, is there a certain way that is good to think about these issues in the vernacular culture and the culture as represented by the media? Given the larger cultural prejudice about how to think about a question, is there then a particular "scientific" discipline that is more easily selected to think about this question because its prejudgments conform to the larger cultural prejudgments?

The question "Is this trouble a problem?" cannot be answered without asking "Who says that this trouble is a problem of a certain kind?" "What kind of a problem is it said to be?" and, if it is an ongoing problem, "Who has been previously authorized to provide a solution?" Any trouble, no matter how novel it appears to be, can be fitted into any previously existing problem-solving apparatus, since as soon as the trouble is assigned to such an apparatus, the apparatus will begin to shape the trouble into the kind of problem that it can manage. Even if a trouble would be better left alone or treated as a different kind of problem, the individuals and institutions which are assigned to deal with the trouble will turn it into a problem for which they have the tools.

The decision that certain kinds of troubles are problems is often taken too quickly; these troubles are usually assigned willy-nilly to individuals and institutions that appear to be appropriate.[3] It is rarely understood that the decision to assign a trouble to a particular problem-solving institution is not a neutral process, but one that ineluctably molds the trouble to conform to whatever problem the selected institution or discipline solves best. To choose whether troubling drug use is a crime problem or a health problem calls into play different social institutions with different problem-solving methods and capacities and different public constituencies and media representations (see the current debate over the efficacy of the War on Drugs). Similarly, to decide that a problem is appropriate to one or another scientific discipline elicits the kinds of prejudgments that constitute the cognitive and material bases for that scientific discipline. The decision that a particular trouble is a psychological, sociological, or economics problem results in calling forth the appropriate disciplinarian in the expectation that he or she will use their understandings of the world to solve the problem. To those armed with a hammer, the environment has nails in abundance.

This rule-bound response is necessary if there is to be a scientific discipline, that is, if advantage is to be taken of what Kenneth Burke once called the "bureaucratization of the imaginative" (Burke 1937). The only reason the scientific work of others is trusted is the belief that they have obeyed the rules of their discipline in designing instruments, in making observations, and in grounding their explanations. They must be disciplined members as well as members of a discipline. Shared instrumentation, observations, and explanations are what Thomas Kuhn labeled a *paradigm* (Kuhn 1970). A paradigm is more than a set of ideas; it is a set of stable social practices that come into play when a trouble is defined as a problem of a given kind appropriate to a certain discipline. It is thus more than a set of individual practices, it is a set of social practices (which include specific explanatory stories or narratives) that characterize an ongoing collectivity of actors.

Members of a scientific discipline tell disciplined stories (i.e., specific

---

3. Lee Clarke points out in his instructive study that a governmental building in New York State in which dioxins (carcinogenic substances) were spread into every nook and cranny by a fire was first assigned to the state agency which was responsible for building cleanliness. The agency promptly sent in unprotected janitors to sweep and dust because the problem was "cleanliness" rather than "decontamination" (Clarke 1989).

genres of tales) to each other about the problems of their disciplines in seminars, grant applications, peer-reviewed journals, and published books (Plummer 1995). Out of this constant chattering and scribbling a community of thought is sustained, something Ludwig Fleck seventy years ago called a "thought-collective" with a characteristic "thought-style" (Fleck [1935] 1979). Aspirants to membership in these scientific collectives are "disciplined" to conduct themselves in ways that their ancestors (i.e., mentors) behaved by attending graduate school and writing dissertations. The stories and practices that constitute the disciplines have large areas of agreement and some small areas of difference—what Kuhn labeled *normal science* (Kuhn 1970). Across divides of greater or lesser intellectual distance, scientific disciplines reproduce themselves and instruct their members about how to imagine the social world differently (it is the difference that creates the discipline). These disciplines are of course more than "thought-collectives," they are also departments, institutes, and centers with office space, names on doors, persons with differing ranks and honors, laboratories, assistants, grants, budgets—all of the material paraphernalia of job spaces. The "thought" and the stories are embodied in lives, in careers, in getting ahead, even in getting replaced. It is this shared thought and materiality that constitute the resistance to interdisciplinarity and to wild hypotheses.

However necessary these disciplines may be for normal science, they also need to be resisted, primarily because within these disciplines rests the power to construct a specific kind of problem out of a diffuse trouble. Once a trouble is defined as a problem appropriate to a discipline, there is a significant narrowing of the possibilities of thought. Hence in the opening moments, as a trouble is being turned into a problem, there should be a pause. A distinguished theoretician and field researcher in ecology, a field similar to sociology in the fundamentally historical character of its subject matter, once said that the most profitable way to think about troubles was analogous to untangling a knot in a line of rope. He said that, "The best procedure should be pick up the knot and gently shake it, the worst procedure would be pull aggressively on the loose ends" (Slobodkin 1972).[4] This metaphor is exactly right; once a tangle has been identified as a potential trouble, then it is best to proceed tentatively, perhaps

---

4. Professor Slobodkin has informed me that the correct quotation is: "To untangle a snarl, loosen all jams or knots and open a hole through the mass at the point where the longest end leaves a snarl. Then proceed to roll or wind through the center exactly as a stocking is rolled up. Keep the snarl open and loose at all times and do not pull at the end; permit it to unfold itself. As the process is continued the end gradually emerges. No snarl is too complicated to be solved by this method; only patience is required." It comes from Clifford W. Ashley, *The Ashley Book of Knots* (NY: Doubleday, 1944), 29, fig. 141.

even agnostically, to determine what kind of tangle you have in hand and how best to comprehend it.

This procedure of problem identification (in the sense of deciding there is a problem and what kind of problem it is) has parallels to the "holism" arguments of Kenneth Burke about essentializing and proportionalizing strategies in literary interpretation. He writes:

> The tendency in Freud is toward [the essentializing strategy]. That is, if one found a complex of, let us say, seven ingredients in a man's motivation, the Freudian tendency would be to take one of these as the essence of the motivation and to consider the other six as sublimated variants. We could imagine, for instance, manifestations of sexual impotence accompanying a conflict in one's relations with his familiars and one's relations at the office. The proportional strategy would involve the study of these three as a cluster. The motivation would be synonymous with the interrelationships among them. But the essentializing strategy would, in Freud's case, place the emphasis upon the sexual manifestation, as causal ancestor of the other two. The essentializing strategy is linked with a normal ideal of science: to explain the complex in terms of the simple. (Burke 1973, 261–62)

Burke goes on to point out that it is actually the complex which needs explaining, and it is unclear whether the complex can be reassembled from the simplified scientized bits. The level of organization of the problem may resist interpretations that break it into elementary parts or primitive relations. After we dissect the frog, we should not be surprised that it does not croak.

The process of untangling the knot by gently shaking it or resisting the impulse to interpret a complex problem in simple ways does not produce "theories," but it does express attitudes or stances toward what are offered to us as "problems" that need to be theorized. What these attitudes or stances entail, to use Burke again, is a "tolerance for ambiguity" (Burke 1936). Thus the first step in a process of theorizing or problem solving is to take a step backward, to disengage from the definition of the problem as first offered. The first questions should not be "What kind of a problem is this (according to my expertise) and what is the theory that is appropriate (according to my expertise)?" This is the equivalent to pulling vigorously on the free strands of the tangled rope, a choice that may lead to having to cut the resulting knot with a sword. Shaking the tangle gently is equivalent to asking some or all of the following kinds of questions: "Is this a problem?" "Who says so?" "What are their interests in defining this trouble a problem?" "What evidence do they provide that this is a problem?" "What solutions have they put forth?" "Who will profit from these solutions?" "Who is praised and who is blamed in the stories they tell about this problem?" The first response should be to problematize how the trouble was made a problem.

Disciplinary Theory and Concrete Circumstances

To properly understand the scientific question "Why do individuals vary in their propensities to engage in risky sex?" requires additional steps backward or, perhaps, sideways. In disciplinary terms this formulation is a psychological question; it concerns the conduct of individuals and will require the measurement of internal states of individuals. It falls directly into the tradition of individual difference research, that is, research which examines the differential response of individuals to what appears to be a common environmental circumstance. As a question in the mainstream of psychological imagining it is highly abstract, ahistorical, and acultural. The question is posed universally and makes number of assumptions about each of the elements in its question. It assumes that single individuals are proper units of assessment and the locus of agency, that propensities are the basis for conduct, that the calculus of risk can be measured, and that certain forms of sex are risky.

The problem as stated already invites a limited range of solutions, disciplinary and otherwise. It assumes a certain level of analysis; in Burke's terms, individuals and their propensities are the essentialized node of interpretation, the causal agents. Such an individualized interpretation, to use Ken Plummer's recent formulations, demands a certain kind of story in which the outcomes will be based on individual differences, either psychological or moral (Plummer 1995). Finally, the question conflates two important domains of action, both replete with historical and cultural implications—risk and sex. How immediately we are engaged with this question, in terms of personal biography (Who has not had sex? Who has not taken a risk?), career (Do our answers generate grants and promotions?), and the practices of our disciplines (How does what we know digest this problem?), suggests that we are on dangerous ground. Now is the time to take the step backward or sideways, to count to ten or a hundred, to become tentative.

Questions need to be raised about the question: Why do we want to explain or theorize the intersect between risk and sex? What persons have called our attention to the intersect between risk and sex, and what are their interests in doing so? The answers to these questions require lowering the level of abstraction, turning our attention away from the "experts" and their theorizing in quiet rooms, disturbed only by the hum of the fluorescent lights and computer fans, to the everyday world in which risk and sex appear to fuse together.

The problem of risk and sex as a secular scientific problem has been primarily generated by experts in public health (and other associated medical researchers), community activists, research funders, and other interested elites worried about the potential transmission of HIV. The concrete problem as specified by the psychologists, epidemiologists, and physicians who dominated the National Institutes of Health Consensus Panel on HIV Prevention is, "How do we understand and, by implication, prevent individuals, both infected and uninfected, from engaging in those forms of sexual conduct that are most likely to transmit HIV?" (National Institutes of Health 1997). The focus on "risk" of transmission or "risky behaviors" is in fact a novel formulation since it takes the prevalence or incidence of risky behaviors as a proxy for risk of transmission. Given the near-fatality of HIV/AIDS and the lack of treatments for AIDS (prior to the use of the new antiviral therapies in the 1990s), and the long delay between infection and mortality, it is not surprising that the proof of success in prevention has moved away from measuring the reduction in numbers of transmissions to the reduction of risky behaviors.

This decision was also influenced by the realities that new transmissions are rare in most regions in the United States, and to focus on hard-to-measure rare events would reduce the authority of the public health message. Measuring and reporting that reported condom use is rising or declining is far easier than measuring and reporting the rate of new infections that might be the result of that condom use or nonuse (or of other unmeasured variables). This represents a movement away from end-state measures of identifiable disease events (how many infections are prevented) to end-state behavioral measures that are often only weakly related to disease transmission. The success of the public health institutions concerned with HIV/AIDS in moving attention toward risky behaviors is part of a more general dependence in health research on the use of behavior change as a proxy for changes in rates of morbidity and mortality. This same question is asked by similar, but not overlapping, interest groups about risk and sexuality in young women (more rarely about young men): "How do we prevent young women from engaging in those risky forms of sexual conduct that are likely to result in pregnancy?"

This similarity in abstract problem formulation makes it appear that all of the players in these two arenas of problem identification and problem solving (HIV prevention and adolescent pregnancy prevention) have similar theories of why individuals take risks with their sexuality or what might be done to prevent these risky outcomes. However, those who "theorize" risk and sexuality in these two domains do so in the context of an ongoing political struggle about the meaning and value of sexuality itself. The concrete question (as opposed to the abstract question) asked by the public health/behavioral science/gay community constituencies in the area of HIV prevention is, "Why do some men who have sex with men and some injection drug users and their sexual partners differ from other persons in the same class of actors in their propensity to have unprotected penetrative sex (anal or vaginal sex) when they know that the risk of transmission of the HIV virus (and other STIs) is increased?" The concrete question asked by the parallel public health/population control community in the area of adolescent pregnancy prevention is, "Why do some young women differ from other young women in their propensity to have uncontracepted penile-vaginal sex when they know that the risk of unwanted pregnancy is increased?" (See any issue of the journal *Family Planning Perspectives*.) This concreteness can be increased by specifying that these questions are being asked about specific gendered, raced, and classed sets of actors in the United States in the 1990s whose sexual conduct has already been the subject of years of scientific, political, and ideological dispute.

These two formulations share a common moral presumption: that at least in some cases the sexual conduct is legitimate, that what makes the sex risky is the failure to take precautions. No member of the secular HIV/AIDS prevention constituencies argues that gay men should not have sex at all. While numbers of partners, oral sex, and drug use are often worrisome to certain absolute zero transmission constituencies, it is usually not that having sex is thought to be risky; it is the lack of precautions that creates the risk (i.e., driving is not risky, driving without a seatbelt or while drinking is risky). A somewhat different picture emerges among the public health/population control/adolescent health constituencies that are interested in preventing adolescent pregnancy. In this example youthful sex is usually viewed ambivalently, most often as an unpreventable, but rarely virtuous, aspect of young people's growing up. Abstinence would be best, it is often argued, but given that it is unlikely in many cases, successful contraception is better than unwanted births. Practically no one argues that an active sex life is a good in the lives of young people. Even the Sexuality Information and Education Council of the United States (SIECUS) says that it agrees with the idea of abstinence.

In this example "risky sex" is both the inability to avoid sex (which is defined as penile-vaginal intercourse) and the inability to use contraception that generates the risk.[5]

The other political and ideological contenders in the HIV and pregnancy prevention domains (i.e., conservative political and religious elites and their constituencies) agree that it is the individual with certain propensities who is at fault in the transmission of HIV and adolescent pregnancy. However, the risk is not the absence of precautions, but the doing of sex. Individuals who are unable to control their sexual impulses, either because they are somehow perverted (i.e., homosexuals) or are simply untutored in proper techniques of restraint (either this-worldly or other-worldly in origin), put themselves at risk of being damned as well as vulnerable to disease or pregnancy. Conservative elites, advocates for the traditional family, and members of the religious right (often the same individuals) focus on eliminating "deviant" sexuality. They argue, correctly, that once this goal is accomplished HIV transmission (as well as other STIs) and adolescent pregnancy will simply disappear. Even if those who are HIV positive do not behave safely in all instances, those infections would be eliminated in one generation under such a sexual regime.

To a remarkable degree these two major contenders in the struggles for HIV prevention share a number of theoretical cum ideological commonalities—it is the individual and his or her propensities that are at issue. In the minds of the public and the sexual health establishment is a question of rational versus irrational action: "Do individuals calculate risk properly according to the public health actuarial table, and do they act on that calculus?" Among the religious conservatives the problem is the issue of moral versus immoral action: "Do people properly observe the moral rules that should govern the sexual?" Both groups also agree that "sex" is hard to control and is often out of control—they differ, though not as much as one might think, about whether sex itself is a problem or a natural manifestation of human development.

The disciplinary theoretical question "Why do individuals differ in

5. The systematic use of "sex," "sexually experienced," and "sexually active" to refer only to vaginal intercourse and exclude the repertoire of other sexual techniques used by young people is a conceptual failure that demographers and others who manage teen pregnancy research share with everyday college students. Sanders and Reinisch (1999) report that many contemporary college students do not view oral sex as "real" sex. This emphasis on vaginal intercourse by experts and everyday folks as the primary goal of sexual relationships has unfortunate consequences. By making vaginal intercourse the only form of "real sex," demographers misunderstand the actual complexity of sexual practice in adolescence, and they contribute to the simplification of youthful sexuality in the public mind. Finally, by limiting considerations of sex to vaginal intercourse, the pleasures of nonvaginal sex as well as masturbation as alternative appropriate endpoints for sexual pleasure are undermined.

their propensities to engage in risky sex?" is thus directly abstracted from certain concrete situations involving everyday actors. "Why do gay men have unsafe penetrative sex with other men, which increases the likelihood of disease transmission?" "Why do injection drug users have unsafe penetrative sex with their sexual partners, which could result in disease transmission?" "Why do young men and women have uncontracepted sex, which could result in pregnancy?" What these questions have in common in terms of risk and sex is that the conduct of these individuals can be interpreted as the voluntary outcome of a ratiocinative process. Not conforming to the rational calculus of safe sex can be attributed to failures of learning, the interposition of other values or preferences, or irrationalities induced by sexual desires or behavior altering chemicals.

Not All Dangerous Sex Is "Risky Sex"

This theoretical connection that is made between "individuals," "propensities," "risk," and "sex" in the domains of HIV/AIDS and adolescent pregnancy cases would be more persuasive if such a connection were applied more generally to other areas of sexuality in which there are easily identified dangers.[6] However, in two other important areas of sexuality a previously held theoretical connection between individual agency and risky sexual conduct has been rejected. The first is in the explanations of sexual violence against women and girls (including sexual harassment), and the second is in the explanations of the sexual abuse of children and adolescents. In both of these areas prior explanations of at least some of these occurrences (described as "rape" and "child molestation" in the criminological literature) focused on the role of the woman or child in provoking these events. The question was posed: "What propensities make a woman or a child put themselves at risk for dangerous sex?" The resulting theoretical questions, which directly parallel the questions "Why do gay men differ among themselves in their propensity to engage in risky sex that transmits HIV?" and "Why do adolescent girls

6. In the area of sexuality perhaps the most dangerous sexual practices for women are sexual/affectional and reproductive relationships with men (Heise 1995). Women are in intermittent danger from men in sexual situations from adolescence to old age. As children and girls they are at risk from heterosexual men who molest them, as adolescents they are at risk from boys and men who force them to have sex or who have sex with them without protection from pregnancy or disease, and as adolescents and adult women they are in danger from men who assault them for sexual as well as nonsexual motives. Women are also sexually harassed in the workplace, face the dangers of childbirth as a result of sex with men, and are often left with their children as their spouses leave them to marry younger women. All of these assertions are easily documented, but none of them are interpreted by scientists as meaning that "heterosexuality" is a form of risky sex for women.

differ among themselves in their propensity to engage in risky sex that results in inappropriate pregnancies?" can no longer be asked.

Consider the following formulations: "Why do women and girls differ among themselves in their propensity to engage in or expose themselves to risky sex?" and "Why do children differ among themselves in their propensity to engage in sexual contacts with adults?" These are questions that are no longer good to think, though they were once thought regularly by scientists who published their research in the scientific literature, and they remain extant sexual theories in some vernacular cultures. In a recent edition of the *New York Times* there was a report of a gang rape of one twelve-year-old and two thirteen-year-old runaway girls by a group of twenty men in Fresno, California. It appears from the press report that the rape was planned. A young man who promised to drive the girls to their homes delivered them to a motel room where the other men were waiting. After the event reached the press, a rape crisis center reported receiving the following calls: "The director [of the center] . . . said people had called her office asking if the girls had been wearing sexy clothing or if they had done something to provoke the attack. One man called to say that because the girls had walked into the motel room, it was not fair to call it rape" ("Gang Rape of Three," A18).

Not very long ago, the concept of "rape-proneness" or "rape provocation" was a well-accepted concept in the scientific, media, and legal discussions of the causes of rape. How the woman was dressed, whether she was drinking, whether she was alone ("alone" meaning without a man escort) in an inappropriate place, her prior sexual relationship to the person or persons accused, or her entire prior sexual history were elements to be assessed in deciding whether she was a woman who had differential propensities to expose herself to risky sexual situations.

Much of the postfeminist scientific literature about rape has been an attempt to identify these once-respected "scientific" ideas as part of a widely accepted cultural syndrome of rape myths. (This exposure of science as ideology is similar to the early feminist critique of "natural" gender differences [Sanday 1996; Roberts and Mohr 1994; Baron and Straus 1989; Holmstrom and Burgess 1978].) Social scientists no longer include the question "Does an individual who has been sexually assaulted differ in his or her propensities to engage in risky sex?" in the class of questions they ask about sexual violence. It does, however, remain a legitimate question in courts of law, where lawyers feel free to theorize in ways that are not permitted in many other venues.

A similar transformation has occurred in the area of adult-child sexual contacts, which is now universally labeled child sexual abuse; often with the definition of "child" ranging upward to age 17 in scientific reports (La Fontaine 1990; Driver and Droisen 1989; Finkelhor 1986; Li, West, and Woodhouse 1990).[7] Thus in contemporary media and vernacular versions of child sexual abuse stories, the child is conventionally thought of as being "at risk" of abuse by certain classes of adult actors, often persons who are strangers to the child and who have prior records of sexual offenses. The child in these stories is not thought of as capable of "taking risks" as a result of internal propensities. This, of course, has not always been so. From the 1930s to 1950s there was a genre of "expert" (supported by vernacular beliefs and practices) stories about adult-child sexual contacts that proposed that children played a significant role by provoking such contacts. The "seductive" or "flirtatious" child might engage in provocative behavior (perhaps not even for sexual motives) that induced a vulnerable adult to act out sexually (see Gagnon 1965 for a review).

That story was rooted on the expert side in the psychoanalytic doctrines of the sexualized child and in other elements of middle-European high cultural thought about the sexualized preadolescent (Werkner 1994). Such a risk story is no longer possible on primarily ideological or political grounds. The dominant contemporary narrative assumes the child to be entirely reactive and a victim of uncontrolled adult sexual interests. While such a narrative often ignores expert knowledge about the ongoing social relationships that usually exist between abused children and the adults who abuse them, the idea of a more proactive, though not necessarily sexual, role on the part of the child cannot be discussed (Laumann et al. 1994).

It is apparent from these examples that only some important concrete instances of the intersect between risk and sex can be used to test a theory about how individual differences produce differences in sexual risk taking. Clearly gay men, individuals who are intravenous drug users, and teenage girls can fall into the imaginary domain of those who are more likely to have "risky sex." The point here is that only certain kinds of actors are assumed to be agentive in sexual matters, to possess propensities that increase their likelihood to put themselves at sexual risk. The instability of what it is possible to think suggests a deep connection between what it is possible to theorize and the cultural and historical context in which the theory is proposed.

At the present moment, although a strong theoretical argument exists

---

7. The elasticity of age in these matters is demonstrated by references on the same television news program to Monica Lewinsky as a "girl" of twenty-one, while two boys aged twelve and thirteen, charged with killing four classmates and a teacher, were referred to as "young men." Perhaps news readers do not listen as they speak.

that the sexual conduct of adolescent girls (including those who are 18 and 19) can be understood as risk taking, it is clear that recent trends in research and policy making seek to alter this conception. The "discoveries" that pregnant adolescent girls in clinical samples report having been "victims" of child sexual abuse more often than never-pregnant controls or that girls in other studies report that they have more often had sex with considerably older men may undermine the conception that such girls have differential internal propensities to engage in risky sex (unless one wants to argue that they had earlier propensities to be victims of child abuse or to have sex with older men) (Lindberg et al. 1997; Luster and Small 1997; Stock et al. 1997). The authors of these studies argue that the degree to which the sexual acts of the girls in this social group were voluntary was severely reduced by their prior or contemporary victimization. In this scenario the question becomes, "Do individuals have prior predisposing experiences that increase the likelihood that they will be unable to prevent exposures to risky sex?"

These prior considerations raise an important question about the cultural conception of the sexuality of gay men and adolescent young women (particularly young women of color) that makes them vulnerable to certain kinds of theories about their behavior, theories which argue that they have either some defect in character or possess certain psychological propensities that result in engaging in risky sex. Other persons, women and girls who have been sexually assaulted or children who have had sexual contacts with adults, are exempted from such explanations by virtue of a specific claim to "victim" status. This is not to argue that the latter two groups should not be treated as victims, but rather to suggest that the scientific hypothesis about the relation between individuals, propensities, risk, and sex is a culturally restricted one. One question we could ask about sex and risk in the exploratory phase of our investigations might be, "Why is it good to think about gay men and adolescent women in this fashion and bad to think in the same way about those who have been sexually assaulted or molested?" The answer to such a question would necessarily involve the issue of agency and who has it, whether the propensities to take risks are the same in all groups, whether risks are gauged in the same way by various actors, and whether all sex has similar risks associated with it.

Scientific and Vernacular Theories

It should be clear that the vast majority of theorizing about "risky sex" takes place outside of the domain of scientifically authorized theorizers about risk, sex, and risky sex. These are the vernacular theories and explanations about risky sex which are embedded in the everyday sex and risk stories that people tell each other.[8] Such vernacular theories can be found in everyday conversations and gossip as individuals tell various audiences about what is happening in their personal lives, the lives of persons immediately around them, and the media versions of the stories of the sexually notorious. It is this process of social reproduction through sexual storytelling of all kinds (both within and across generations) which forms the basis for local and ancillary sexual cultures within the dominant culture. Such vernacular sexual stories are not told randomly, but travel through and are conditioned by proximate social networks structured by gender, class, ethnicity, age, and marital status. Who tells what sexual stories to whom is part of the scripted nature of social life. Talk shows on the radio and chat rooms on the Internet are modern media formulations of these everyday stories. When such stories are gathered from "respondents" by scientists it is the theories and experiences embedded in these stories which provide the data for the research mills of experts who will fashion their expert theories from the reported grist of everyday life.

It is usually not noted, but all experts on sex and risk were once non-experts on these topics, and the personal sex-and-risk lives of most experts are often not guided by their expertise on these matters. The point is that all experts in a culture were raised with the usual vernacular theories of sex and risk prevalent in their cultures at a given historical moment and had to unlearn or refine these theories in the process of becoming an expert of one sort or another. The vernacular theories known to scientific experts (before they were experts) had to be refined or replaced with new theories during their lives as graduate students and as participants in the research process. Few would claim that prior vernacular learning about sex and risk is completely erased by experience with expert representations of sex and risk; indeed, it is probably true that in practice most budding experts on sex and risk have sex-and-risk lives that are much like those who share their educational and social aspirations and experiences. The fact that experts often use their own sex-and-risk autobiographies

---

8. How to refer to "the people" is a contentious issue. "The common people" is too archaic and contains the implication that there are "uncommon people" who are somehow better or more knowing than their fellow citizens (recall the phrase: people of the common sort). "Folk" is not much better and also has the negative racial connotation of "Volk." In this case the only distinction that is being made is between expert theorists and the theories shared by the "non-expert" people and the mass media. It is clear that the actual content of theories held by experts and nonexperts is not actually very different except that expert theories are expressed in expert jargon by credentialed speakers.

as a way of understanding the sex-and-risk lives of others (as in the self-stories of risky sexual conduct) suggests that experts are not strangers to the risky sex experiences that others report. Indeed, in order to participate meaningfully with nonexpert others in social life, experts may have to act as if they hold the vernacular theories held by their partners in social interaction.

The research mills of experts not only use the stories of risky sex and experiences of everyday folks as "data" to theorize and debate issues of risk and sex with their fellow experts, but these experts also have a variety of opportunities to influence the lives of those who provided the data. First, the process of higher education influences young people. Previously they were the recipients only of vernacular stories of risky sex (stories which have "theories" of risk and sex embedded in them) that were generated by their parents, their teachers, their religious spokespersons, their peers, and the media; now they are exposed to expert stories of risky sex (and expert theories) in the form of text books and lectures. Such expert risky sex theories may even influence and in certain storytelling situations, replace, various elements of young people's vernacular stories of risky sex and come to be the basis of new vernacular forms.

Second, in the process of policy formation the theories of experts about risky sex are sometimes influential in those social formations that are composed of other experts whose job it is to manage what they view as risky sex and its negative sequelae. Bureaucracies that manage people— e.g., social welfare systems, educational institutions, healthcare corporations, the business community, and the military—use some, though not all, of the expert theories about risky sex to support lines of action which are of interest to them. Thus the lives of everyday folks will be impacted by the stories that they have told to experts who have transformed these stories into the basis for social policy.

Third, the stories experts tell about risky sex interface with the media through "science reporting" and interviews with experts and pseudo-experts with varying degrees of storytelling competencies and ideologies. These stories experts tell about risky sex are transmitted through the mass media and may come to influence stories about risky sex in the general public.

In consumer-based infotainment societies stories about risky sex with their embedded theories of sex and risk are retailed each day in all forms of the print and electronic media. Stories about risky sex appear in "news" reports, advertisements, advice columns, short stories and novels, talk shows, soap operas (afternoon and evening versions), sitcoms, made-for-TV films, Hollywood movies, and documentaries. No genre is free of the story about risky sex. This massive system of storytelling has an important but complex relationship with the stories told by members of the general public and the stories told by experts. In a cheerfully promiscuous and profitable manner the infotainment system calls on everyday folks for their experiences of and opinions about risky sex and calls on the research and talking heads of experts about risky sex and fuses them together with the opinions of news readers and pundits to produce a third force in the telling of stories about risky sex.

What I am describing is a highly conflated storytelling environment with a diverse set of storytellers who tell overlapping, conflicting, and often mendacious stories (usually based on unexamined theories) to serve many different interests. The image of a culture as an ongoing communication machine which is based on producing and reproducing conduct through socially structured storytelling is implicit in the critical work of Kenneth Burke and explicit in some aspects of the sociological work of Nicolas Lumann. Perhaps the most important point is that such a society does not separate "expert" storytelling from vernacular storytelling or media-based storytelling.

This larger context of theorizing has an important implication for theorizing sex and risk within the disciplines. The intimate relationship between individualized explanations of risky sex, explanations of risky sex given in vernacular cultures, and the explanations given by the mass media profoundly influence the content of expert theories. In each of these overlapping domains there is a cultural prejudgment that it is the individual who is the primary causal agent of risk and sex. This overlap means that scientific theory of the relation between risk and sex is not free of bias and prejudgment.

The Individual and Social Theories of Risky Sex

It is clear from the foregoing discussion that the formulation of the concrete questions about the sexual conduct of some gay men and some teenage girls—"Why do individuals differ in their propensities to engage in risky sex?"—carries a good deal of cultural baggage in the United States. This is a culture which treats many forms of conduct, most commonly those that are stigmatized, as matters of successes or failures in individual self-control.[9] The consequence for problem identification and

9. This same prejudice toward blaming the individual can be found in all attributions of cause in accidents. "Human error" is always operator error rather than system designer error, equipment designer or manufacturer error, or errors in the way the system is operated by the corporation that owns it. Such attributions of accident causation to individuals are always profitable

problem solving is that morality tales of internal struggles against temptation are isomorphically mapped over by the scientific categories of individualistic psychology. That individuals who do not succeed in avoiding "risky sexual conduct" differ in some internal characteristics from those who do is a view held by the person in the street, the mass media, religious tradition, medical belief, economic theory, political rhetoric, and individualistic psychology. The fact that there are unexamined assumptions made in this formulation of the relation between risk and sex does not change this nearly hegemonic cultural view of the relation between risk and sex.

Alternative theories of both sex and risk are often hard to propose (and harder to sell) in such an environment. In a recent lecture sociologist-historian Charles Tilly argued that cultural elites and ordinary people in most societies support certain kinds of widely held stories (what were once called zeitgeists or worldviews) which justify taken-for-granted courses of action or explanations of conduct (Tilly forthcoming). Tilly was referring to the stories held and retold by ordinary citizens and elites about the origins of their nation (he was referring to Canada), and he argued that sociological stories of a structural sort which contradicted stories of great men and important events were not easily assimilated into national tale telling. So it is with both risk and sexuality in the United States. Pointing to the structural or contextual variables that might create the separate and joint situations of sexuality and risk taking requires explanations that either do not implicate the individual or that implicate the differences between individuals only within narrow contexts of action. As a consequence such explanations do not easily fit into the taken-for-granted and *dominant* explanations of risk and sexuality in the society.

What this suggests is that where an explanation starts in the continuum from gene to individual to small group to the macrostructure of society has important consequences in terms of theory, data gathering, and policy recommendations. The selection of this or that starting point depends on the cultural perspectives of the society and the theoretical orientations of the specific discipline. In "individual difference" research one starts with the conduct of individuals and works back into the mental life of individuals to identify those internal propensities that might account

---

in economic and other terms to manufacturers, insurance companies, government regulators, and the like. Attributions of operator error are ways of off-loading the blame and costs of accidents to those who are least able to prevent them. For examples of this practice see Gusfield 1981 and 1996 for a discussion of drunken driving and Perrow 1984 (170–231) for a discussion of shipping accidents.

for the different behavioral outcomes. While some environmental variables, both historical and current, might be included in the analysis (e.g., birth order in the explanation of "homosexuality" or alcohol use in the explanation of unsafe sex), the historical variables are assumed to have been internalized by the individual in such a way that they have become propensities for current actions and the situational variables are treated as evidence of other propensities (e.g., alcohol use is further evidence of risk-taking propensities or disinhibition). The locus of explanation or the potential for behavioral change is internal to the individual. The larger social, cultural, and historical factors are usually treated as relatively constant or primarily operative through the individual. In general the psychologist of individual differences starts with the individual and works her or his way out from the interior of the individual to local contexts of action and assumes that the individual has the ability to choose one line of conduct or another.

Structural and cultural forms of explanation start at the levels of organization that are far removed from the individual level and seek explanations of variations in individual conduct in the constraints and opportunities offered individuals by the world around them. The patterns of conduct (including those of sexuality and risk taking) displayed by individuals are the result of growing up in a specific socially structured milieu in a given historical and cultural situation. The search for explanation often starts at a level distant from the individual (e.g., "Is the economy capitalist or socialist?" or "Is the health care system dominated by fee-for-service or health maintenance organizations or by the state?"), and the theorist works his or her way back toward the individual. It is not that individual agency does not count, but that the preexisting social and cultural world constrains forms of sexuality, forms of risk taking, and the relationship between those two factors (Campenhoudt et al. 1997; Singer 1998).

Theoretically working from structure and culture to the individual enables us to identify additional sources of "causation" and additional opportunities to change individual conduct by changing elements of the environment rather than propensities of individuals. In the case of risky sex and HIV transmission such sources of policy change can range from providing free needles (thus reducing sexual transmission from injection drug users [IDUs] to their sexual partners and children) to legalizing gay marriage (for needle exchange see Normand, Vlahov, and Moses 1995). Neither of these policies directly depends on changing the sexual or risk-taking propensities of individuals, though these individual propensities may change in new environments.

Structural and cultural analyses provide alternative environmental explanations of what is considered "risky sexual conduct" in other arenas of sexual conduct. An analysis of the work situation of commercial sex workers suggests that the risks to which women in this industry are exposed in most countries are related to the criminalized and man-dominated contexts in which they work. Many sex workers are harassed and exploited by agents of the criminal justice system, public health workers, clients, pimps and other "managers," and middle-class profiteers who own the work sites in which the trade is practiced. Women who work through escort services are in less danger of exploitation than women who work on the street, in bars, in bordellos, or in most red-light districts. Thus the problem of risk associated with sex is not dependent on the internal propensities of the women to take risks, but is associated with the environments in which sex work takes place. The most recent United Nations recommendations on controlling HIV transmission among sex workers in the Third World recognize how important these factors are in exposing sex workers to risk, recommendations that could be extended to sex workers in the First World as well (Joint UN Programme on HIV/AIDS 1999).

Structural and cultural theories of sexuality provide a movement away from differences among individual actors toward the ways in which the environments for sexual action are organized by the social, economic, and political structures and the cultural meaning systems of the society. This disciplinary perspective moves the attention of the theorist away from the individual to those processes and structures which offer opportunities and constraints on sexual action. Theorizing at this level changes the policy levers that can be pushed and pulled to get the outcomes that are desired. The possibility or impossibility of changing policy at the collective level also teaches us about the actual environments in which sexuality goes forward and how it is associated with risk. If condoms are not easily accessible in the high school (a structural variable) then the riskiness of sexuality for students in those schools differs from those of students in schools where they are available (Jonson and Stryker 1993). Similarly, if a society creates opportunities for responsible sexuality for its youth and supports that sexuality structurally, the riskiness of sex for young people is reduced. Propensities to take risks which are attributed to the individual are in fact responses of individuals to the riskiness of the environments in which they operate.

Theorizing sex and risk from a structural or cultural perspective also allows (though it does not guarantee) a more holistic perspective which includes the agentive actor but does not make assumptions about causal priority of the individual. The actions of an individual are examined first from the point of view of the settings in which the actions take place. The problem of risk often resides in the setting, and individuals may have little choice about whether to be in such a setting or not. Changing the level of risk may involve changes in the setting rather than changes in the individual. Treating the problem of risky sex as a property of the individual often simply blames the individual for structural conditions about which he or she can do nothing. In this way the situation is justified by placing the blame for risk taking on the individuals in the situation.[10]

The difficulty of applying structural theories and solutions to identified problems which are supra-individual is more than a question of ideology or cultural beliefs. Ongoing social problems and the ongoing solutions applied to those problems involve important stakeholders who have material interests in the problems, in the solutions, and in the cultural beliefs about the problems. Identifying those who profit from a problem, from its solution, or from cultural beliefs about the problem means that powerful interest groups are mobilized against such alternative theories. Structural change involves changing ongoing social arrangements which benefit, in a variety of ways, interested individuals and organizations. Treating teen pregnancy as a problem caused by poverty, a lack of jobs, racial inequality in the imprisonment of young men, and the lack of availability of birth control and sex education requires a change in focus to matters of residential segregation (Massey and Denton 1993), urban poverty (Wilson 1990, 1996), the War on Drugs (Bertram 1996; Goode 1997), and political/ideological movements that emphasize absolutist sexual values. Theories that emphasize structure also make poor media stories since they do not focus on praising or blaming individuals. This kind of structural approach does not merely identify "bad guys" but also raises issues about "good guys"—whose institutionalized solutions to the problem have become integrated into the problem itself. Thus, in a

10. The argument here is that risk is allocated by social arrangements rather than by individual propensities and that persons at higher risk of nearly all hazards are members of populations who are marginalized in one fashion or another. Such a perspective means that the first recommended policy step would be to change social arrangements and equalize the distribution of risk across the population (to stop red-lining certain social groups). Once this was done it might be appropriate to examine the degree to which there were individual differences in risk taking which could be attributed to "propensities." Examples of the social allocation of risk or the red-lining of certain social groups abound. For instance, when this chapter was being written, the *New York Times* reported that in New York City a series of companies that tear down buildings were discovered to have hired homeless men, whom they paid less than minimum wage to tear out asbestos insulation. The men were not informed of the risk, trained to deal with asbestos removal, or provided adequate protective equipment. The problem was only "discovered" when asbestos dust began to threaten nonworkers (i.e., the nonhomeless or nonmarginalized citizens).

best-case scenario, incorrect solutions to the problem absorb resources that could be better spent (or left unspent) in other ways; in a worst-case scenario those solutions become self-interested impediments to alternative solutions.

Sexual Theorizing in Social Conte(s/x)t

In the prior sections of this essay I made a number of related arguments that attempt to make the question "Why do individuals vary in their propensities to engage in risky sex? problematic in both a pretheoretical and a disciplinary theoretical sense. These arguments were:

1. Before a trouble is treated as a problem and assigned to a discipline there is a good deal of pretheoretical work to be done. This involves an examination of the ideological and political interests of those who propose that this trouble be treated as a problem and the interests of those who are assigned (or volunteer) to deal with it. Since defining a trouble as a problem will nearly always generate proposals to improve the situation by modifying the problem, a cautious approach to problem identification should be taken. This is particularly true since solutions when adopted are rarely evaluated and often become part of a problem. This caution should applied to all problem identification, regardless of its social origins or disciplinary orientation.

2. It is important to recognize that when a problem has been defined as belonging to a specific class of problems which are the property of specific disciplines, the problem will become reformulated in the terms routinely available to the specific culture and technology of that discipline. This is true of all assignments of a specific problem, or even a general topic (e.g., sexuality, religion, politics), to a specific discipline. Psychologists, sociologists, economists, and anthropologists imagine in different ways and call upon different cultures of explanation both within and outside their disciplines. Theoretical conflicts between disciplines are routine because disciplines are different ways of conceiving and mastering the world.

3. It is necessary to concretize abstract propositions and ask whether the concrete case that is hiding behind the abstract formulation is somehow a special case which makes it more amenable to inclusion as an example in the abstract category. Researchers should also seek comparative examples of concrete cases that might be included, but that may be excluded for ideological reasons. It is espe-

cially useful if one can find cases that were once included as examples but are no longer so included, or cases that were once excluded but now are included. The changing cultural and historical boundaries and contexts of a theorized category are evidence of the limitations of its claims to universality and generalizability.

4. The selection of what instances can be defined as "risky sex" from the larger arena of sexual relations that are dangerous to one or another of the participants suggests that there are cultural limitations on theorizing the connection between individual risk taking and sexuality. These constraints on what is good to think in sexual matters demonstrate that the procedures by which disciplines identify problems are not independent of views held by social groups or movements outside of the discipline. Such exogenous influences on scientific choices are of course deeply influential in social scientific disciplines.

5. The lack of insulation between disciplinary theories of the sexual and the vernacular theories of sexuality held by "the people" in a society and those sexual theories which are represented in the collective culture of modern societies (i.e., the mass media) must be constantly considered. Indeed the everyday sexual stories told by both the "folk," the mass media, and disciplines that are based on individual attributes focus on the lack of self-control exhibited by individuals and the irrationalities of sexual passion as the driving forces for sexual misconduct. In addition, authorized experts about sexuality in a given culture share by reasons of upbringing and sexual histories to a greater or lesser degree the folk beliefs of the culture and are only to a limited extent free of these cultural prejudgments. These are the cultural underpinnings of the individualistic theories of sexual risk taking, but not necessarily the underpinnings of nonindividualistic theories (which are also not free of vernacular and media theories).

Rather than construct local, historically situated, structuralist, or culturalist theories, the dominant arguments in this paper have deconstructed individualized, abstract, and universalized theories of sexual conduct. This is because structural or cultural theories, although I prefer them, are often vulnerable in many ways to the same pretheoretical arguments. A trouble that is defined as a problem appropriate to structuralist theorizing will be reconstituted as a "structural" problem and will be submitted to structuralist explanations and policy making. Structuralists often develop special territorial interests and claims over a problem and become participants in the institutional struggles over resources and rights and honors associated with "solving" the problem. Also structuralists often do not think systematically and comparatively about the historical and cultural situation out of which their theories emerge or their concrete cases are selected. Finally, structuralist and culturalist theorists are often seduced by scientistic claims to the universal applicability of their theories and problem-solving machinery.

Given that structuralist and culturalist theorists of the sexual are vulnerable to many of the ills of individualist theories, why are they preferable? Because such structural and cultural theories can be more attentive to the historical and cultural situation of theory building and problem identification and solving. Such theories can be, but are not always, more holistic and interactional in their approach. It is also somewhat easier for such theories to include more sources of causation. Finally, such theories are preferable because they often go against the grain of accepted theorizing and can offer some resistance to the dominant social, cultural, economic, and political status quo. Once again we are back to a stance which is pretheoretical.

In sum, scientific theorizing of sexuality in the social sciences takes place in a contested social and political world with important scientific and nonscientific stakeholders in the outcomes of what theory is chosen to guide what research programs to support what policies. Unlike astronomy, whose starry subject matter is indifferent to the theories of Ptolmey, Galileo, Newton, and Einstein, the people who are the subject matter of sexual theorizing are active, complicit, and resistant participants in the theorizing and policy formation process. Sexual theorizing is consequential. It is part of the day-to-day struggle to direct, manage, control, and invent human sexuality.

Coda

In this deconstructive exercise readers will note that the focus has been more on sex and less on risk. In part this is a function of what the author knows and what the assignment for the paper was. Risky sex represents the overlap in a Venn diagram between the domain of risk and the domain of sex. Most of the argumentation of the paper has addressed this conjunction from the perspective of sexuality. It would be very profitable to approach this conjoint domain from the perspective of risk. For instance, it would be useful to explore how the elite in the society promote and praise risk taking as a useful force in entrepreneurial conduct in the marketplace, in recreational behavior (skiing, surfing, rock climbing, and scuba diving), and in innovative conduct in the arts, science, and technology.

Such an analysis might lead to an assessment of risk management, risk evaluation, and risk allocation in the nonsexual domain and examine how the practices and ideologies involved could provide theoretical and policy alternatives when dealing with risk in sexual matters. For instance, risk is often dealt with in nonsexual domains by insurance or other mechanisms that spread the risk across larger populations. Would it be culturally plausible to "insure" against the negative outcomes of sexual relationships (stalking insurance, divorce insurance, or adultery insurance)? Such considerations may work back toward the sexual, as in the phrase "sexy risk," by asking questions about how the culture makes "risky sex" attractive to various subgroups of the population and how these subgroups are treated when they take such risks (see Vance 1984).

Epidemics and Researchers: AIDS and the Practice of Social Studies (1992)

Doing Science and Doing Authority

If the AIDS epidemics[1] have done nothing else, they have emphasized the interpenetration of science and power in all of its forms, including the politics of reality, and in this emphasis have demonstrated that the authority claims of the sciences rest in large measure upon their appearance as objective, detached, and pure of purpose. This is not a new recognition, but it takes on a greater salience at the current moment because science as constituted in certain research communities has become identified as the lead agency in providing solutions for the epidemics. The biomedical sciences are charged with understanding the virus and its impacts on the immune system and discovering both a vaccine to prevent further spread and treatments for the opportunistic infections as well as the direct effects of the virus. The social and behavioral sciences are to produce recipes for behavior change that will prevent transmission as well as compliance with healthy lifestyles (until the "magic bullet" comes along). These tasks are

Originally published in *Social Analysis in the Time of AIDS*, edited by Gilbert Herdt and Shirley Lindenbaum (Newbury Park, CA: Sage, 1992), 27–40. Reprinted by permission.

1. The plural form of *epidemics* is a deliberate usage. The epidemics do not have some "natural course" even as the disease HIV/AIDS is a different epidemic among the inner-city poor than it is among various groups of men who have sex with men, and the epidemic is not the same in the Soviet Union, Zaire, or Thailand. The social and cultural ecology of the AIDS epidemics has created the social, cultural, and political responses to the disease. These national and international responses, usually heedless of local ecologies, have in turn shaped the course of the epidemics in any given society or sector of a society. Similarly, the presence or absence of specific cultures of illness and health and available technologies and infrastructures of health care will be the armature of the sociomedical history of HIV/AIDS.

to be accomplished in the face of rapidly changing epidemics that are cross-cultural in scope and interdisciplinary in their methodological and theoretical demands on the scientific community. An adequate technical response to HIV disease demands that scientists quickly acquire reliable knowledge that can be turned into applied programs that work. However, beyond the technical requirements of such a task, there is the matter of implementing these programs in actual cultural and social contexts, implementations that will have impacts on far more aspects of social life than HIV/AIDS treatment or prevention. Behavior change is required not only of those at risk but of the widest range of both direct and indirect participants in the epidemics in all of the affected cultures.

The medical profession, which is the conduit for the delivery of the work of biomedical scientists, provides a relatively complete apparatus of legitimation that produces the ability of the individual physician to tell people what to do to reduce illness. This moment of assured superordination in the doctor-patient encounter is the result of an entire system of symbols and institutions of healing that bulk large in the structure of Western societies. As a result, physicians and their surrogates have been willing to give advice or make rules with a confidence that occurs less often among social or behavioral scientists. Yet, by taking on a similar role in the epidemics, the behavioral and social sciences are running the risk of having to take on a similar mantle of authority. They are expected to produce results in the form of tried and tested interventions that will reduce the rate of infection or increase compliance with drug regimes. They are to gather precise data usable in regression equations that model the epidemic, or they are to conduct randomized trials of educational programs that mimic the drug trials of their medical betters. In the context of the epidemics, social scientists are expected to tell people what to do in conditions of uncertainty.

Epidemics and Accidents

One of the images that comes to mind during reflections on the course of the HIV/AIDS epidemics is the behavior of the operators in the control room of the nuclear power plant at Three Mile Island in the first moments of the accident. Untoward and unexpected events were occurring with incredible rapidity in the bowels of the reactor vessel, and lights were flashing in the control room that were believed (within some limits) to provide information to the operators about what was going on inside the great machine. The operators had a "theory of the machine," which had been constituted in their training and in the everyday practice of running the plant, and that theory of the machine was the basis on which they (1) formulated their beliefs about what could and could not happen in the machine, (2) chose which control board lights to believe and which to ignore, and (3) decided what actions to take next. Everyone knows the results (for a description of this process, see Perrow 1984).

The application of this metaphor to the HIV/AIDS epidemic is not exact—but there were many features in common during the first years of the epidemics. In the early 1980s, a dangerous and unknown disease suddenly appeared in the United States that required a rapid response by agencies and individuals responsible for the nation's health, a response that would necessarily be based on inadequate knowledge. The designated operators of the affected parts of the social machine need to react and to do something. In the opening stages of the epidemics, when they had a multiplicity of theories and a paucity of data, they nevertheless conducted research guided by these theories, and they gave advice to their masters as well as those who were ill. In addition to these directly illness-related activities, the designated operators worried about their own careers and protected their institutional interests, they took notice of the interests of others in the system, and they took for granted "how the system works." These responses of the designated operators of the system were part of the ecology of the epidemics and central to shaping the character of the epidemic/accident (see Shilts 1987 for one representation of the opening years of the epidemic and Crimp 1987 for one of many counter representations).

There are some differences both in fact and in the application of the accident metaphor. Perhaps the most important substantive difference is that Three Mile Island was a far more transient event than the HIV/AIDS epidemics. In moments, the critical events in the reactor vessel were over, and perhaps a week passed before the major events in the machine were concluded. It was the work of the next decade to assign the blame, sanitize the rubble, amortize the costs, and hopefully learn the lessons that would prevent similar untoward events in the future. The costs to the nuclear power industry were profound, but the damage to those living near the plant as well as to the social order at large was limited.

One major difference between TMI and HIV/AIDS is that the epidemics will continue to evolve over time (we are now in their second decade in the United States and there will assuredly be a third), with their character constantly being reshaped by attempts to deal with them. Another difference is that, unlike the great but passive and dedicated machine that is a nuclear power plant, the HIV/AIDS epidemics are embodied in an active set of human collectivities. In the case of the epidemics, the designated operators were and are part of the social machine that they wish to manage. While management of the epidemics has become more stabilized in their second decade, there is a continuing stream of potential operators who press into the control room offering new advice, point to ignored lights on the control board, and attempt to press levers to make things happen.

The Lines of Cleavage

As the epidemics move into their second decade, the coalitions formed in the opening days of the epidemics are eroding. In 1985, the activists and the biomedical researchers covertly combined against the Reagan administration; now that these researchers are better funded and have taken traditional stances about what is good science, the activists attack them. A few years ago, nearly everyone was against contact tracing; now, with new modes of treatment available, old opponents of contact tracing believe it has a new usefulness. New alliances are forming based on ethnic interests, and struggles between drug activists and traditional community leaders opposed to needle exchange have continued in the African American community. The temporary nature of factional and ideological alliances that constitute all social relations in modern life have become accentuated by the dynamic character of the epidemics.

Notes from a Meeting Day

The opening addresses at the Sixth International Conference on AIDS in San Francisco focused on a common theme: every person who was in the great exposition hall of the Moscone Convention Center (perhaps excluding the police, the janitors, and the service personnel, but including the journalists), as well as those who boycotted or could not come to the meeting because of immigration restrictions on those with HIV/AIDS, shared a common cause and a common enemy—the AIDS virus. Everyone, it was said, was engaged in a great crusade—persons living with HIV and AIDS, social workers, activists, virologists, pharmaceutical houses, the GPA of the WHO, community workers, sociologists, direct care physicians, the CDC, the NIAID, Genentech, grant reviewers at NIH, and on and on. The ubiquitous inclusionary phrase was "physicians and scientists and activists."

If persons with HIV/AIDS or those at risk for infection had any enemies other than the "diabolical virus" that insinuates itself into the cell, they were surely not among us. Everybody mentioned how they opposed the Immigration and Naturalization Service restrictions on travel, which had no scientific basis, especially to scientific meetings where the free interchange of ideas was the only goal. A few speakers mentioned the abstractions of racism and sexism and poverty without mentioning the names of the guilty. The mayor of San Francisco said that AIDS was a disaster similar to the recent earthquake that had shattered parts of his community and that it should be addressed with the same levels of outpouring of moral and fiscal support. The mayor, a Democrat, mentioned that the Republicans in the executive branch of the national government might be part of the problem.

Only the speaker from ACT UP offered a more political analysis by remarking that he was losing his faith in the whole enterprise represented by AIDS International, Inc. In a rhetorical move artfully posed to raise the anxieties of the audience, he suggested that he was considering Larry Kramer's advice that he become an AIDS terrorist. He named the names of those who, from the ACT UP perspective, made life difficult for PLWH/As: these included members of the doctors group at the NIH that approved clinical trials, Burroughs Welcome, George Bush, and Jessie Helms. He invited the audience, many of whom had voted for George Bush, to shout in common chorus with the activists, who had gathered in front of the hall, anti-Bush slogans. In the end, he too called for unity; we were, by our presence at the meeting, honorary members of ACT UP.

And after these many speeches, the plenary speaker, a Kenyan woman dressed in modernized traditional dress, spoke in a quiet and dignified, but quite predictable way, naming no names, about HIV/AIDS and the situation of women and children in Africa. As she spoke, a quarter, perhaps a third, of the audience drifted out of the halls toward the wine and cheese and fruit heaped on tables around the exhibits set up by the great international medical-pharmaceutical institutions.

A postmodernist pendant: earlier in the evening, the San Francisco Symphony played, the San Francisco Gay Chorus sang, and we could all watch the speakers and ourselves and little video statements by a rainbow coalition of persons living with HIV and AIDS on giant video screens spread across the hall.

***

What the plenary speakers at the International AIDS Conference wanted to deny, even though some knew it to be true, is that the AIDS epidemics and the individual and collective response to them are part of a struggle between contending factions over how to define what the epidemics are and, in consequence, how to allocate resources to deal with them (or not deal with them). Everybody in that great hall was not on the same side. Even those persons living with HIV/AIDS differed on what to do (will it be ACT UP or GMHC or Queer Nation or some combination of the three?), and their concerns with staying alive in a quality way were related only to the work of a very small proportion of the scientists and physicians who were present. The cleavages and the potential for cleavage ran through the hall, the pharmaceutical houses versus the third-party payers and the patients, one virology laboratory pitted against another in a race for publication, the sociologist who wanted a grant versus the physician who had the grant, those in on the ground floor versus the new contenders, the women and African Americans and Latino Americans against "white middle-class gay men," the Third World against the First, the sick against the well.

Consider simply the problem of usage. Acronyms have disappeared: GRID, ARC, HTLV3. More "correct" usages appear: AIDS victims gave way to persons with AIDS and that gives way to persons living with HIV/AIDS. Usages clash across group boundaries: African American, Hispanic American, and Asian American are proposed as parallels to European American, as alliances based on color words may be in decline. Multicultural speak contests with race speak as the appropriate language for distinguishing between groups. Each step in this process of renaming involves both the embracing of fictions as well as the articulation of truths. What cultures does the Asian American label disguise, and what new cultures and constituencies will its usage create? Is this a temporary "necessary fiction" in much the same way that Hispanic was before Latino and Latina?

Each of these contentious moments of naming are mini crises of meaning for both the practice and the ideology of social studies as science. Such mini crises, if taken seriously, should have (but rarely do have) consequences for the actual doing of science: if one is serious about issues of gender, then the stubs of tables need to contain the words woman/women or man/men rather than the biological female and male. Consider what this does to data series such as the census in which reports on females and males over one hundred years assumed that biological continuity is a surrogate for cultural continuity. Or the shift in emphasis that would be required to take adequate notice that women and men in West Africa are not the same cultural creatures as women and men in

Sweden, to take seriously the contention that persons are differently gendered in different cultures. Similarly, if one thinks about the new names for ethnic groups, should one ask the question: "Do you consider yourself Black, White, . . ." or "African American, Hispanic American, European American, . . .," and how should the stub at the end of the table read?

The Distribution of Doubt

The willingness to dress in the cloak of authority demanded by the practical considerations of epidemics varies among students of cultural and social life; indeed, there are a fair number who wonder about the label "science" when it is applied to social and cultural studies, not because they share the doubts of the hard sciences about the soft sciences but because they have doubts about positivist science, hard or soft (Fleck [1935] 1979; Kuhn 1970, 1977). The relativist historians and anthropologists of science, feminist scholars as well as the older traditions of the sociology of knowledge, with its roots in Freud and Marx, have been deeply influential in producing a serious crisis of confidence in social and cultural studies, a crisis characterized by an increased prevalence of "epistemological doubters." This kind of doubt goes well beyond the issues raised by even serious "methodological doubters," among whom it is recognized that theories are limited, techniques are imperfect, and data are often error laden. However, such methodological doubters believe that theories may be refined, techniques improved, error reduced, and bias accounted for, and that there are some true parameters in nature that human efforts at discovery may approximate. "Nature does not lie," the physical scientist says, "it must only be asked the right question." It is methodological doubt that characterizes the majority of mainline social science professionals who have strong personal and professional commitments to participation in programs of behavior monitoring and change and whose career lines have been defined by giving programmatic advice to policymakers about what to do when faced with various social problems.

Those whose doubt is epistemological go further than those whose doubts extend only to issues of method. For the epistemological doubters, the problem is not in the method or the technique, it is in the practice of doing social science. Put succinctly, it is argued that social researchers do not discover social facts, they participate in their production and reproduction (Geertz 1973, 1983). This view is at the core of Foucault, the strong theories of social constructionism and symbolic interactionism, relativist theories of the production of scientific knowledge, as well as the pragmatist tradition from Pierce to Dewey to Mead to Rorty (1979). The actions of knowledge producers in the social world are part of the production and reproduction of that world: knowledge is what is good to think, and beliefs are deployed in systems of power and authority. It is not that truth displaces error but that current ideology and practice are replaced by new ideologies and new practices.

The argument is made that the right to explain social phenomenon is not neutral and that who explains a phenomena and how it is explained is central to the control—or, more strongly, the construction—of that phenomenon (Foucault 1978, 1979; Peckham 1969, 1979). The analytic distinction between control in the weak sense of participating in the social management of a phenomenon and control in the strong sense that involves the social construction of a phenomenon is one of emphasis. Clearly, one merges into the other; medical doctors, when diagnosing and treating "homosexuals and bisexuals with AIDS," participate in both the management of the behavior of the patient and the maintenance of the "culturally approved" social category, the "homosexual." In both of these senses of control—management and construction—scientists and their explanations are part and parcel of the production of the phenomenon that they study.

Both methodological and epistemological doubt are problematic in the changing contexts of the epidemics, though the effects of the latter are far more extensive than the former. Methodological doubt can be solved by better methods, though there are methodological doubters who believe that the problems of method cannot be solved with sufficient promptness to offer proper guidance either to individuals or to institutions that wish to take pathways that will reduce the risks associated with HIV/AIDS. Epistemological doubters worry whether the information produced in the research process may be so tainted by ideology and by the potential for affirming oppressive social and cultural practices that it will do more harm than good.

Stances and Standing

Many of the students of social and cultural life were attracted to the AIDS epidemics for personal reasons or because their prior work was of special relevance to the populations who were infected with HIV in the United States. The marginality of the populations infected was reflected in the marginality to the professions of many of the social scientists who were first engaged by the epidemics. Persons in social and cultural studies who have research interests in sexuality, drug use, poverty, ethnicity, or women are often as marginal to their professions as the persons studied are to the societies in which they live. Some researchers are members of the groups they study. This is particularly true of women (many of whom are feminists, some of who are lesbians), gay men, members of cultural minorities, and the formerly poor. There are, however, only a few currently poor, intravenous drug users, or current members of the "underclass" to be found in the cadres of HIV/AIDS researchers (yet they are found among community "representatives" and "contacts," though they may differ from the natives in the same way that informants differ from those on whom they inform). Many of these researchers, though not all, came to the HIV/AIDS epidemics with more than medicalized visions of what needed to be done.

Indeed, it was among this group of social and cultural researchers that "epistemological doubt" was most common, in part because either they or the persons they had studied had been the targets of "scientific objectivism." At first- or secondhand, they knew that science had been an important element in both the system of social control as well as the construction of social reality. Women researchers knew about sexism, ethnic minority researchers about racism, gay male and lesbian researchers about homophobia, and the formerly poor about poverty.

It was clear to many that the traditional medical approaches to HIV/AIDS and persons living with HIV/AIDS were deeply inadequate and in many cases harmful. Doctors still believed that there were homosexuals in the sense of the late-nineteenth-century version of the word and had to be reeducated at nearly every turn about gay life. Medical professionals still need to be disabused of the notion that intravenous drug users are universally sneaky, unreliable, weak willed, and treacherous in addition to being noncompliant with medical regimes. If the medical profession's gaze rarely rises above the level of the symptom in normal times, in HIV/AIDS times, it often focuses on the level of the cell, the gene, or the molecule. As persons living with HIV/AIDS struggle to be persons (and not an acronym: PLWH/A), scientists are interested in arcane measures of biological functions in the immune system. It is true that the attention given to this level of the organism is what will make people well in the magic bullet sense—AZT does extend life somewhat, aerosolized pentamidine does prevent and treat PCP for a time, the hoped-for vaccine will prevent transmission—however, in the view from the laboratory, the patient may appear to be more and more like the genetically similar white rats that can be ordered from some breeding colony.

At least some of the social scientists who were called to the cause felt uneasy about their new collaboration with the biomedical sciences because they had been at the forefront of criticizing the medical model in health care as well as the medicalization of all social problems. It is hard to tell what has happened to this uneasiness as the traditional medical establishment has successfully occupied the terrain of AIDS and HIV disease. There is (or ought to be) an exquisite tension created for the gay scientist who opposes the essentialist psychiatric vision of "homosexuality" while working in a research unit that tests for and diagnoses "AIDS dementia" or studies the psychiatric natural history of AIDS among "homosexuals and bisexuals." Similarly, a certain anguish should be felt by the woman researcher who studies the social networks of women patients in hospitals where the same women do not participate in drug trials. Perhaps in the daily struggle of "doing" the work, the anomalies are ignored or swallowed or reduced in significance because of the larger goals.

The capture of the high ground of epidemic by biomedical science is expressed in more ways than by the fact that they receive three-quarters of the money allocated by the federal government for HIV/AIDS research or that the studies that the social scientists do usually mimic the studies that the doctors do. Consider the roles that social scientists play at the interface between the biomedical profession and the "community" or their role as "prevention scientists." The interface role is often played by social scientists who are members of "the afflicted communities" when they use their community membership to explain the culture of their community to biomedical scientists and when they aid biomedical scientists in securing the cooperation of the community in the production of serum, social data, and behavioral compliance. The representation of this relationship in all of its individual and collective complexity is very difficult. The job of the "prevention scientist" is to find ways to reduce transmission at the individual and community levels, and this involves attempts to create "behavioral interventions" that can be proven to "work." Here again, membership in either afflicted or potentially afflicted communities is an important source of authority in intervention design even if measurement strategies are quite conventional. These roles can be experienced as either being required by the epidemic (as a natural force) or as the result of the structures of domination that exist between the biomedical establishment and their social and behavioral science coworkers/subordinates.

The Decline of Scientific Sanctity

The participation of social and behavioral scientists who are members of the "afflicted communities"[2] and others who are marginal to the larger scientific enterprise in the epidemic is made more complex by the social mobilization of cultural groups to resist "scientific" queries and methods and answers. The most obvious of these forms of resistance has been participation in randomized placebo-control drug trials by persons living with HIV/AIDS. It is easy to forget how normal such trials, or approximations to them, have become in biomedical science since the 1950s. There have been many trials in which persons with fatal illnesses have passively allowed themselves to be allocated by the luck of the draw to no-treatment conditions in which the physician could be sure that the patient was not being helped in ways that were better than normal practice. The willingness to resist medical authority has not always been very strong even in extremis (though there is considerable evidence of noncompliance in many other drug trials).

This recent challenge to medical authority has been abetted by an accumulating list of medical catastrophes. Thalidomide babies, the increased incidence of vaginal cancer among those treated with DES, the deaths of patients as a result of the Cutter vaccine, and the resistance of surgeons to lumpectomies (versus radical mastectomies) are constant reminders of the fragility of medical knowledge and practice. Such disasters are, of course, swords with two edges—biomedical researchers use them to argue for increased care and control in the production of new treatments, critics of biomedical research use them to point out the scientific and ideological failures of medicine as well as, in some cases, the venality of the scientists. Outside of medicine, the failed promises of science (per-

---

2. The HIV/AIDS epidemics can best be understood theoretically as an "ecology of games" (Long 1958). As Long points out, even bounded communities are a complex of individuals who play many roles and have many personal and organizational allegiances (which constitute groups and institutions). In such communities individuals and groups contend both directly and indirectly with each other, often not even realizing that they are in opposition. Even individuals have divided interests such that, when they play the role of parent, it may conflict with their role as worker, not only in private and psychologically, where most role conflict is thought to occur, but in the public arena as well. Parent wants better schools, taxpayer wants lower taxes, worker wants to get to work faster, mother wants more stop signs, and so on. In situations of recognized community conflict, the calls of community leaders for individuals to subordinate their interests to the higher interests of the community are not simply appeals for community. Such situations are more often those in which the "higher interests" of the community coincide with the interests of those who make the calls for the community. Such a perspective that points up that social life is the outcome of contending groups is particularly appropriate to the inchoate and ad hoc aggregate of groups and individuals that make up the AIDS epidemics and their constituencies.

haps only defined as such by the "risk averse") that are manifested in Three Mile Island and Chernobyl, Love Canal and Rocky Flats—and lest social scientists forget, the War on Poverty and public housing projects— have increased the level of collective mistrust in the scientific/technological sense, even among scientists.

The increased vulnerability of science to external criticism rests on more than its mistakes. Accusations of "materialism" and greed and politicking for the Nobel Prize have become increasingly common. Arrowsmith and Madame Curie seem to have made a deal with Genentech or Burroughs Welcome and, in making a deal, they have given up even the appearance of virtue. In this scramble for the material rewards, can fraud be far behind? Here the crucial point is that extrascientific groups become more central in deciding on what the scientific standards are and how they should be applied. From the Right, there is a new breed of religious critics who are intervening in science not only in a larger arena (e.g., creationism and evolution), but more particularly in the management of HIV/AIDS itself. Religious groups have had an impact on government funding of intervention programs that are "too sexually explicit," have killed condom education programs, have prevented surveys of sexual conduct, and have engaged in television campaigns against the reports of scientific bodies. Finally, political groups both in local areas and at the national level have resisted programs of needle exchange on the grounds that this would result in "sending the wrong message about drugs."

In each of these examples of external intervention in scientific affairs, there is evidence of a larger agenda (the problem of fraud in science, the struggle between science and religion, and the "war on drugs") in which the HIV/AIDS epidemics have supplied an additional opportunity for conflict. In this set of conflicts, the social scientist is particularly vulnerable, for in the above list it is only the problem of fraud and profiteering that is aimed at the biomedical sciences. It is the behavioral intervention programs and the data gathering efforts of the social scientists that are most likely to be attacked by traditional religious and political groups. It is perhaps an irony that many social and behavioral scientists who are pleased by the interventions of the "community" in the scientific process are themselves the target of intervention by other communities.

Doubt and Participation

The demands of the HIV/AIDS epidemics have been and will be practical and immediate. Many students of social and cultural life, even those with deep "epistemological doubts," have and will participate as social scientists in goal-oriented research, do surveys that they know are flawed, and compare statistical results even though they know the limits of statistics. They will conduct applied ethnographies that focus on the part and not the whole, prepare and score psychological tests even though they do not believe in traits, engage in thin description, and, all in all, submit themselves to the rigors of positivist science. The goal of such activities will surely be worthy: saving lives. At the same time, the speed at which the epidemic and its representations are moving means that today's facts and today's advice might be tomorrow's falsehoods. Many social scientists have been and will be caught between their impulse to doubt (either methodologically or epistemologically) and the consequent pressures to disengage and criticize and the pressures of the epidemics to participate, to engage in research that has the primary goal of managing and changing the lives of those who are its subject/victims rather than the social and cultural order in which they live.

Researchers in social and cultural social studies have a peculiar place in the history of the epidemics because some of these researchers do understand the particular tension between the practical necessity of research participation that may be of some use and the understanding that such participation may result in the reproduction of oppression. The experience of this tension should be understood as a trouble, not a pain. The ultimate pain of the epidemics is inflicted on those who are living with and dying of HIV/AIDS; other pains, even those experienced by those most intimate with those who are living and dying with the disease, usually recede, albeit slowly, with forgetfulness.

Notes from a Conference: Day 5

The closing speeches of the conference were directed at unity. There will be no meeting in Boston if U.S. immigration rules against the entry of persons living with HIV/AIDS are maintained, said an important speaker. Applause. Cheers. But there was a profound uneasiness in the hall. There was a rumor that ACT UP had a copy of the remarks that were to be made by Louis Sullivan, Secretary of the Department of Health and Human Services, and there would be a ZAP. It was clear that those on the podium were anxiously aware of the movement in the audience as activists handed out flyers to physicians and researchers. Anthony Fauci condemned ACT UP for condemning members of the clinical trials group, particularly for naming names, while holding out the kind of olive branch that would continue the symbiosis between the ill and the physicians and researchers. The place of Louis Sullivan on the program was changed to the end. As he rose to speak, the activists gathered around the front of the room began to shout so loudly that Sullivan, when he spoke, could not be heard. Many in the audience who were not shouting stood and turned their backs to the speaker. Others drifted out the door, some deafened, others angry, many wondering what this had to do with their epidemic.

Captain Cook and the Penetration
of the Pacific (1997)

The Deadly Embrace

It is only recently in the history of an expanding Euro-American global cultural hegemony that there has been careful reflection on what the natives of other cultures, large and small, advanced and simple, must have thought when first confronted by (usually) white-faced bearers of advanced armaments, religious and commercial fervor, and genocidal impulses based on racist or evolutionary principles. Even those traditional cultures that are currently being recorded by anthropologists are ending with silence as they are erased by nation-building, entry-level positions in the global economy, and the worldwide media (Wilford 1994).

The encounter of Captain Cook with the "Indians" of the South Seas at the end of the eighteenth century, fatal to Cook as an individual and to the "Indians" as individuals and as cultures, represents a paradigmatic meeting of cultures that is regularly revisited for a variety of contemporary purposes. This chapter, written in the era of AIDS and global human movement, had its origins in an attempt to make sense of the sexual aspects of this specific historic encounter between cultural strangers, in this case Europeans and Polynesians (primarily Tahitians), in the late eighteenth century. It is an encounter in which the participants were not only "other to each other" at the historical moment, but in which both sets of

Reprinted by permission from *Sexual Cultures, Migration, and AIDS: Anthropological and Demographic Perspectives,* edited by Gilbert Herdt. (Oxford: Oxford University Press, 1997), 23–38.

historic participants are "other" to their cultural descendants. The quality of this "otherness" between ancestors and descendants is, however, somewhat different for the cultures of these two regions.

The Tahitians, as well as other Pacific Islanders, depending on their utility to the national interests of states that were and are more advanced in the violent arts, have been subjected to either continuous or intermittent commercial, military, biological, linguistic, and religious interventions for nearly two hundred years. As a result of this process of domination the descendants of the preintervention populations often see their own past through a dark and refracted prism, sometimes recovering fragments of their own historic cultures through the records kept by cultural aliens.[1]

Following a different trajectory, the primary colonizing cultures of the Pacific Basin—the Netherlands, England, France, the United States, Germany, and more recently, Japan—have accelerated into diverse examples of urban-industrial nation-states that are vastly different from their historic cultures. Even Spain and Portugal, who were early participants in the wave of Pacific colonization, but who have lagged behind their Northern European peers in economic development, differ dramatically from even their nineteenth-century pasts. The agrarian, preindustrial, sometimes peasant and quasifeudal ways of life that dominated all these European societies two centuries ago have been extinguished and in many cases these social worlds now exist only in repositories of the more durable traces of the past. The living cultures that produced and used these surviving artifacts are dead, and the artifacts themselves survive either in alien contexts such as museums, libraries, and scholarly texts or in monuments that are given life through historical reenactments and the gaze of tourists (Selwyn 1996).

However, these cultures, the subordinated and the superordinate, both separated from their pasts, remain in chronic tension in the present. The tourists, business persons, soldiers, sailors, and government administrators who land at the airports and docks at Papeete or Honolulu bear with them expectations about the South Seas that were first generated nearly two hundred years ago by European explorers in their sailing ships. At the center of these expectations are the ghosts of sexual encounters between sailors and "native girls" that have been rerepresented for two centuries.

Trying to understand the sexual aspects of this late-eighteenth-century

1.The journals of Cook and other early explorers are the only written or visual records of the state of preliterate Pacific societies at the time of first contact.

encounter from the perspective of the very late twentieth century requires a recognition of the dense assemblage of collective myth and individual fantasy that these first as well as subsequent encounters in the Pacific, particularly with Polynesians, have deposited in the Euro-American consciousness. Any contemporary observer must have internalized some portion of these myths and fantasies (sexual and otherwise) that make up the current Western view of the Pacific Islanders (as they existed then and now) as well as the contemporary counter-strategies recommended by modernists and postmodernists that are believed to be able to counteract or adjust the gaze of the other on the other.

The urtexts for English speakers for the first encounters of Europeans with Polynesians are the journals of Captain James Cook and his literate colleagues (Banks 1962; Cook 1955–1974). Written in the last third of the eighteenth century they are in toto an extraordinary document of late-eighteenth-century English culture and mental life. They contain a limited record of the sexual aspects of these first encounters with Polynesia, encounters that provided the original framework for Anglo-American fantasies about the "South Seas." While the majority of the sexual myths and fantasies are heteroerotic and have been reiterated in combination with themes of innocence and corruption, discovery and loss, in Hollywood films such as *Hurricane, Rain, South Pacific,* and *Return to Paradise,* the journeys of Captain Cook continue to resonate in many other ways in modern Western societies.[2]

---

2. For instance, we might consider the direct parallels between Captain James Cook and Captain James Kirk of the television program *Star Trek.* Echoes of both Cook's journeys and the attitudes of the Enlightenment that are associated with them can be found in this modern rerepresentation of Cook in the fictional Captain Kirk of the starship *Enterprise.* Each episode of the series begins with a dated entry (a Stardate rather than an Earthdate), usually in the captain's log. Over the musical theme the following words are spoken: "Space, the Final Frontier. These are the voyages of the starship *Enterprise.* Her five-year mission: to explore strange new worlds, to seek out new life and new civilizations, to boldly go where no man has gone before."

In the next version of this series, *Star Trek: The Next Generation,* the offending sexist terms "her" and "man" have been changed to "its" and "one"; however, the mission remains the same and so do the other parallels with the exploration of the Pacific. The only traces of these encounters with "strange new worlds" are in the logs of the starship *Enterprise*—as they were in the logs of Cook's voyages (no log is kept by indigenous peoples, or at least we don't know of them). And Kirk/Cook is bound by the "prime directive" (taken from the Enlightenment and anthropology) not to change the new worlds which are visited by the introduction of new technical or social forms.

In the most recent version of the series, *Star Trek: Voyager,* there is a story that explicitly focuses on the "prime directive." A species of "robots" or "androids" built by a vanished race of humanoids will become extinct if they are not provided with technology commonplace to the crew of the starship. The moral crux of the story is whether supplying the technology will involve an unwarranted intervention in the course of another culture. The fact that the other culture is composed of artificial beings makes the conflict more piquant.

Who Was That Man?

These resonances of Cook's voyages in present-day Euro-American culture, from low to high, from sex tourism to academic anthropology, suggest that transforming an everyday member of the Euro-American culture complex into an objective scientific hero of modern anthropology or sociology may be more difficult than was previously thought. Acquiring an academic doctorate from a Euro-American university after a couple of years of "studying a people" is not a sufficient basis for membership of a new culture of "positivistes," freed from their culture of origin and attached to no culture of destination. Since these "disciplines" are an integral part of the expansionist Euro-American culture (as is the space of positivism), the anthropological traveler shares the subtle attachments to the cultural past that are threaded unnoticed through the cultural present. As a consequence, in the contemporary collision between cultures (a collision that includes anthropologists and their practices), myth and fantasy are fused with data and theory in the constructed space of objectivity.

Thus the current anthropological controversy over who Captain Cook was to the "Indians" of Hawaii is also a controversy about who Captain Cook is to the core and peripheral cultures of the contemporary world order. The manifest content of this controversy focuses on whether Cook was believed to be a god when he and his crew encountered the indigenous peoples of the Hawaiian Islands in the late eighteenth century. As part of a complex argument about the ways in which cultures change, Marshall Sahlins (1981, 1985) has argued that Cook was believed by the Hawaiians to be an incarnation of the Hawaiian god Lono. Sahlins contends that the Hawaiians were required to fit Cook into their previously received cultural system and that their interpretations of the historical events that unfolded after first contact were primarily contingent on the interpretive resources provided to the Hawaiians by this fixed symbol system. Sahlins provides a rereading of the events of the Hawaiian encounter, as recorded in the logs and journals of the Europeans, interpreting each event as fitting the return and death myth of Lono. According to Sahlins, the killing of Cook during a melee on the beach was interpreted by the Hawaiians as fitting the correct ending of the Lono myth cycle, which allowed for the apotheosis.

Countering these views, Gananath Obeysekere (1992), an academic anthropologist but Sri Lankan in origin and Third World in allegiance, provides a detailed critique of Sahlins's readings of the events, particularly focusing on whether Cook was apotheosized by the culture-bound natives. The theoretical dispute centers on whether the Hawaiians were captives of their preexisting cultural system (Sahlins's view) and therefore required in the opening phase of the encounter to interact with Cook and his crew in fixed symbolic terms (that is, the actual events are interpreted to fit the mythic template, therefore Cook equals Lono) or whether the Hawaiians had a pragmatic understanding that Cook was an important man, but only a man, and as a man had resources that could be taken and a body that could be killed.

If the latter interpretation is accepted, Cook's apotheosis would be the result of the continued colonization of Hawaii in the years after his death, a colonization that required a god myth as the continuation of the legitimization of the Euro-American conquest. The belief that Cook became a god to the Hawaiians would then be an example of European myth imposition, not Hawaiian myth fulfilling. There is evidence that Europeans often believed that they were viewed as gods by the natives they conquered (Todorov 1987), and this view of Cook would fit into the myth-making potential of European cultures. In these myths, Europeans (and later Americans and Japanese) come as saviors to raise the benighted heathen from their lives of degradation and error. This myth conceals the genocidal and culturocidal effects of the economic, military, religious, and disease-producing incursions of more militarily advanced cultures into less well defended cultures.

There are two ways in which the anthropology of the late nineteenth and the twentieth centuries support this concealment of the historical record. The first way is in acting as if the postcontact cultures were untainted descendants of the precontact cultures. Professional anthropologists arrived in many numbers in the South Seas nearly 150 years after first contact. The decision of anthropologists to examine the social lives that they were recording for Western consumption as if they closely represented precontact cultures, rather than hybrids of various sorts, both allowed anthropologists to conduct "comparative social research" and concealed the extent of European influence (e.g., churches, prisons, forced labor, modesty, clothing). In addition the anthropological treatment of natives as static products of their culture and social structure (see Douglas [1966] 1970) while the anthropologists were members of dynamic, reflexive, and interpreting cultures continued the mythology of Captain Cook and his "Indians." In this mythology the behavior of Europeans, North Americans, and Japanese is treated as practical and empirical—nearly freed from culture (or at least possessing a superior culture)—and preserving a belief in surviving indigenous cultures passively waiting to be studied, classified, and added to the collective cultural encyclopedia and the individual curriculum vitae.

Obeyesekere's point is that the colonizers' side of the encounter remains unanalyzed. What did these eighteenth-century Englishmen believe about "Indians" prior to dropping anchor? How did the eighteenth-century culture of England condition the beliefs, actions, and records of the sailors ("scientists," officers, and men) during and after the encounter? And, in this case, what purpose did it and does it serve for Westerners, then and now, to believe that the natives believed Cook was a God?

Unnatural Conjunctions

Each of these questions about Cook's apotheosis is relevant to the far more modest question of why sexual relations developed so quickly and with such apparent ease between the Englishmen and certain "Indian" women on the island of Tahiti. While these apparently facile sexual contacts have been core elements of popular Western fantasies about the South Seas, there has been little reflection on how the members of two very different cultures could so easily get to what are now considered extremely "intimate" and affectively loaded interactions without a common language or knowledge of each other's cultures. Who were these men to these women? Who were these women to these men? Why did each find copulation so easy to accomplish?

Usually these questions are treated as a nonquestions. An interest in copulation with women is assumed to be a natural attribute of men as a species, and the lack of sexual "inhibition" on the part of the women is assumed to result from the special circumstances of a Polynesian culture that was closer to nature in its lack of sexual repression. In this analysis, the conduct of the men is based in their fundamental natures and strong sex drives even in the presence of repression (which would have been weak for sailors long deprived of sex), and (in a twentieth-century post-Freudian interpretation) the sexual desires and behavior of women is closer to nature under these special cultural conditions. In this Western mythic state of nature, unrestrained and guiltless copulation is part of the expected order of things.

Such an analysis based on nature leaves unanswered the very questions that a social constructionist might ask about this highly unnatural state of affairs. How were these women and men culturally constituted, and why did their prior cultural training in sexual practices allow for such apparently easy copulation? In the light of these questions, how sexual conduct is accomplished between members of culturally different peoples is of importance to larger theoretical understandings.

Social constructionism as a theoretical stance can vary along a continuum from weak to strong. Weak social construction simply means that the social practices of a naive "people" derive from their own sociocultural history, but these social practices can be objectively understood by a "nonmember" of the culture trained in the appropriate discipline. This posture is no different from a culturally informed "objectivism." In contrast, holding a strong social constructionism position mean that all interpretations of social life, including those which aspire to the privileged status of science, are emergent and contingent. That is, they are the transient results of struggles over meaning between differing groups and individuals and are entirely dependent on the historical and cultural circumstances in which they are announced and repeated. There are no statements or observations which are independent of the time and place in which they are made, and all statements are part and parcel of the phenomena which they attempt to describe. Thus a scientific article, a news release, even an academic seminar about gay men and lesbians or prostitution or HIV are as much part of the social construction of these phenomena as is the conduct that such intellectual exercises observe, interpret, or represent.

This latter perspective, which emphasizes the rootedness of all action in local meaning systems, raises the critical problem of how shared meanings are acquired and actions are coordinated across cultural boundaries. How does a cultural stranger make sense of a new environment and coordinate his or her desires with those of others? In the particular case at hand:

> How does a person from eighteenth-century England with its specific sexual scripts have "sex" with a person who comes from a culture with entirely or nearly entirely different sexual scripts (for a more extended discussion of sexual scripts, see Gagnon and Simon 1973 and Gagnon 1990b)?
>
> How are the differing elements—the who, what, when, where and why—of the sexual scripts of the differing cultures identified and coordinated?
>
> What are the mechanisms of identifying with whom it is appropriate to have "sex"?
>
> Under what circumstances of time and place should the conduct be undertaken?

What elements of a previously acquired "sexual repertoire" are appropriate in these new circumstances?

What reasons can the other party have to engage in sexuality, that is, what are the practical motives of the other, and is there any need to attend to these motives?

In sum, what are the points of contact between the systems of scripts that make a coordinated sexual encounter (including its cultural, interpersonal, and mental aspects) possible?

These specific concerns about the possibilities/difficulties of cross-cultural sexual encounters have emerged subsequent to a discussion by the author and his colleague William Simon about the cultural and historical specificity of sexual meanings and action (Gagnon and Simon 1973). At that time, our intellectual concerns were different, but the underlying arguments remain the same. We wished to demonstrate the cultural specificity of sexual practice in order to critique the regnant naturalistic and biologistic paradigms (what has recently been labeled *sexual essentialism*) that dominated thought about sexuality until that time. As one part of this program we attempted to deconstruct the category "homosexual" by arguing that the physical acts between two men in Classical Greece (Dover 1978), in late-nineteenth-century London (Bartlett 1988), and in the period of gay liberation in San Francisco in the pre-AIDS era (Bell and Weinberg 1978) might be physically identical but culturally incommensurate.[3] We argued further that even within a specific culture both processes of social and cultural change and differences in social position could create different kinds of "homosexualities." In our view "men" of the 1920s and 1930s in the United States were not the same cultural creatures as "gay men" of the 1990s, and the working-class boy who prostituted himself to his "queer" customer (here used in an older sense of *queer*) came to the encounter with a different set of scripts for the occasion than did his client (Chauncey 1995).

The goal of this deconstructive exercise was to point out that the category "homosexual" and by implication, all other sexual categories, including the category "heterosexual," were historical and cultural productions, not human universals (Katz 1995). From this perspective the

---

3. If one lives long enough, it is possible to be overtaken by new terms for what one has already been doing for some period of time. To be understood in the new context one must use current nomenclature. The view that the meaning of statements is equivocal and that all talk and text (now called discourse) can be infinitely reinterpreted is part and parcel of the pragmatist tradition from Charles Pierce to John Dewey and George Herbert Mead. The work of Kenneth Burke contains many formal examples of these interpretative strategies dating from the early 1930s. Such analytic tactics are now called deconstruction. So be it.

enacting of sexuality required the orchestration of a reflexive mental life, sequences of interpersonal actions in socially structured environments, and an attention to cultural instructions rather than the simple unfolding of biological imperatives. The problem of sexuality, indeed of all social life, was, for us, one of meanings and actions which emerged from specific cultures and social structures, rather than a natural sequence of bodily movements that were grounded in evolutionary or other behavioral programs. In such a version of the sexual, meaning as the grounds for action is found both in the mind and in the culture, but not immediately in the body. The concrete social event is understood as the confluence of the mental life of individuals as they are situated in the great social divisions of any specific culture or society. The interpretive move is from both the public world of meaning and social structure and the private world of memories, plans, fantasies, and desires toward the concrete sexual performance. This strategy of understanding clearly involves a different conception of the sexual from one that starts with coupling bodies or lubricated organs and argues that the content of the mind and the structure of the society are responses to the necessities of reproduction or an imperious sex drive.

There is, however, a difficulty which is created by such a robust vision of the cultural discontinuities of sexual life—this is the empirical observation that many persons from quite separate cultures manage to get their bodies together in ways that are interpretable as "sexual" according to most Western definitions. This may not appear to be a very difficult question to those who view sex as "doing what comes naturally"; however, for those with constructionist predilections, the problem only begins with an observation of coupling.

Who Were Those "Indians"?

To return to Captain Cook and Tahiti. Clearly the case is a prejudiced one, but the choice is not entirely idiosyncratic. Many of those from the European cultural area, particularly from Northern Europe and the United States, share the belief that an exemplary sexual encounter between strangers is the one between Europeans or Euro-Americans and Pacific Islanders, especially between Polynesian women and European men.[4] This exemplary symbolic sexual status is recognized and responded to

4. Perhaps this paper can at least raise the question of why certain European sexual encounters with "others" are sexualized or eroticized and others are not. It is clear that the contacts of Spanish and Portuguese conquerors and the indigenous populations of the 'new world' have produced a very large population with mixed ancestry. It would be useful to know whether these

by Euro-American women as well as men (though for different reasons) and captivates men who desire sex with men as well as those who desire sex with women. From Cook, Bougainville, and Diderot in the eighteenth century to Herman Melville and Gauguin in the nineteenth to Bronislaw Malinowski, Margaret Mead, James Michener, and Hollywood in the twentieth, the physical beauty of Polynesian settings and peoples, the abundance of nature, the ease of life, and the appearance of innocence have had a continuous fascination for the Euro-American imagination (Moorehead 1966).[5] Polynesia is either Eden before the fall or Eden corrupted, but unlike the biblical Eden, sexuality is a Western myth of Eden's cultural core.

The presence of these secondary and tertiary cultural accretions have to be assumed in a reading of the primary and secondary literatures that chronicle the fatal impact of European contact on the cultures of the Pacific that began in the eighteenth century. The reports of the "willingness" of certain Polynesian women to have sexual intercourse with the men on Cook's (and other explorers') ships seemed to require no further explanation either in the eighteenth century or now. Notice the cautious description of these events and the deliberate imprecision of the term "willingness." It is no longer possible in the late twentieth century, given the evidence of widespread sexual violence against women and the pervasiveness of gender inequality, to treat what appears to be the eager participation of women in sexual activity as evidence of desire or consent (Heise 1995). At the same time to deny the capacity of women to "demand" sexual relations with men may also deny women's own agency within their own culture.

In contrast to this twentieth-century caution, one of the journal keepers reported that, on first contact, the gestures of the women in approaching canoes indicated "their intentions of gratifying us in all of the pleasures the Sex [that is, women] can give" (quoted in Sahlins 1981, from the Hawaiian encounter in 1788, p. 38; parenthetical clarification added).

Another journal keeper reports: "We now live in the greatest of luxury, and as to the choice of fine women there is hardly one among us who

---

pre-Enlightenment invasions by Southern European cultures during the sixteenth and seventeenth centuries generated similar erotic mythologies.

5. While Cook treats his arrival as a "first," there is sure evidence that Bougainville arrived first, and there is some evidence that at least one Spanish ship arrived earlier. Could the Tahitians have learned from these prior encounters ways to deal with these newcomers? As far as I know no one has attempted to locate the records of earlier arrivals that may have affected Cook's reception (Moorehead 1966).

may not vie with the grand Turk himself" (quoted from Samwell in Sahlins 1981, 38).

While these reports of sexual willingness seem straightforward enough, the reader removed by two centuries and half a world wonders exactly what sexual practices are meant by the phrase "all of the pleasures" women can offer. The allusion to the seraglio and the Turk suggests the resources of comparison possessed by the European mind of the time, in which orientalism serves as the resonant symbol for organizing "astonishing" sexual experiences. That these questions have not been asked before suggests a tendency to treat the journals as records of fact (that is, field notes) rather than as historical documents that require detailed interpretation. As narratives, the journals are documents of the time, influenced by all the cultural baggage of the educated Englishman and written in full awareness of the audiences back home. Like all travel journals the documents produced by Cook and others have many faces, looking backward and forward, to and from home, while seeming to look only at the new world.

That the entire record of these encounters is written by a few literate men on board the European ships should give us serious pause. However, more serious is the profound silence when we try to locate the voices of the other half of the sexual encounter. If we can trust the observers, these women were young, unmarried, and not members of the ruling class (Sahlins 1981). But how much else can be trusted? What were the sexual theories of these Englishmen, and how do they determine the record? More importantly, and impossible to know, What were the sexual theories of the Polynesians, particularly the women? Did they even have theories that included something called "the sexual" as a separate domain of meaning and action? More distantly and even less well understood, at least from the perspective of Euro-American traditions of sexual exclusivity and the property value of women, What were the sexual theories of Polynesian men?

It is clear from other sources that the sexual theories of the eighteenth-century British and French explorers may have been both alike and different. The literate on these ships were viewing the world from the last bright glow of the sunset of the Enlightenment and reporting on a region of the world which, for that short moment, did not invite the exploitative energies of European civilization (Pagden 1993). Very soon these men and the social worlds that they inhabited would disappear, just as surely as the eighteenth-century worlds of Tahitians, Tongans, and Hawaiians would disappear. The journal-keeping Europeans (as distinguished from the common sailors) came from the rising middle levels of a quasi-urban society that was in the opening stages of applied technological development. The worlds of the common sailor are recorded in ships' logs and public and private maritime records as well as in fictions of the time—but these records have not yet been fully explored. All of these worlds would dissolve in the acid onrush of the American Revolution, the Napoleonic Wars, the subsequent economic and political restructuring of Europe, and the opening of the steam, coal, iron, and railroad phase of the industrial revolution.

The sexual language of the journals is preindustrial, but not preempirical. It is the language of a sexuality that was grounded in the "natural." The sexual world of the late eighteenth century remains primarily a rural world in its theory, very different than the peculiar repressions and celebrations of sexuality that characterized the Victorian era.[6] The sexual conduct of men and women of the times was largely understood in terms of their natural lusts or bodily passions. The English background is the language of the gentry and the countryside; Moll Flanders and Tom Jones and Robinson Crusoe are alive and well. At no point are the astonished sailors reported to find the sexual accessibility of the women repellent, disgusting, or sinful, unlike the religionists who would follow them to the Pacific Islands in only a few decades.

The French sexual tradition appears to be, at least theoretically, considerably more complex since this was also the time of Choderlos de Laclos, Restif de la Bretonne, and the Marquis de Sade. The libertine tradition of a decaying aristocracy was still present, as were the intellectual speculations of the encyclopaedists, but these traditions and speculations rested on largely peasant society. Who the French common seamen might have been remains unknown, though the French maritime tradition was a vigorous one. One need only consider the French fishing fleets off the Grand Banks and the slaving activities that contributed to the wealth of Bordeaux and Nantes. Reactions to the explorers' journals suggest the differences between these two cultures; Diderot, reflecting on Bougain-

---

6. While Foucault's observations about the rising level of discourse about sexuality in the nineteenth century are an important corrective to the view that there was only silence about sexuality at that time, a silence that was ended by progressive sexual reformers in the late nineteenth and early twentieth centuries, his views are aimed at current disputes rather than attending to the historical record. Foucault was quarrelling with his contemporaries who viewed the sexual changes of the last century as evidence of human progress and human liberation from oppression. A more accurate version of the sexual transformations of the nineteenth century would take account of the actual repression *or* sexual cultures of differing social formations as well as the censorship of sexual materials in the public world and the formation of new sexual cultures in the expanding middle classes. The efflorescence of discourse justifying these transformations and facilitating them were only part of a new sexual practice that was in formation. Both silencing and speaking were part of the process.

ville, warns the Tahitians to protect themselves: "one day they (the Christians) will come, with crucifix in one hand and dagger in the other, to cut your throats or force you to accept their customs and opinions, one day under their rule you will be almost as unhappy as they are." In contrast, after the first rush of interest in Tahiti, emerging English cultural insularity was evident as Walpole responded that he had no interest in the behavior of a lot of savages (both cited in Moorehead 1966).

The "wantonness" of the Polynesian women and the apparent indifference of the Polynesian men to the women's sexual assertiveness was puzzling to the journal keepers, but they seemed to accept it in the spirit of unrestraint and play rather than as sexual lawlessness. Sexual irregularity was surely more acceptable to the English visitors than the tendency of the natives to take (the Europeans thought it "stealing") all shiny baubles and trinkets. It is the struggle over property (rather than sexuality) that produces the most serious conflicts between the Europeans and the natives.[7] Indeed it was one of these European incursions to recover stolen property that resulted in Cook's death in Hawaii. While taking immediate pleasure in the sexual arrangements, the journal keepers do wonder why sex appears to have little to do with those great organizers of sexual life in Europe, shame, guilt, sin, privacy, social distinctions, economic exchange, and marriage. The women are wanton, but not "bawds"; "they visited us with no other view, than to make a surrender of their persons" (quoted in Sahlins 1981). Consider the gender assumptions in the word *surrender.*

What did these women want? Marshall Sahlins's twentieth-century answer is that there was a general cultural propensity among the Polynesians (specifically Hawaiians) of the precontact period to seek masters, and as the chiefs submitted to the mastery of Cook, so the women submitted to the mastery of the sailors (Sahlins 1981). My twentieth-century answer is that the women were products of a social order in which sex was an unmarked form of pleasurable sociability on the part

---

7. Usually little is made of the amount of intimidation and violence that accompanied these first encounters. Cannon were often fired to remind the local people of the advanced technology of the Europeans, and natives were killed or injured without much concern. A native who snatched a musket away from a guard was shot down without much concern. Mr. Parkinson, a Quaker, described the events: "Giving orders to fire, they [the guards] obeyed with the greatest glee imaginable, as if they had been shooting at ducks, killing one stout man, and wounding many others . . ." (Cook 1955, 81, n. 2). Cook himself reports that after the killing, he sought to persuade them (the natives) "that the man was killed for taking away the musquet [*sic*] and that we still would be friends with them." (Cook 1955, 81). Obeysekere (1992) reports that Cook himself ordered more severe floggings than did his contemporary Captain Bligh, but this report is largely directed at discrediting Cook's sainted image among the white populations of the Pacific Islands, particularly in New Zealand and Australia.

of both women and men before marriage. This must have been impossible to understand for eighteenth-century Europeans, for whom sexuality was a marked category: "there are no people in the world who indulge themselves more in their appetites than these; indeed they carry it to a most scandalous degree." (quoted from Ellis 1792 in Sahlins 1981). Sex as an unmarked pleasure is perhaps more difficult for twentieth-century Euro-Americans to understand than for their eighteenth-century predecessors, given the new ways in which sex has been marked in the last two centuries.

For the eighteenth-century sailor this way of framing copulatory life (there is no reference to procreation) may have been impossible to understand, given his cultural limitations, but not impossible to practice. It may be impossible to practice for the twentieth-century anthropologist—note the contemporary rules on not taking sexual advantage of the data (Vance 1991; Herdt and Stoller 1990). The Polynesian women and the European men both knew about how to fit their bodies together in penile-vaginal intercourse and make movements that seemed appropriate (think how much more complicated all this would have been if either the men or the women had a cultural taste for oral sex or tongue kissing and tried to introduce these tastes into the script, or if the Polynesian men wanted sex with the European men). Both parties to the activity are reported as being pleased by their actions, though there is no testimony from the women or the common seamen. Both partners probably assumed that the other (and both were "other" to each other in this case) were engaged in the acts for similar purposes to their own. It was indeed fortunate that neither party seemed to have very esoteric tastes in sexual practices and that the "willingness" of the women, while surprising, did not challenge the gender power assumptions of the men.

However, such interactions, no matter how pleasing and simple-appearing in the beginning, could not have been undertaken between cultural strangers without evoking new meanings and possibilities. Willy-nilly, new elements were included as part of the behavioral script for sexual intercourse. In addition to the sexual encounters, the times spent with the Englishmen provided opportunities for the women to eat tabooed foods (for example, pig) and to engage in tabooed actions (for example, on board the English ships they ate in the presence of men), and they were given gifts by the Englishmen with whom they had intercourse. The activity of the Polynesian and European bodies became conflated with the exchange of goods and the violation of correct relations between Tahitian women and Tahitian men. Only a short time passed before the activity of the bodies increasingly became contingent on the goods and the women appeared to be less and less under the control of the Polynesian men. Europeans were willing to pay for that which appeared to be freely given. In this process of gift-giving the sailors began the creation of the forms of prostitution of women which in later periods characterized the main ports of call in Polynesia. In scripting terms, these practices, initiated by the Europeans, commenced the transformation of the wanton into the bawd.

The changes in everyday social and sexual practice in Polynesia began to occur almost immediately as a result of the encounter with Europeans. The first effects resulted from the disease-ridden bodies (carcasses, said Diderot) of the Europeans themselves. Pox- and virus-ridden, they began the first stages of the decimation of Eden (Moorehead 1966). The changes in social and sexual practice in Europe were more indirect and abstract. They were provoked by the representations of experience rather than by experience itself. The personal experience of these few sailors was publicized across Europe, where the idea of Eden was more important than Eden itself. An alternative sexual world to Christian shame and guilt or to a world of economic calculation became part of the counter-cultural ideals from the time of the early Romantics until the end of the twentieth century.

The Erasure of the "Other"

How do these reflections on this historic instance of cultural contact relate to the larger purposes of a volume on migration, sexual risk, and HIV/AIDS? It was, after all, long ago and far away; not only are the sailors and the women dead, so too are their cultures. I propose that there are a number of useful reflections that can be drawn from it.

First, to return to the initial question: How did these particular cultural strangers solve the problem of knowing what to do sexually? Fortunately the case was a simple one; indeed, this is why it is so well remembered. Neither the Europeans nor the Polynesians had particularly divergent bodily expectations, women and men had physical sex together, and by implication, it was "sex" without the additional eroticism that was surely known to both officers and sailors at the time (remember that the erotic novel *Fanny Hill* had been published forty years before). Further, the encounters were apparently welcomed by the women, which meant that men did not engage in predatory acts of sexual violence that characterized other European encounters with other cultures. Finally, during the initial encounters the sex did not depend on significant convergences between cultural meaning systems since it did not extend into the larger networks of cultural life beyond the confines of the harbors where the ships were anchored. The eventual extension of Euro-American cultural penetration to the interiors of the islands would be carried out by the agents of commerce and religion and tourism, rather than by simple sailors.

When sexual tastes are more complex, and in later stages of the cultural encounter, identifiable zones (formal or informal) are set up in which sexual encounters are structured, often on a commercial basis. In Mexican border communities with the United States these were areas of prostitution named in some cases "la Zona." These are examples of what John and Ruth Useem once called "third cultures," which are specialized locales or ways of life that are differentiated from the "usual cultures" of both sets of participants. These zones are often as clearly marked in their instructions as a well-designed airport, so that the interpersonal organization of the sexual encounter is externally scripted. In some cases, these zones develop attractions of their own for certain groups of men. Men often find desired forms of sociability in ports of call, bright-light areas, and brothel districts (Greene 1980). These districts often serve to protect women in the rest of the society from social contact with strangers interested in sex, in the same way that tourist buses protect local drivers from untrained drivers from other cultures.

Second, one of the lessons of rereading these explorers' journals (as well the secondary literature) as historical texts, is that such a reading emphasizes that both sides of the sexual encounter were/are bearers of culture, as are those who interpret these encounters and their consequences. This particular encounter suggests most poignantly the ways in which Euro-American sexual cultures have come to dominate and transform those cultures that had/have alternative sexual practices. They were and we are, after all, sons (and increasingly daughters) of particular social, intellectual, and sexual cultures. In this process of cultural penetration, domination is usually confused with knowledge since only a fool will disagree with the interpretations of a better armed and obviously dangerous intruder.[8]

Third, the Polynesian encounter is instructive in the way it has provided one element of the ideological framework for the ways in which Europeans, as visitors, tourists, researchers, have organized their sexual

8. The "ethno-theories" of local populations are always treated "respectfully" by anthropologists when they are acquiring them. These theories are then converted into "data" for the anthropologists' theories, but this is usually accomplished in another language and for other audiences. A native who gets his or her hands on an anthropologist's report and challenges its objectivity is probably in less danger than a native who challenges the commercial exploitation of the local workforce (e.g., for road building) by colonial administrations.

intrusions into other cultures during the last two centuries. The "other" as sexual innocent or as sexual savage (often linked to differences in ethnicity or race) are part of the erotic life of the modern West (Schweder 1982). The journey outside of one's own culture that has been so characteristic of nineteenth- and twentieth-century life often was and remains a sexual journey for both men who had sex with men and men who had sex with women.

Aftermaths

There are two further observations that are linked to the Polynesian case. The first is the worldwide decline in cultural diversity and, usually unmentioned, sexual diversity as indigenous peoples are threatened by physical destruction or cultural transformation (recall that 1993 was the Year of Indigenous People). Demographically small and culturally different cultures everywhere in the world are in danger as a result of changes in local habitats and the incursions of representatives of centralizing or expanding nation-states or economic enterprises (Wilford 1994). In the absence of the creation of protected regions (cultural zoos?) it is clear that many small-scale experiments in human living will disappear in the next century.

But equally importantly there is a new homogenizing incursion into the cultural and sexual life of all societies, great and small, by the mass media, centered primarily in the United States and Europe. Here the danger is not to bodies, but to the actual content of diverse sexual scripts in many societies (Cohen 1994). The popularity of American soap operas and situation comedies not only creates a taste for middle-class goods, but conflates the good sexual life with the good consumer life. Perhaps we should rephrase Diderot as "one day they will come, with a satellite dish in one hand and a credit card in the other, to fill your minds and pockets and entice you to accept their customs and opinions; one day under their rule you will be almost as unhappy as they."[9]

9. On Thanksgiving Day 1994, I was channel surfing on the television and came upon the Macy's Thanksgiving Day Parade, which is held annually to celebrate the commercial opening of the Christmas season. While I was watching the telecast of the parade in New York the venue of the broadcast was switched to Hawaii, where a similar parade was being held. A high school marching band was preceded by two groups of young women, one of which was wearing the kinds of hula costumes and dancing in ways familiar to tourists in Hawaii or viewers of Hollywood movies of the South Seas. As they wended their way through downtown Honolulu, shaking their hula skirts modestly, the woman announcer gushed: "Isn't it wonderful the way they continue to celebrate native Hawaiian culture?"

Who Was That Girl? (2000)

I take my title and the organizing impulse for these reflections from Neil Bartlett's *Who Was That Man? A Present for Mr. Oscar Wilde* (1988).[1] The title of Bartlett's work poses the crucial question Is "homosexuality" at the core of Oscar Wilde's story? Was Oscar Wilde the ur-gay man, were his writings the genetic tests for camp, does Oscar Wilde deserve to be the most widely known "homosexual" of them all? Can the modern detective/historian/literary critic decipher from the body of Wilde's writings, from his and others' letters, from thickening layers of interpretive texts a "true" Oscar Wilde?

One of Bartlett's answers is

> After 25 May 1895 ("Guilty") Wilde could no longer pass. Everyone knew that Oscar was a forgery, a fake. He was not what he appeared to be. It was no defense that he himself had never claimed to be anything other than both forger and forgery. ("The first duty in life is to be as artificial as possible.") *He was entirely lacking in*

Originally published in *The Obscure Object of Desire: Freud's Female Homosexual Revisited*, edited by Erica Schoenberg and Ronnie Lesser (New York: Routledge, 1999), 76–86. Reprinted by permission. Support for the writing of this chapter came from a Research Leave from the College of Arts and Sciences of the State University of New York at Stony Brook and a grant from the Ford Foundation.

1. Bartlett's subtitle is double—the work is a gift, a present to Mr. Oscar Wilde, but it is more than that. It offers Mr. Oscar Wilde a place in the present, a contemporaneousness that attempts to overwrite (it cannot erase) the layers of interpretation that have papered over his historicity.

wholeness and completeness of nature. He wished, in fact, to be completely unnatural. He was a creator of copies, borrowing and reprocessing fragments of his own and other people's works. He assiduously composed his public life as father, husband, and moralist and he created a career for himself as a playwright whose plays are littered with the wrecks of fathers, husbands, and moralists, who are struggling to prove that they are who and what they say they are. His "private" homosexual life was an elaborate drama of deception, lies, and most of all, inspired invention. He could not, even in 1895, after concealment had failed, reveal his true nature. There was no real Oscar Wilde, if by real we mean homosexual. He did not, like us, have the alibi of "being like that." London in 1895 had no conception of a man being "naturally homosexual." A man who loved other men could only be described as an invert, an inversion of something else, a pervert, an exotic, a disease, a victim, a variation. Wilde was an artist as well. He was entirely uninterested in authenticity. (163–64, emphasis in original)

I chose this paragraph to legitimate various forms of the question Who was that girl who plays one of the two central roles (Freud plays the other) in the essay "The Psychogenesis of a Case of Homosexuality in a Woman"? If we cannot be sure about the homosexuality of Mr. Oscar Wilde, there may be similar questions about the homosexuality of this young woman. What is it about this young woman that makes Freud so sure that she is "homosexual"?

We are more restricted in answering this question about "the girl" than was Bartlett about Wilde. Wilde left behind volumes of works in his own hand; there are a vast number of commenting contemporaries; there are letters to and from a variety of others—even the streets of the city of London that Wilde frequented look much as they did then. One can slowly immerse oneself in Wilde and Wildeana until one has the illusion of being at one with the Other. Of course this metaphor for knowing is not unlike the archaeological dig. Though both methods draw upon the romantic impulses of the nineteenth century, the latter requires an objective and scientific supervisor of the excavation. The exemplary searcher in Freud is the archaeologist. The mound on the plain contains the hidden ruins of the city; the diggers unearth pottery shards, figurines, sometimes a completed tomb that has escaped the grave robbers. The mound yields up its secrets to the prepared hand and mind. The layers that represent the ruined cities, one built upon the other, are obviously the layers of repressed materials, down through which the analyst sifts his or her way. The metaphor is too passive to be complete, for the active role of the analysand is missing—indeed it is the analysand, like the native digger, who unearths the psychic fragments for the analyst to evaluate and interpret.

What is left of the girl? All that we know is in the essay from which all of the identifying characteristics have been expunged. We know that we are in Vienna, a vast imperial city, now shorn from its territorial and cultural periphery by the vagaries of World War I. Left only with its German majority, this East Reich will welcome its inclusion in the Third Reich in 1938. In 1920 it is an impoverished city, seething with discontents and resentments and anti-Semitism. The girl is brought to Freud by her father, and she walks up the steps to the consulting room at Bergstrasse 19 for only a few months. The case report is published in 1920, so perhaps she was a patient during 1918 or 1919, perhaps born in 1900 or 1901. We are told that she is eighteen and that she comes from still well-to-do parents, used to summering in resorts even during the war. These are the modest facts with which a detective might start. There are probably a few newspaper clippings about her suicide attempt that could lead us further in deciphering who the historical girl was and who she might have become.

Freud is now in his mid-sixties. He too has been diminished by the end of Empire. His international reputation is growing, but the actual circumstances of daily life are problematic. His professorship counts for less than he paid for it, as does the medical establishment in which he works.[2] Indeed, psychoanalysis itself does not seem to have achieved its proper role in the sciences as Freud ([1920] 1953–1974) notes: "The low estimation in which psychoanalysis is so generally held in Vienna did not prevent him [the girl's father] from turning to it for help" (149). Indeed, psychoanalysis was only the girl's father's penultimate alternative before a "speedy marriage [that] was to awaken the natural instincts of the girl and stifle her unnatural tendencies" (149).

My desire to know more about the historical girl is dual. Knowing about the historical girl would answer questions about whether her "natural instincts" or "unnatural tendencies" triumphed during the course of the next decades. It is a crude test of whether Freud's analysis of her past would have predicted her future. Second, it might answer questions about Freud's reactions to her. The rejection by the girl of both psychoanalysis

2. "Paid for it" refers to Freud's decision to use personal influence to be given his much delayed professorship.

as science and Freud as analyst has resulted in a profoundly defensive response by Freud in the essay itself.[3] What were the attributes of the girl
that allowed her to defend herself against the wishes of her natural father
and his psychoanalytic surrogate? Perhaps we would learn nothing about
"homosexuality" from this exercise in detective work, though we could
learn something about Freud.

One important note. It is clear that unlike Wilde's London, Freud's
Vienna does have a concept of the homosexual, perhaps not the "natural
homosexual," but at least the "unnatural homosexual" or the pervert. Indeed, Freud is one the shapers of the category "homosexual," both in
explanations of its etiology and of its adult enactment. The theater, literature, and fine arts of fin-de-siècle Vienna were highly eroticized (an
eroticization that is the context for Freud's own erotic works). The cross-
cutting margins between ethnic groups and social classes, Jew and non-
Jew, Austrian, Czech, Bohemian, Slav, and Hungarian, decaying aristo-
crats and rising bourgeoisie, employers and domestic servants are the
fertile edges around which the erotic imagination and sexual practice
flourished (Dabrowski and Leopold 1997; Schorske 1961; Werkner 1994).
It is hard to imagine Sigmund Freud beginning his work in late-
nineteenth-century London, although it is easy enough to find him near
the end of his life in a Bloomsbury he helped create.

A Girl in Love

The narrative structure of this profoundly digressive and incoherent essay does not make the behavioral facts of the case very accessible. And as
usual, the only voice that is heard in the writing is Freud's. The present-
ing conduct relevant to the classification of this "beautiful and clever girl"
(147) as homosexual appears in two widely separated sections of the essay. The first evidence is that the young woman has developed a passion
(perhaps a "crush" in contemporary terms) for an attractive woman some

3. Indeed, there are moments of splenetic narcissism, when Freud is angry at the world and
humanity (most of whom had never heard of him or his ideas) for not accepting his vision of the
world and its purposes (or lack thereof): "I know, indeed, that the craving of mankind for mysticism is ineradicable, and that it makes ceaseless efforts to win back for mysticism the territory
that it has been deprived of by *The Interpretation of Dreams*" and "my astonishment that
human beings can go through such great and important moments of their erotic life without
noticing them much. Sometimes even, indeed without having the faintest suspicion of their existence. . . . This happens not only under neurotic conditions, but also seems common enough in
ordinary life" (166). But even if human beings consciously noted these events they would not
have the appropriate psychoanalytic explanations for them.

ten years older than she. The older woman, who is of high social origins (perhaps the upper bourgeoisie or aristocracy), has fallen upon economic hard times—perhaps because of the dire effects of World War I in dismembering the Austro-Hungarian empire. The older woman lives with a married woman (whether there is a husband present is unclear, as are all other characteristics of this third woman and her relation to the beloved) and is said to have sexual relations with a number of men in exchange for economic support. (Freud nowhere specifies whether this support is in the form of gifts, cash, or other resources). Freud uneasily describes this woman as a "cocotte," by which he means something more serious than a coquette, perhaps a prostitute or at least a woman of ill-repute.

The girl (given her age, why Freud refers to her as a woman is unclear; in current terms she is still a "teenager," but she may have become a "woman" because she resists his advances) is entirely open to Freud about her attachment to her older friend. In the period before the girl is brought to Freud for "treatment," she hung about various places where her beloved could be seen (outside the beloved's door and at tram stops), and the girl took every opportunity to spend time with her beloved (though she lied to her parents about her activities). Of particular concern to the parents was that the girl and her beloved walked (how often is unspecified) arm in arm in the crowded pedestrian districts of the city, sometimes near her father's offices.

One day while strolling together, the girl and her beloved met the girl's father, who gave them only an angry glance and passed on. When the girl told her beloved who that angry man was, the beloved told the girl that their relationship must end—whether because the father knew or because the father disapproved is not clear. Rejected by both her father and her beloved, the girl then threw herself into a suburban railway cutting in an unsuccessful attempt at suicide. The girl was rescued, and after a six-month recovery at home once again began to see her beloved in a more open fashion than before. Her attempted suicide both made the girl's beloved take the girl's passion more seriously (or the beloved took the girl more seriously because she worried about the girl's self-destructive behavior)[4] and was the event that provoked the father to bring the girl to Freud.

Freud reports that these facts of the case are readily admitted by the

---

4. As evidence for this view, "the lady used to recommend [to] the girl every time they met to withdraw her affection from herself and from women in general, and she had persistently rejected the girl's advances up to the time of the attempted suicide" (153). Given the girl's insistence on physical purity, it is difficult to know what these "advances" involved.

girl. In addition, the girl reports other attachments to somewhat older women (often young mothers) in the girl's early teens (perhaps when she was thirteen or fourteen). During one summer in this period, she also eagerly sought out the company of a film actress, though this attachment was curtailed by her father. Yet with all of these passions, even with this relationship to an older woman now lasting (perhaps) nearly two years, she has never had a physical sexual relationship with either a woman or a man. As far as one can tell from the text, not even passionate kissing has occurred (153). She reports that she has rejected what she interpreted as homosexual advances from a young woman of her own age. The reason for this lack of physical sexual expression was that "[s]he was after all a well brought up and modest girl, who had avoided sexual adventures herself, and who regarded coarsely sensual satisfactions as unaesthetic" (161). And, "[w]ith none of the objects of her adoration had the patient enjoyed beyond a few kisses and embraces; her genital chastity . . . had remained intact" (153).

Are we to conclude from this interpreted evidence of what appear to be unconventional emotional attachments to women that the girl is "homosexual"? The evidence of attachments has clearly been selected and ordered first by the girl and then by Freud, and this is some species of interpretation. However, from the evidence, up until Freud terminates the sessions, the girl remains physically chaste. Further, Freud never says that girl labels herself as a homosexual or a lesbian (a word also well-known in Vienna). While she is articulate about the social aspects of sexual relationships, there is no evidence that she has had sex with either a woman or a man, nor that she is well-informed about the physical aspects of sex. Is evidence of such a "passion" by a "modest" girl, even one that includes a suicide attempt, sufficient evidence for inclusion in the category "homosexual"?

Clearly, just the fact that a woman has had or has not had sex with another woman is not enough to make any contemporary observer decide that a woman is a "homosexual" or lesbian. Even the psychoanalytic tradition has left spaces for acts without identity (the situational homosexual) or desires without action (the latent homosexual). Indeed, it is this issue that is at the heart of much of the recent discussion of the distinction between identity and behavior in gay and lesbian politics and studies. Similarly strong emotional attachments, even strong romantic attachments between men or between women, are not sufficient evidence of "homosexuality." From the evidence at hand, the girl only says "that she could not conceive of any other way of being in love" (153).

Was This Girl a Boy?

"The beautiful and well made girl had, it is true, her father's tall figure, and her features were sharp rather than soft and girlish, traits which might be regarded as indicating a physical masculinity. Some of her intellectual attributes could also be connected with masculinity: for instance, her acuteness of comprehension and her lucid objectivity, in so far as she was not dominated by her passion. But these distinctions are conventional rather than scientific" (154).

The girl is not a boy, at least in terms of "physical hermaphroditism," the ghost of nineteenth-century anatomic theories of the intersexes (see also p. 171) (Engelstein 1989). Freud seems to consign these constitutional views of the origins of homosexuality to the realm of those who are "unversed in psychoanalysis" (154). But biology remains prior to psychoanalysis in a tangled series of arguments that shift from "on the one hand" to "on the other hand": "It is possible here to attribute to the impress of the operation of external influence in early life something which one would have liked to regard as a constitutional peculiarity. On the other hand, a part even of this acquired disposition (if it was really acquired) has to be ascribed to inborn constitution" (169). And therefore, "it is rather a case of congenital homosexuality which, as usual, became fixed and unmistakenly manifest in the period following puberty" (169–70). So the ghost of constitutionalism still lives.

But then what about the relation between masculinity and femininity (in modern parlance, *gender identity* and *role*) and the gender of the sexual object-choice? "A man with predominantly male characteristics and also masculine in his erotic life may still be inverted in his erotic life in respect to his object. . . . A man in whose character feminine attributes obviously predominate . . . may nevertheless be heterosexual. . . . The same is true of women; here also mental sexual character and object-choice do not necessarily coincide" (170).[5] This is the contemporary view, except among the biologists of sexual orientation. And yet the girl may be a boy, if only in her romantic style. "What is certainly of greater importance is that in her behaviour toward her love-object she had throughout assumed the masculine part . . . the preference for being the lover rather than the

---

5. Here Freud shares with Kinsey the observation that there is no necessary relation between "obviousness" and same-gender preference in erotic relations. At the same time the "masculine in his erotic life" must refer to being a "top" or inserter rather than a "bottom" or insertee in sexual relations. Here styles of sexual activity become indicators of "masculinity" and "femininity."

beloved. She had thus not only chosen a feminine love-object, but had also developed a masculine attitude towards that object" (160).

The girl behaves as a boy in love "even to the smallest details" (160). Prior to finding her "*cocotte,*" the girl's desires were focused on women of marginal heterosexual respectability ("coquettes in the ordinary sense of the word" [161]); now she is bent on "rescuing her beloved from these ignoble circumstances" in which "she lived simply by giving her bodily favors" (161). The girl, by playing the role conventionally taken by a young man (as in the question What is a nice girl like you doing in a place like this?) in seeking to rescue a fallen woman through the purity of her love, somehow becomes "homosexual."

Or perhaps the girl is a tomboy? She is "a spirited girl, always ready for romping and fighting" (169), she has a "strongly marked 'masculinity complex' . . . She has developed a pronounced envy of the penis" (169). It then follows that "[s]he was in fact a feminist; she felt it unjust that girls should not enjoy the same freedom as boys, and rebelled against the lot of women in general" (169).

The girl's social "boyness" in her affectional styles of dealing with her beloved—that is, her gender role nonconformity—is central to Freud's decision to classify her as "homosexual," but a more critical theme is the girl's unwillingness to share "the lot of women in general" (169), which for Freud is uniquely manifested in childbearing. During the girl's puberty her mother gave birth to a child, and Freud's interpretation is that at puberty, when the girl most strongly wished to have a male child by her father, her mother gave birth to her brother. Therefore, "[a]fter this first great reverse she forswore her womanhood and sought another goal for her libido" (157). "[T]his girl had entirely repudiated her wish for a child, her love for men, and the feminine role in general" (158). "She changed into a man and took her mother in place of her father as the object of her love" (158). The first renunciation is the wish for the child, the second is the love of men, and the third is the feminine. If she is homosexual, she cannot be a woman.

A Journey Not Taken and a Suitor Rejected

Participation in psychoanalysis follows the pattern of all forms of romantic self-exploration during the nineteenth and twentieth centuries. It is a journey, either physical or psychical. But unlike the great solo journeys to other cultures and climes (here consider such examples as Byron to Greece, Gauguin to Tahiti, even Freud to Italy), the psychoanalytic journey into the land of the unconscious requires engaging a tour guide, the analyst. Only Freud has ever gone alone, and upon his return, he (like all great romantic explorers) wishes to make his journey available to others. The training of others in psychoanalysis creates a tour company similar to Thomas Cook's, and Freud's own writings become a Baedeker for the curious.

The role of the journey, particularly the train journey, was central to the development of psychoanalysis. It is on the train that Freud comes across those fertile slips of the tongue that are the empirical evidence for the unconscious. It is his own aborted train journeys to Rome that are central to his own personal history (Schorske 1961). It is in "Psychogenesis" that Freud uses the metaphor of the train journey to characterize the two parts of the psychoanalytic journey: "The first [part] comprises all the necessary preparations, today so complicated and hard to effect, before ticket in hand, one can at last go on to the platform and secure a seat on the train. One then has the right, and the possibility, of traveling to a distant country; but after all these preliminary exertions one is not yet there—indeed, one is not a single mile nearer to one's goal. For this to happen one has to make the journey itself from one station to the other, and this second part of the performance may well be compared to the second phase of the analysis (152).[6]

The first part of the journey has been that period when the girl has told Freud all of the facts, and Freud has shared with her the psychoanalytic explanations relevant to her condition. In Freud's words, "The analysis went forward almost without any signs of resistance, the patient participating actively with her intellect, though absolutely tranquil emotionally" (163). The girl has willingly participated in the "necessary preparations, today so complicated and hard to effect," yet she is unwilling to get on the train and make the journey with this guide: "Everything that has been accomplished is subject to a mental reservation of doubt" (163). Freud cannot accept that there has been no transference, yet the transference must have been insufficient. Faith has not repeated the history of its own origins. Freud then conceals his own individual failure by attributing it to a generalized hatred of men.

Freud has been rejected as a tour guide and as a theorist. "Once when I expounded to her a specially important part of the theory, one touching her nearly, she replied in an inimitable tone, 'How very interesting,' as though she were a *grande dame* being taken over a museum and glancing through her lorgnon at objects to which she was completely indifferent"

---

6. It is difficult not to believe that the phrase "today so complicated and hard to effect" does not refer to the actual difficulties of travel in the early postwar period in contrast to the pleasures of Freud's many train journeys of the prewar period.

(163). The metaphor is rich with ambiguity. On Freud's desk are the antiquities (museum objects) that he has collected, signaling the end products of the archaeological dig, objects to which the girl is indifferent. The *grande dame* looks down from a higher social position on the servant-doctor, perhaps even on the old Jewish man.[7] The intellectual seduction has failed. Unable to persuade the girl to get on the train, Freud protects himself, and psychoanalysis, by terminating the journey.

An Unpredictable Future

Despite this rejection (or perhaps because of it) Freud is sure of his diagnosis; indeed, he tells us many times that he is very sure:

> "to trace its origin and development in the mind with complete certainty" (147)

> "a full confirmation of my constructions" (152)

> "It was established beyond all doubt." (156)

> "The analysis revealed beyond all shadow of doubt" (156)

> "This position on affairs . . . is not a product of my inventive powers. . . . I can claim objective validity for it." (156)

> "I was right." (165)

> "but surely in the case under consideration everything is simple enough" (165)

> Except: "The amount of information about her seems meagre enough nor can I guarantee that it is complete." (155)

Even in the face of an analysis truncated by a contemptuous rejection—the most important half of the analytic journey, during which new truths are assimilated, remains untaken—Freud has no doubts of his objective powers.

However, it is in his response to this case that Freud denies psychoanalysis a capacity for prediction—a denial that casts the greatest doubt on psychoanalysis as positive science. Consider this long quotation:

> So long as we trace the development from its final outcome backwards, the chain of events appears continuous, and we feel that we

---

7. It would be interesting to know if the girl were Jewish or whether her distance from Freud was a combination of her superior economic situation and religious-ethnic difference.

have gained an insight that is completely satisfactory or even exhaustive. But if we proceed in the reverse way, if we start from the premises inferred from the analysis and try to follow these up to the final result, then we no longer get the impression of an inevitable sequence of events that could not have been otherwise determined. We notice at once that there might have been another result and that we might have just as well been able to understand and explain the latter. The synthesis is thus not so satisfactory as the analysis; in other words, from a knowledge of the premises we could not have foretold the nature of the result." (167)

What then is psychoanalysis? Perhaps only a reinterpretation of the analysand's story offering a new set of explanations for the set of facts. As such, psychoanalysis is part of that archaeology of explanation in which one hermeneutic interpretation is layered over another. In the first part of the ideal analytic journey, the analysand tells her story and should place her faith in the physician's healing powers (both as ideology and persona); in the second half of the journey, the physician uses this faith to rewrite her interpretations. However, this ideal analysis cannot predict the future. Even a satisfactory construction has no predictive power. While the girl may be a "homosexual" at eighteen, what will she be in 1938 when she is thirty-six? Depending on when in the patient's life the analysis begins, perhaps another "exhaustive insight" might be produced. What is important is not the actual life of the analysand, which is lived forward, but the reconstructions of the analyst, in which the life of the analysand is interpreted backward.

Who Was That Man?

In the last analysis, there is no last analysis. Freud and each of his interpreters, as well as the interpreters of this specific essay (Appignanesi and Forrester 1992; Merck 1993; Jacobus 1995), stand between us and the girl. Was she "actually" a homosexual girl of eighteen in 1918 or 1919 in post–World War I Vienna? Does the answer to this question matter? Perhaps the debate about the girl is actually a debate about Freud and his authority to tell her story to us (Fuss 1993).

The question is not Who was that girl? but Who was that man who stands between us and that girl, perhaps between us and all girls? The girl is pretext for avoiding the confrontation with Freud and Freudiana. This question brings us closer to Bartlett on Wilde. Perhaps a paraphrase of the opening quotation from Bartlett on Wilde may help: "Freud was a creator of copies, borrowing and reprocessing fragments of his own and other people's lives. He assiduously composed his public life as father, husband, and moralist, and he created a career for himself as a physician whose essays are littered with the wrecks of fathers, mothers, and children, who are struggling to prove that they are who and what they say they are. Freud's life was an elaborate drama of deception, lies, and most of all, inspired invention. There was no real Sigmund Freud. Freud was an artist as well. He was entirely uninterested in authenticity."[8] And so the question might be reformulated one more time. The question is not who was that girl or even who was that man, but who are we and why are we still so interested in this girl and this man?

8. Recall that Wilde (born 1854) and Freud (born 1856) were contemporaries and are equally guilty of helping to invent modernity. Freud lived thirty-eight years longer than Wilde.

Epilogue

Sexual Conduct Revisited (1998)

Gunter Schmidt: Twenty-five years ago you and William Simon published Sexual Conduct, *a "pathbreaking study" as Ken Plummer put it recently, "constituting the approach which now is commonly known as the 'social constructionist approach.'" Do you share this evaluation?*

John Gagnon: My answer has two parts. The first part is to agree that the book that we wrote offered an original alternative to prior ways of thinking about sexuality. So in that sense it can be described as pathbreaking. I am not sure that's exactly the right word; perhaps we only remapped what was thought to be a well-understood terrain. The second part is to say I don't think we have viewed ourselves as social constructionists. We have never had any sense of ourselves being directly influenced by the German constructionist tradition exemplified by Alfred Schutz, Peter Berger, or Thomas Luckman. That tradition had no direct connection to us. Our thinking was much more rooted in the tradition of pragmatism in the United States, an intellectual orientation that is very, very American, especially in terms of its attempt to declare independence from its European origins.

GS: What persons are you thinking of?

Translated, by permission, from *Zeitschrift fuer Sexualforschung* 11, pp. 353–66. This interview with John Gagnon on *Sexual Conduct* was conducted June 5, 1998, in Sermione, Italy, in a hotel on the shores of Lake Garda. The area, which includes the site of the ruin of a spectacular Roman villa, is now a summer resort.

JG: Simon and I had been trained in sociology at the University of Chicago, but the Chicago department was changing dramatically when we were there in the 1950s. George Herbert Mead, Robert Park, and Herbert Blumer were no longer heroes of Chicago sociology. Young people, who were influenced by the Chicago school, primarily in the person of Everett Hughes—students like Erving Goffman and Howard Becker and others who would continue some aspects of the Chicago tradition—had all left. The old faculty had been replaced by a new generation trained at Columbia University. The Chicago tradition was replaced by the middle-range sociology of Robert Merton and Paul Lazarsfeld, a perspective which dominated the intellectual climate at the end of our careers at the University of Chicago. Actually there are two other intellectual threads which connected the two of us. First is the work of a man named Kenneth Burke, who was a profound influence on Bill and me. Burke is not widely known either internationally or even in the American sociology anymore, though there has been a revival of interest since his death two years ago.

GS: *He was a sociologist?*

JG: No, he was a music critic, a book reviewer, a literary critic and scholar, an intellectual. He belongs to the tradition of American eccentrics, people who are outside the mainstream, who are not academics, but who are public intellectuals. Bill and I were influenced independently by Burke. He began reading Burke when he was in literary studies at the University of Michigan. Before that Bill was an activist in the far left of the American labor movement. I started reading Burke in college because I was interested in his ideas about interpretation. We actually used fragments of Burke's work, but these were critical elements in our shared perspective.

GS: *We will come back to Burke. But which was the second thread of connection between Gagnon and Simon?*

JG: The second connection was and is that tradition in the Chicago school of thinking about nonoccupational aspects of social life metaphorically as "careers." The career model offered a processual and contingent perspective on how people assimilated new ways of living, how they enacted them, and how life choices changed the self. This perspective goes back into the roots of Chicago criminology, when Clifford Shaw and Henry McKay began to write about criminal careers in the same way that others wrote about conventional occupational careers. The metaphor could then be extended to marijuana smoking, pregnancies out of wedlock, homosexuality. Also thinking about alternate life paths as careers allowed a certain moral neutrality while thinking about deviance. The careers of a banker and a gangster could be analyzed in exactly the same way: learning how to do a job, acquiring skills and insider knowledge, learning how to deal with all of the other social actors in a particular social milieu. By emphasizing the common features of learning and performing the usual moral differences between occupational and lifestyle categories could disappear. The concept of social careers was an important idea in conceiving of certain parts of *Sexual Conduct.*

GS: Let's come back to Kenneth Burke and read a few sentences from your book. "Part of the legacy of Freud is that we had all become adept at seeking out the sexual ingredient in many forms of non-sexual behavior and symbolism. We are suggesting what in essence the insight of Kenneth Burke is: it is just as plausible to examine sexual behavior for its capacity to express and serve non-sexual motives as the reverse." Is this one of the central messages of Sexual Conduct?

JG: Yes, absolutely. Following Burke we began to think about the way in which sex (both symbolically and physically) could be expressive of other interests (work, politics, religion) and that the sexual did *not* have a priority in causal explanation. If there is a network of different influencing factors, Freud always chose the sexual to explain all the others. By this simplification you often eliminate what is most interesting, which is that the sexual is one element in a dynamic network of forces, including gender, class, race/ethnicity, nationality. You may do something sexually dramatic for quite mundane other reasons. That came directly out of the Burkean texts.

GS: What makes the difference between sexual behavior and sexual conduct?

JG: The sexual conduct phrase actually came from Ernest W. Burgess, who worked with Robert Park. Park and Burgess were two of the great figures of the second Chicago school. What Burgess was arguing—this was in a critique of Kinsey—was that behavior is always morally evaluated. There is no human behavior without moral, hence social, evaluation. So you don't have biologically naked sex behavior, you have socially clothed sexual conduct. And so we took the phrase "conduct," because we wanted to say we are not talking about socially unevaluated behavior. The crucial issue is, sexual behavior is socially constituted so that it becomes sexual conduct. Actually this formulation is backwards and wrong. It probably should be said that thinking about sex as behavior is one aspect of the way we conduct ourselves sexually. Sex becomes behavior when we decide to take off the cultural clothing of sexuality, which is its socially "natural" condition, to reveal the unnatural condition of sex as naked behavior.

GS: Three years after the publication of Sexual Conduct *the psychoanalyst Robert Stoller developed similar thoughts in his theory of perversion and in his theory of sexual excitement stressing the sexualizing effect of meanings. Did you know something about Stoller when you were writing* Sexual Conduct?

JG: No. And I don't think Bill did either. Bill and Stoller developed a very close relationship later on. And I recall that an interesting correspondence then resulted, in which Stoller indicated the importance of the ideas of *Sexual Conduct* for his own work. He had read the book and he had used some of the ideas in it. I am less persuaded by Stoller's notion of the microdot. Stoller's microdots have their origins too early in childhood for me and remain influential far later in life than I give them credit for. We did however take a critical microdot-like example from the novelist Jerzy Kosinski in a discussion of the independent role of the intrapsychic in arousal.

GS: I remember this story, where a man is attracted by his female colleague, and it doesn't work because she was accessible?

JG: Yes. So he fantasies about an airline stewardess raising her arms above her head to put away a bag in an overhead bin. Her breasts are pulled up by her brassiere, and this becomes an erotic provocation in a way that is similar to the microdot. However, we preferred a less restrictive source of erotic symbols, a more general menu of arousing symbols, than did Stoller.

GS: However, similar ideas developed in quite different places, in quite different disciplines, in quite different schools of thinking in those years. You and Stoller get rid of traditional approaches of sexuality — the naturalization of sex and the concept of sex drive.

JG: Stoller began in the context of psychoanalysis as a practitioner and theorist. Consequently, he has had a more difficult intellectual task in revising Freud, given the centrality of libido theory to psychoanalytic practice, than we did. We resisted Freud in general.

GS: And admired him at the same time.

JG: Freud was one of the great men we had to push aside in order to establish our own point of view. And so we may have simplified him more than we should have. But we were young and he was in the way. I don't think we were as generous as we should have been, or even as thoughtful about what he could have given us. Stoller's position was much more complicated than ours because he had to keep Freud, and he had to selectively retain and honor those elements that still worked for him as a practicing psychoanalyst. And so his reading of Freud is much more nuanced than ours was, at least in that first version. I think that Bill in his own work has reconstituted his relationship to Freud in important ways. I think I have done that less than he has.

GS: So one hero you tried to put aside as a young man was Freud, the second was Kinsey. Is there a connection between Freud and Kinsey?

JG: Well, I think that I resist the label "sexology" because it has at its core the theory of sexual naturalization; that idea that stretches from Krafft-Ebing to Masters and Johnson that sex is a natural phenomenon. Kinsey's naturalism is very different than Freud's. Freud's notion is that nature must be resisted to create civilization. Kinsey's view of nature is much more beneficent. In his view nature produces a variety of opportunities to be sexual. For Kinsey the problem of civilized sexual culture is that it's like agriculture. It produces only one sexual product, one sexual crop. The only approved crop is heterosexuality.

GS: Destroying variability . . .

JG: That's right. Kinsey—and I think this is why he is so badly misunderstood—really was a taxonomist of evolution. He believed in the beauty of diversity in nature. Nature provided you with all these variations. And what culture did was to place limits on nature. This turns Freud upside down. However, nature remains for Kinsey the origin of desire. And so we had to get rid of both of them in order to get a completely socially determined sexuality. We had to eliminate nature.

GS: And you did it by creating what you call the script theory?

JG: We created script theory in an attempt to have a device to describe how people go about doing sex socially and to demonstrate the importance of social elements in the doing of the sexual.

GS: What would you say script theory is in your sense today?

JG: Where did it go? I think we lost control of it. You know, one loses control of every idea. When I hear people say the word *script* at a meeting, I often don't recognize what they are talking about. But that's inevitable. I think that at this moment neither Bill nor I have made a fully coherent argument about scripts.

GS: In your recent book The Social Organization of Sexuality *there is a small and very comprehensive description of script theory. In its shortness it's quite informing. Can you respond to this?*

JG: I am actually quite labile in my intellectual relationship to people I respect intellectually. When I talk to them I am always actively influenced or resistant to what they are saying, and I often revise my own ideas as they talk. In a way there is sort of a Gagnon-Laumann script theory in the book you mentioned, and there is a Gagnon-Simon script theory, and there is a Gagnon script theory. As I listened to Ed Laumann talking about social networks and the importance of networks, scripting linked into those ideas. One can think about a sequence of events (such as all the separable events that make up a wedding) as a sequence of scripts, and then think about who is present or absent at various moments in the unfolding of the larger set of events. The key ideas are the copresence or absence of actors and the ordering of the scripts. And so you get a matrix which is "scripted events" on one axis and "actors" on the other, and the social arrangement then becomes the matrix of actors and events. In the work which I did with Bill there was a much greater concern with what went on inside people's heads—with the intrapsychic and the social origins of mental life.

GS: Do you still stick to the three levels of scripting, the cultural scripts, the interpersonal scripts, and the just mentioned intrapsychic scripts?

JG: The reason that we invented the three levels of scripting was to deal with the quasi-independent relation between the agentive individual, the interactional situation, and the surrounding sociocultural order. This was always the weakness of traditional culture-personality theory in anthropology. The individual often appeared to be a simple replicate of the sociocultural order. The same simplification appeared in robust sociological theories which emphasized the dominance of the social order in the production of social life. The problem for such theories is that they could not account for variations in individual conduct in what appeared to be the same socially structured situation.

We formulated the concept of cultural scenarios somewhat later than the intrapsychic and the interpersonal levels of scripting, though this idea was implicit in *Sexual Conduct*. Cultural scenarios was the name we gave to the instructional semiotic system that is the intersubjective space of the sociocultural. All social institutions have instructions of how to behave built into them, and these instructions are not internal properties of individuals, they are the property of the organized collection of individuals who were enacting that institution or situation. In between these two levels was the interpersonal, social conduct in the presence of other individuals. I think that *Sexual Conduct* was good on dyads (perhaps guided by the dyadic nature of much of sexuality), but less good on complex social situations or complex sequences of events. This is what Ed Laumann was good at, understanding the contribution of audiences to ongoing social action. My work with Laumann made me more sensitive to the role of "stake holders," both individual and institutional, in what appear to be purely interpersonal interactions.

Finally to preserve the independently acting individual (this has some connection to Meade's "I") we needed intrapsychic scripting, a socially based form of mental life. What went on in people's heads was critically important since it embodied planning, remembering, fantasy. I actually think at the time we wrote *Sexual Conduct,* Bill was better at theorizing about mental life than I was, better at thinking about the intrapsychic.

GS: More interested I think. Is that the connection to Stoller?

JG: That's the connection to Stoller. It is also the connection to poetry.

GS: To poetry?

JG: Yes, he had read a lot of poetry, and in our discussion of the intra-psychic he was always arguing that thought processes are not always linear, but there are always masses of unrelated associations. So creating the poem, particularly the modern poem, means disrupting conventional prose/speech, calling on private images and experiences. Essentially everyday thought is noisy, messy, chaotic. I think it was this conception of the symbolic that brought him back to Freud.

And from my point of view it is abnormal to think scientifically. Most thought processes, as you go through the world, are impressions and fragments and pieces. You have to create an environment in which linear and highly coherent thought can go forward: you find a quiet room, you close the doors, you turn on the computer, you look at the screen, you type, you pretend like there is nothing else going on in the world or in your head. But that describes a specialized environment for a very specialized form of thinking.

GS: Is the differentiation of cultural scripts, interpersonal scripts, and in-trapsychic scripts still reasonable for you?

JG: It remains an analytic device for me. In my new thinking the critical tension in the individual is managing the relationship between the public and the private. The private is the domain of the intrapsychic. Both cultural scenarios and interpersonal scripts are enacted in the public domain. It's not that the intrapsychic does not depend on these other two domains. It's that you can manipulate mental life more freely than you can manipulate either other people or the culture at large.

GS: It gives way to more variance?

JG: That's right. You can allow fantasy to flourish. And the flourishing of fantasy is not only sexual. Political and social fantasies abound. For instance in order to make a better world we must first fantasize, How can we make this a better world? Marxist communalism was first of all a fantasy in a burgeoning capitalist world about how to create a postcapitalist world. Certain social orders create a need for this more complicated mental world. And as modern social orders get more complicated, there is actually an increase in the density and significance of intrapsychic life. As concrete situations get more various, psychic life has to get even more various. Dealing with a concrete social situation requires a concomitant mental effort. And as we come in contact with an increasingly sexually complex world, we have to bring more mental resources to bear to understand that the person you are going to deal with is not only a man, but a man of a certain culture and history and biography. We can deal with that by narrowing and simplifying the other to their body or their organs. However if we want to have a shared social relationship we have to take account of the variousness of this sexual situation from all the other sexual situations we have been in. And that requires a great deal of mental agility in private matters.

GS: Is that what other sociologists call "reflexivity"?

JG: I think so, it's a version of reflexivity, but hopefully more highly elaborated version than the usual version. Again it is closer to Burke and perhaps Freud. Sometimes when social scientists talk about reflexivity, it's too automatic, too simple. It is as if reflexivity did not cost anything. Being reflexive is enormously complex because the actor has to think of many possibilities and many consequences, not only for others, but for the constitution of the self. The pressure to select, to choose one of many lines of action, increases the more you get into the public world, but at the same time the integrity of the fantasy must be maintained. This relationship between mental life and other levels of scripting is the aspect of scripting about which I have been thinking. The other part is the ways in which the cultural and interpersonal order are connected in mental life. Culture has no direct relationship to interpersonal relations. It must go through the heads of the actors. The task of the actor is to continually link and adjust and transform and stabilize the interpersonal and the cultural while maintaining the plausibility of the self. At the same time the interpersonal and cultural worlds the actor inhabits are not passive, for other individuals and social institutions are always trying to either constrain or change the individual. The levels now become interactive. I think in our first version it was a bit more static. There was culture, the interpersonal, the intrapsychic, sort of freestanding.

GS: In Sexual Conduct, *your first version of script theory, you don't have the cultural scripts.*

JG: It's largely implicit and it's actually more visible in the chapter on pornography than in other places. *Sexual Conduct* as a book is enormously uneven. It's trying out a lot of different ideas.

GS: It convenes a number of essays on quite different areas.

JG: Yes, I think that's a real difficulty. But on the other hand approaching each topic separately allowed us to try out our theoretical perspectives deductively. When we wrote about homosexuality among men, we emphasized the concept of careers. It is in this essay where the idea of "career" is very visible. When we wrote about lesbianism our concern was the relationship between gender differences and sexuality. In both of those essays we also addressed what we called the specious problem of etiology. When we wrote about pornography, we were interested in how culture offered people sexual stories which they then bring into their own lives. Pornography was also a textual testing ground for the script concept.

GS: And then you were talking about childhood and adolescence, a very broad chapter in this book.

JG: Yes, it's a rich chapter full of underdeveloped ideas. For instance it's where we invent the concept "homosocial." As a concept it is now absolutely ubiquitous, and nobody knows where it came from. But it's first used there, though perhaps in a different spirit. We were looking for a word to substitute for "homosexual." At the time, when thinking of the affiliative behavior of boys in adolescence, the available language of psychoanalysis was "these are homosexual groups" or "this is a homosexual period." We invented the word homosocial exactly to get rid of the idea of the casual centrality of sexuality; first the social, we argued, then the sexual, second.

GS: It could include sexual act, too?

JG: Yes, but it subordinated the sexual acts to social processes. These are groups of boys in whose social practices the sexual is embedded, but it is performed for other social purposes. It doesn't give priority to the sexual. The sex is interesting to the boys, but not nearly as important as the approval of other young men. And once again this was the concrete version of the Burkean notion, that you do sexual things for other social purposes.

GS: Let's come back to the intrapsychic scripts. Was Stoller a specialist in this?

JG: I don't want to psychoanalyze Stoller. But I think that his situation was different, the kinds of people he saw were different. He sought out more dramatic instances of sexuality to analyze.

GS: And around you?

JG: We were working primarily in the world of the mundane, and Stoller remained, as a psychoanalyst must, in the world of the drama, of powerful emotions, of events filled with affective intensity. If there was a weakness in Stoller, it was his belief in the intensity of the sexual. He still believed that the sexual was powerful.

GS: But only because it took over emotions and energy from nonsexual sources.

JG: Right. But essentially it was still powerful. It was still a drama. And for Bill and I, at that time, we saw the sexual at a much lower level of emotional intensity. The script for us was not *Faust*. And I think that Stoller and psychoanalysis in general invites dramatic stories, important stories. We were interested in ordinary people and everyday tasks: How did people get home from work, have dinner, turn on the television, watch the television, have sex together, then go to sleep? And in a way we were the voice of the common man and woman, which is what sociology pretends to be. It's the story of everyday life. We were in fact the enemies of the traditions that stressed the power of the sexual for purposes of social change or appealing to sexuality as a source of personal or political redemption, or as the primary terrain of social meaning. We said that sexuality was routine, and that it was produced by routine social causes.

GS: Quite unromantic!

JG: Quite unromantic. But I think both Bill and I are romantics as individuals! But being in this crazy discipline of the everyday and of the unremarkable and the nonmiraculous, we worked against our own personal interests. For many people sex remains the only place where there are miracles. Sex and love remain the world of the miracle. You cross a crowded room, you fall in love, you change your life—something transformative happens. And what we were saying was: the feeling of transformation is socially orchestrated, you feel transformed, but you are enacting the script of transformation. My work with Laumann went somewhat further; the argument is: Of course you can fall in love across a crowded room. The question to ask is, How did the two of you get into the same crowded room? And the answer is, Everyone in the room has the appropriate social characteristics to be in the same crowded room. The emotions are real, but arranged by social structure and enacted through sexual scripts.

GS: Coming back to the cultural scripts, do you think that Foucault is some expert on cultural scripts? Are discourses cultural scripts?

JG: I have lots of ambivalence about Foucault. I think he was a poor historian, but I also think that he asked more general questions than we did. He tried to grasp other, perhaps larger issues. And I think he is wrong in a number of ways. For instance, I think that the impulse to reduce things to texts, discourses, is an error. Because what social life is really about is performances. It's really people performing in social spaces. Scripts are closer to the performative than is discourse. I think what Foucault does is too texty; it's too parochially French, with in its interest in discourse and the power of discourse.

GS: You said ambivalence, so there must be something that you could take from Foucault?

JG: I am not sure. In many cases I don't understand his arguments and I don't know where they take me intellectually, what these ideas do for my thinking. If we interpret what he says as meaning that people have power over other people, and they use discourses to do so, well, I would suggest a reading of Marx. Often I think much of Foucault is not very new except to folks who are not well read in history and the other social sciences. Other people have made his arguments better, or at least more clearly and less infused with the local intellectual circumstances of Paris in the 1970s. Foucault is sort of an intellectual figure whom I worry about and push against largely because of his importance to others, but I don't think I actually have ever really been engaged by him.

GS: *Looking at American social constructionists, be they feminist or gay theoreticians, they much more refer to Foucault, it seems to me, than to Simon and Gagnon. Is that embarrassing for you? Disappointing?*

JG: Well, disappointing. I think we were there first. And at least some people think that we said it better. Most of the non–social science people who do gay and lesbian studies and cultural studies have not read very much in the relevant social sciences. What they have read is their business, but for instance they don't know anything about the American pragmatist tradition. They don't realize that the notion of the meaning is in the response, which is at the core of Derrida, was said by George Herbert Mead and Kenneth Burke decades ago. Only Richard Rorty seems to have recognized the common roots of these ideas in Hegel. It's the usual American provincialism—that if they say it in France, it must be so. There is a deference to French intellectual life by Americans, that in fact, I don't think it always deserves. Being knowledgeable about France and French ideas is a way American intellectuals separate themselves from the common herd.

GS: *You say it as a person who really loves France.*

JG: Oh, yes, absolutely. I think the French probably more than anybody else in the Western world are resisting being Americanized. They value their language, they think that speaking French is better than speaking English. It is admirable, a way to avoid being Coca-Cola-ed to death. But at the same time French intellectuals don't read anybody else either. And they don't read anybody who writes in Lyon either. If you don't write from inside Paris, you aren't anybody. The deference which contemporary Americans show to French intellectuals is similar to the deference Americans showed to European culture in general at the end of the nineteenth century. Members of a colonial society showing deference to their intellectual superiors. If you say "Foucault," you don't have to make any more arguments.

GS: *Your rejection of the naturalism in the Freudian and Kinseyan sense offered quite new perspective on social change in sexuality.*

JG: Well, I think what we were trying to do is actually in the last line of the book.

GS: *We have to cite it.*

JG:(Reads) "The critical posture to maintain is that the future will not be better or worse, only different." This sentence was our attempt to say that the future of sexuality was not a matter of "progress" or moral improvement or utopia or dystopia. We are always involved in the human struggle to make the future. But the future that is being created is just going to be different than the present, not better or worse. This phrase also signaled our belief in the historical/cultural constitution of mental life, which we alluded to in the beginning of the book. When the future comes, who and what we are now will be lost. Each generation is always the dinosaurs to the future. We have lost the nineteenth century, the twenty-first century will lose us. The past is always the worlds we have lost.

GS: *In contrast to some Freudians, for example, Wilhelm Reich or Herbert Marcuse, or in contrast to Kinsey, you then cannot have a positive utopia of sexual change.*

JG: Yes, that's the root theme that ran through all of this work: the antiutopian, the antidramatic, the antimagical, the antiromantic.

GS: *De-dramatizing sexuality?*

JG: That's right. I think perhaps that was really the key idea. The fact that there was no magic in the world. We were really searching for disenchantment. The world is no longer enchanted, and it cannot be enchanted again. And the search for enchantment in sexuality must end in failure.

GS: *This means, too, that you have no sympathy for the cultural pessimistic attitude many social philosophers present?*

JG: The notion that culture is declining? No, it's just going to be different. If you asked me how I would like the world to be, I could only repeat to you the standard democratic platitudes: equality, democracy, justice. I would repeat all those catch phrases, like everybody would. What else would you say? But the world is not going to be like that.

GS: *What should it be sexually?*

JG: I think the only way that you can make the world sexually the way you want it to be is to have ambition for your ideals as the psychoanalyst Heinz Kohut put it. This is what Marx was: he was ambitious for his ideals. I don't see anyone, or any movement, which has new ambitions for sexuality. And particularly given the posture I took, how can you have ambitions for the mundane? It doesn't go together, to be ambitious for the commonplace. The desire to make orgasm better, to help men to have more erections—that is like improving cooking. You have to construct something interesting out of the sexual. If that something has to be richer than the behavioral, then sexuality has to be transformed. But then, into what? Into better communication? Into Haberemas's just communication?

GS: Sociological research shows, that many people are looking for authentic emotions, passion, exciting thrills coming from sexuality. So they are ambitious.

JG: Well, I think that in the everyday world the belief in the romantic is still very powerful. And I think it's not just the sexual; I think it's about love. I think we underestimate the importance of the intensity of love. People are looking for intensity, spontaneity. Our argument was that spontaneity is scripted. We had already undermined ourselves. It wasn't that life was not variable, it was only scripted variously. Spontaneity is always bounded, even in fantasy. You are always enacting a script. Even when you are playing with it, trying to make it anew, you are making up a system of scripted action. And in a way there is only the social. It's actually a much darker vision than the notion of decline. Because the notion is that at one time sexuality was something important, and now there is decline. And our argument was: there never was anything wonderful. And it's not going to get better or worse. We simply say: In 1940 they did it that way, in the year 2040 they're going to do it this other way. That's what the creature does. It's a cultural animal. A gloomy perspective, I must say.

GS: In what respect gloomy?

JG: Because there was never anything special. Or if there was something special, it was only because we as cultural/historical creatures made it special in the ways the culture dictated. So many social theories begin with the notion that from out of nowhere we will eventually be blessed. Perhaps this is the source of the current alien craze. Or that there is some larger purpose to human life. I think that our book is a celebration of purposelessness. That the only purpose to sexuality is the one we create in a given time and place. God, evolution, the state, patriotism, progress, communism, capitalism—those are all collectivist notions which we have imposed on ourselves to avoid purposelessness.

GS: You have made a lot of predictions in your book, or speculations about the future. Please imagine for a minute that you are a sleeping beauty, falling asleep in 1973 and being kissed awake by a princess or a prince in these days. What would you be astonished about and what would you be not astonished about, seeing today's sexual landscapes?

JG: Starting now, I think I would have been struck by the transformation of gay and lesbian life and feminism in the West. The intellectual bravura of the gay and lesbian movements and feminism is deeply surprising, if you start in 1973. In *Sexual Conduct* we had a sentence which said that the homosexual community is primarily a sexual marketplace. And I don't think that anyone can make the claim today. The gay world is an immensely rich and complicated social world, a community created and creating an identity. It is a fascinating set of options. And the amount of original thought which is going on—it is really a very rich intellectual world. I am not sure I agree with all of it, but it's clearly an interesting place.

We probably overestimated the sexual originality of American culture at the behavioral level. I don't think that I would have been surprised by the amount of pornography. The erotic landscape seemed to me already on it's way to current development in 1973.

GS: What about the heterosexuals?

JG: I don't think they changed very much; that's really been kind of remarkably stable. What does happen actually? Well, they have intercourse a little bit sooner. They have a few more partners.

GS: Not only sex partners but love partners.

JG: Love partners. Basically serial monogamy now begins at fifteen to sixteen and proceeds through life.

GS: That's a difference. If you look on their grandparents . . .

JG: That is a difference. But in a sense even if it is not the same couple over the life course, but many couples, the Durkheimian effects may remain the same. The opposite gender couple remains the primary way of organizing emotional and psychic life, children, houses, cars, ownership. Actually maybe the triumph of capitalism is its capacity to maintain at the individual level large numbers of satisfied consuming and reproducing couples. I think what's most interesting is the remarkable disconnection between the cultural erotic life of the society—the amount of erotica—and the absolute conventionality of the people.

GS: A discrepancy between . . .

JG: . . . this level of the production of erotic cultural scenarios and this level of what people in fact do.

GS: Do you have an explanation for it?

JG: I do, but it will sound a little crazy.

GS: That sounds interesting!

JG: I think there are really two arenas of sexual action which don't have anything to do with each other most of the time. There is the domain of the symbolic and the domain of the behavioral. People go to the domain of the symbolic not because it compensates for how dull things are; people in fact are perfectly happy with their dull sexual lives. It's because what the symbolic domain offers you, and now this is a much more general argument about capitalism, is a world without social friction, a world without cost. You can play, you can have contact with beautiful bodies, you can look at lovely things without investment. That's the difference between owning an automobile and looking at an advertisement for an automobile.

GS: Different worlds, but both are important.

JG: But they are independent in many ways. They come together every once in a while. In moments of cultural crises, you may have people saying, "My fantasies are not the same as my behavior." But otherwise people do not compare the world of fantasy and the world of what they do every day, and neither has a natural priority. The most important thing is that it is very pleasant.

We have to move outside the sexual, and we can see it everywhere—fantasy consumption, fantasy celebrity. If you want to know that you are watching a movie and you are not sure—you think you may be hallucinating, but you won't know—you know it's a movie when the car pulls up to park in New York City and there is no other car parked on the block. Well, fantasy copulation has the same quality. You don't have to pull next to other cars, look and see how big the parking space is, block traffic and listen to the horns blowing, go through all the maneuvers of parking—there is always a space available in fantasy.

Why are you satisfied emotionally from an advertisement in which a beautiful person drives a fancy car up in front of a fancy building and stops? An advertisement that calls the BMW the ultimate driving machine. In reality everyone in New York knows that the ultimate driving machine will only go 15 miles an hour in city traffic, if they are lucky. It's the psychic independence that exists between real world driving and the fantasy of driving. One does not criticize the other. Similarly there is real world sexuality and the fantasy of sexuality. And they are simply separate. Fantasy is a world without friction. No one denies you, and you can turn it off. I think that's how people live in the postmodern world.

GS: In what respect?

JG: There is an increase in the importance of intrapsychic life which is absolutely crucial. To survive the modern world requires more mental activity rather than less.

GS: Are you going to reprint Sexual Conduct?

JG: We have made an agreement with the original publisher. The new version, we think at this moment, will have an introduction about the origins of the key ideas, the circumstances of invention. What were the biographical, cultural, historical circumstances of writing the book, including the fact it was written during the sixties. It was written during a period of crisis, by two people who had a tangential relationship to that crisis. At the end of each chapter we will put a few comments, trying to not destroy the original structure. And then at the end there will be a discussion of where the central ideas of the book have gone. We will leave the original text the same, only making it nonsexist in its language.

GS: It is sexist?

JG: Yes, it was the 1960s, so we were not yet aware of gender neutral language.

GS: More than twenty-five years ago, I met you and Bill Simon in a New York Hotel. And by chatting around you said, "We have just one problem: to know who is Marx and who is Engels" Did you decide upon this question?

JG: (Laugh) A revolutionary remark!

GS: I was deeply impressed!

JG: I think that I had the wrong people in mind. The better choice would have been "Who is Freud and who is Durkheim?"

GS: Thank you very much, John, for this talk.

References

Abelson, R. F. 1981. Psychological Status of the Script Concept. *American Psychologist* 36:715–29.

Altman, L. K. 1982. New Homosexual Disorder Worries Health Officials. *New York Times*, 11 May, C1, C6.

Appignanesi, L., and J. Forrester. 1992. *Freud's Women: Family, Patients, Followers.* New York: Basic Books.

Aries, P. 1962. *Centuries of Childhood: A Social History of Family Life.* New York: Vintage Books.

Ashley, C. W. 1944. *The Ashley Book of Knots.* New York: Doubleday.

Atwater, L. 1982. *The Extramarital Connection: Sex, Intimacy, and Identity.* New York: Irvington.

Atwood, J. 1981. *The Role of Masturbation in Socio-Sexual Development.* Ph.D. diss., Department of Sociology, SUNY at Stony Brook, Stony Brook, NY.

Atwood, J., and J. H. Gagnon. 1987. Masturbatory Behavior in College Youth. *Journal of Sex Education and Therapy* 3:5–42.

Averill, J. R. 1982. *Anger and Aggression: An Essay on Emotion.* New York: Springer-Verlag.

———. 1984. The Acquisition of the Emotions in Adulthood. In *Emotion in Adult Development*, edited by C. Z. Malatesta and C. K Izard. Beverly Hills: Sage.

Baldwin, A. L. 1969. A Cognitive Theory of Socialization. In *Handbook of Socialization Theory and Research*, edited by D. A. Goslin, 322–345. Chicago: Rand McNally.

Banks, Sir J. 1962. *The Endeavour Journal of Joseph Banks, 1768–1771.* Edited by J. C. Beaglehole. Sydney: Trustees of the Public Library of New South Wales in association with Angus and Robertson.

Baron, L., and M. A. Straus.1989. *Four Theories of Rape in American Society: A State-Level Analysis.* New Haven, CT: Yale University Press.

Bartlett, N. 1988. *Who Was That Man?: A Present for Mr. Oscar Wilde.* London: Serpent's Tail.

Baudrillard, J. 1968. *Simulations.* New York: Semiotext(e).

Bebel, A. [1883] 1971. *Woman under Socialism.* New York: Shocken Books.

Becker, H. S. 1973. *Outsiders: Studies in the Sociology of Deviance.* New York: Free Press.

Bell, A., and M. Weinberg. 1978. *Homosexualities: A Study of Diversity among Men and Women.* New York: Simon and Schuster.

Bell, A., M. Weinberg, and S. K. Hammersmith. 1981. *Sexual Preference.* New York: Simon and Schuster.

Bell, R. R., S. Turner, and L. A. Rosen. 1975. A Multivariate Analysis of Female Extramarital Coitus. *Journal of Marriage and the Family* 37:375–84.

Bendix, R., and S. M. Lipset, eds. 1953. *Class, Status, and Power.* New York: Free Press.

Berne, E. 1966. *Games People Play.* New York: Grove Press.

Bertram, E. 1996. *Drug War Politics: The Price of Denial.* Berkeley: University of California Press.

Blumstein, P., and P. Schwartz. 1983. *American Couples: Money, Work, and Sex.* New York: Wm. Morrow.

Boswell, J. 1980. *Christianity, Social Tolerance, and Homosexuality: Gay People in Western Europe from the Beginning of the Christian Era to the Fourteenth Century.* Chicago: University of Chicago Press.

Brecher, R., and E. Brecher, eds. 1966. *An Analysis of Human Sexual Response.* Boston: Little, Brown.

Brody, J. E. 1981. Kinsey Study Finds Homosexuals Show Early Predisposition. *New York Times,* 23 August, 1, 30.

———. 1984. Homosexual Study Cites Hormone Link. *New York Times,* 21 September, A16.

Brownmiller, S. 1975. *Against Our Will: Men, Women, and Rape.* New York: Simon and Schuster.

Burke, K. 1936. *Permanence and Change: An Anatomy of Purpose.* New York: New Republic.

———. [1937] 1964. *Attitudes toward History.* Berkeley: University of California Press.

———. 1966. *Language as Symbolic Action: Essays on Life, Literature, and Method.* Berkeley: University of California Press.

———. 1974. The Philosophy of Literary Form. Berkeley: University of California Press.

Bumpuss, L., and J. Sweet. 1988. Preliminary Findings on Cohabitation from the 1987 National Survey of Families and Households. Paper presented at the annual meetings of the Population Association of America, New Orleans.

Burt, M. R. 1980. Cultural Myths and Support for Rape. *Journal of Personality and Social Psychology* 38:217–20.

Byers, E. S. 1988. Effects of Sexual Arousal on Men's and Women's Behavior in Sexual Disagreement Situations. *Journal of Sex Research* 25:235–54.

Calder-Marshall, A. C. 1959. *Havelock Ellis.* London: Rupert Hart Davis.

Califia, P. 1983. Gay Men, Lesbians, and Sex: Doing It Together. *Advocate,* July, 24–27.

Campenhoudt, L. V., M. Cohen, G. Guizzardi., and D. Hauser, eds. 1997. *Sexual Interactions and HIV Risk: New Conceptual Perspectives in European Research.* London: Taylor and Francis.

Cannon, K. L., and R. Long. 1971. Premarital Sexual Behavior in the Sixties. *Journal of Marriage and the Family* 33 (1): 36–49.

Carrier, J. 1976. Cultural Factors Affecting Urban Mexican Male Homosexual Behavior. *Archives of Sexual Behavior* 5:103–24.

Chauncey, G. 1995. *Gay New York*. New York: Basic Books.

Check, J. V. P., and N. M. Malamuth. 1983. Sex Role Stereotyping and Responses to Depictions of Stranger vs. Acquaintance Rape. *Journal of Personality and Social Psychology* 45:344–56.

Chilman, C. S. 1978. *Adolescent Sexuality in a Changing American Society*. Washington, DC: National Institutes of Health.

Clark, R. D., and E. Hatfield. 1989. Gender Differences in Receptivity to Sexual Offers. *Journal of Psychology and Human Sexuality* 1:39–55.

Clarke, L. B. 1989. *Acceptable Risk? Making Decisions in a Toxic Environment*. Berkeley: University of California Press.

Clayton, R. R., and J. L. Bokemeier. 1980. Premarital Sexual Behavior in the Seventies. *Journal of Marriage and Family* 42:759–78.

Cobham, R. 1992. Misgendering the Nation: African Nationalist Fictions and Nuruddin Farah's Maps. In *Nationalisms and Sexualities,* edited by A. Parker, M. Russo, D. Sommer, and P. Yaeger. New York: Routledge.

Cochran, W., F. Mosteller, and J. Tukey. 1953. Statistical Problems of the Kinsey Report. *Journal of the American Statistical Association* 48:673–716.

Cohen, J. B., et al. 1988. Changes in Risk Behavior for HIV Infection and Transmission in a Prospective Study of Sexually Active Women in San Francisco. Paper presented at the Fourth International Conference on AIDS, June, Stockholm.

Cohen, R. 1994. Aux Armes! France Rallies to Battle Sly and T. Rex. *New York Times,* 2 January, 2:1, 22.

Coles, R., and G. Stokes. 1985. *Sex and the American Teenager*. New York: Harper.

Collis, J. S. 1959. *An Artist of Life*. London: Casall.

Connell, R. W., and S. Kippax. 1990. Sexuality in the AIDS Crisis: Patterns of Pleasure and Practice in an Australian Sample of Gay and Bisexual Men. *Journal of Sex Research* 27:167–98.

Cook, J. 1955–74. *The Journals of Captain James Cook on His Voyages of Discovery,* edited by J. C. Beaglehole. Cambridge: Cambridge University Press, for the Hakluyt Society.

Coser, L. 1974. *Greedy Institutions: Patterns of Undivided Commitment*. New York: Free Press.

Crimp, D. 1987. How to Have Promiscuity in an Epidemic. *October* 43:237–68.

Crompton, L. 1985. *Byron and Greek Love: Homophobia in Nineteenth-Century England*. Berkeley: University of California Press.

Dabrowski, M., and R. Leopold. 1997. *Egon Schiele: The Leopold Collection, Vienna*. Museum exhibition catalog. New York: Museum of Modern Art.

Dank, B. 1971. Coming Out in the Gay World. *Psychiatry* 34:180–97.

Darnton, R. 1984. *The Great Cat Massacre and Other Episodes in French Cultural History*. New York: Free Press.

Darrow, W., et al. 1987. Multicenter Study of HIV Antibody in U.S. Prostitutes. Paper presented at the Third International Conference on AIDS, June, Washington, DC.

Davis, K. B. 1929. *Factors in the Sex Life of 2,200 Women*. New York: Harper.

Davison, G. S. 1968. Elimination of a Sadistic Fantasy by a Client Controlled Counter Conditioning Technique. *Journal of Abnormal Psychology* 77:84–90.

Day, S., et al. 1988. HIV and London Prostitutes. Paper presented at the Fourth International Conference on AIDS, June, Stockholm.

De Cecco, J. 1987. Homosexuality's Brief Recovery: From Sickness to Health and Back Again. *The Journal of Sex Research* 23:106–14.

Delacoste, F., and P. Alexander. 1987. *Sex Work*. Pittsburgh, PA: Cleis Press.

DeLameter, J. 1987. Gender Differences in Sexual Scenarios. In *Females, Males, and Sexuality*, edited by K. Kelley. Albany: SUNY Press.

DeLameter, J., and P. MacCorquodale. 1979. *Premarital Sexuality: Attitudes, Relationships, Behavior*. Madison: University of Wisconsin Press.

D'Emilio, J. 1983. *Sexual Politics, Sexual Communities: The Making of a Homosexual Minority in the United States, 1940–1970*. Chicago: University of Chicago Press.

Dickinson, R. L., and L. Beam. 1931. *One Thousand Marriages*. Baltimore: Williams and Wilkins.

Donnerstein, E., and D. Linz. 1988. A Critical Analysis of "A Critical Analysis of Recent Research on Violent Erotics." *Journal of Sex Research* 24:348–52.

Douglas, M. [1966] 1970. *Purity and Danger: An Analysis of Concepts of Pollution and Taboo*. London: Pelican Books.

Dover, K. J. 1978. *Greek Homosexuality*. Cambridge, MA: Harvard University Press.

Driver, E., and A. Droisen. eds. 1989. *Child Sexual Abuse: A Feminist Reader*. New York: New York University Press.

Duberman, M. B. 1974. The Bisexual Debate. *New Times*, 28 June, 34–41.

Ellis, H. 1932. *Views and Reviews: A Selection of Uncollected Articles*. 2 vols. (1884–1919; 1920–1932). London: D. Harmsworth.

———. [1899] 1936. *Studies in the Psychology of Sex*. Vol.1, no.1. New York: Random House.

Ellul, J. 1964. *The Technological Society*. New York: Knopf.

Englestein, L. 1989. *Keys to Happiness: Sex and the Search for Modernity in Fin de Siècle Russia*. Ithaca, NY: Cornell University Press.

Erikson, E. 1963. *Childhood and Society*. 2d ed. New York: Norton.

Fay, F., C. Turner, A. Klassen, and J. H. Gagnon, 1989. Prevalence and Patterns of Same Gender Contact with Men. *Science* 243 (20 January): 338–48.

Feyerabend, P. K. 1976. On the Critique of Scientific Reason. In *Essays in Memory of Imre Lakatos*, edited by R. S. Cohen, P. K. Feyerabend, and M. W. Wartofsky. Dordrecht, Holland: D. Riedel.

Fine, M. 1984. Coping with Rape: Critical Perspectives on Consciousness. *Imagination, Cognition, and Personality: The Scientific Study of Consciousness* 3:249–67.

———. 1988. Sexuality, Schooling, and Adolescent Females: The Missing Discourse of Desire. *Harvard Educational Review* 38:29–53.

Finkelhor, D. 1986. *A Sourcebook on Child Sexual Abuse*. Beverly Hills: Sage.

Finkelhor, D., and K. Yllo. 1981. Forced Sex in Marriage: A Sociological View. Paper presented at the annual meetings of the American Orthopsychiatric Association, New York.

Fleck, L. [1935] 1979. *The Genesis of a Scientific Fact.* Chicago: University of Chicago Press.

Foucault, M. 1978. *The History of Sexuality.* Vol.1, *An Introduction.* New York: Pantheon.

———. 1979. *Discipline and Punish: The Birth of the Prison.* New York: Pantheon.

Fowles, J. 1970. *The French Lieutenant's Woman.* London: Panther Books.

Freilich, M., ed. 1970. *Marginal Natives: Anthropologists at Work.* New York: Harper and Row.

Freud, S. [1920] 1953–1974. The Psychogenesis of a Case of Homosexuality in a Woman. In *The Standard Edition of the Complete Psychological Works of Sigmund Freud,* edited and translated by J. Strachey, 18:145–72. London: Hogarth.

Furstenberg Jr., F. F. 1982. Conjugal Succession: Reentering Marriage after Divorce. In *Life Span Developmental Psychology, Non-Normative Life Events,* edited by E. J. Callahan and K. A. McCluskey. New York: Academic Press.

Fuss, D. 1993. Freud's Fallen Women: Identification, Desire, and a Case of Homosexuality in a Woman. *Yale Journal of Criticism* 6 (1): 1–23.

Gagnon, J. H. 1965. Female Child Victims of Sex Offenses. *Social Problems* 13 (2): 176–92.

———. 1968. Prostitution. In *The International Encyclopedia of the Social Sciences.* New York: Crowell-Collier.

———. 1972. The Creation of the Sexual in Early Adolescence. In *Twelve to Sixteen: Early Adolescence,* edited by J. Kagan and R. Coles. New York: Norton.

———. 1974. Scripts and the Coordination of Sexual Conduct. In *Proceedings of the Nebraska Symposium on Motivation,* edited by J. K. Cole and R. Dienstbier. Lincoln: University of Nebraska Press.

———. 1975. Sex Research and Social Change. *Archives of Sexual Behavior* 4:111–41.

———. 1977. *Human Sexualities,* Glenview, IL: Scott Foresman.

———. 1978. Reconsiderations: A. C. Kinsey et al., *Sexual Behavior in the Human Male* and *Sexual Behavior in the Human Female. Human Nature* 1 (10): 92–95.

———. 1979. The Interaction of Gender Roles and Sexual Conduct. In *Human Sexuality: A Comparative and Developmental Approach,* edited by H. Katchadourian. Berkeley: University of California Press.

———. 1983. Sex Research and Social Change. In *Challenges in Sexual Science,* edited by C. M. Davis. Philadelphia: Society for the Scientific Study of Sex.

———. 1985. Attitudes and Responses of Parents to Pre-adolescent Masturbation. *Archives of Sexual Behavior* 14:451–66.

———. 1987. Masturbation in Two College Educated Cohorts. Paper presented at the annual meetings of the International Academy of Sex Research, June, Tutzing, West Germany.

———. 1988. Sex Research and Sexual Conduct in the Age of AIDS. *Journal of Acquired Immune Deficiency Syndromes* 1 (6): 593–601.

———. 1990a. Gender Preference in Erotic Relations, the Kinsey Scale, and Sexual Scripts. In *Heterosexuality, Homosexuality, and the Kinsey Scale,* edited by D. McWhirter, S. Sanders, and J. Reinisch. Oxford: Oxford University Press.

———. 1990b. The Implicit and Explicit Use of the Scripting Perspective in Sex Research. In *Annual Review of Sex Research,* edited by John Bancroft, 1:1–43.

Gagnon, J. H., and C. S. Greenblat. 1978. *Life Designs: Individuals, Marriages, and Families.* Glenview: Scott Foresman.

Gagnon, J. H., R. C. Rosen, and S. Leiblum. 1982. Cognitive and Social Aspects of Sexual Dysfunction: Sexual Scripts in Sex Therapy. *Journal of Sex and Marital Therapy* 8 (1): 44–56.

Gagnon, J. H., and W. Simon. 1967a. Femininity in the Lesbian Community. *Social Problems* 15 (2): 212–21.

———. 1967b. Pornography: Raging Menace or Paper Tiger? *Trans Action* 4:41–48.

———, eds.1967c. *Sexual Deviance: A Reader.* New York: Harper and Row. Reprint, J. J. Harper edition, 1969.

———. 1973. *Sexual Conduct: The Social Sources of Human Sexuality.* Chicago: Aldine.

———. 1987. The Scripting of Oral-Genital Conduct. *Archives of Sexual Behavior* 16 (1): 1–25.

Gebhard, P. H., J. H. Gagnon, W. B. Pomeroy, and C. V. Christenson. 1965. *Sex Offenders: An Analysis of Types.* New York: Harper and Row.

Gang Rape of Three Girls Leaves Fresno Shaken, and Questioning. 1998. *New York Times,* 1 May, A18.

Gebhard, P. H., and A. B. Johnson. 1979. *The Kinsey Data.* Philadelphia: Saunders.

Geertz, C. 1973. *The Interpretation of Cultures.* New York: Basic Books.

———. 1983. *Local Knowledge.* New York: Basic Books.

Giola, D. A., and P. A. Poole. 1984. Scripts in Organization Behavior. *Academy Management Review* 9:449–59.

Gladue, B. A., R. Green, and R. E. Hellman. 1984. Neurendocrine Response to Estrogen and Sexual Orientation. *Science* 225:1496–99.

Goffman, Erving. 1971. *Relations in Public.* New York: Basic Books.

Goode, E. 1997. *Between Politics and Reason: The Drug Legalization Debate.* New York: St. Martin's.

Gould, S. J. 1981. *The Mismeasure of Man.* New York: Norton.

Greene, G. 1980. *Ways of Escape.* New York: Simon and Schuster.

Groth, A. N. 1979. *Men Who Rape: The Psychology of the Offender.* New York: Plenum.

Gusfield, J. R. 1981. *The Culture of Public Problems: Drinking-Driving and the Symbolic Order.* Chicago: University of Chicago Press.

———. 1996. *Contested Meanings: The Construction of Alcohol Problems.* Madison: University of Wisconsin Press.

Hamilton, G. V. 1929. *A Study in Marriage.* New York: Alfred and Charles Boni.

Herdt, G. 1981. *Guardians of the Flute.* New York: McGraw-Hill.

———. 1984. *Ritualized Homosexuality in Melanesia.* Berkeley: University of California Press.

Herdt, G., and R. Stoller. 1990. *Intimate Communications: Erotics and the Study of a Culture*. New York: Columbia University Press.

Heise, L. L. 1995. Violence, Sexuality, and Women's Lives. In *Conceiving Sexuality*, edited by R. Parker and J. H. Gagnon. New York: Routledge.

Hessol, N. 1987. The Natural History of Human Immunodeficiency Virus in a Cohort of Homosexual and Bisexual Men: A Seven-Year Prospective Study. Paper presented at the Third International Conference on AIDS, June, Washington, DC.

Hochschild, A. R. 1983. *The Managed Heart: Commercialization of Human Feeling*. Berkeley: University of California.

Hocquenghem, G. 1978. *Homosexual Desire*. London: Allison and Busby; New York: Schocken Books. Originally published in French, 1972.

Hofferth, S. L., and C. D. Hayes. 1987. *Risking the Future, Adolescent Sexuality, Pregnancy and Childbearing*. Vol. 2. Washington, DC: National Academy Press.

Hofferth, S. L., J. R. Kahn, and W. Baldwin. 1987. Premarital Sexual Activity among U.S. Teenage Women over the Past Three Decades. *Family Planning Perspectives* 19:46–52.

Holmstrom, L. L., and A. W. Burgess. 1978. *The Victim of Rape: Institutional Re-actions*. New York: Wiley.

Hooker, E. 1966. The Homosexual Community. In *Perspectives in Pathology*, edited by J. C. Palmer and M. J. Goldstein. Oxford: Oxford University Press.

Humphreys, L. 1970. *Tearoom Trade: Impersonal Sex in Public Places*. Chicago: Aldine.

———. 1972. *Out of the Closets: The Sociology of Homosexual Liberation*. Englewood Cliffs: Prentice Hall.

Institute of Medicine. 1988. *Confronting AIDS: Update*. Washington, DC: National Academy Press.

Irving, J. 1990. *Disorders of Desire: Sex and Gender in Modern American Sexology*. Philadelphia: Temple.

Jackson, S. 1978. The Social Context of Rape: Sexual Scripts and Motivation. *Women's Studies International Quarterly* 1:27–38.

Jacobus, M. 1995. Russian Tactics: Freud's "Case of Homosexuality in a Woman." *GLQ: A Journal of Gay and Lesbian Studies* 2 (1–2): 65–97.

James, J. 1977. Prostitutes and Prostitution. In *Deviants: Voluntary Actors in a Hostile World*, edited by E. Sagarin and F. Montanino. Glenview, IL: Scott Foresman.

Jay, K., and A. Young. 1979. *The Gay Report: Lesbian and Gay Men Speak Out about Sexual Experiences and Life Styles*. New York: Summit Books.

Joint UN Programme on HIV/AIDS. 1999. *The UN AIDS Report*. Geneva: United Nations.

Jones, E. F., et al., eds. 1986. *Teenage Pregnancy in Industrialized Countries*. New Haven: Yale University Press.

Jonsen, A. R., and J. Stryker. 1993. *The Social Impact of AIDS in the United States*. Washington, DC: National Academy Press.

Joseph, J. G. 1987. Two-Year Longitudinal Behavioral Risk Reduction in a Cohort of Homosexual Men. Paper presented at the Third International Conference on AIDS, June, Washington, DC.

Kantner, J., and M. Zelnik. 1972. Sexual Experiences of Young Unmarried Women in the United States. *Family Planing Perspectives* 4:9–17.

Katz, J. 1983. *Gay/Lesbian Almanac: A New Documentary.* New York: Harper and Row.

———. 1995. *The Invention of Heterosexuality.* New York: Dutton.

Kinsey, A. C., W. B. Pomeroy, and C. E. Martin. 1948. *Sexual Behavior in the Human Male.* Philadelphia: Saunders.

Kinsey, A. C., W. B. Pomeroy, C. E. Martin, and P. H. Gebhard. 1953. *Sexual Behavior in the Human Female.* Philadelphia: Saunders.

Kohut, H. 1977. *The Restoration of the Self.* New York: International University Press.

Kuhn, T. S. 1970. *The Structure of Scientific Revolutions.* 2d ed. Chicago: University of Chicago Press.

———. 1977. *The Essential Tension.* Chicago: University of Chicago Press.

Kutchinsky, B. 1973. Eroticism without Censorship: Sociological Investigation on the Production and Consumption of Pornographic Literature in Denmark. *Journal of Criminology and Penology* 1:217–25.

LaFitte, F. 1967. Inaugural lecture of the Havelock Ellis Society, May, London.

La Fontaine, J. S. 1990. *Child Sexual Abuse.* Cambridge: Polity Press.

Lakatos, L., and A. Musgrave, eds. 1970. *Criticism and the Growth of Knowledge.* Cambridge: Cambridge University Press.

Langer, E. J. 1978. Rethinking the Role of Thought in Social Interaction. In *New Directions in Attribution Research,* vol. 2, edited by J. Harvey, W. Ickes, and R. Kidd. Hillsdale, NJ: Erlbaum.

Langer, E. J., A. Blank, and B. Chanowitz. 1978. The Mindlessness of Ostensibly Thoughtful Action. *Journal of Personality and Social Psychology.* 36:635–42.

LaPlante, M. N., N. McCormick, and G. G. Brannigan. 1980. Living the Sexual Script: College Student's Views of Influence in Sexual Encounters. *Journal of Sex Research* 16:338–55.

Laumann, E. O., J. H. Gagnon, and R. Michael. 1987. Social and Behavioral Aspects of Health and Fertility Related Behavior: Technical Proposal in Response to Request for Proposals No. NICHD-PHS-DBS-97–13. Chicago: NORC.

Laumann, E. O., J. H. Gagnon, R. Michael, and S. Michaels. 1994. *The Social Organization of Sexuality: Sexual Practices in the United States.* Chicago: University of Chicago Press.

Lederer, L., ed. 1980. *Take Back the Night: Women on Pornography.* New York: Morrow.

Leiblum, S. L., and L. A. Pervin, eds. 1980. *Principles and Practices of Sex Therapy.* New York: Guilford.

Leiblum, S. L., and R. C. Rosen, eds. 1988. *Sexual Desire Disorders.* New York: Guilford.

Levine, M. P. 1987a. Eros and Romance among Gay Men. Paper presented at the Fifty-Seventh Annual Meetings of the Eastern Sociological Society, March, Boston, MA.

———. 1987b. *Gay Macho: Ethnography of the Homosexual Clone.* Ph.D. diss., Department of Sociology, New York University.

———. 1988. Reconstructing Gay Eroticism: Changing Patterns of Sexuality among Clones. Paper presented at the Annual Meetings of the American Sociological Association, August, Atlanta, GA.

Levine, M. P., P. M. Nardi, and J. H. Gagnon, eds. 1997. *Encounters with AIDS: The Impact of the HIV/AIDS Epidemic on the Gay and Lesbian Communities.* Chicago: University of Chicago Press.

Lewis, S. G. 1979. *Sunday's Women: A Report on Lesbian Life Today.* Boston: Beacon Press.

Li, T., D. J. West, T. P. Woodhouse. 1990. *Children's Sexual Encounters with Adults.* London: Duckworth.

Lindberg, L. D., F. L. Sonenstein, L. Ku, and G. Martinez.1997. Age Differences between Minors Who Give Birth and Their Adult Partners. *Family Planning Perspectives* 29:61–66.

Linz, D. E. 1989. Exposure to Sexually Explicit Materials and Attitudes toward Rape: A Comparison of Study Results. *Journal of Sex Research* 26:50–84.

Lobitz, W. C., and J. Lopiccolo. 1972. New Methods in the Treatment of Sexual Dysfunction. *Journal of Behavior Therapy and Experimental Psychiatry* 3:265–71.

Long, N. 1958. The Local Community as an Ecology of Games. *American Journal of Sociology* 64 (3): 251–61.

Loomis, K. 1989a. AIDS: The Numbers Game. *New York Magazine* 22 (10): 44–49.

———. 1989b. Voodoo Statistics: The Health Department's AIDS Mess. *Village Voice,* 4 April, 3–34, 137.

Lopiccolo, J., and W. C. Lobitz. 1972. The Role of Masturbation in the Treatment of Orgasmic Dysfunction. *Archives of Sexual Behavior* 2:163–71.

Luster, T., and S. A. Small. 1997. Sexual Abuse History and Number of Sex Partners among Female Adolescents. *Family Planning Perspectives* 29:204–11.

MacKinnon, C. A. 1987. A Feminist/Political Approach. In *Theories and Paradigms of Human Sexuality,* edited by J. Geer and W. O'Donoghue. New York: Plenum Press.

Madge, J. 1962. *The Origins of Scientific Sociology.* New York: Free Press.

Malamuth, N. M. 1988. Research on Violent Erotica: A Reply. *Journal of Sex Research* 24:340–48.

Malamuth, N. M., and J. Check. 1980. Penile Tumescence and Perceptual Responses to Rape as a Function of Victim's Perceived Reactions. *Journal of Applied Social Psychology* 10:528–47.

Malamuth, N. M., and K. Donnerstein. 1982. The Effects of Aggressive Pornographic Mass Media Sexual Stimuli. *Advances in Experimental Social Psychology* 15:104–36.

———. 1984. *Pornography and Sexual Expression.* Orlando, FL: Academic Press.

Malamuth, N. M., M. Heim, and S. Feshbach. 1980. Sexual Responses of College Students to Rape Depictions: Inhibitory and Disinhibitory Effects. *Journal of Personality and Social Psychology* 38:399–408.

Marmor, J. 1980. *Homosexual Behavior: A Modern Reappraisal.* New York: Basic Books.

Marshall, D., and R. Suggs, eds. 1971. *Human Sexual Behavior: Variations in the Ethnographic Spectrum.* Englewood, NJ: Prentice Hall.

Massey, D. S., and N. A. Denton. 1993. *American Apartheid: Segregation and the Making of the Underclass.* Cambridge, MA: Harvard University Press.

Masters, W. H., and V. E. Johnson. 1966. *Human Sexual Response.* Boston: Little, Brown.

———. 1970. *Human Sexual Inadequacy.* Boston: Little, Brown.

———. 1979. *Homosexuality in Perspective.* Boston: Little, Brown.

Matalene, W. H. 1989. Sexual Scripting in Montaigne and Stern. *Comparative Literature* 41:360–77.

McCormick, N. B. 1979. Come-Ons and Put-Offs: Unmarried Students' Strategies for Having and Avoiding Sexual Intercourse. *Psychology of Women Quarterly* 4:194–211.

———. 1987. Sexual Scripts: Social and Therapeutic Implications. *Sexual and Marital Therapy* 2:3–27.

McCormick, N. B., and C. J. Jesser. 1983. The Courtship Game: Power in the Sexual Encounter. In *Changing Boundaries: Gender Roles and Sexual Behavior,* edited by E. R. Allgeier and N. B. McCormick. Palo Alto, CA: Mayfield.

McWhirter, D, and D. Mattison,. 1984. *The Male Couple.* Englewood Cliffs, NJ: Prentice Hall.

Merck, M. 1993. *Perversions: Deviant Readings.* London: Virago.

Merton, R. K. 1975a. The Bearing of Sociological Theory on Empirical Research. In *Social Theory and Social Structure,* edited by R. K. Merton. Glencoe, IL: Free Press.

———. 1975b. The Sociology of Knowledge. In *Social Theory and Social Structure,* edited by R. K. Merton. Glencoe, IL: Free Press.

Michael, R. T., J. H. Gagnon, E. O. Laumann, and G. Kolata. 1994. *Sex in America.* New York: Little, Brown. Translations into German (1994), Dutch (1995), Japanese (1996), and Chinese (1997).

Michael, R. T., E. O. Laumann, J. H. Gagnon, and T. Smith. 1988. Number of Sexual Partners and Potential Risk of Sexual Exposure to Human Immunodeficiency Virus. *Morbidity and Mortality Weekly Report* 3 (37): 564–67.

Miller, G. A., E. Galanter, and K. H. Pribram. 1960. *Plans and the Structure of Behavior.* New York: Holt.

Miller, P. Y., C. Cottrell, and W. Simon. 1973. Some Social and Psychological Correlates of Adolescent Sexuality. Paper presented at the Pacific Sociological Association annual meetings, Tucson, AZ.

Miller, P.Y., and W. Simon. 1974. Adolescent Sexual Behavior: Context and Change. *Social Problems* 22:52–76.

Modell, J., F. Furstenburg, and D. Strong. The Timing of Marriage in the Transition to Adulthood. *American Journal of Sociology* 84 (Suppl.): S120–50.

Moore, K. A., C. W. Nord, and J. L. Peterson. 1989. Nonvoluntary Sexual Activity among Adolescents. *Family Planning Perspectives* 21:110–14.

Moorehead, A. 1966. *The Fatal Impact: An Account of the Invasion of the South Pacific 1767–1840.* New York: Harper and Row.

Mosher, D., and S. S. Tomkins. 1988. Scripting the Macho Man: Hyper-masculine Socialization and Enculturation. *Journal of Sex Research* 25:60–84.

Mould, D. E. 1988. A Critical Analysis of Recent Research on Violent Erotica. *Journal of Sex Research* 24:326–40.

Murnen, S. K., A. Perot, and D. Byrne. 1989. Coping with Unwanted Sexual Activity: Normative Responses, Situational Determinants, and Individual Differences. *Journal of Sex Research* 26:85–106.

Nathanson, C. A. 1991. *Dangerous Passage: The Social Control of Sexuality in Women's Adolescence.* Philadelphia: Temple University Press.

National Institutes of Health Consensus Statement. 1997. *Interventions to Prevent HIV Risk Behaviors* 15 (2): 1–41.

Newcomer, S. F., and J. R. Udry. 1985. Oral Sex in an Adolescent Population. *Archives of Sexual Behavior* 14:41–46.

New York Times. 1989. Science Watch. 4 April.

Nichols, M. 1988. Low Sexual Desire in Lesbian Couples. In *Sexual Desire Disorders,* edited by S. R. Lieblum and R. C. Rosen. New York: Guilford.

Normand, J., D. Vlahov, and L. Moses, eds. 1995. *Preventing HIV Transmission: The Role of Sterile Needles and Bleach.* Washington, DC: National Academy Press.

Obeyesekere, G. 1992. *The Apotheosis of Captain Cook.* Princeton: Princeton University Press.

Ortner, S. B., and H. Whitehead, eds. 1981. *Sexual Meanings: The Cultural Construction of Gender and Sexuality.* Cambridge: Cambridge University Press.

Padian, N., et al. 1987. Male-to-Female Transmission of Human Immunodeficiency Virus. *Journal of the American Medical Association* 258 (6): 788–97.

Pagden, A. 1993. *European Encounters with the New World.* New Haven: Yale University Press.

Parker, R., and J. H. Gagnon, eds. 1995. *Conceiving Sexuality: Approaches to Sex Research in a Post Modern Era.* New York: Routledge.

Peckham, M. 1969. *Art and Pornography: An Experiment in Explanation.* New York: Basic Books.

———. 1979. *Explanation and Power: The Control of Human Behavior.* New York: Seabury.

Peplau, L., Z. Rubin, and C. Hill. 1977. Sexual Intimacy in Dating Relationships. *Journal of Social Issues* 33 (2): 86–109.

Perrow, C., 1984. *Normal Accidents.* New York: Basic Books.

Person, E. S. 1987. A Psychoanalytic Approach. In *Theories and Paradigms of Human Sexuality,* edited by J. Geer and W. O'Donoghue. New York: Plenum Press.

Peterson, J. 1989. Center for AIDS Prevention, University of California, San Francisco, personal communication, February.

Piot, P., et al. 1987. Heterosexual Transmission of HIV. *AIDS* 1 (19): 199–206.

Plummer, K., ed., 1981. *The Making of the Modern Homosexual*. London: Hutchinson.

———. 1995. *Telling Sexual Stories: Power, Change, and Social Worlds*. London: Routledge.

Polanyi, Michael. 1964. *Personal Knowledge: Towards a Post-Critical Philosophy*. New York: Harper Torchbooks.

Pomeroy, W. B. 1972. *Doctor Kinsey and the Institute for Sex Research*. New York: Harper and Row.

Reiss, A. J. 1961. The Social Organization of Queers and Peers. *Social Problems* 9:102–20.

Reiss, I. L. 1960. *Premarital Sexual Standards in America*. New York: Free Press.

———. 1967. *The Social Context of Pre-marital Permissiveness*. New York: Holt, Rinehart, and Winston.

———. 1983. *Heterosexual Relationships Inside and Outside of Marriage*. Morristown, NJ: General Learning Press.

Reiss, I. L., E. E. Anderson, and G. C. Spoonagle. 1980. A Multivariate Model of the Determinants of Extramarital Sexual Permissiveness. *Journal of Marriage and the Family* 45:395–411.

Richardson, L. 1985. *The New Other Woman*. New York: Free Press.

Roberts, E. J. 1980. *Children's Sexual Learning*. Cambridge: Ballinger.

Roberts, J. V., and R. M. Mohr, eds. 1994. *Confronting Sexual Assault: A Decade of Legal and Social Change*. Toronto: University of Toronto Press.

Robinson, P. 1976. *The Modernization of Sex*. New York: Harper and Row.

Rorty, R. 1979. *Philosophy and the Mirror of Nature*. Princeton, NJ: Princeton University Press.

———. 1989. *Contingency, Irony, and Solidarity*. Cambridge: Cambridge University Press.

Rosen, R. C., and S. R. Leiblum. 1988. A Sexual Scripting Approach to Problems of Desire. In *Sexual Desire Disorders*, edited by S. R. Leiblum and R. C. Rosen. New York: Guilford.

Rubin, G. 1975. The Traffic in Women. In *Toward an Anthropology of Women*, edited by R. R. Reiter. New York: Monthly Review.

———. 1984. Thinking Sex. In *Pleasure and Danger*, edited by C. Vance. London: Routledge, Kegan Paul.

Sanday, P. R. 1996. *A Woman Scorned: Acquaintance Rape on Trial*. New York: Doubleday.

Sanders, S. A., and J. M. Reinisch. 1999. Would You Say You Had Sex If . . . ? *Journal of the American Medical Association* 281 (3): 275–77.

Sahlins, M. 1981. *Historical Metaphors and Mythical Realities: Structure in the Early History of the Sandwich Islands Kingdom*. Association for Social Anthropology in Oceania. Ann Arbor, MI: University of Michigan Press.

———. 1985. *Islands of History*. Chicago: University of Chicago Press.

Schank, R. C. 1982. *Dynamic Memory: A Theory of Reminding and Learning in Computers and People*. Cambridge: Cambridge University Press.

Schank, R. C., and Abelson, R. P. 1977. *Scripts, Plans, Goals, and Understanding: An Inquiry into Human Knowledge Structures*. Hillside, NJ: Lawrence Erlbaum.

Scheff, T. 1968. *Being Mentally Ill: A Sociological Theory*. Chicago: Aldine.

Schmidt, G. 1984. Allies and Persecutors: Science and Medicine in the Homosexuality Issue. *Journal of Homosexuality* 10:127–40.

Schorske, C. 1961. *Fin de Siècle Vienna: Politics and Culture*. New York: Random House.

Schwartz, P., and P. M. Blumstein. 1977. Bisexuality. *Journal of Social Issues* 33:132–45.

Schweder, R. 1982. On Savages and Other Children. *American Anthropologist* 84:354–66.

Selwyn, T., ed. 1996. *The Tourist Image: Myths and Myth Making in Tourism*. London: Wiley.

Shaw, G. B. 1970. *Collected Plays with Their Prefaces*. Vol.1. Edited by Max Reinhardt. London: Bodley Head.

Sheehy, G. 1972. The Landlords of Hell's Bedroom. *New York* 5 (47).

Shilts, R. 1987. *And the Band Played On*. New York: St. Martin's.

Shostak, A. 1981. Oral Sex: New Standard of Intimacy and Old Standard of Troubled Sex. *Deviant Behavior* 2: 127–44.

Sigusch, V., E. Schorsch, M. Dannecker, and G. Schmidt. 1982. Official Statement by the German Society of Sex Research on the Research of Dr. Gunter Dorner on the Subject of Homosexuality. *Archives of Sexual Behavior* 11:445–50.

Simon, W. 1974. The Social, the Erotic, the Sensual: The Complexities of Sexual Scripts. In *The Nebraska Symposium on Motivation*, edited by J. K. Cole and R. Dienstbier. Lincoln: University of Nebraska Press.

———. 1982. The Scripting of Aggression: A Sociological Perspective. Paper presented at the Symposium on Violence and Aggression, Southwest Science Forum, May, Houston, TX.

———. 1989. The Postmodernization of Sex. *Journal of Psychology and Human Sexuality* 2:9–37.

———. 1996. *Post-Modern Sexualities*. London: Routledge.

Simon, W., A. S. Berger, and J. H. Gagnon. 1972. Beyond Anxiety and Fantasy: The Coital Experiences of College Youth. *Journal of Youth and Adolescence*. 1:203–32.

Simon, W., and J. H. Gagnon. 1967. Homosexuality: The Formulation of a Sociological Perspective. *Journal of Health and Social Behavior* 8:177–85.

———. 1969. On Psychosexual Development. In *Handbook of Socialization Theory and Research*, edited by D. A. Goslin. Chicago: Rand McNally.

———. 1986. Sexual Scripts: Permanence and Change. *Archives of Sexual Behavior* 13:97–120.

———. 1987. A Sexual Scripts Approach. In *Theories of Human Sexuality*, edited by J. H. Geer and O'Donohue. New York: Plenum.

———, eds. 1970. *The Sexual Scene*. New Brunswick: Trans-Action Books.

————, eds. 1970. *Sexuelle Aussenseiter.* Hamburg: Rowohlt Verlag. Germans translation of *The Sexual Scene,* 1st ed.

————, eds. 1971. *Il Fourlegge del Sesso,* Rome: Bompiani. Italian translation of *The Sexual Scene,* 1st ed.

————, eds. 1972. *Seksuele Zijwegen.* Utrecht, Antwerp, Uitgeverij Jet Spectrum B.V. Dutch translation of *The Sexual Scene,* 1st ed.

————, eds. 1973. *The Sexual Scene.* 2d ed. Trans-Action Society Books. No. 5. New York: E. P. Dutton.

Simon, W., and D. Kraft. 1990. Oral Sex: A Critical Overview. In *AIDS and Sex An Integrated Biomedical and Behavioral Approach,* edited by J Reinisch, B. Voeller, and F. Goldstein. New York: Oxford University Press.

Singer, M. 1998. Political Economy of AIDS. Amityville, NY: Baywood Publishing.

Singh, V. J., B. L. Walton, and J. S. Williams. 1976. Extramarital Sexual Permissiveness: Conditions and Contingencies. *Journal of Marriage and the Family* 38:701–12.

Slobodkin, L. 1972. Department of Ecology and Evolution, State University of New York at Stony Brook, personal communication.

————. 1999. Department of Ecology and Evolution, State University of New York at Stony Brook, personal communication.

Smith, D. A., and A. C. Graesser. 1981. Memory for Actions in Scripted Activities as a Function of Typicality, Retention Interval, and Retrieval Task. *Memory and Cognition* 9:550–59.

Snitow, A., C. Stansell, and S. Thompson, eds. 1984. *Desire: The Politics of Sexuality.* London: Virago.

Socarides, C. W. 1978. *Homosexuality.* New York: Jason Aronson.

Spanier, G. B., and R. L. Margolis. 1983. Marital Separation and Extramarital Sex. *Journal of Sex Research* 19 (1): 23–48.

Stearns, C. Z., and P. N. Stearns. 1986. *Anger: The Struggle for Emotional Control in America.* Chicago: University of Chicago Press.

Steiner, G. 1984. The Distribution of Discourse. In *A Reader,* edited by G. Steiner. London: Pelican.

Stock, J. L., M. A. Bell, D. K. Boyer, and F. A. Connell. 1997. Adolescent Pregnancy and Sexual Risk-Taking among Sexually Abused Girls. *Family Planning Perspectives* 29:200–203, 227.

Stoller, R. J. 1976. Sexual Excitement. *Archives of General Psychiatry* 33:899–909.

Straver, C. 1980. Competence in and Rules of Erotic Overtures. Paper presented at the meetings of the Society for Symbolic Interaction, August, New York.

Szasz, T. 1961. *The Myth of Mental Illness.* New York: Dell.

Tavris, C. 1982. *Anger: The Misunderstood Emotion.* New York: Simon and Schuster.

Thompson, A. B. 1983. Extramarital Sex: A Review of the Scientific Literature. *Journal of Sex Research* 19:1–22.

Thorne, B., and Z. Luria. 1986. Sexuality and Gender in Children's Daily Worlds. *Social Problems* 33:176–90.

Tiefer, L. 1986. In Pursuit of the Perfect Penis: The Medicalization of Male Sexuality. *American Behavioral Scientist* 5:579–99.

————. 1987. Social Constructionism and the Study of Human Sexuality. In *Sex and Gender*, edited by P. Shaver and R. Kendrick. Beverly Hills, CA: Sage.

Tilly, C. Forthcoming. The Trouble with Stories. In *Teaching for the 21st Century*, edited by R. Aminzade and B. Pescosolido. Thousand Oaks, CA: Pine Forge Press.

Todorov, T. 1987. *The Conquest of America: The Question of the Other.* New York: Harper Torchbooks.

Tomkins, S. S. 1978. Script Theory, Differential Magnification of Effects. *Nebraska Symposium on Motivation* 26:201–36.

Trilling, L. 1950. *The Liberal Imagination.* New York: Viking Press.

Turner, C., H. Miller, and L. Moses, eds. 1989. *AIDS, Sexual Behavior and Intravenous Drug Use.* Washington, DC: National Academy Press.

U.S. Public Health Service. 1987. Human Immunodeficiency Virus Infections in the United States: A Review of Current Knowledge and Plans for Expansion of HIV Surveillance Activities. Report to the Domestic Policy Council, 30 November.

————. 1988. The Coolfont Report: The PHS Plan for Prevention and Control of AIDS and AIDS Virus. *Public Health Reports* 101 (4): 341–48.

Vance, C. S. 1984. *Pleasure and Danger.* London: Routledge, Kegan Paul.

————. 1991. Anthropology Rediscovers Sexuality: A Theoretical Comment. *Social Science and Medicine* 3 (8): 876–84.

Van den Berg, J. H. [1961] 1975. *The Changing Historical Nature of Man: Introduction to a Historical Psychology.* New York: Delta.

Veblen, T. [1914] 1964. *The Instinct of Workmanship and the Industrial Arts.* New York: W. W. Norton.

Wagner, R. 1981. *The Invention of Culture.* Chicago: University of Chicago Press.

Warren, C. A. B. 1974. *Identity and Community in the Gay World.* New York: John Wiley.

Weeks, J. 1981. *Sex, Politics, and Society: The Regulation of Sexuality since 1800.* London: Longmans.

Werkner, P., ed. 1994. *Egon Schiele: Art, Sexuality, and Viennese Modernism.* Palo Alto, CA: Society for the Promotion of Science and Scholarship.

White, E. 1980. *States of Desire: Travels in Gay America.* New York: E. P. Dutton.

————. 1983. *A Boy's Own Story.* New York: E. P. Dutton.

White, R. W. 1960. Competence and Psychosexual Stages of Development. In *Nebraska Symposium on Motivation*, edited by M. R. Jones. Lincoln: University of Nebraska Press.

Wiley, J. A., and S. J. Herschkorn. 1990. Homosexual Role Separation and AIDS Epidemics: Insights from Elementary Models. *Journal of Sex Research* 26:434–49.

Wilford, J. N. 1994. Among the Dying Species Are Lost Tribes of Mankind. *New York Times,* 2 January, The Week in Review, 1, 3.

Willis, R., and R. Michael. 1988. Innovation in Family Formation: Cohabitational Unions from the 1986 Follow-up of the NLS/72 Sample. Paper presented at the annual meetings of the Population Association of America, New Orleans.

Wilson, W. J. 1990. *The Truly Disadvantaged: The Inner City, the Underclass, and Public Policy.* Chicago: University of Chicago Press.

———. 1996. *When Work Disappears: The World of the New Urban Poor.* New York: Knopf.

Wolf, D. G. 1979. *The Lesbian Community.* Berkeley: University of California Press.

Zelnick, M., and J. E. Kantner. 1972. *National Survey for the Commission on Population Growth and the American Future.* Washington, DC: Government Printing Office.

Index

activism: and HIV/AIDS, 231–32, 240–41; of gay men, xx, 53, 104, 116, 154, 180

AIDS. *See* HIV/AIDS

aggression: and sexual scripts, 156–58

anal sex: and gay liberation, 154–55; and HIV/AIDS, 155; and masculinity, 153–54; sex research on, 150; and sexual scripts, 148, 149

anthropology: cultural biases of, 245–46, 257–58; in Pacific Islands, 246–47

Baldwin, Albert, 62

Bartlett, Neil, 259, 269–70

Beam, Louise, 36

Bebel, August, 57

Becker, Howard, xvii–xviii, 272

bisexuality: and HIV/AIDS, 183–87, 199; as identity, 116, 127; Kinsey on, 115, 184

blood donations: and HIV/AIDS, 183

Blumer, Herbert, xvii, 272

Brake, Mike, xx

breasts: as sexual objects, 78

Brown, Norman O., xiv

Burgess, Ernest W., 273

Burke, Kenneth, xix, 41, 206–8, 219, 272–73, 281

Bush, George H. W., 232

Califia, Pat, 156

censorship: of mass media, 49; and political opinion, 50–51; and social control, 34

Centers for Disease Control: and HIV/AIDS, 188–89

Chomsky, Noam, 73

Clifford, Ruth, 76

coitus. *See* intercourse

coming out, 123, 154–55

contraception: availability of, 38, 191–92; and obscenity laws, 40

Cook, James: apotheosis of, 245–46; journals of, 244; in South Seas, 242

Corner, George, 43–44

criminality: cultural beliefs about, 39–40; and sexuality, 47

culture: and gender, 135–36; and HIV/AIDS, 233–34; and homosexuality, 105, 115–16,

249–50; and intercourse, 133; and rape, 213–14; and sexual scripts, 135–36, 169–70, 248–49, 255–56, 276–78; and sexuality, 104–5, 133–35, 167, 196, 248–50, 255–56

Davis, Katherine, 36

De Cecco, J., 95

Derrida, Jacques, 281

desire: and gender, 95–96, 98, 125, 265–66; and mental life, 137–38; and sexual dysfunction, 168–69; and sexual scripts, 119–21, 136

Dickinson, Robert, 36

Diderot, Denis, 253–54

Durkheim, Emile, xvii

Ehrhardt, Anke, xxiii

Ellis, Havelock: compared to Freud, 31; influence of, 32–33; and history of sex research, 25, 28, 30, 88, 101; on women, 57

Ellul, J., 107

epidemics: defined, 233; and gay men, 179–83; HIV/AIDS as, 177–79, 228n, 229–30

epistemology: and science, 234–35

erectile dysfunction: and therapy, 165–66

Erikson, Erik, 60

exploration: and anthropology, 245; and cultural contact, 256–57; in Pacific, 243; and sexuality, 242–43, 247–48, 250–52; and violence, 254n

fantasy: and sexual scripts, 61, 75, 138–39, 277–78, 285

Fauci, Anthony, 240

feminism, xx, 214, 283–84

Fleck, Ludwig, 207

folklore: as explanatory paradigm, 106–7

Foucault, Michel: on discourse, 280–81; *History of Sexuality*, xx–xxii, 253n

Fowles, John, 70–71

Freud, Sigmund, xv, xxi, 270; compared to Ellis, 31; on homosexuality, 52, 260; and history of sex research, 25, 100–101; influence of, 31–33, 40, 273–74;